COLOR BLEACH

KOREAN BARBECUE BATTLE ROYAL AT THE KUROSAKIS'

ILLUSTRATED MANUSCRIPT OF DAILY IDLENESS

Part 1

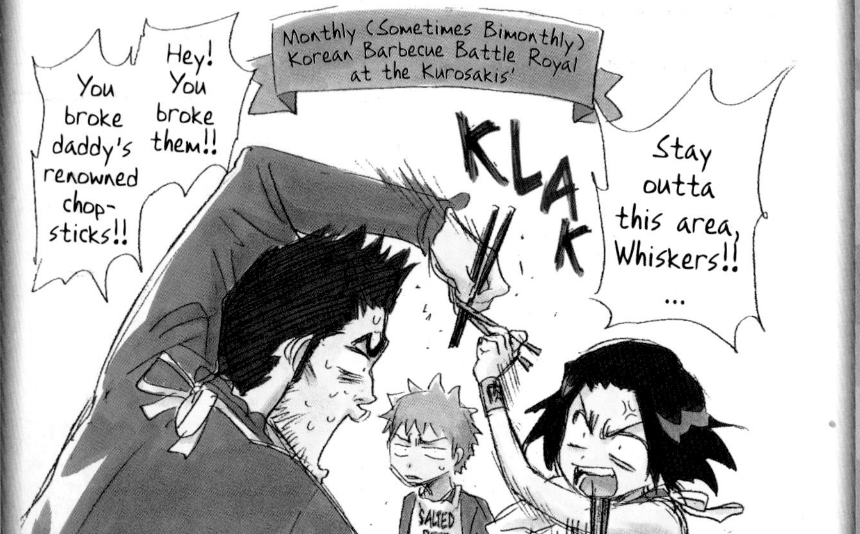
Monthly (Sometimes Bimonthly) Korean Barbecue Battle Royal at the Kurosakis'
KLAK
Stay outta this area, Whiskers!! ...
SNAP
Hey! You broke them!!
You broke daddy's renowned chop-sticks!!
SALTED BEEF TONGUE
PORK BELLY

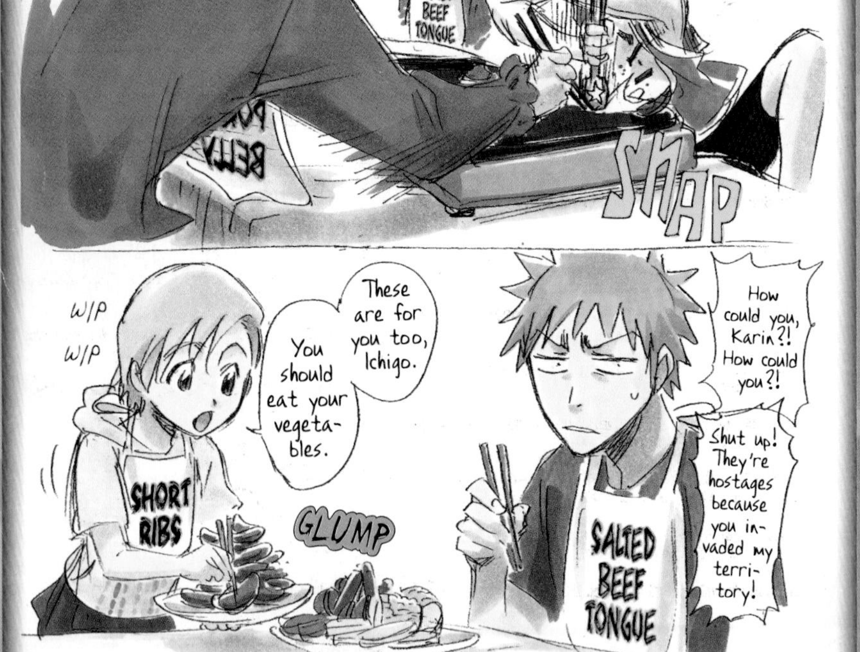
W/P
W/P
You should eat your vegeta-bles.
These are for you too, Ichigo.
SHORT RIBS
GLUMP
How could you, Karin?! How could you?!
Shut up! They're hostages because you in-vaded my terri-tory!
SALTED BEEF TONGUE

CHIZURU'S SUMMER HOMEWORK

ILLUSTRATED MANUSCRIPT OF DAILY IDLENESS
Part 2

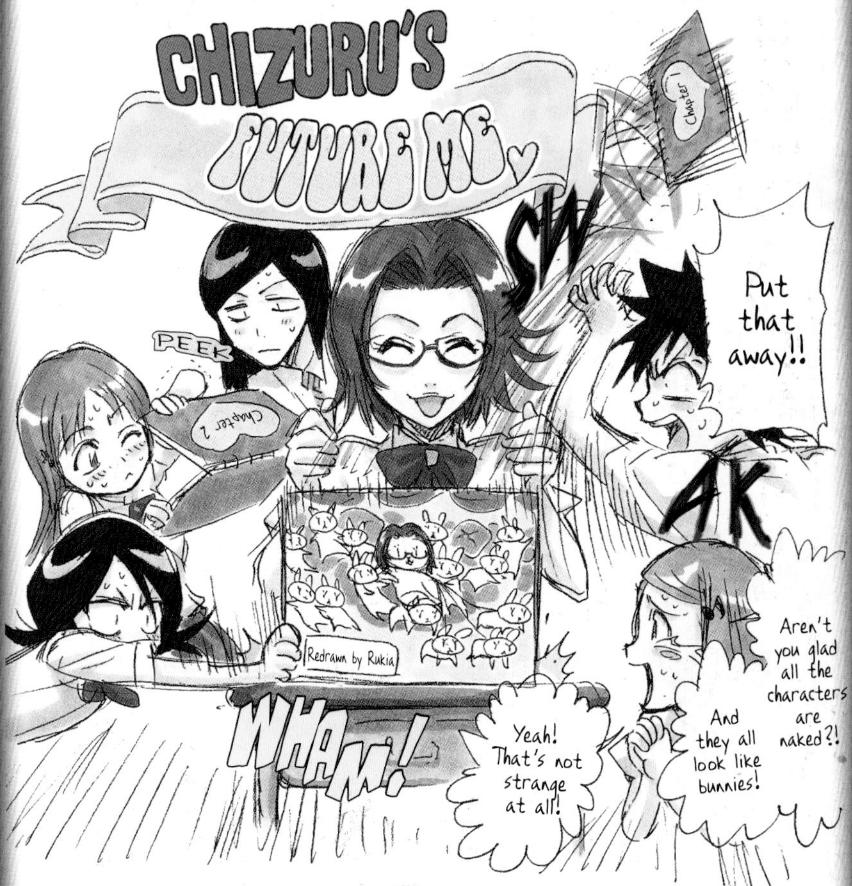
CHIZURU'S FUTURE ME♥
Chapter 1
SW
AK
Put that away!!
PEEK
Chapter 2
Redrawn by Rukia
WHAM!
Aren't you glad all the characters are naked?!
And they all look like bunnies!
Yeah! That's not strange at all!

CAUTION!

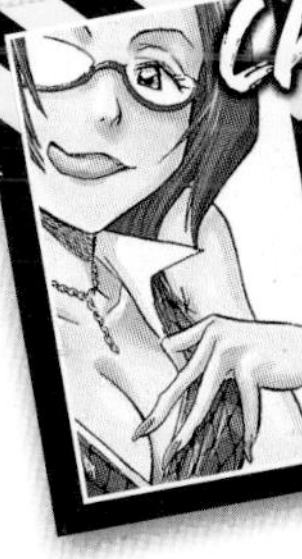

Chizuru Honshô is full of beans 24 hours a day, 365 days a year. She likes to lie in wait for Orihime but is always thwarted by the ever-vigilant Tatsuki.

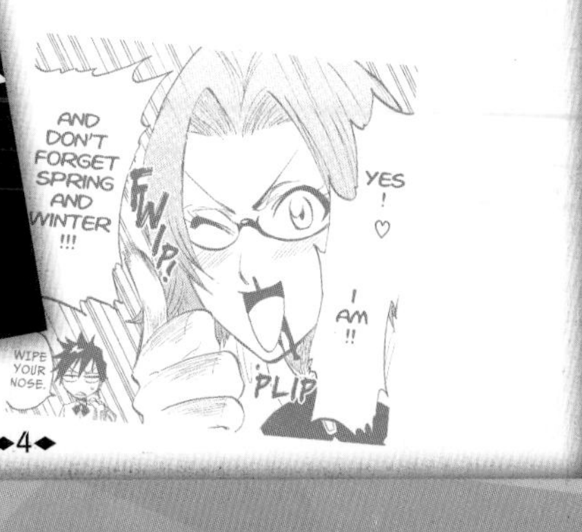
AND DON'T FORGET SPRING AND WINTER!!!
FWIP
YES! ♡ I AM!!
WIPE YOUR NOSE.
PLIP

COLOR BLEACH

SPRING AT URAHARA SHÔTEN

ILLUSTRATED MANUSCRIPT OF DAILY IDLENESS

Part 3

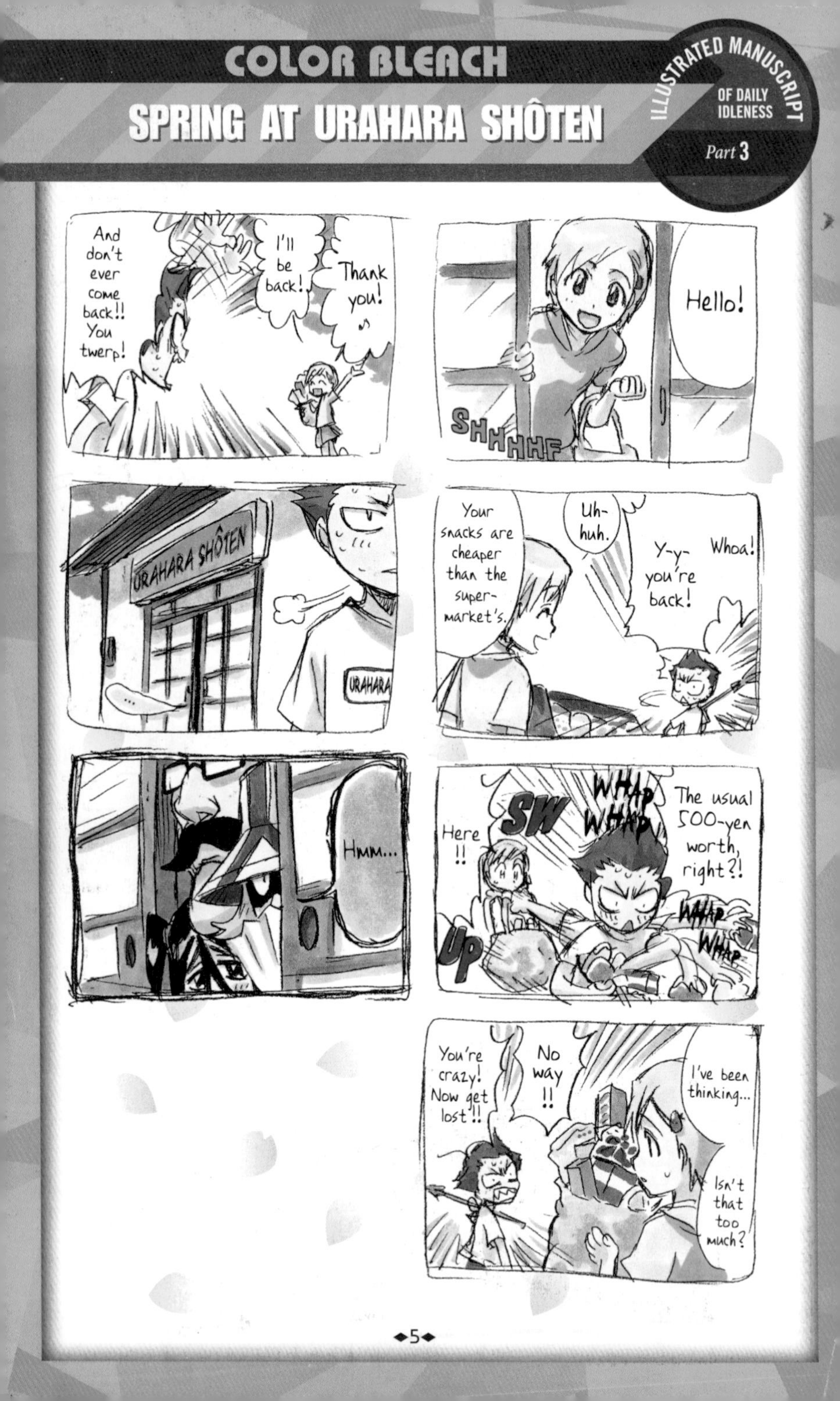

Hello!
SHHHHF
Whoa!
Y-y-you're back!
Uh-huh.
Your snacks are cheaper than the super-market's.
The usual 500-yen worth, right?!
WHAP WHAP
SW
Here!!
WHAP
WHAP
UP
I've been thinking...
Isn't that too much?
No way!!
You're crazy! Now get lost!!
Hmm...
URAHARA SHÔTEN
URAHARA
...
Thank you!
I'll be back!
And don't ever come back!! You twerp!

COLOR BLEACH

NANAO ISE'S VALENTINE'S DAY

ILLUSTRATED MANUSCRIPT OF DAILY IDLENESS

Part 4

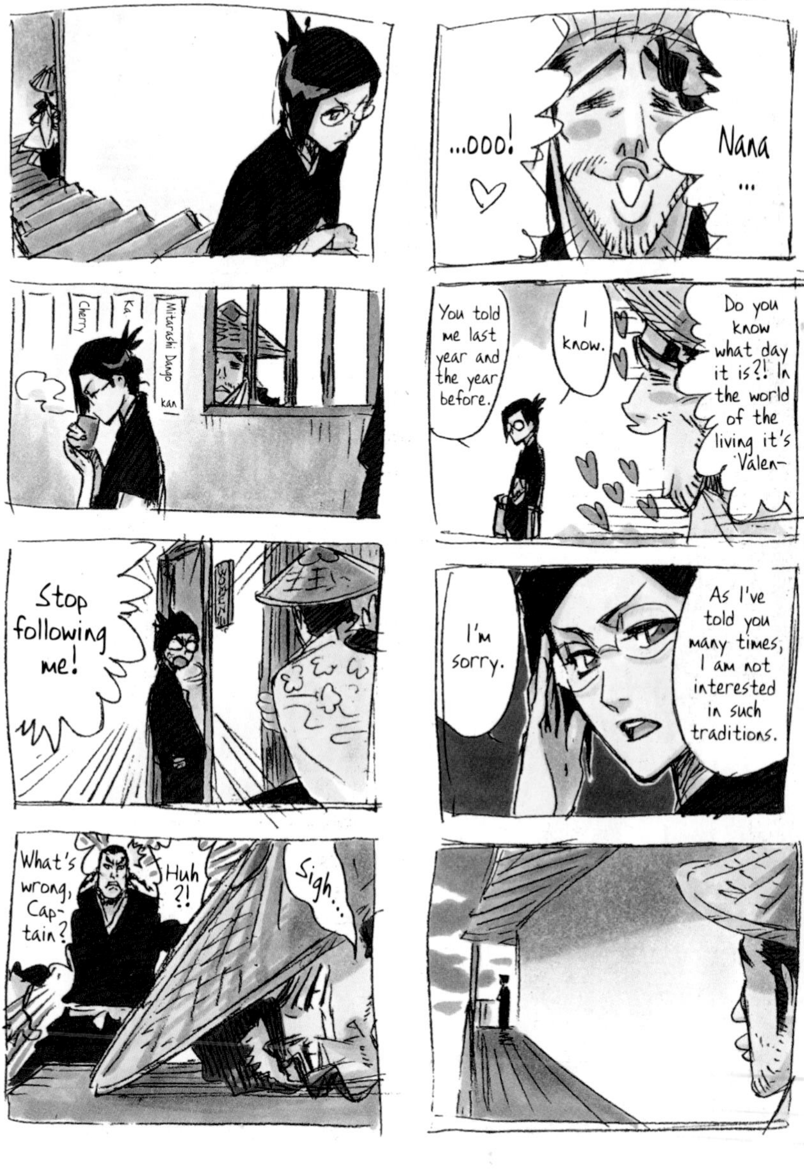
Nana
...ooo!
Do you know what day it is?! In the world of the living it's Valen-
I know.
You told me last year and the year before.
As I've told you many times, I am not interested in such traditions.
I'm sorry.
Mitarashi Dango
kan
Ka
Cherry
WOMEN
Stop following me!
Sigh...
Huh ?!
What's wrong, Cap-tain?

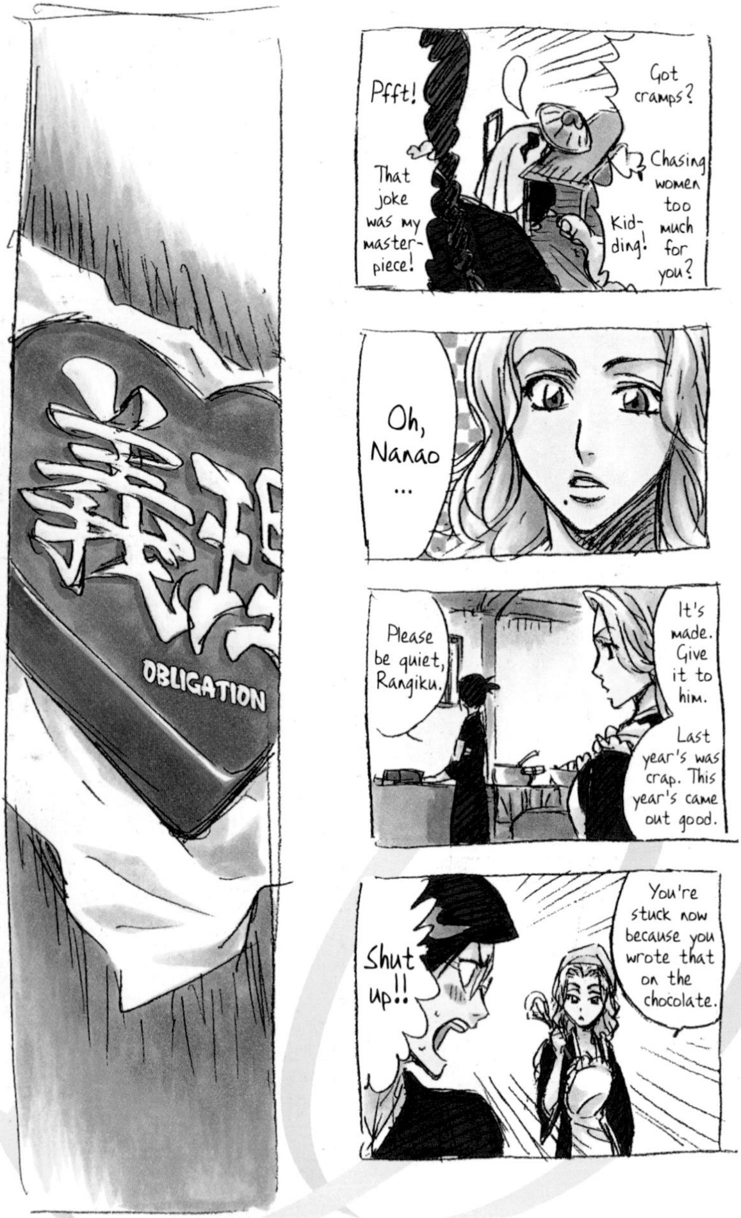
Got cramps?
Chasing women too much for you?
Kid-ding!
Pfft!
That joke was my master-piece!
Oh, Nanao ...
It's made. Give it to him.
Last year's was crap. This year's came out good.
Please be quiet, Rangiku.
You're stuck now because you wrote that on the chocolate.
Shut up!!
OBLIGATION

COLOR BLEACH
THE THIRTEEN COURT GUARD COMPANIES GAME

ILLUSTRATED MANUSCRIPT OF DAILY IDLENESS Part 5

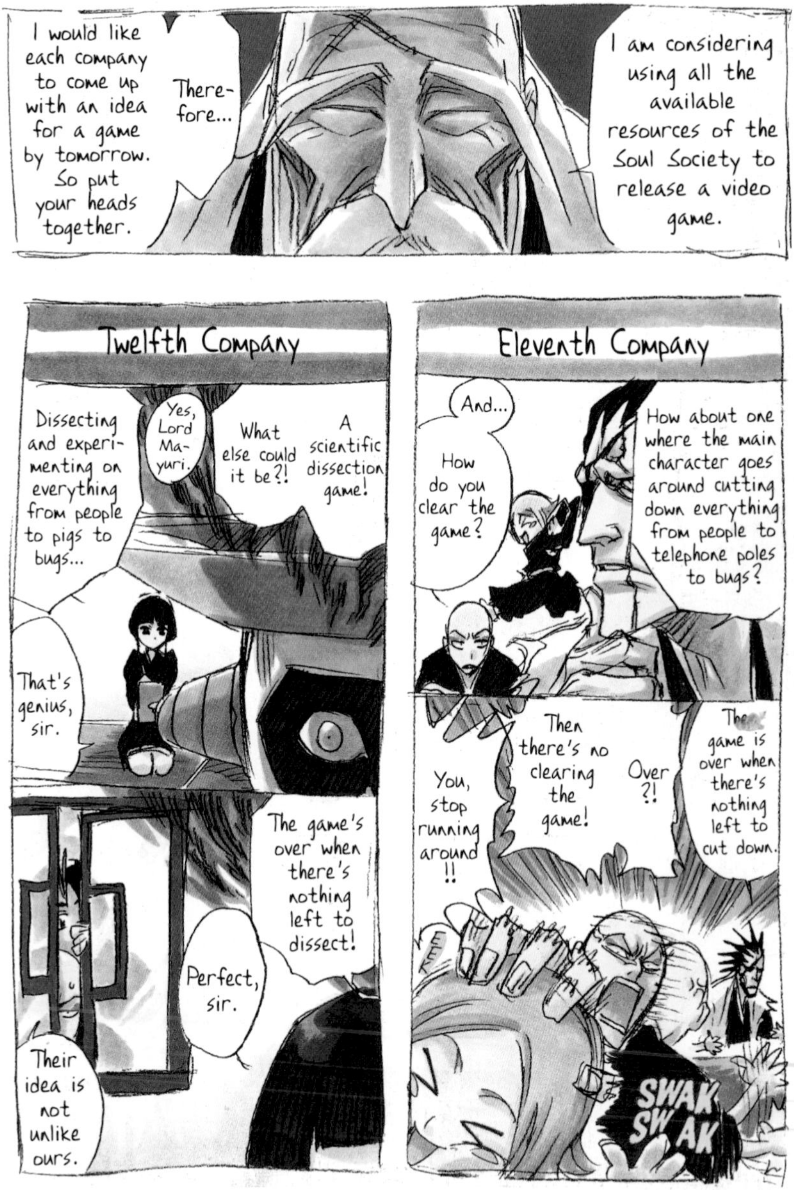
I am considering using all the available resources of the Soul Society to release a video game.
Therefore...
I would like each company to come up with an idea for a game by tomorrow. So put your heads together.
Eleventh Company
How about one where the main character goes around cutting down everything from people to telephone poles to bugs?
And...
How do you clear the game?
The game is over when there's nothing left to cut down.
Over?!
Then there's no clearing the game!
You, stop running around!!
EEK
SWAK SWAK
Twelfth Company
A scientific dissection game!
What else could it be?!
Yes, Lord Mayuri.
Dissecting and experimenting on everything from people to pigs to bugs...
That's genius, sir.
The game's over when there's nothing left to dissect!
Perfect, sir.
Their idea is not unlike ours.

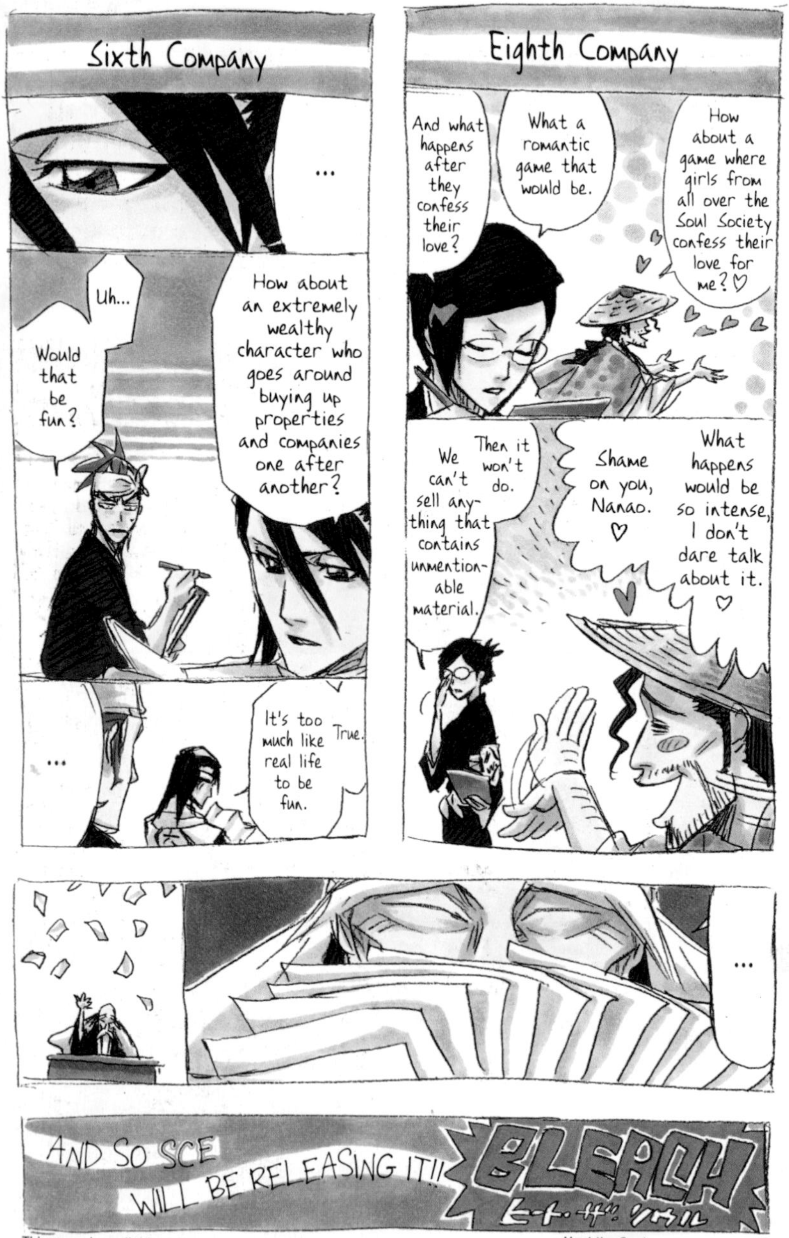
Eighth Company
How about a game where girls from all over the Soul Society confess their love for me? ♡
What a romantic game that would be.
And what happens after they confess their love?
What happens would be so intense, I don't dare talk about it. ♡
Shame on you, Nanao. ♡
Then it won't do.
We can't sell anything that contains unmentionable material.
Sixth Company
...
How about an extremely wealthy character who goes around buying up properties and companies one after another?
Uh...
Would that be fun?
True.
It's too much like real life to be fun.
...
...
AND SO SCE WILL BE RELEASING IT!!
BLEACH

This game is available only in Japan. Heat the Soul

COLOR BLEACH

THE ZANPAKU-TÔ'S SECRET

ILLUSTRATED MANUSCRIPT OF DAILY IDLENESS

Part 6

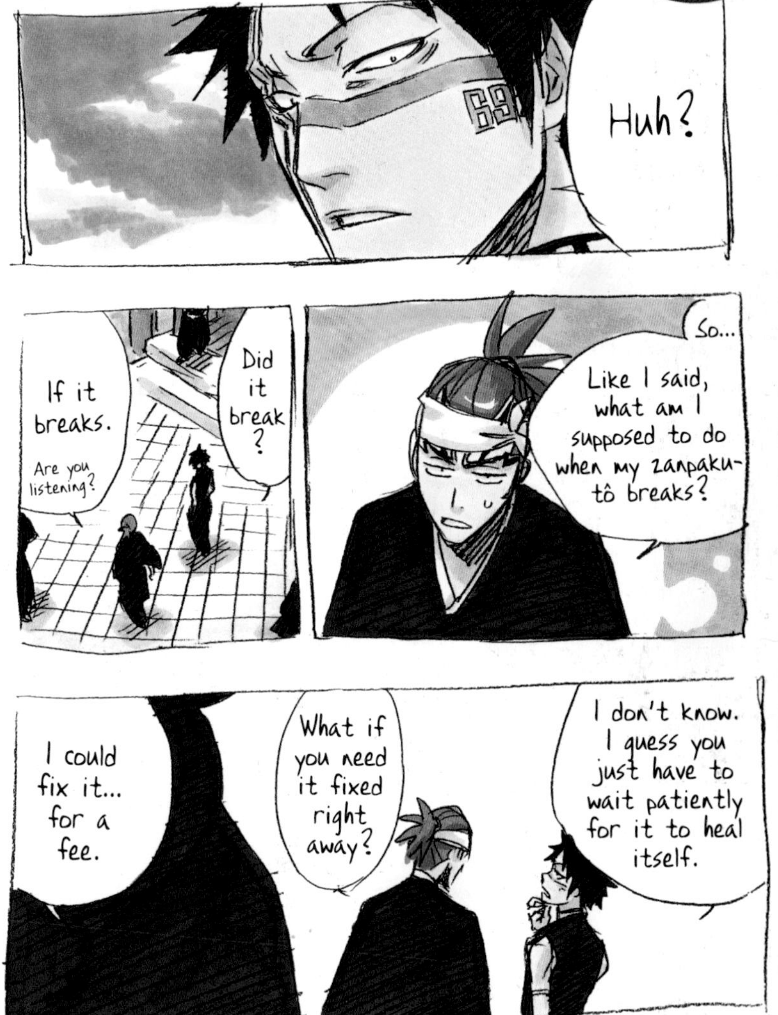
Huh?
So...
Like I said, what am I supposed to do when my zanpaku-tô breaks?
Did it break?
If it breaks.
Are you listening?
I don't know. I guess you just have to wait patiently for it to heal itself.
What if you need it fixed right away?
I could fix it... for a fee.
Huh?

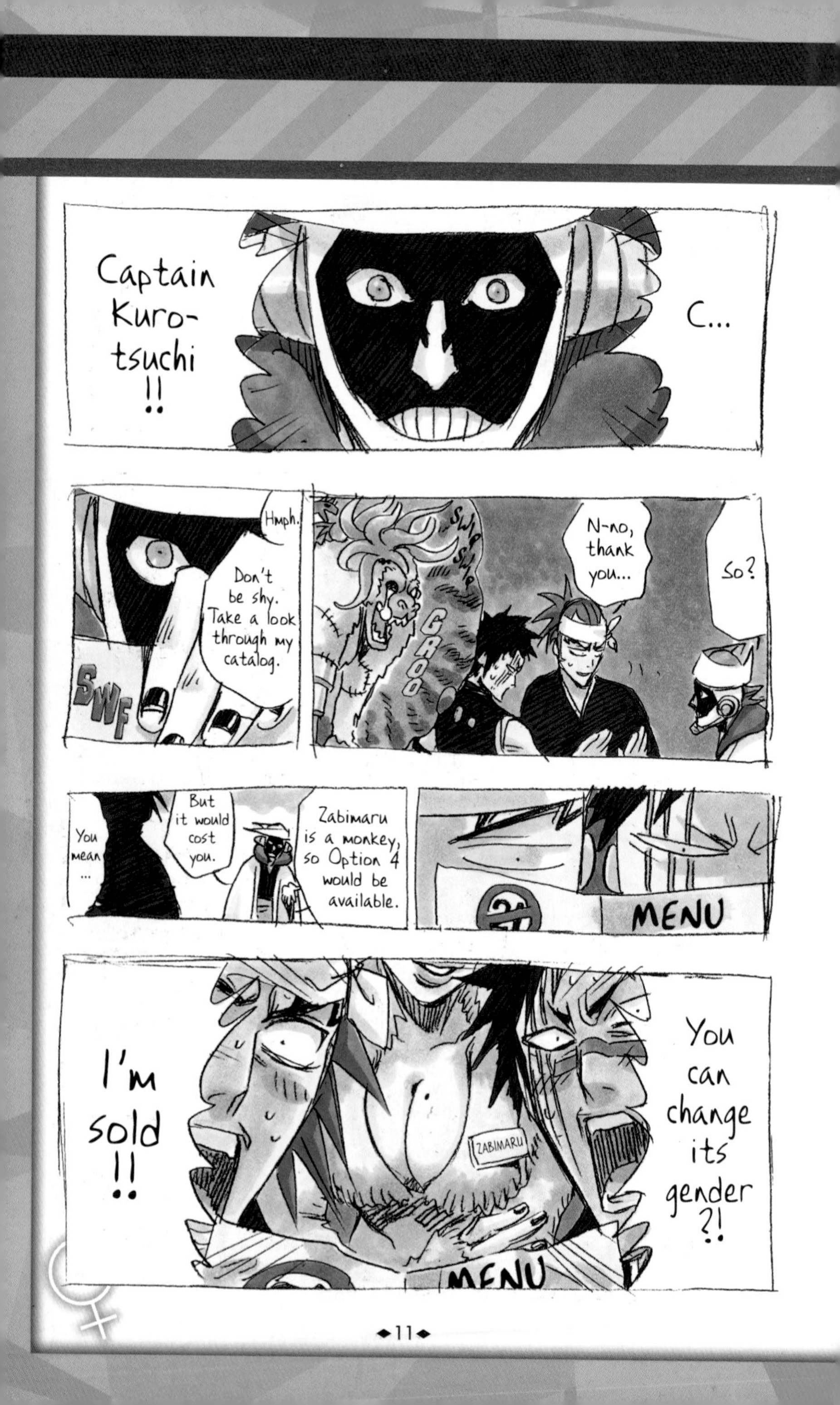
C...
Captain Kuro-tsuchi!!
So?
N-no, thank you...
GROOO
Hmph.
Don't be shy. Take a look through my catalog.
SWF
MENU
Zabimaru is a monkey, so Option 4 would be available.
But it would cost you.
You mean...
You can change its gender?!
I'm sold!!
ZABIMARU
MENU

COLOR BLEACH

A VISIT TO THE ÔMAEDA FAMILY

ILLUSTRATED MANUSCRIPT OF DAILY IDLENESS

Part 7

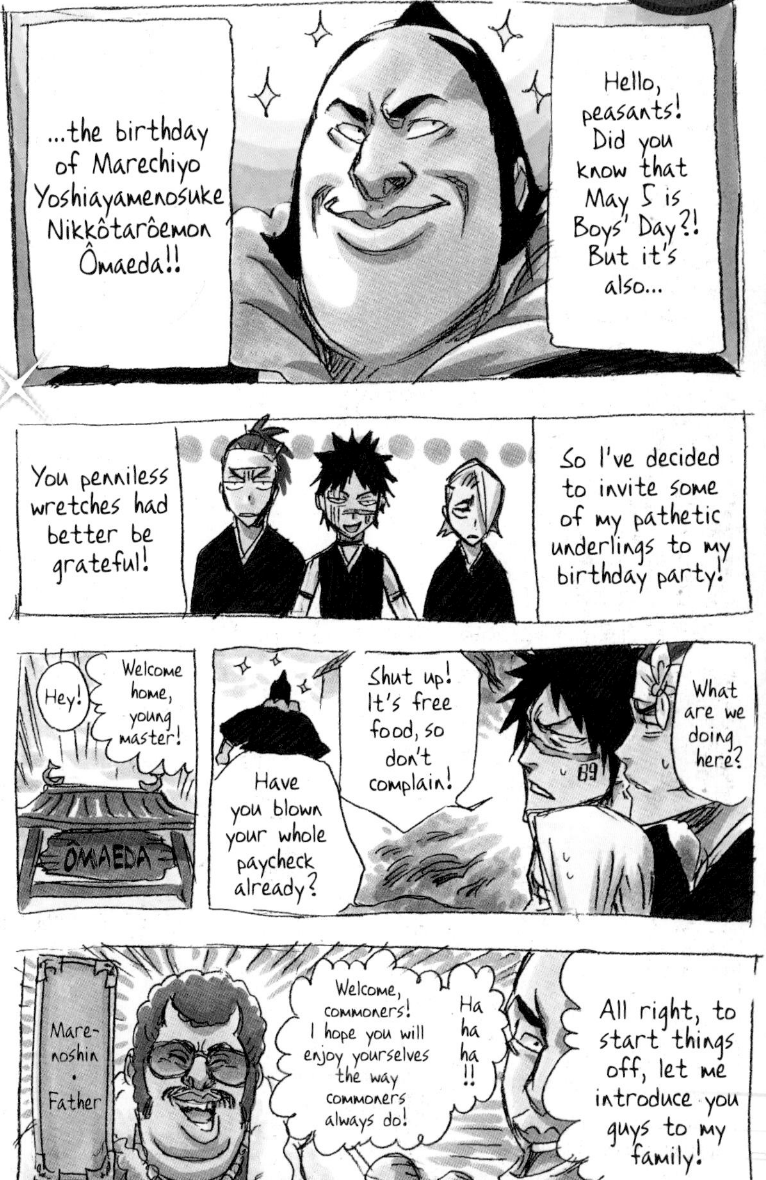

Hello, peasants! Did you know that May 5 is Boys' Day?! But it's also...
...the birthday of Marechiyo Yoshiayamenosuke Nikkôtarôemon Ômaeda!!
So I've decided to invite some of my pathetic underlings to my birthday party!
You penniless wretches had better be grateful!
What are we doing here?
89
Have you blown your whole paycheck already?
Shut up! It's free food, so don't complain!
Welcome home, young master!
Hey!
ÔMAEDA
All right, to start things off, let me introduce you guys to my family!
Ha ha ha!!
Welcome, commoners! I hope you will enjoy yourselves the way commoners always do!
Mare-noshin • Father

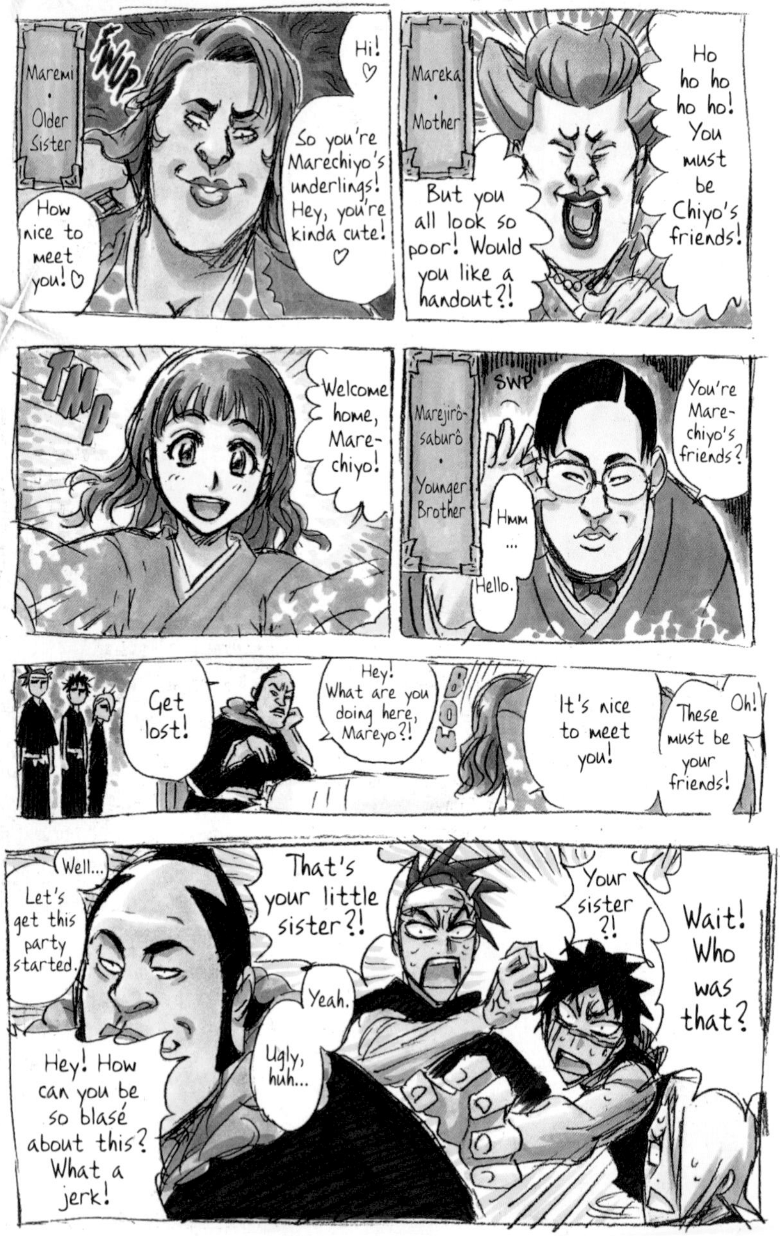
Mareka · Mother
Ho ho ho ho ho! You must be Chiyo's friends!
But you all look so poor! Would you like a handout?!
Maremi · Older Sister
FWUP
Hi! ♡
So you're Marechiyo's underlings! Hey, you're kinda cute! ♡
How nice to meet you! ♡
Marejirô-saburô · Younger Brother
SWP
You're Marechiyo's friends?
Hmm...
Hello.
TMP
Welcome home, Marechiyo!
Oh!
These must be your friends!
It's nice to meet you!
BOW
Hey! What are you doing here, Mareyo?!
Get lost!
Wait! Who was that?
Your sister?!
That's your little sister?!
Yeah.
Ugly, huh...
Well...
Let's get this party started.
Hey! How can you be so blasé about this? What a jerk!

RANGIKU'S ACCURATE HOROSCOPE

ILLUSTRATED MANUSCRIPT OF DAILY IDLENESS

Part **8**

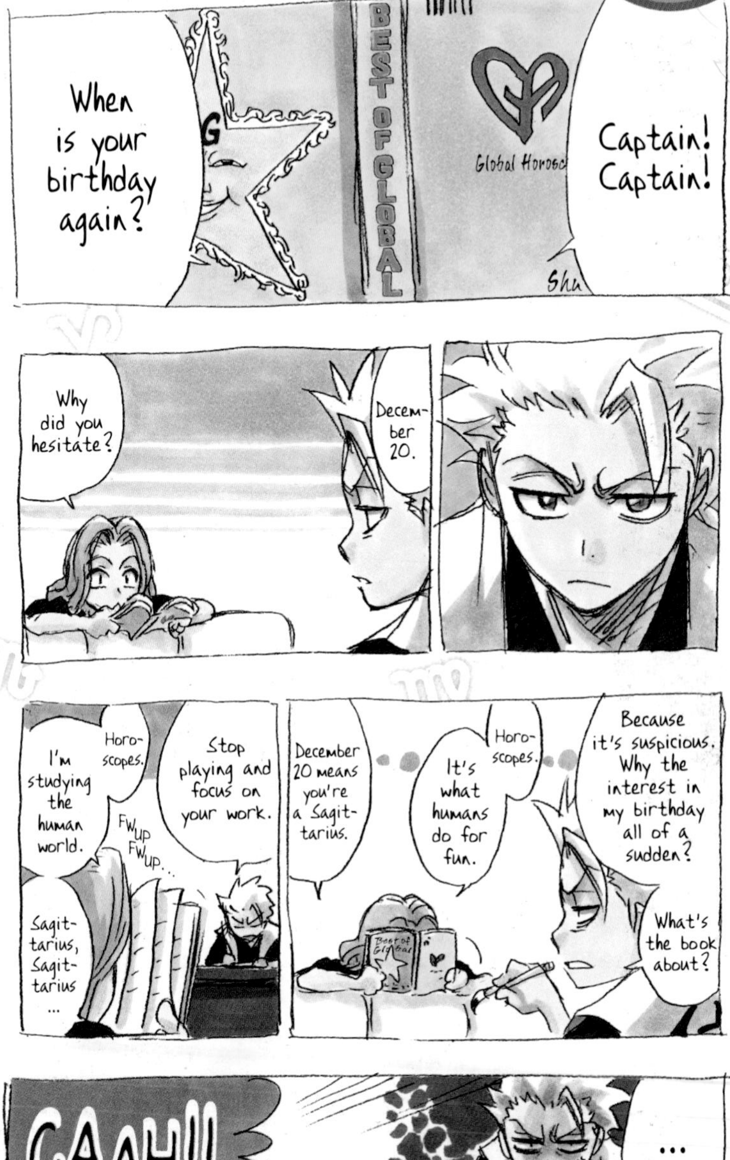
Captain! Captain!
Global Horosc
BEST OF GLOBAL
When is your birthday again?
December 20.
Why did you hesitate?
Because it's suspicious. Why the interest in my birthday all of a sudden?
What's the book about?
Horoscopes.
It's what humans do for fun.
December 20 means you're a Sagittarius.
Best of Global
Stop playing and focus on your work.
Horoscopes.
I'm studying the human world.
FWUP FWUP...
Sagittarius, Sagittarius...
...
GAAH!!

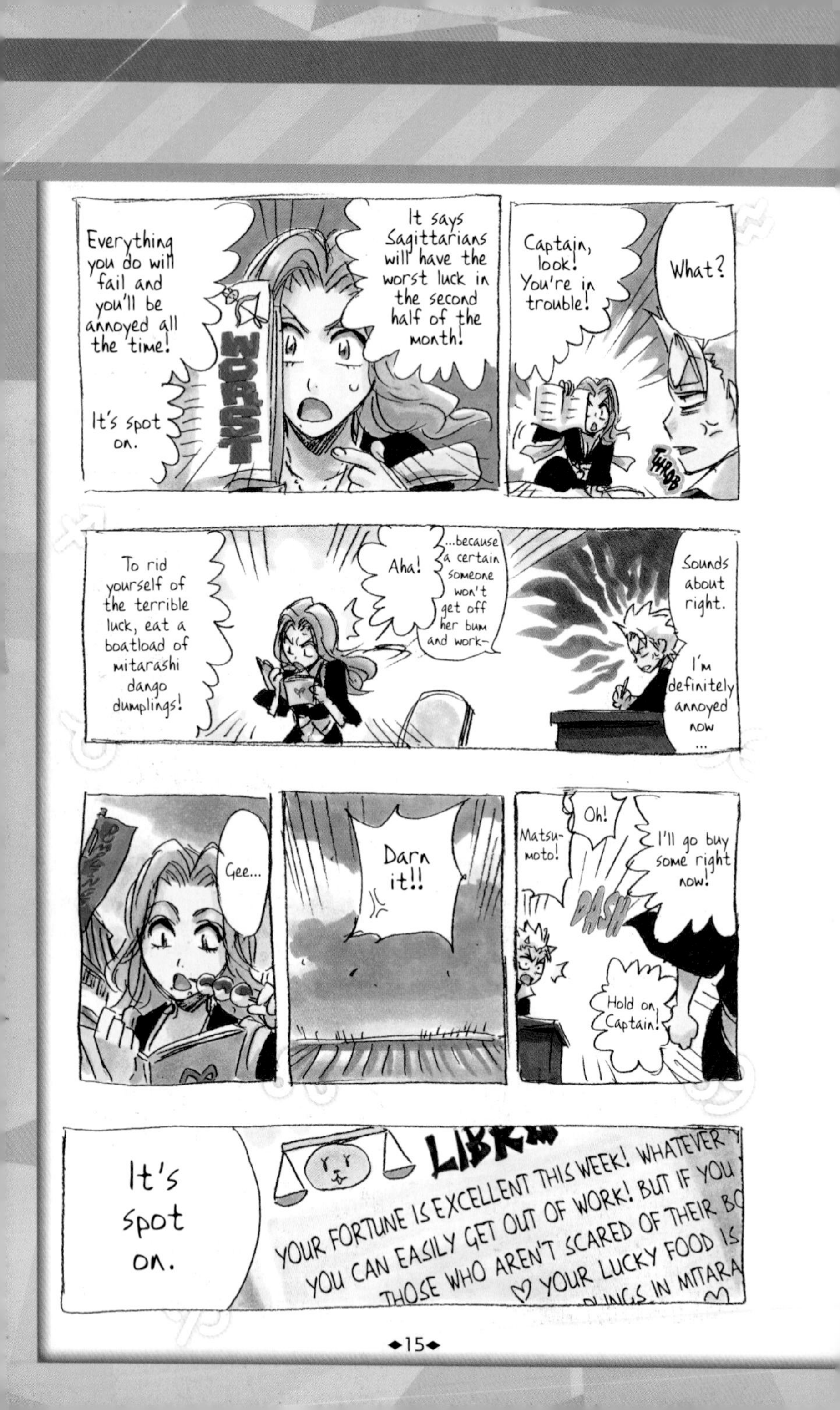
It says Sagittarians will have the worst luck in the second half of the month!
Everything you do will fail and you'll be annoyed all the time!
WORST
It's spot on.
Captain, look! You're in trouble!
What?
THROB
To rid yourself of the terrible luck, eat a boatload of mitarashi dango dumplings!
Aha!
...because a certain someone won't get off her bum and work—
Sounds about right.
I'm definitely annoyed now...
Gee...
Darn it!!
Matsu-moto!
Oh!
I'll go buy some right now!
DASH
Hold on, Captain!
It's spot on.
LIBRA
YOUR FORTUNE IS EXCELLENT THIS WEEK! WHATEVER
YOU CAN EASILY GET OUT OF WORK! BUT IF YOU
THOSE WHO AREN'T SCARED OF THEIR BO
YOUR LUCKY FOOD IS
DUMPLINGS IN MITARA

COLOR BLEACH

CONGRATULATIONS! THE GBA *BLEACH* GAME IS ON SALE!

ILLUSTRATED MANUSCRIPT OF DAILY IDLENESS
Part 9

Congratulations!
You have successfully enlisted in the Thirteen Court Guard Companies!
Which company would you like to join?

Real men join Eleventh Company! Go to 1

You've longed for Tenth Company!! Go to 2

Eighth Company, of course!! Go to 3

Fourth Company seems the nicest... Go to 4

1

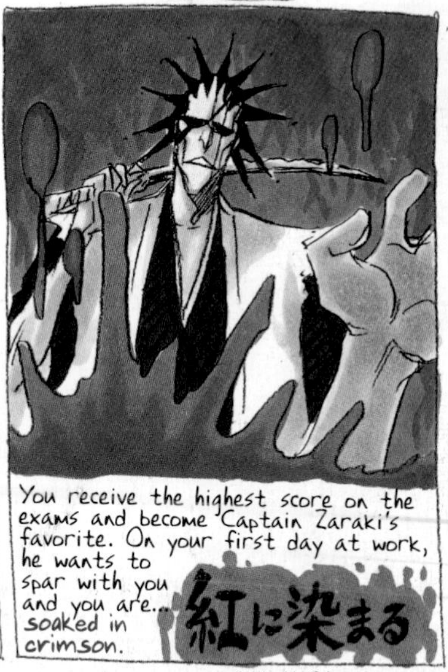

You receive the highest score on the exams and become Captain Zaraki's favorite. On your first day at work, he wants to spar with you and you are... soaked in crimson.
紅に染まる

2

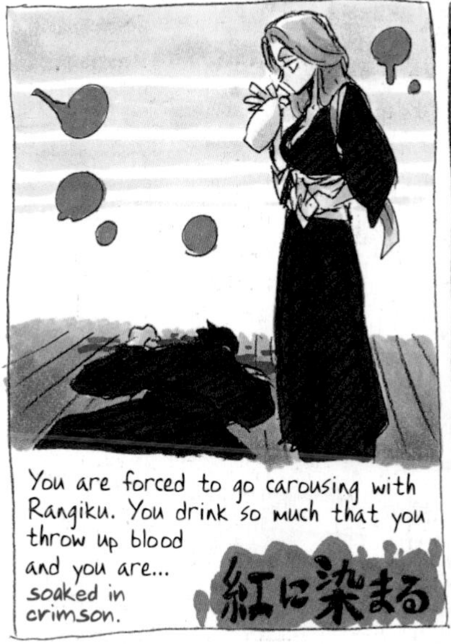

You are forced to go carousing with Rangiku. You drink so much that you throw up blood and you are... soaked in crimson.
紅に染まる

Soaked in Crimson

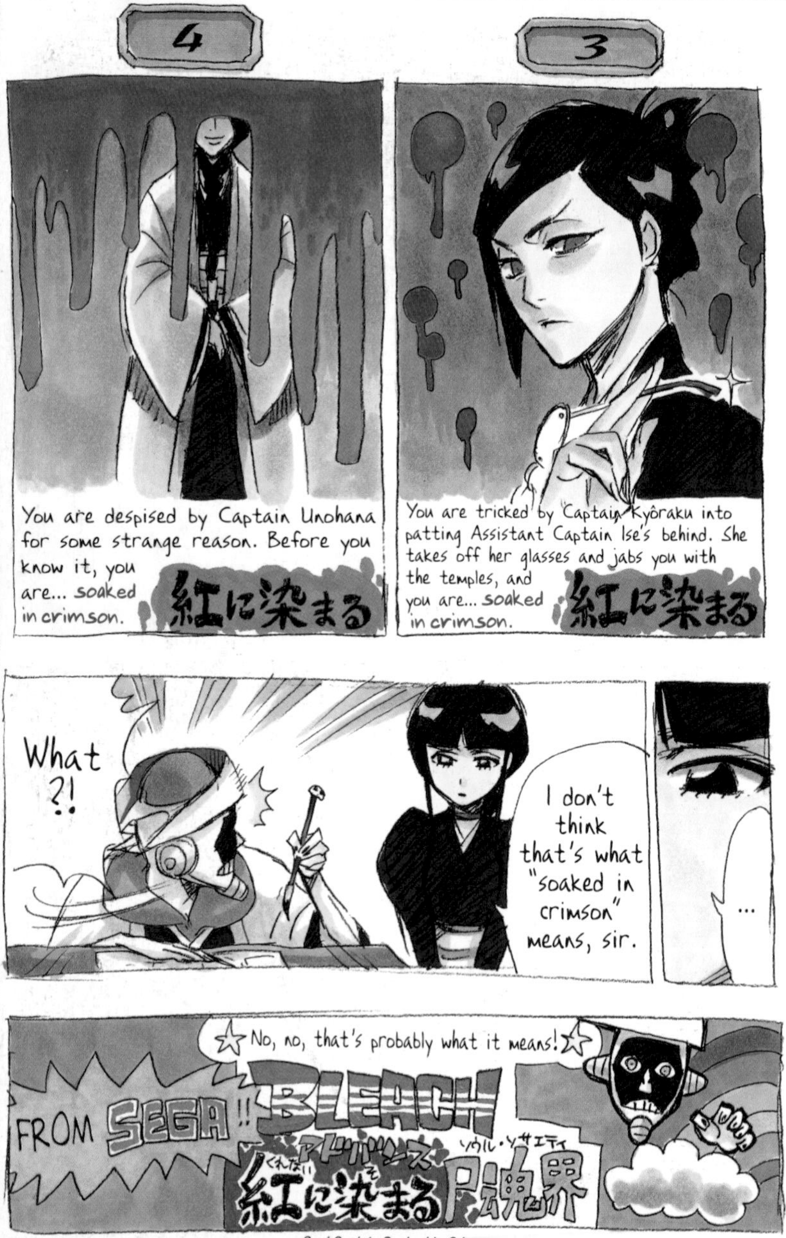
3
You are tricked by Captain Kyôraku into patting Assistant Captain Ise's behind. She takes off her glasses and jabs you with the temples, and you are... soaked in crimson.
紅に染まる
4
You are despised by Captain Unohana for some strange reason. Before you know it, you are... soaked in crimson.
紅に染まる
...
I don't think that's what "soaked in crimson" means, sir.
What?!
No, no, that's probably what it means!
FROM SEGA!!
BLEACH
アドバンス
くれない
紅に染まる
ソウル・ソサエティ
尸魂界

This game is available only in Japan.

Soul Society Soaked in Crimson

COLOR BLEACH

DELUSIONAL MEN OF THE THIRTEEN COURT GUARD COMPANIES

ILLUSTRATED MANUSCRIPT OF DAILY IDLENESS Part 10

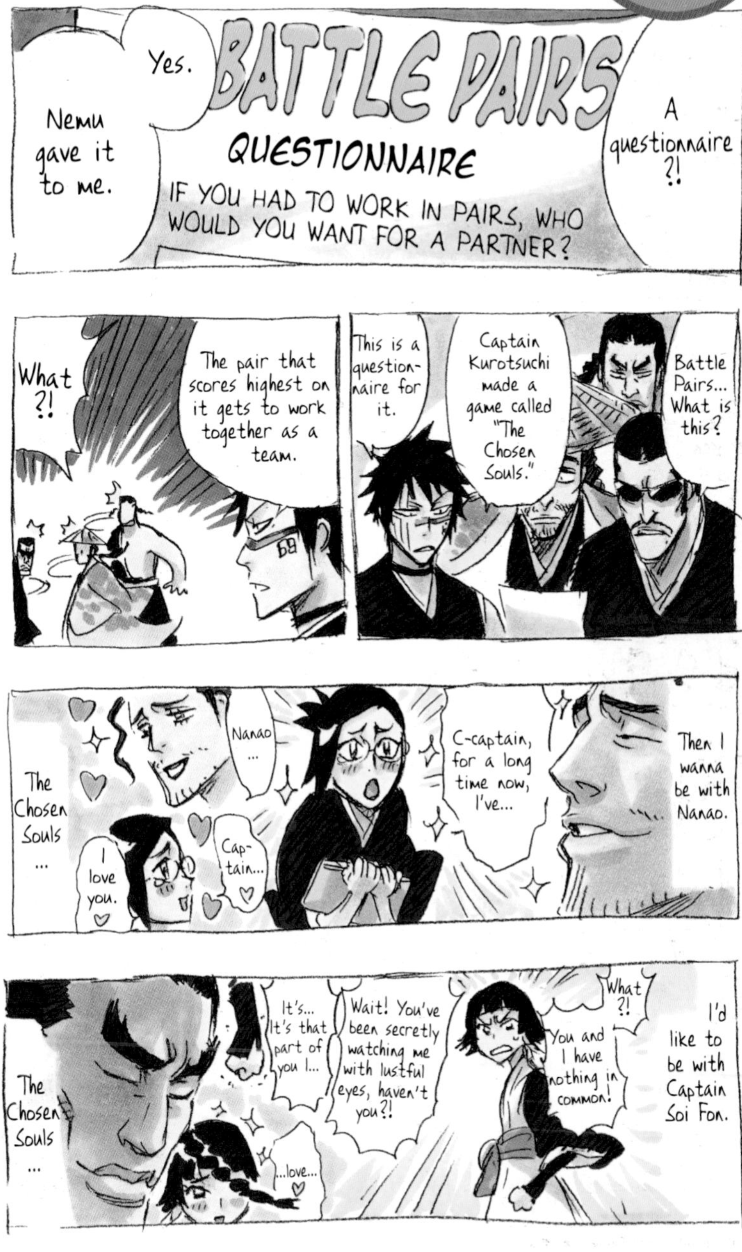
A questionnaire?!
BATTLE PAIRS
QUESTIONNAIRE
IF YOU HAD TO WORK IN PAIRS, WHO WOULD YOU WANT FOR A PARTNER?
Yes.
Nemu gave it to me.
Battle Pairs... What is this?
Captain Kurotsuchi made a game called "The Chosen Souls."
This is a question-naire for it.
The pair that scores highest on it gets to work together as a team.
What?!
Then I wanna be with Nanao.
C-captain, for a long time now, I've...
Nanao...
Cap-tain...
I love you.
The Chosen Souls...
I'd like to be with Captain Soi Fon.
What?!
You and I have nothing in common!
Wait! You've been secretly watching me with lustful eyes, haven't you?!
It's... It's that part of you I...
...love...
The Chosen Souls...

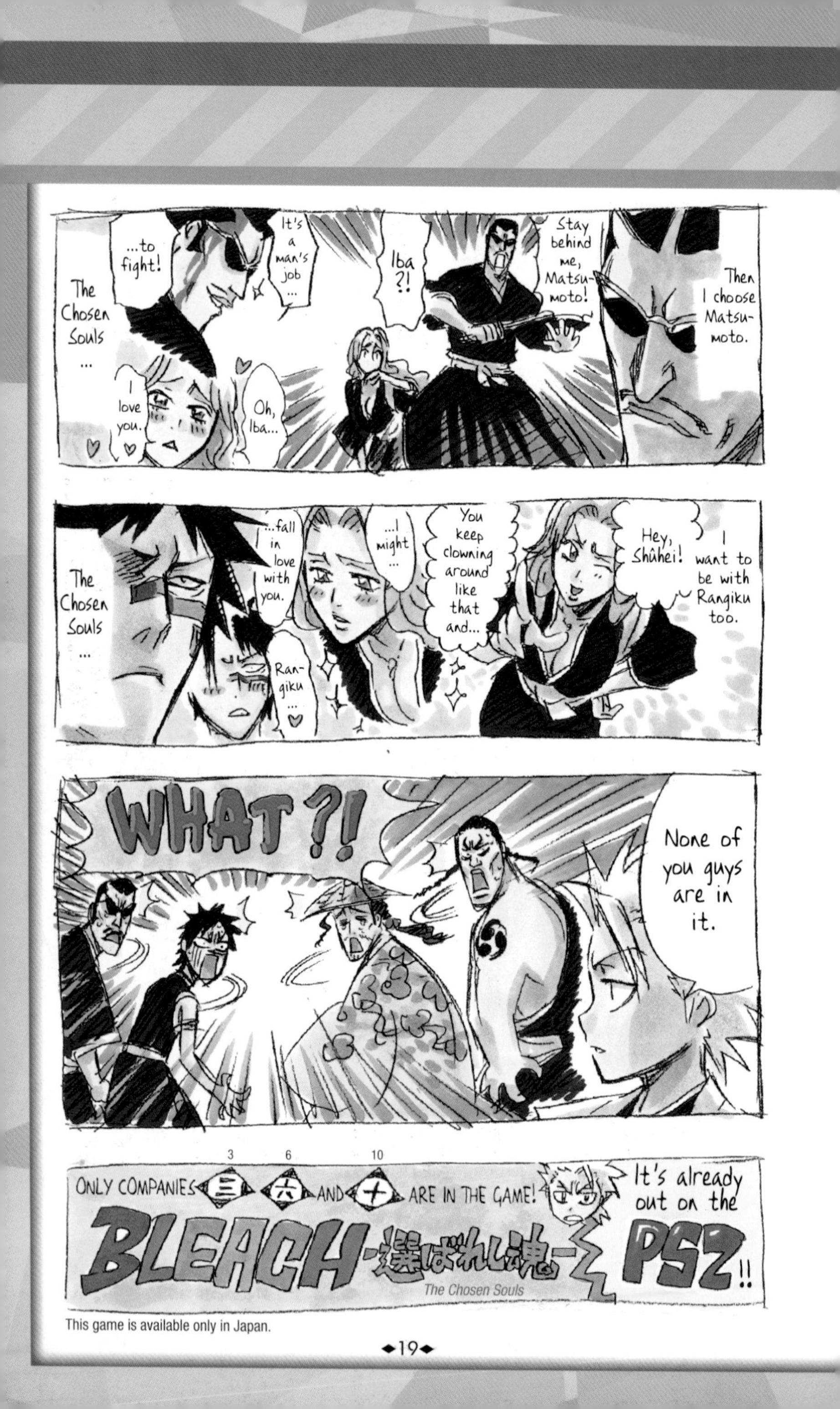
Then I choose Matsumoto.
Stay behind me, Matsumoto!
Iba ?!
It's a man's job...
...to fight!
Oh, Iba...
I love you.
The Chosen Souls...
I want to be with Rangiku too.
Hey, Shûhei!
You keep clowning around like that and...
...I might...
...fall in love with you.
Rangiku...
The Chosen Souls...
None of you guys are in it.
WHAT ?!
ONLY COMPANIES 3 三 6 六 AND 10 十 ARE IN THE GAME!
It's already out on the
BLEACH -選ばれし魂-
The Chosen Souls
PS2!!

This game is available only in Japan.

COLOR BLEACH

GAME IDEAS WELCOME!

ILLUSTRATED MANUSCRIPT OF DAILY IDLENESS *Part* 11

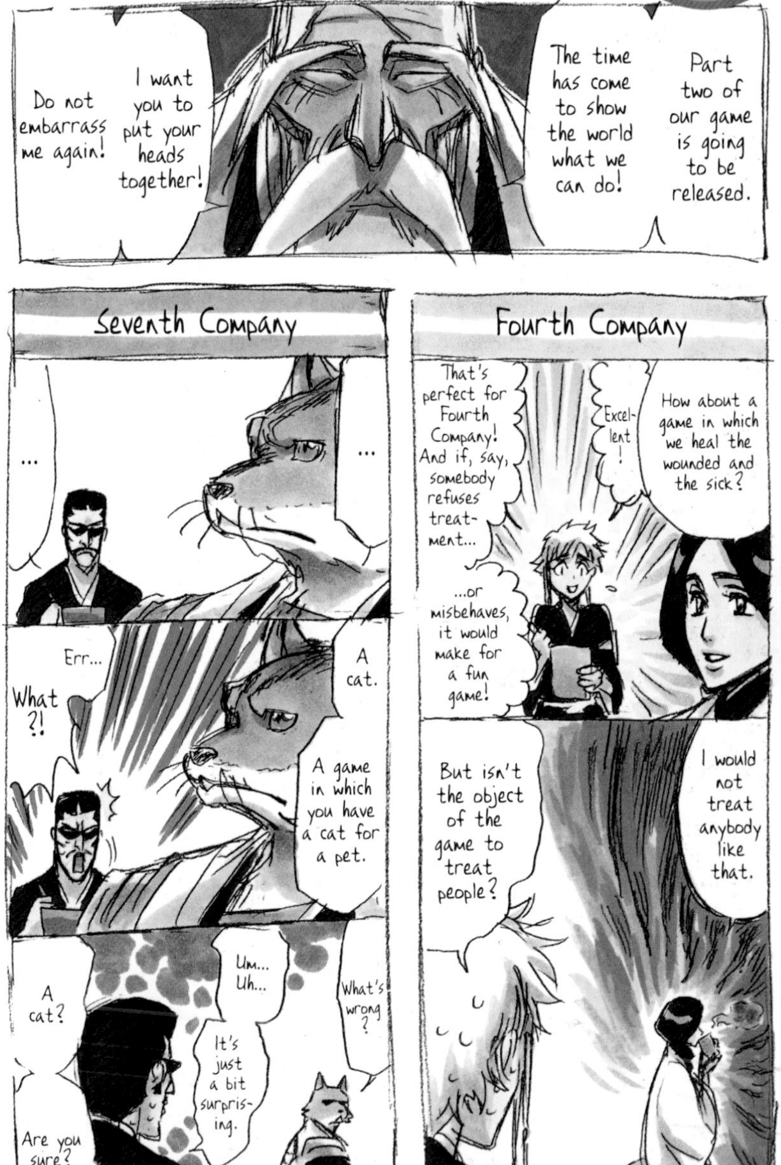
Part two of our game is going to be released.
The time has come to show the world what we can do!
I want you to put your heads together!
Do not embarrass me again!
Fourth Company
How about a game in which we heal the wounded and the sick?
Excel-lent!
That's perfect for Fourth Company! And if, say, somebody refuses treat-ment...
...or misbehaves, it would make for a fun game!
I would not treat anybody like that.
But isn't the object of the game to treat people?
Seventh Company
...
...
A cat.
A game in which you have a cat for a pet.
Err...
What?!
What's wrong?
Um... Uh...
It's just a bit surpris-ing.
A cat?
Are you sure?

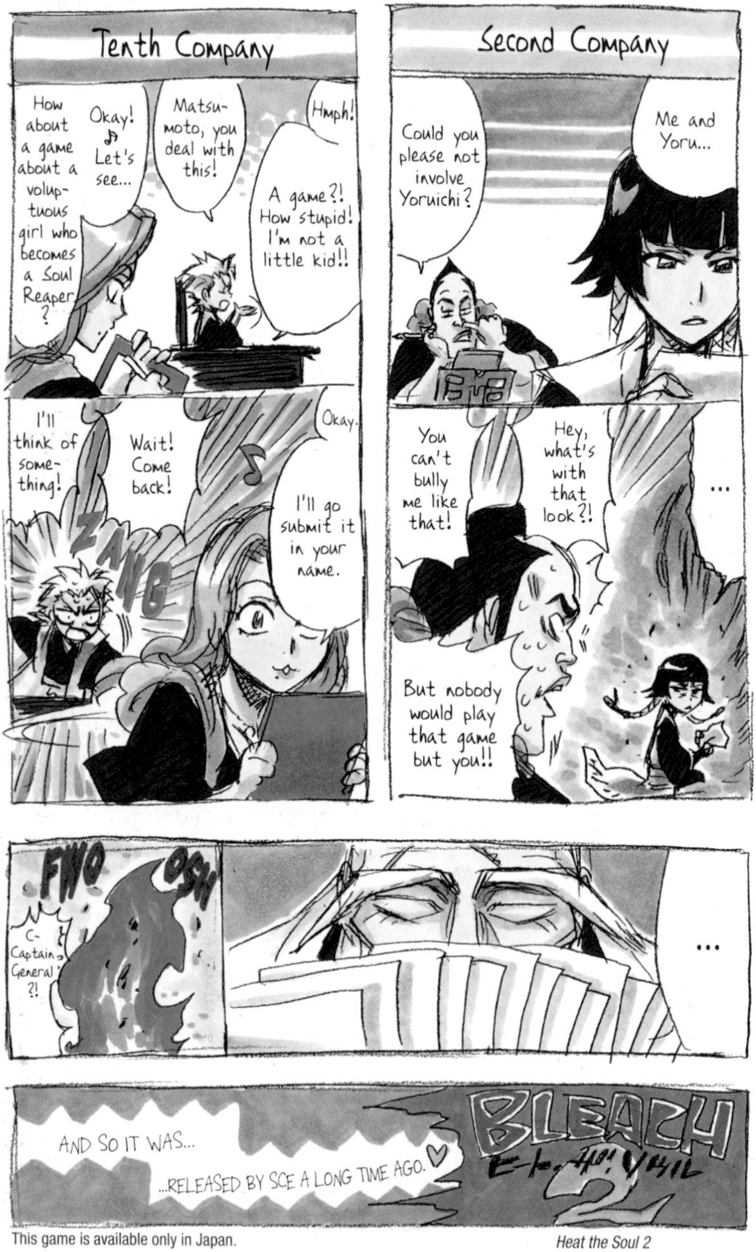
Second Company
Me and Yoru...
Could you please not involve Yoruichi?
...
Hey, what's with that look?!
You can't bully me like that!
But nobody would play that game but you!!
Tenth Company
Hmph!
A game?! How stupid! I'm not a little kid!!
Matsumoto, you deal with this!
Okay! ♪ Let's see...
How about a game about a voluptuous girl who becomes a Soul Reaper?
Okay.
I'll go submit it in your name.
Wait! Come back!
I'll think of something!
ZANG
...
FWOOSH
C-Captain General?!
BLEACH
AND SO IT WAS...
...RELEASED BY SCE A LONG TIME AGO. ♡

This game is available only in Japan.

Heat the Soul 2

COLOR BLEACH

AN ASSASSIN IN THE KUCHIKI HOUSEHOLD

ILLUSTRATED MANUSCRIPT OF DAILY IDLENESS

Part 12

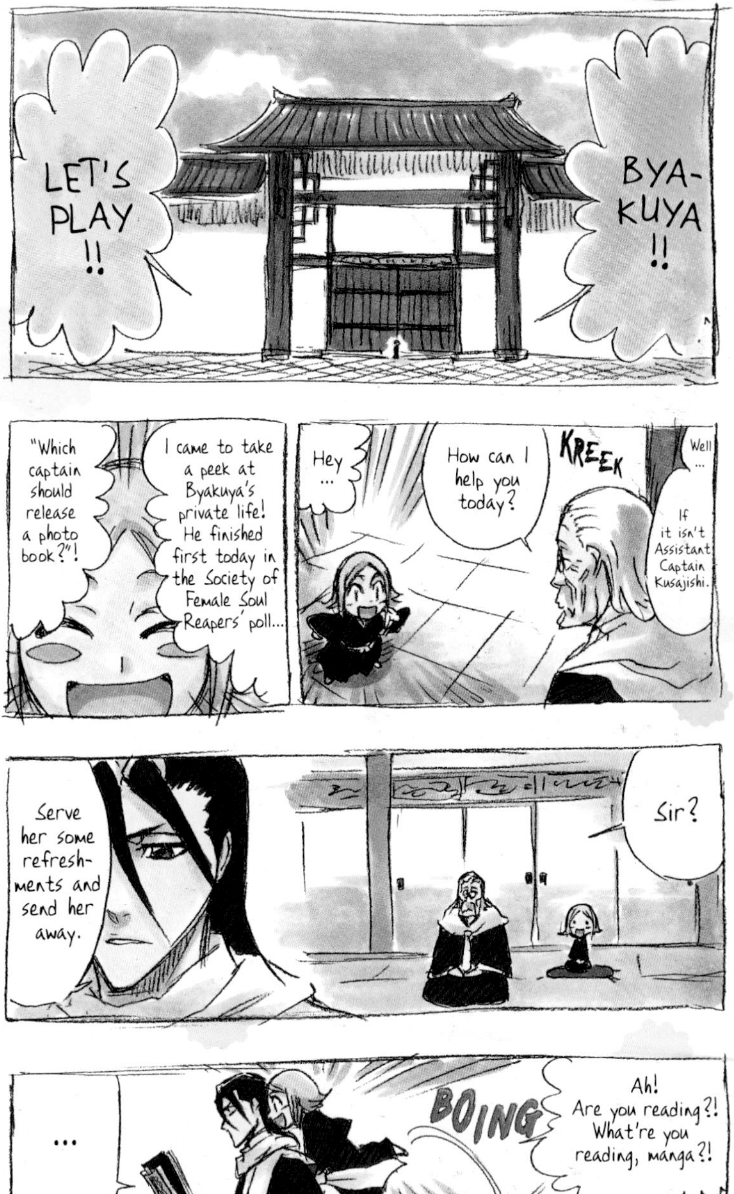
BYA-KUYA!!
LET'S PLAY!!
Well ... If it isn't Assistant Captain Kusajishi.
KREEK
How can I help you today?
Hey ...
I came to take a peek at Byakuya's private life! He finished first today in the Society of Female Soul Reapers' poll...
"Which captain should release a photo book?"!
Sir?
Serve her some refreshments and send her away.
Ah! Are you reading?! What're you reading, manga?!
BOING
...

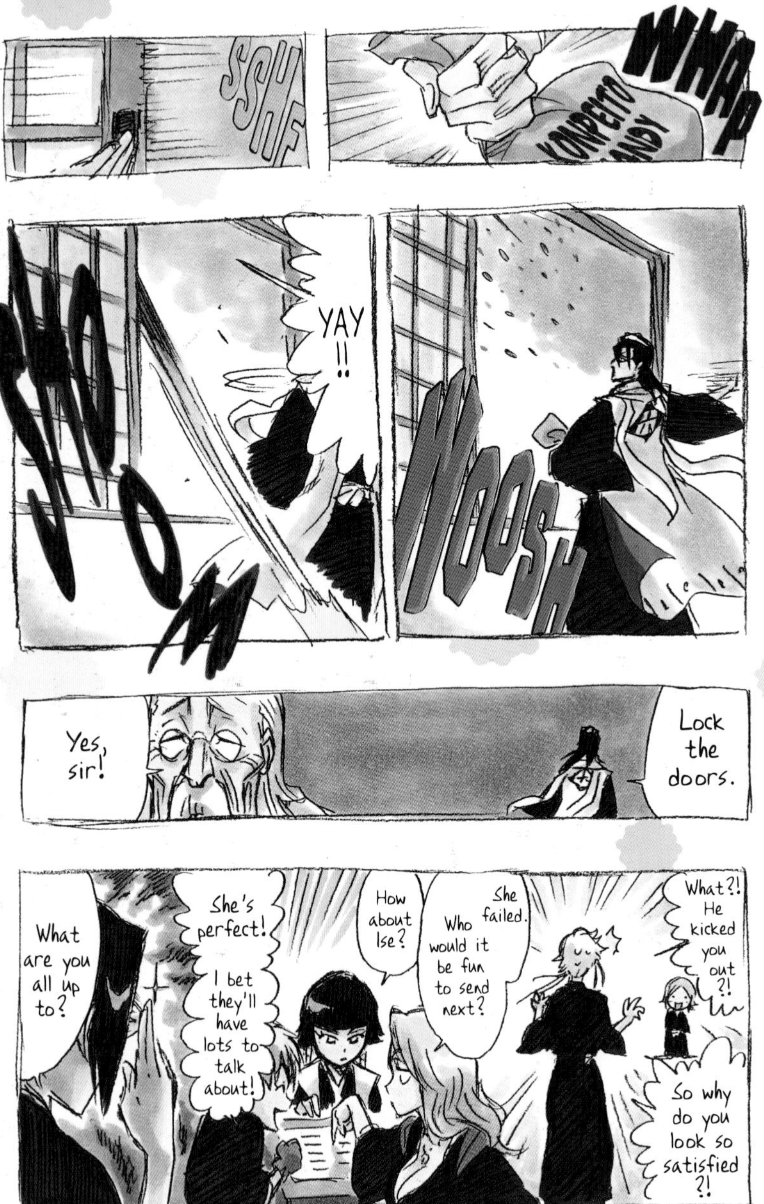
WHAP
KONPEITO CANDY
SSHF
WOOSH
YAY!!
SHOOM
Lock the doors.
Yes, sir!
What?! He kicked you out?!
So why do you look so satisfied?!
She failed.
Who would it be fun to send next?
How about Ise?
She's perfect!
I bet they'll have lots to talk about!
What are you all up to?

COLOR BLEACH

THE LATEST DREAM GAME

ILLUSTRATED MANUSCRIPT OF DAILY IDLENESS

Part 13

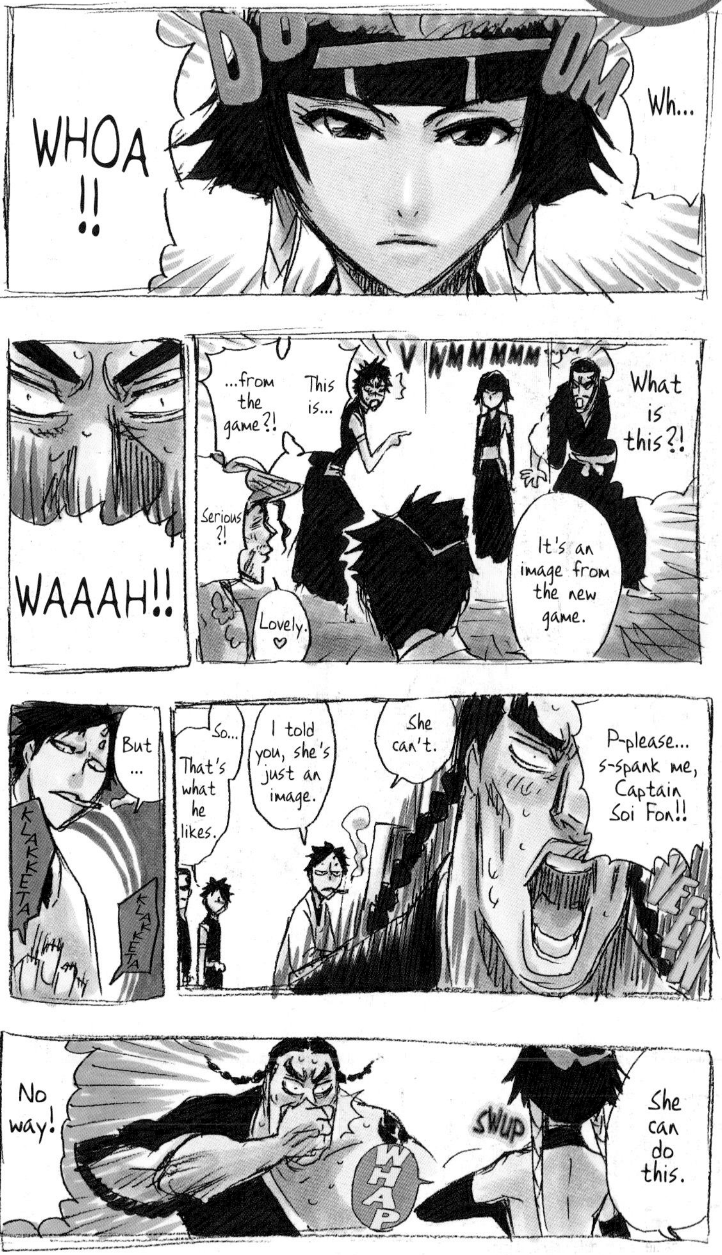
DOOM
Wh...
WHOA!!
VWMMMMM
What is this?!
This is...
...from the game?!
It's an image from the new game.
Serious?!
Lovely. ♡
WAAAH!!
P-please... s-spank me, Captain Soi Fon!!
YEEEN
She can't.
I told you, she's just an image.
So... That's what he likes.
But...
KLAKKETA
KLAKKETA
She can do this.
SWUP
WHAP
No way!

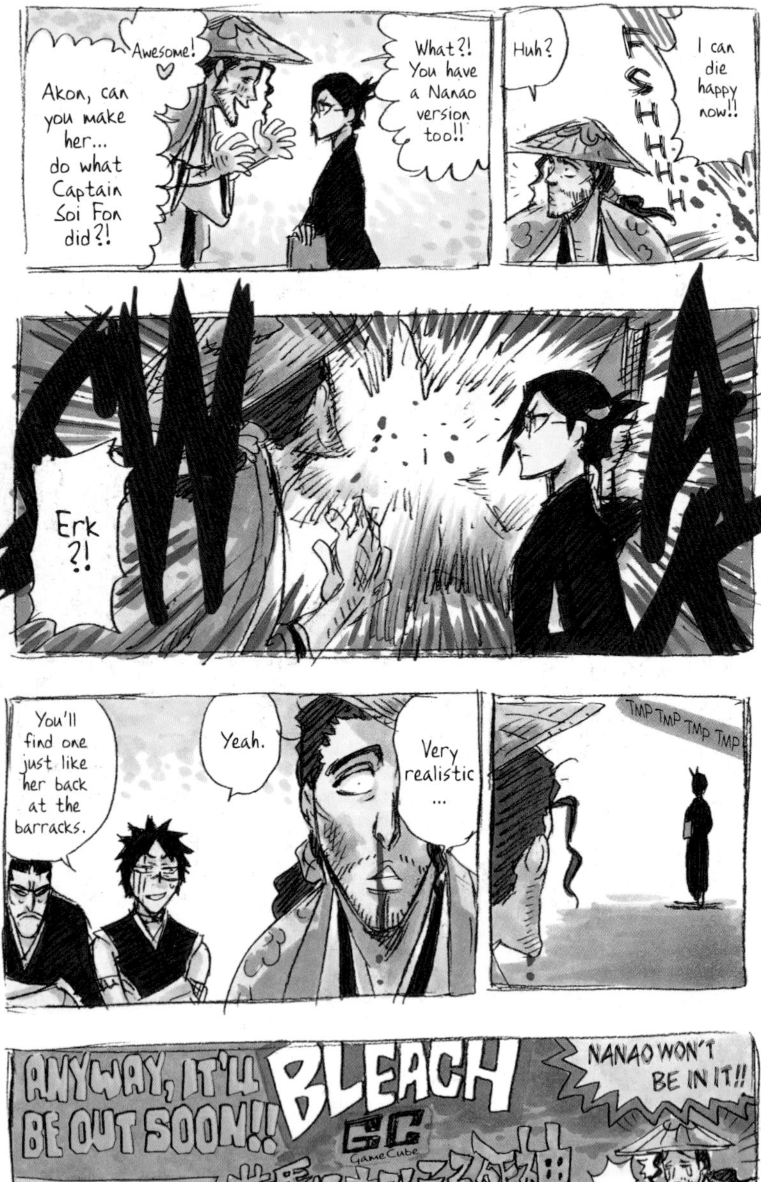
What?! You have a Nanao version too!!
Awesome!
Akon, can you make her... do what Captain Soi Fon did?!
Huh?
FSHHHHH
I can die happy now!!
Erk?!
You'll find one just like her back at the barracks.
Yeah.
Very realistic...
TMP TMP TMP TMP
ANYWAY, IT'LL BE OUT SOON!!
BLEACH
GC GameCube
黄昏にまみえる死神
NANAO WON'T BE IN IT!!
What?!

This game is available only in Japan.

Soul Reapers in the Twilight

COLOR BLEACH
A LIFE-SIZE PRESENT

Illustrated Manuscript of Daily Idleness
Part 14

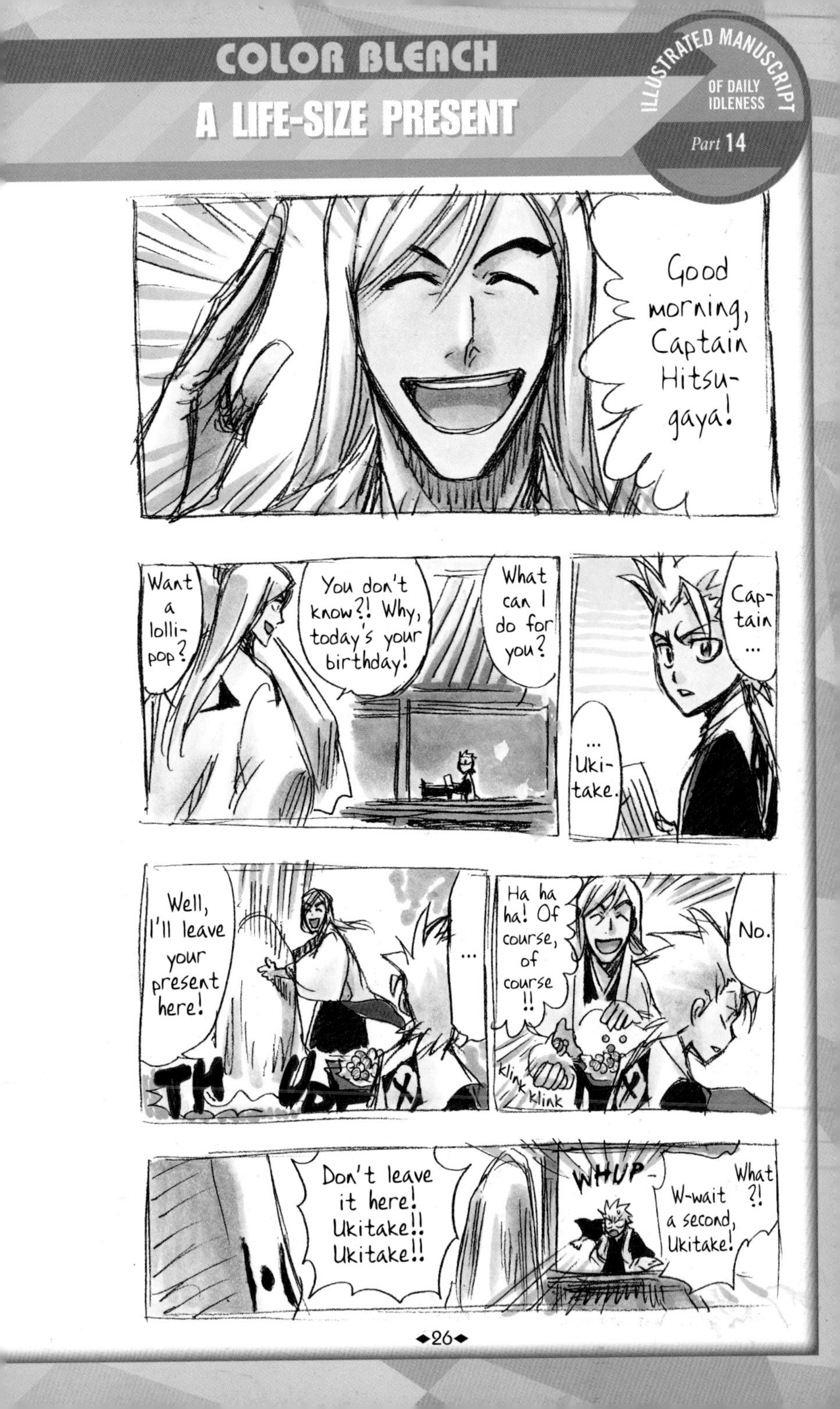
Good morning, Captain Hitsugaya!
Captain ...
... Ukitake.
What can I do for you?
You don't know?! Why, today's your birthday!
Want a lollipop?
No.
Ha ha ha! Of course, of course!!
klink klink
...
Well, I'll leave your present here!
THUD
What?!
W-wait a second, Ukitake!
WHUP
Don't leave it here! Ukitake!! Ukitake!!

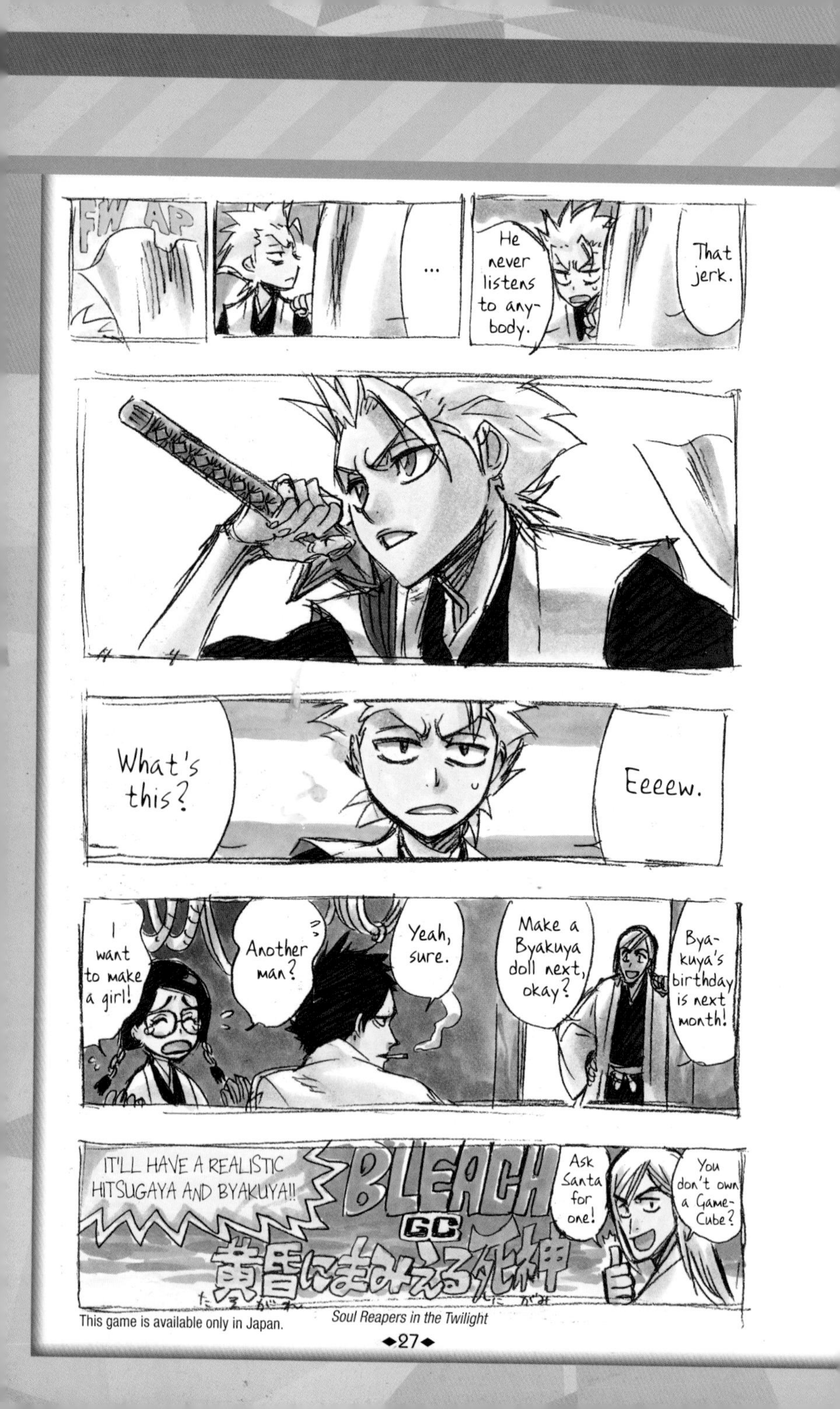
That jerk.
He never listens to anybody.
...
FWAP
Eeeew.
What's this?
Bya-kuya's birthday is next month!
Make a Byakuya doll next, okay?
Yeah, sure.
Another man?
I want to make a girl!
You don't own a Game-Cube?
Ask Santa for one!
BLEACH GC
黄昏にまみえる死神
IT'LL HAVE A REALISTIC HITSUGAYA AND BYAKUYA!!

This game is available only in Japan.

Soul Reapers in the Twilight

COLOR BLEACH

OPERATION FUNDRAISING

ILLUSTRATED MANUSCRIPT OF DAILY IDLENESS

Part 15

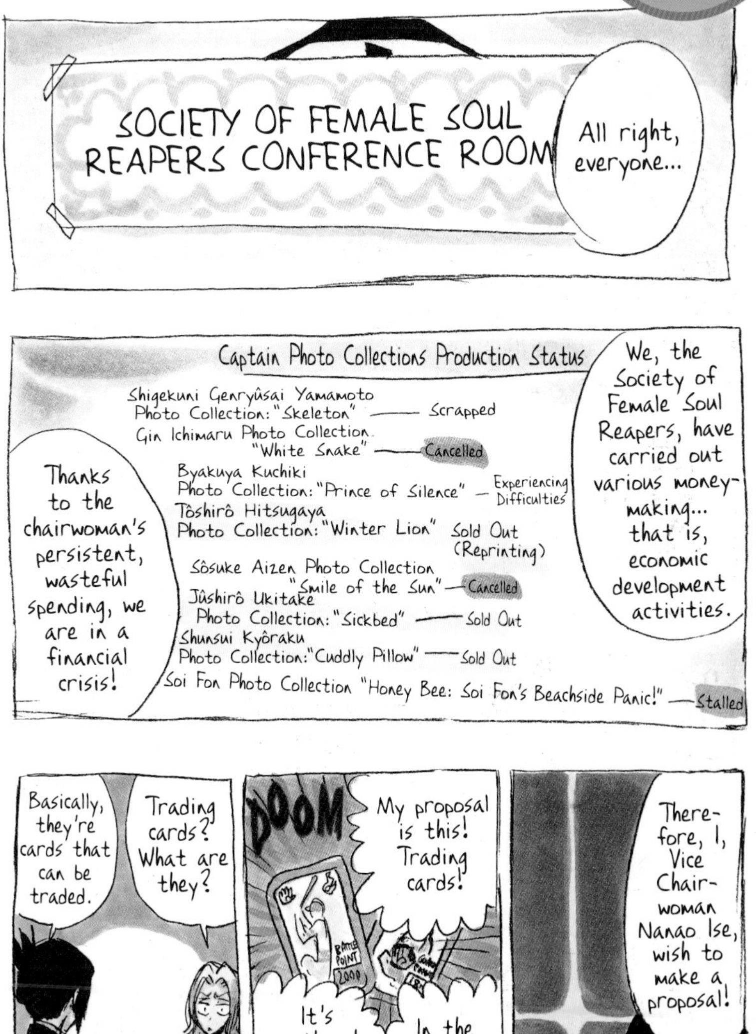
SOCIETY OF FEMALE SOUL REAPERS CONFERENCE ROOM
All right, everyone...
We, the Society of Female Soul Reapers, have carried out various money-making... that is, economic development activities.
Captain Photo Collections Production Status
Shigekuni Genryûsai Yamamoto Photo Collection: "Skeleton" — Scrapped
Gin Ichimaru Photo Collection "White Snake" — Cancelled
Byakuya Kuchiki Photo Collection: "Prince of Silence" — Experiencing Difficulties
Tôshirô Hitsugaya Photo Collection: "Winter Lion" Sold Out (Reprinting)
Sôsuke Aizen Photo Collection "Smile of the Sun" — Cancelled
Jûshirô Ukitake Photo Collection: "Sickbed" — Sold Out
Shunsui Kyôraku Photo Collection: "Cuddly Pillow" — Sold Out
Soi Fon Photo Collection "Honey Bee: Soi Fon's Beachside Panic!" — Stalled
Thanks to the chairwoman's persistent, wasteful spending, we are in a financial crisis!
Therefore, I, Vice Chairwoman Nanao Ise, wish to make a proposal!
My proposal is this! Trading cards!
DOOM
In the world of the living, everyone's crazy about them!
It's as though if you're not on a trading card, you're not human!
Trading cards? What are they?
Basically, they're cards that can be traded.
What's that mean?
I don't know.

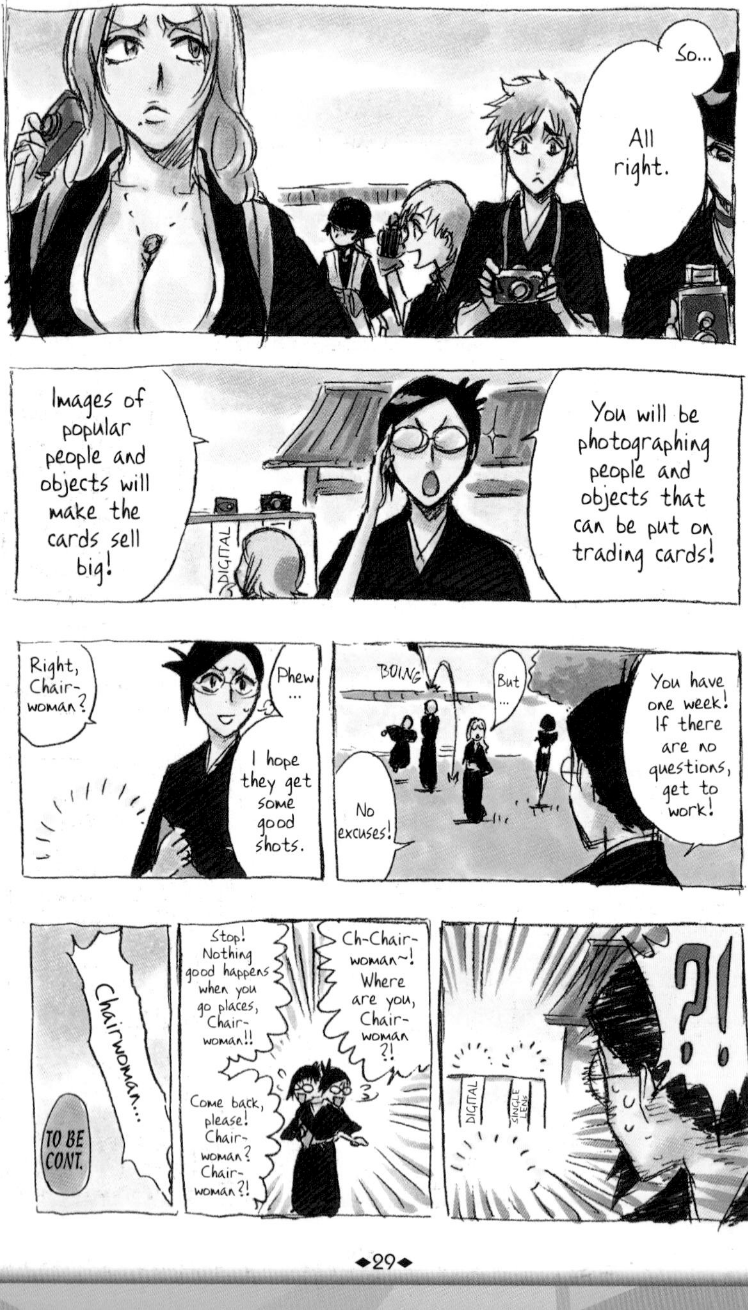
So...
All right.
You will be photographing people and objects that can be put on trading cards!
Images of popular people and objects will make the cards sell big!
DIGITAL
BOING
You have one week! If there are no questions, get to work!
But...
No excuses!
Phew...
Right, Chair-woman?
I hope they get some good shots.
?!
DIGITAL
SINGLE LENS
Ch-Chair-woman~! Where are you, Chair-woman?!
Stop! Nothing good happens when you go places, Chair-woman!!
Come back, please! Chair-woman? Chair-woman?!
Chairwoman...
TO BE CONT.

OPERATION PHOTOGRAPH BYAKUYA

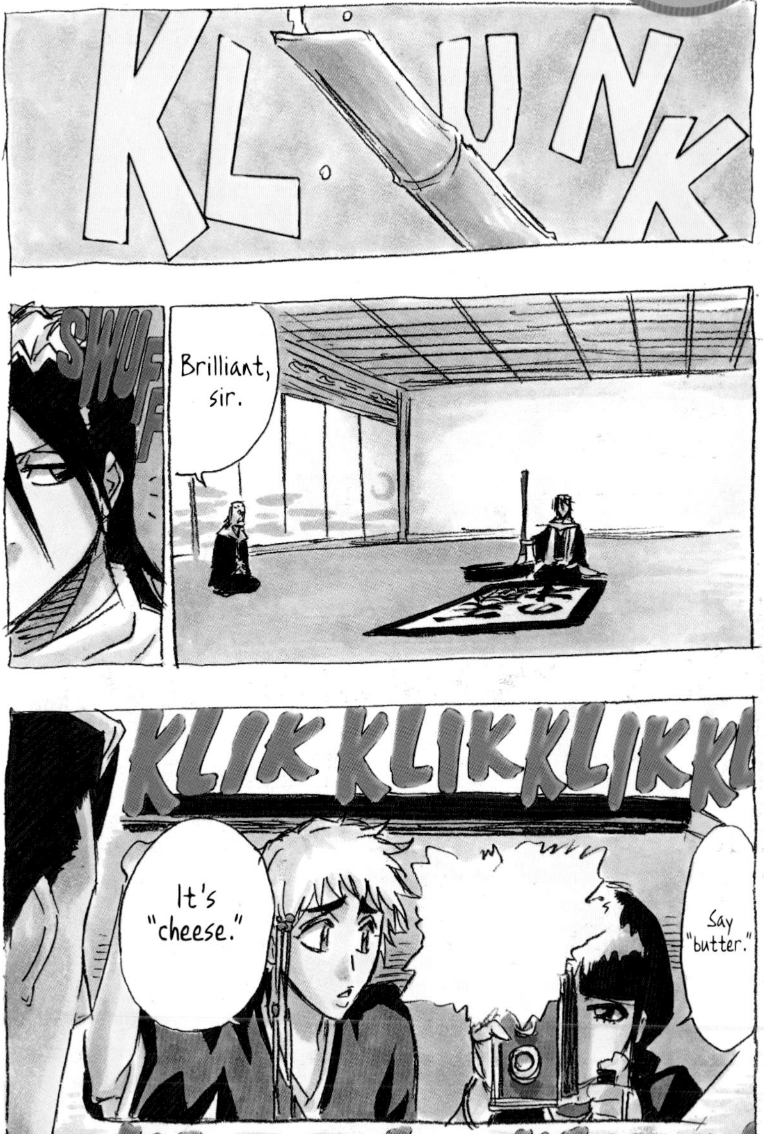
KLUNK
Brilliant, sir.
SWUFF
KLIKKLIKKLIKKL
Say "butter."
It's "cheese."
KLIKKLIKKLIKKLIKKL

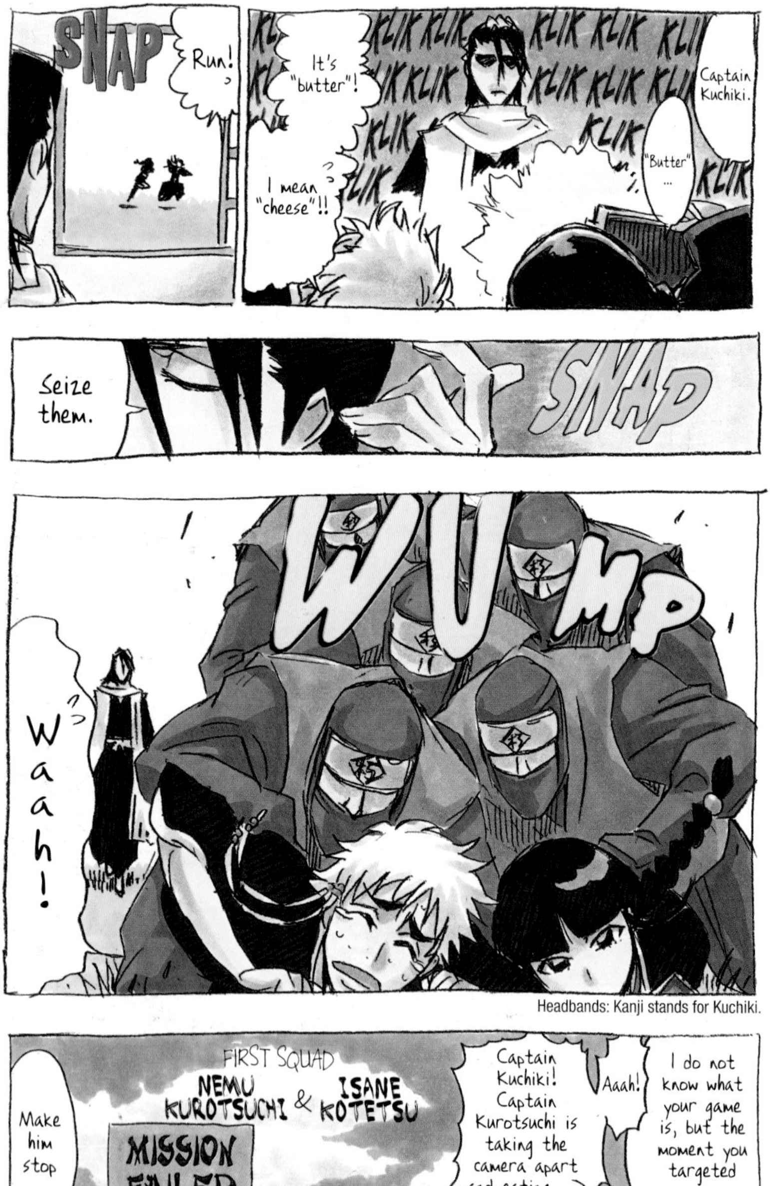
Captain Kuchiki.
"Butter"...
KLIK KLIK KLIK KLIK KLIK
It's "butter"!
I mean "cheese"!!
SNAP
Run!
SNAP
Seize them.
WUMP
Waah!

Headbands: Kanji stands for Kuchiki.

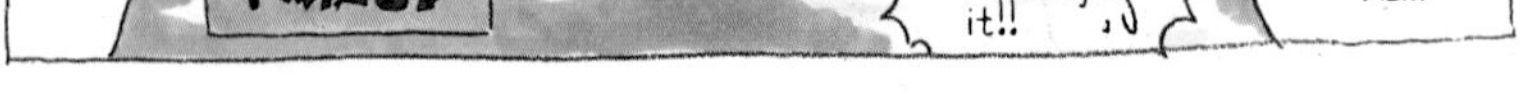
I do not know what your game is, but the moment you targeted me...
Aaah!
Captain Kuchiki! Captain Kurotsuchi is taking the camera apart and eating it!!
FIRST SQUAD
NEMU KUROTSUCHI & ISANE KOTETSU
MISSION FAILED
Make him stop...

HOW DO YOU READ "銀蜻蛉"?

ILLUSTRATED MANUSCRIPT OF DAILY IDLENESS
Part 17

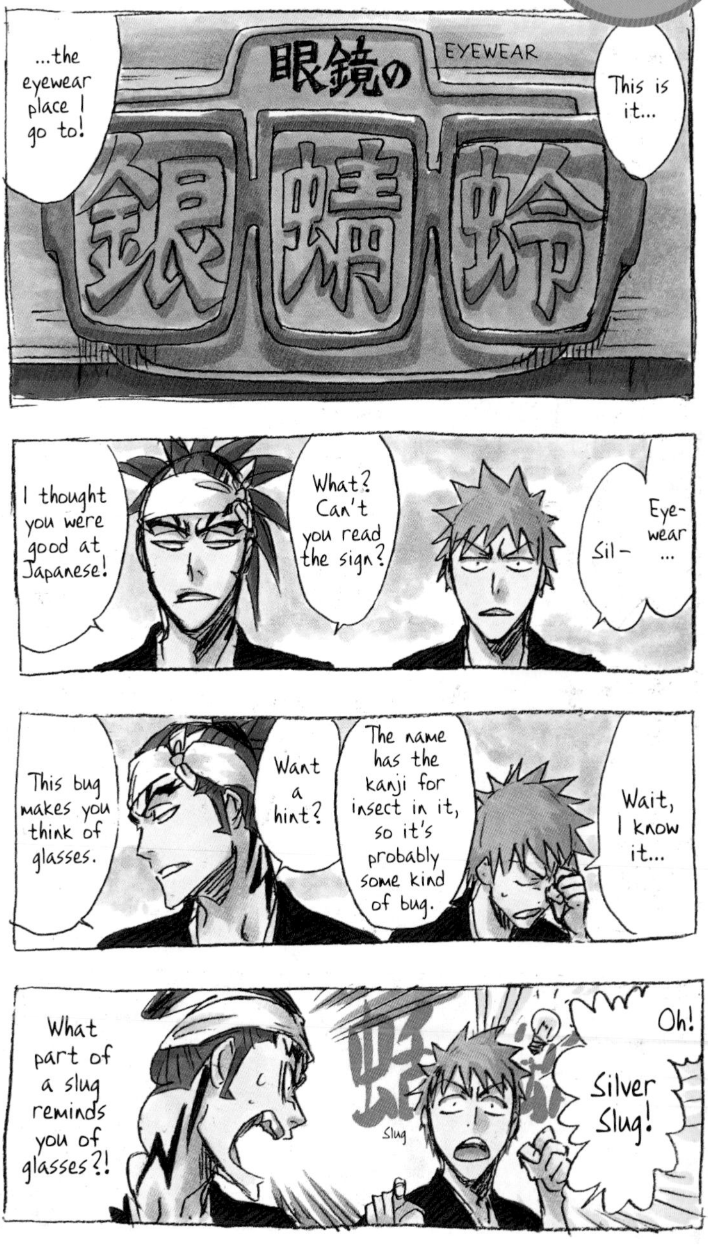
This is it...
眼鏡の
EYEWEAR
銀蜻蛉
...the eyewear place I go to!
Eye-wear...
Sil-
What? Can't you read the sign?
I thought you were good at Japanese!
Wait, I know it...
The name has the kanji for insect in it, so it's probably some kind of bug.
Want a hint?
This bug makes you think of glasses.
Oh!
Silver Slug!
Slug
What part of a slug reminds you of glasses?!

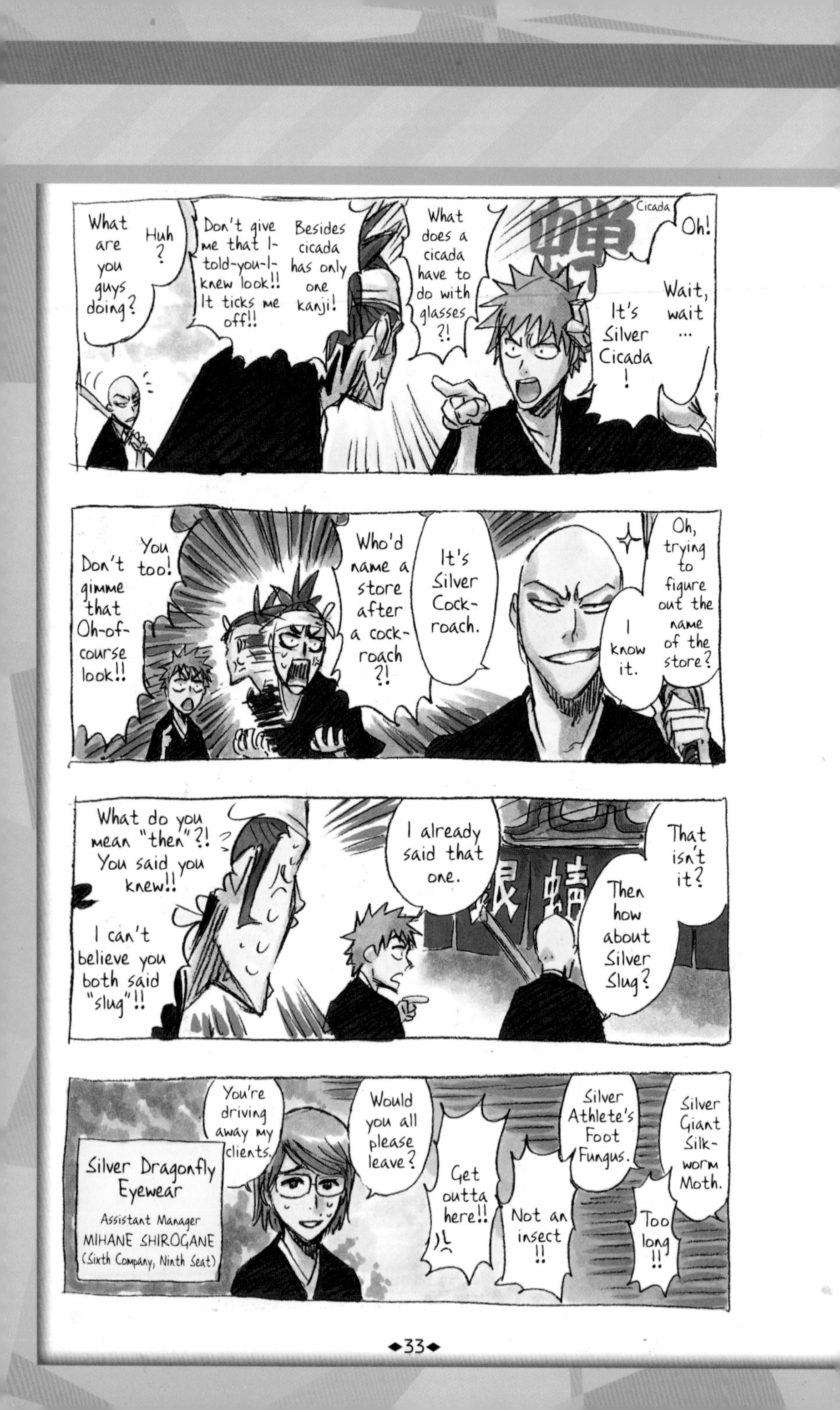
Oh!
Wait, wait ...
Cicada
It's Silver Cicada!
What does a cicada have to do with glasses?!
Besides cicada has only one kanji!
Don't give me that I-told-you-I-knew look!! It ticks me off!!
Huh?
What are you guys doing?
Oh, trying to figure out the name of the store?
I know it.
It's Silver Cock-roach.
Who'd name a store after a cock-roach?!
You too!
Don't gimme that Oh-of-course look!!
That isn't it?
Then how about Silver Slug?
I already said that one.
What do you mean "then"?! You said you knew!!
I can't believe you both said "slug"!!
Silver Giant Silk-worm Moth.
Too long!!
Silver Athlete's Foot Fungus.
Not an insect!!
Would you all please leave?
Get outta here!!
You're driving away my clients.
Silver Dragonfly Eyewear
Assistant Manager
MIHANE SHIROGANE
(Sixth Company, Ninth Seat)

COLOR BLEACH

UKITAKE'S MISFORTUNE

ILLUSTRATED MANUSCRIPT OF DAILY IDLENESS

Part 18

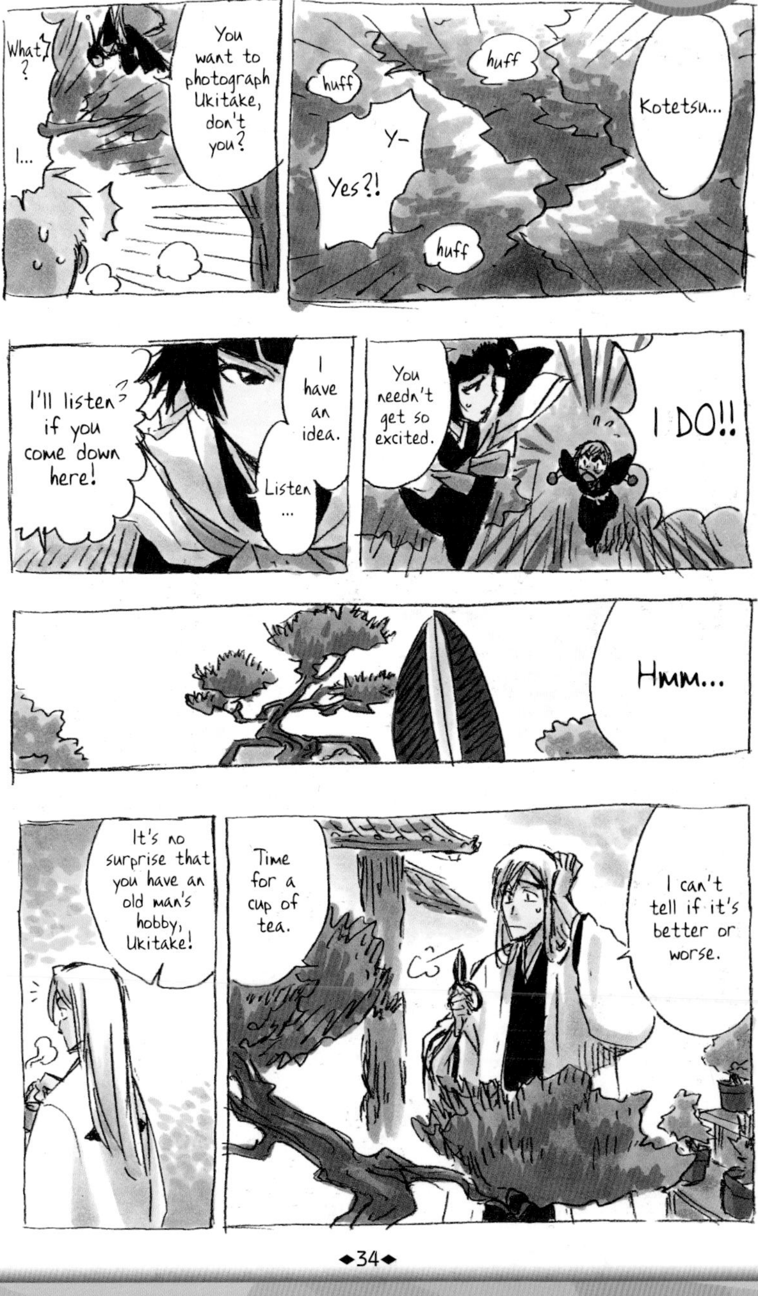
Kotetsu...
huff
huff
Y-
Yes?!
huff
You want to photograph Ukitake, don't you?
What?
I...
I DO!!
You needn't get so excited.
I have an idea.
Listen...
I'll listen if you come down here!
Hmm...
I can't tell if it's better or worse.
Time for a cup of tea.
It's no surprise that you have an old man's hobby, Ukitake!

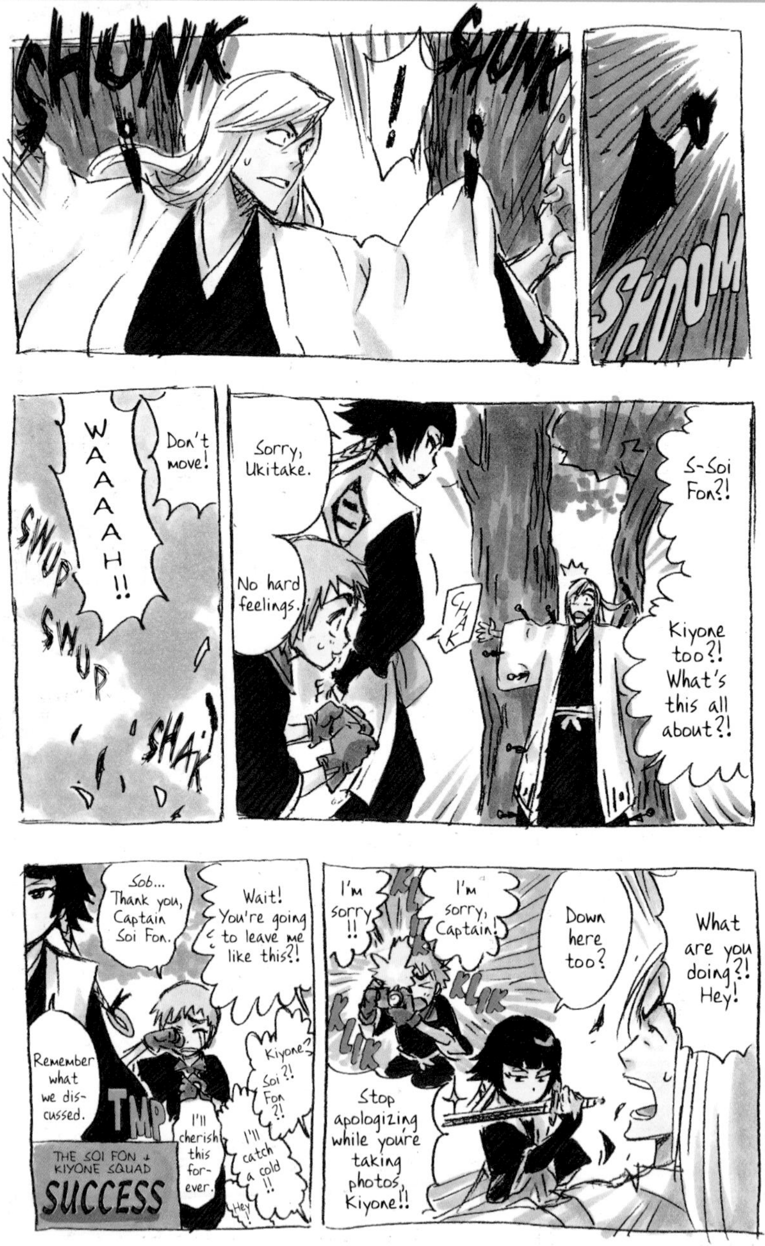
SHOOM
!
SHUNK
SHUNK
S-Soi Fon?!
Kiyone too?! What's this all about?!
CHAK
Sorry, Ukitake.
No hard feelings.
Don't move!
WAAAAAH!!
SWUP
SWUP
SHAK
What are you doing?! Hey!
Down here too?
I'm sorry, Captain!
I'm sorry!!
KLIK
KLIK
KLIK
Stop apologizing while you're taking photos, Kiyone!!
Wait! You're going to leave me like this?!
Sob... Thank you, Captain Soi Fon.
Remember what we discussed.
TMP
Kiyone? Soi Fon?!
I'll catch a cold!!
Hey!
I'll cherish this forever.
THE SOI FON & KIYONE SQUAD
SUCCESS

COLOR BLEACH

WHO WILL BE THE NEXT VICTIM?

ILLUSTRATED MANUSCRIPT OF DAILY IDLENESS

Part 19

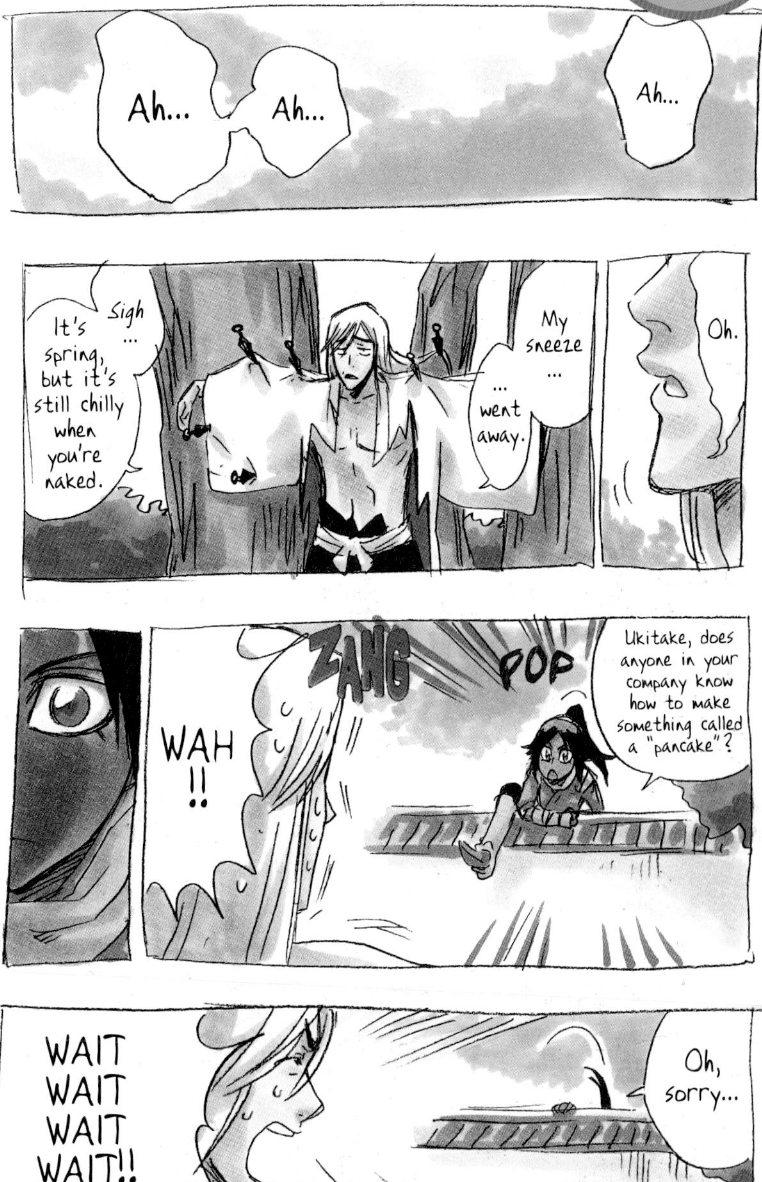

Ah...
Ah...
Ah...
Oh.
My sneeze ... ... went away.
Sigh ...
It's spring, but it's still chilly when you're naked.
Ukitake, does anyone in your company know how to make something called a "pancake"?
POP
ZANG
WAH !!
Oh, sorry...
WAIT WAIT WAIT WAIT!!

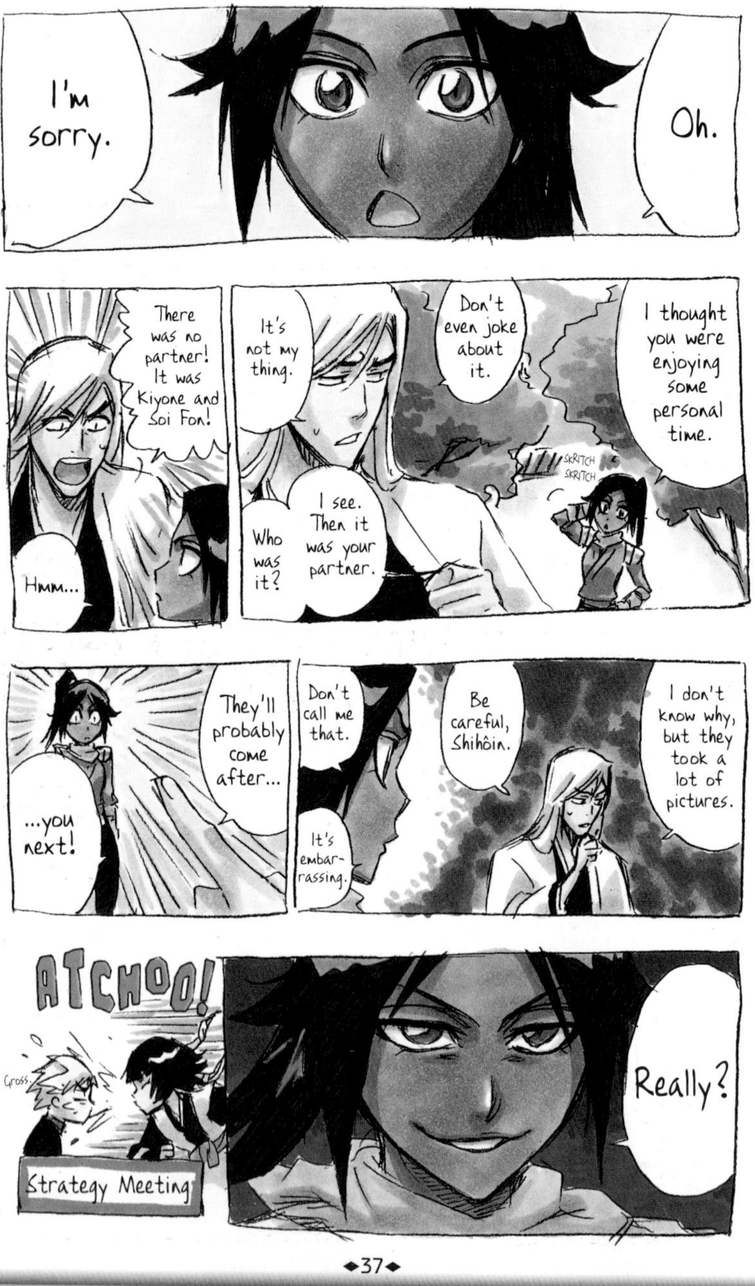
Oh.
I'm sorry.
I thought you were enjoying some personal time.
Don't even joke about it.
SKRITCH SKRITCH
It's not my thing.
I see. Then it was your partner.
Who was it?
There was no partner! It was Kiyone and Soi Fon!
Hmm...
I don't know why, but they took a lot of pictures.
Be careful, Shihôin.
Don't call me that.
It's embarrassing.
They'll probably come after...
...you next!
Really?
ATCHOO!
Gross.
Strategy Meeting

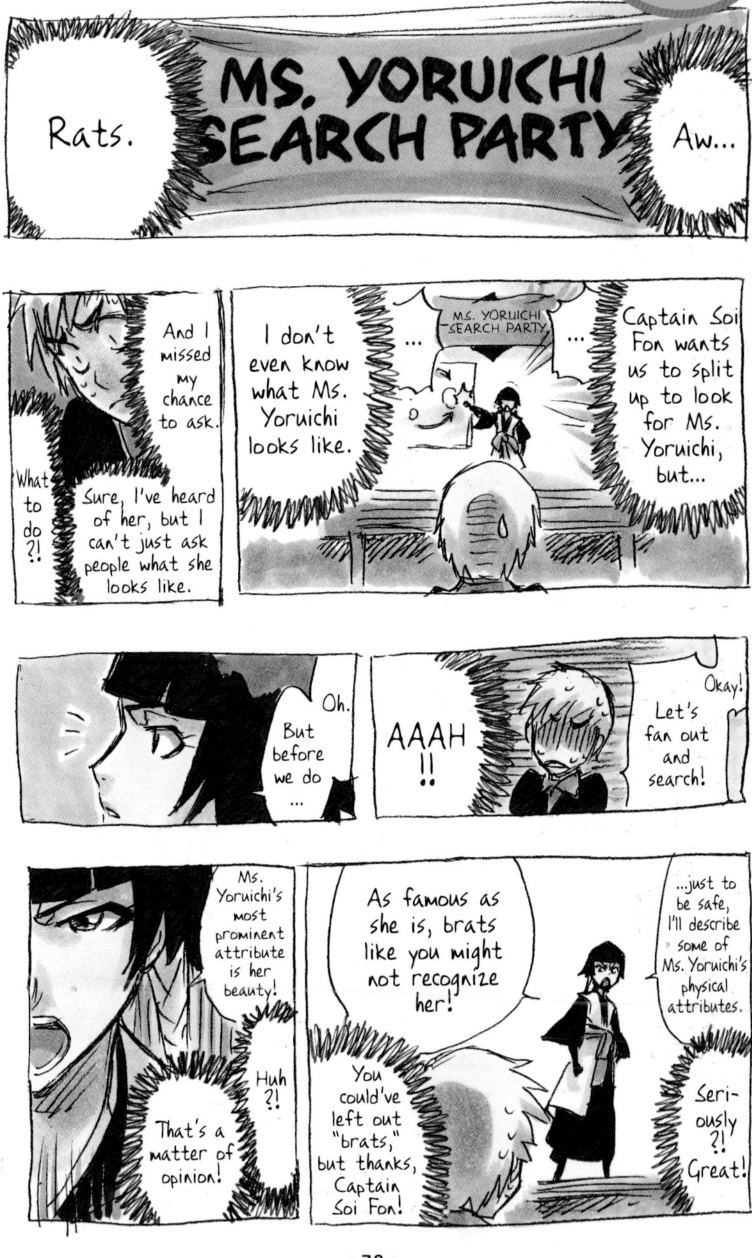
Aw...
MS. YORUICHI SEARCH PARTY
Rats.
Captain Soi Fon wants us to split up to look for Ms. Yoruichi, but...
...
MS. YORUICHI SEARCH PARTY
...
I don't even know what Ms. Yoruichi looks like.
And I missed my chance to ask.
Sure, I've heard of her, but I can't just ask people what she looks like.
What to do?!
Okay!
Let's fan out and search!
AAAH!!
Oh.
But before we do...
...just to be safe, I'll describe some of Ms. Yoruichi's physical attributes.
As famous as she is, brats like you might not recognize her!
Seri-ously?! Great!
You could've left out "brats," but thanks, Captain Soi Fon!
Ms. Yoruichi's most prominent attribute is her beauty!
Huh?!
That's a matter of opinion!

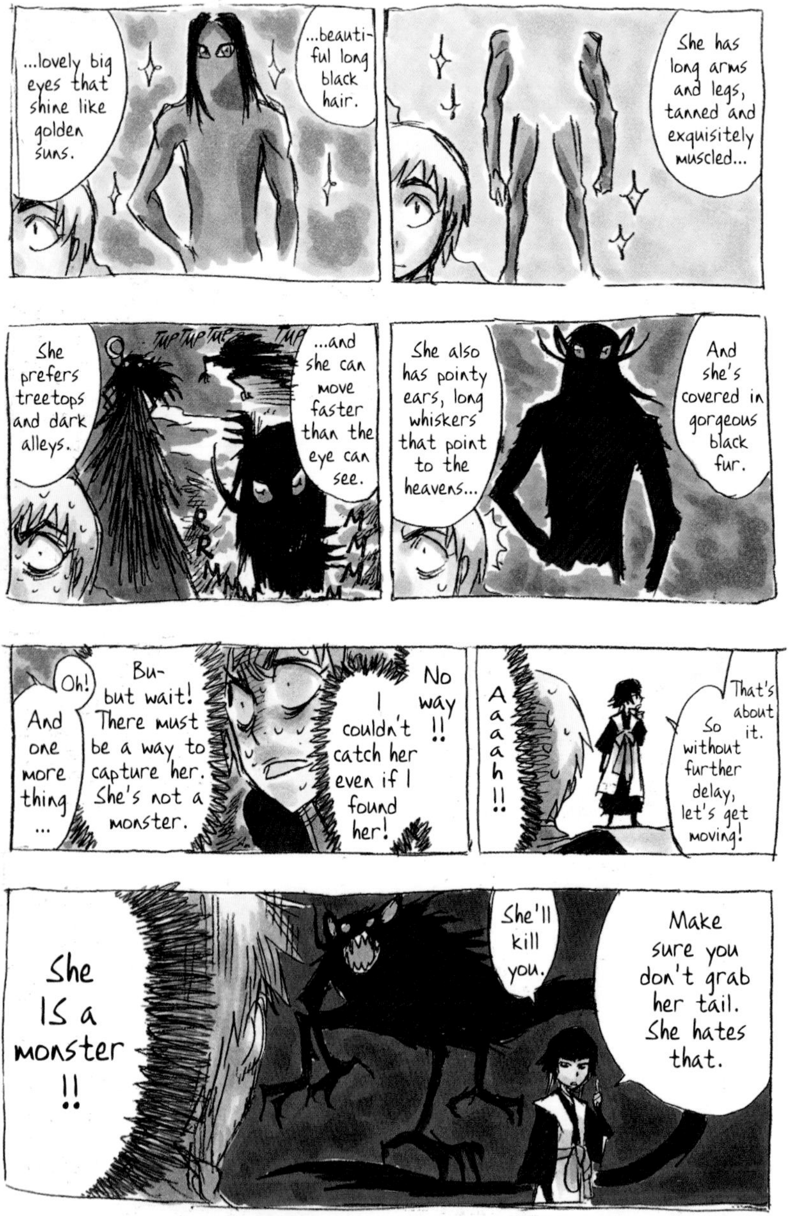
She has long arms and legs, tanned and exquisitely muscled...
...beautiful long black hair.
...lovely big eyes that shine like golden suns.
And she's covered in gorgeous black fur.
She also has pointy ears, long whiskers that point to the heavens...
...and she can move faster than the eye can see.
She prefers treetops and dark alleys.
That's about it. So without further delay, let's get moving!
Aaaah!!
No way!!
I couldn't catch her even if I found her!
Bu-but wait! There must be a way to capture her. She's not a monster.
Oh!
And one more thing...
Make sure you don't grab her tail. She hates that.
She'll kill you.
She IS a monster!!

COLOR BLEACH
THE REAL YORUICHI
(The Sequel)

ILLUSTRATED MANUSCRIPT OF DAILY IDLENESS
Part 21

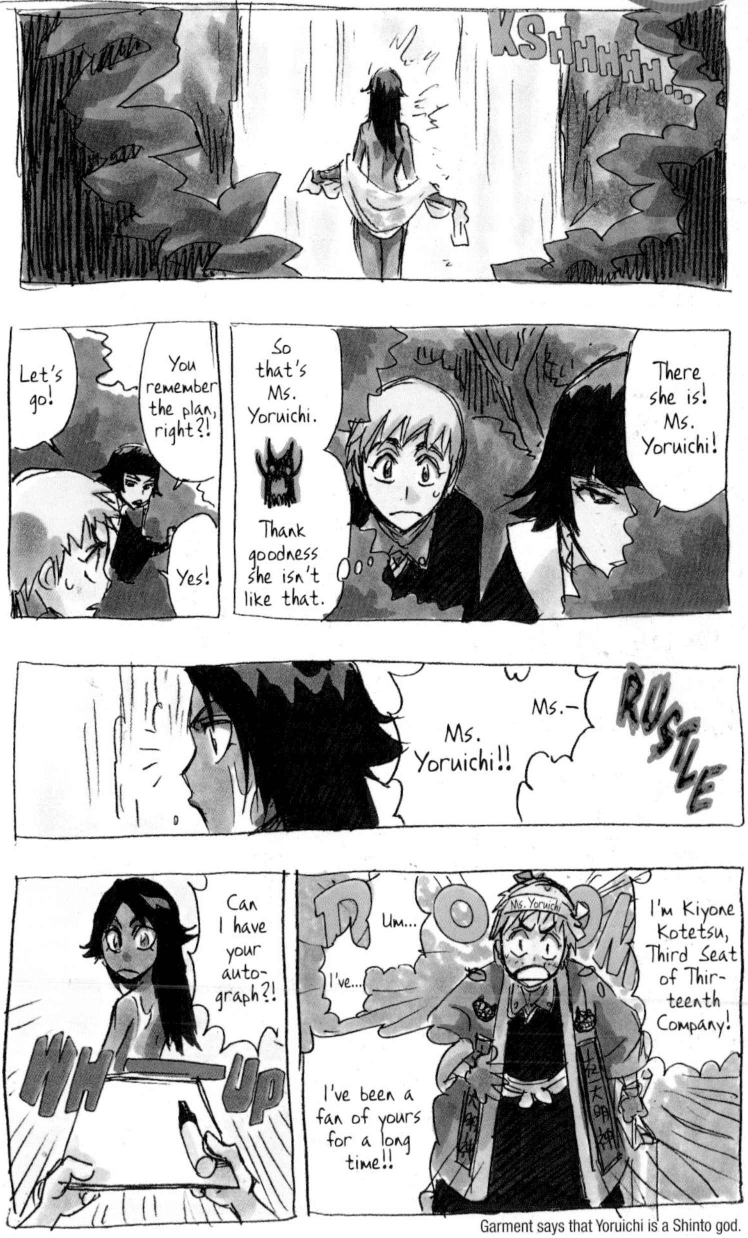
KSHHHHHH...
There she is! Ms. Yoruichi!
So that's Ms. Yoruichi.
Thank goodness she isn't like that.
You remember the plan, right?!
Let's go!
Yes!
RUSTLE
Ms.–
Ms. Yoruichi!!
I'm Kiyone Kotetsu, Third Seat of Thirteenth Company!
Ms. Yoruichi
Um...
I've...
I've been a fan of yours for a long time!!
Can I have your autograph?!
WH–UP

Garment says that Yoruichi is a Shinto god.

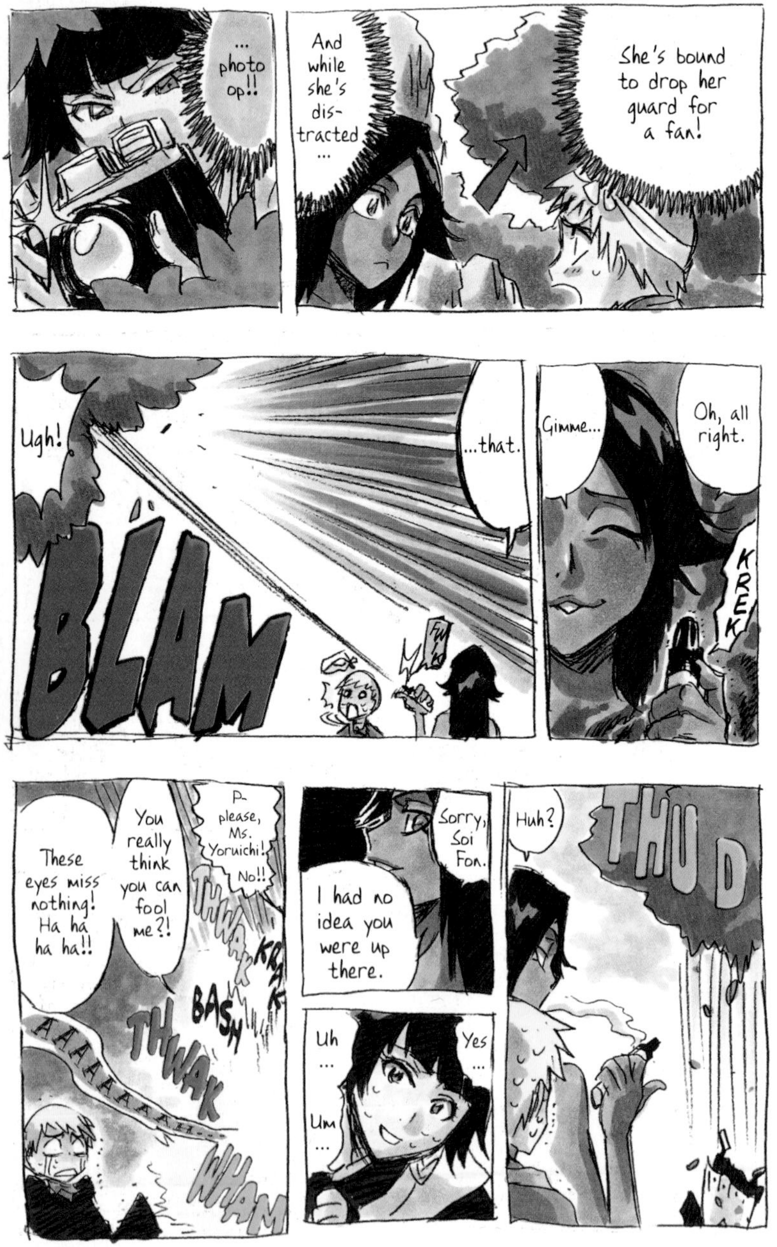

She's bound to drop her guard for a fan!
And while she's dis-tracted...
...photo op!!
Oh, all right.
Gimme...
...that.
KREK
Ugh!
BLAM
Huh?
THUD
Sorry, Soi Fon.
I had no idea you were up there.
Yes...
Uh...
Um...
P-please, Ms. Yoruichi! No!!
You really think you can fool me?!
These eyes miss nothing! Ha ha ha ha!!
THWAK
KRAK
BASH
THWAK
AAAAAAAAAH...
WHAM

♯ THE DRAWING SONG ♪

MAYURI KUROTSUCHI'S DRAWING SONG

SASRAC 0000001

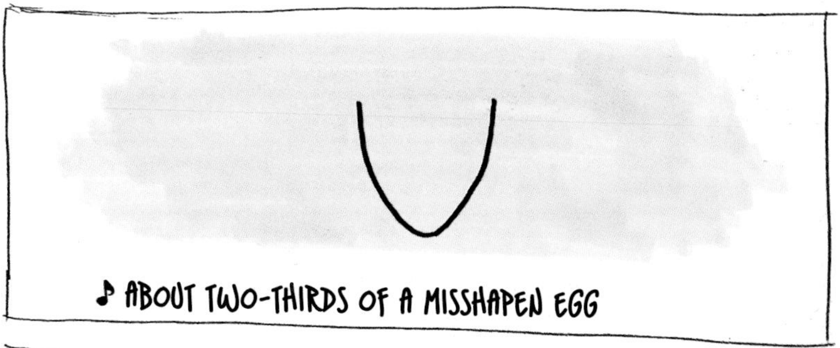
♪ ABOUT TWO-THIRDS OF A MISSHAPEN EGG

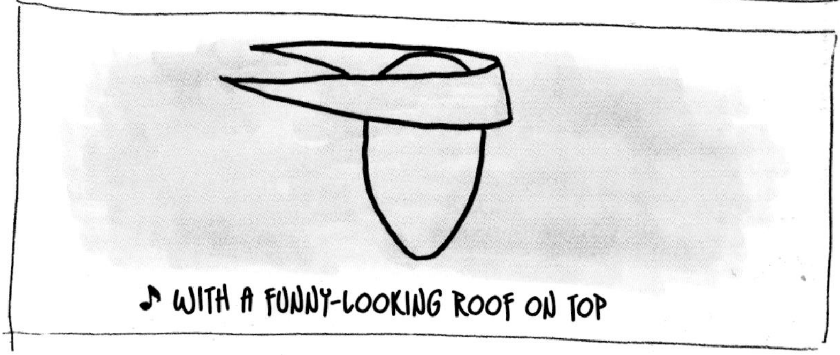
♪ WITH A FUNNY-LOOKING ROOF ON TOP

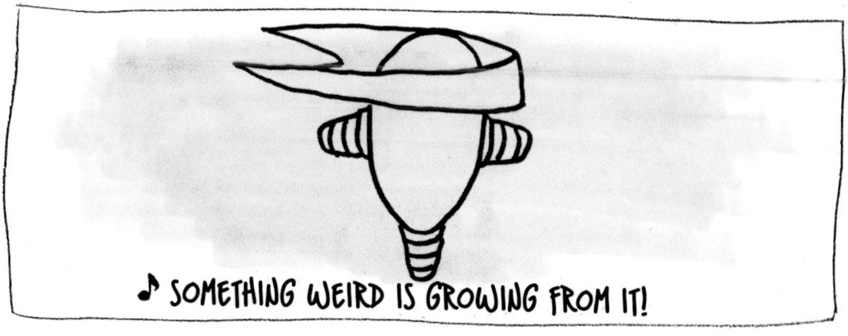
♪ SOMETHING WEIRD IS GROWING FROM IT!

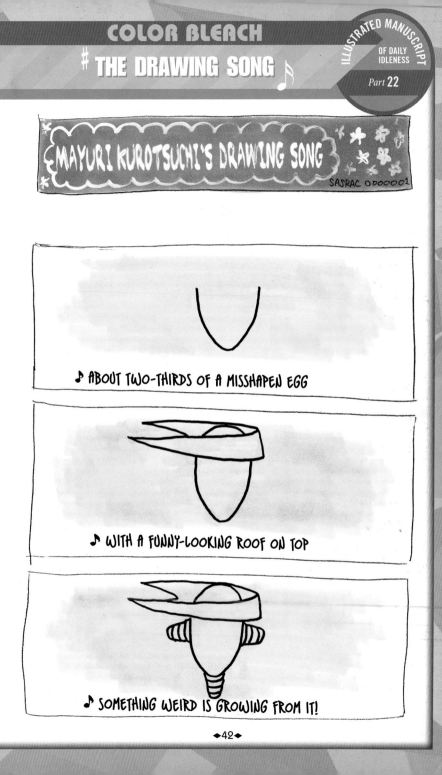

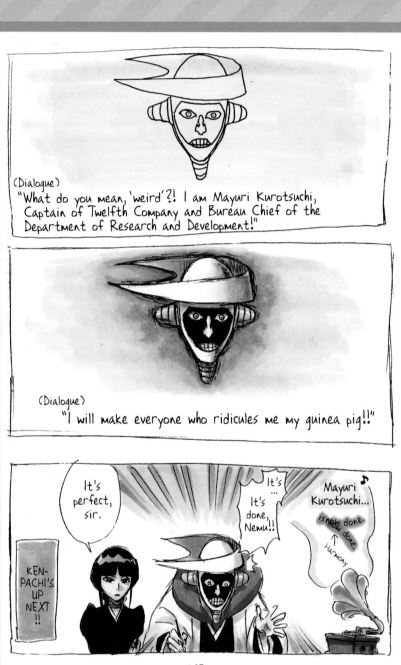

(Dialogue)
"What do you mean, 'weird'?! I am Mayuri Kurotsuchi,
Captain of Twelfth Company and Bureau Chief of the
Department of Research and Development!"

(Dialogue)
"I will make everyone who ridicules me my guinea pig!!"

It's
perfect,
sir.

It's
...
It's
done,
Nemu!!

Mayuri ♪
Kurotsuchi...
is now done.
↑
Harmony

KEN-
PACHI'S
UP
NEXT
!!

◆43◆

THIRTEEN COMPANIES: RARE CARDS

ILLUSTRATED MANUSCRIPT OF DAILY IDLENESS
Part 23

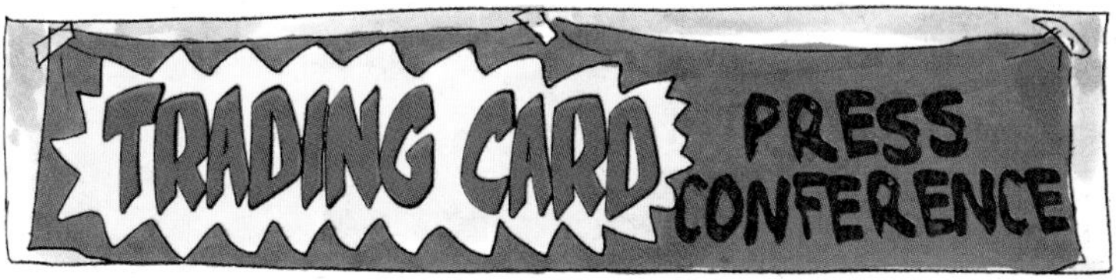
TRADING CARD
PRESS CONFERENCE

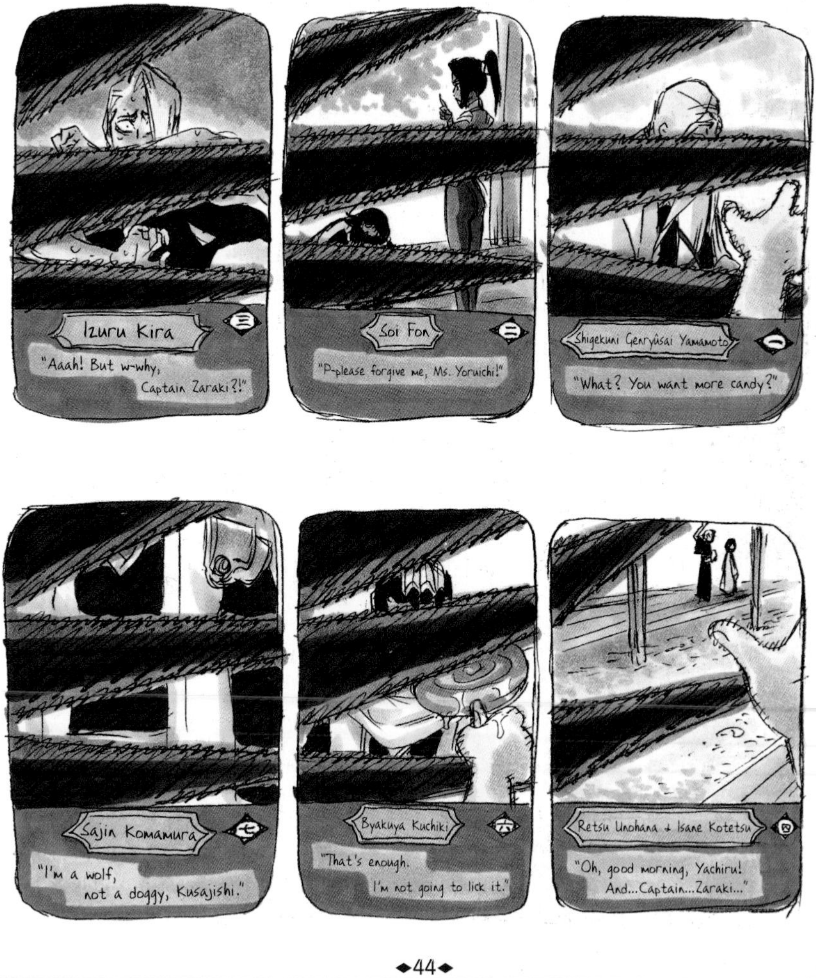
Shigekuni Genryûsai Yamamoto
"What? You want more candy?"
Soi Fon
"P-please forgive me, Ms. Yoruichi!"
Izuru Kira
"Aaah! But w-why, Captain Zaraki?!"
Retsu Unohana + Isane Kotetsu
"Oh, good morning, Yachiru! And...Captain...Zaraki..."
Byakuya Kuchiki
"That's enough. I'm not going to lick it."
Sajin Komamura
"I'm a wolf, not a doggy, Kusajishi."

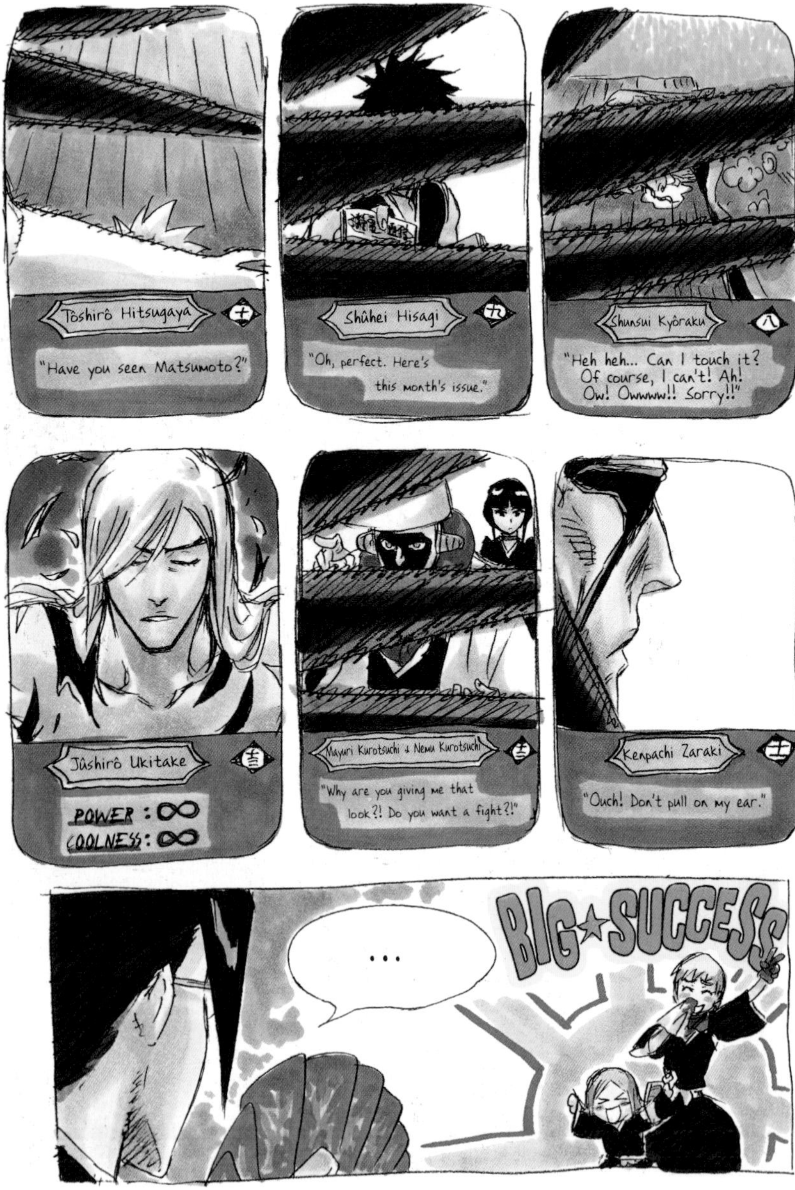

Shunsui Kyôraku
八
"Heh heh... Can I touch it? Of course, I can't! Ah! Ow! Owwww!! Sorry!!"
Shûhei Hisagi
九
"Oh, perfect. Here's this month's issue."
Tôshirô Hitsugaya
十
"Have you seen Matsumoto?"
Kenpachi Zaraki
十一
"Ouch! Don't pull on my ear."
Mayuri Kurotsuchi & Nemu Kurotsuchi
十二
"Why are you giving me that look?! Do you want a fight?!"
Jûshirô Ukitake
十三
POWER : ∞
COOLNESS : ∞
BIG★SUCCESS
...

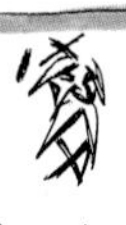

Place stamp here!

Return Postcard
Monthly Seireitei Bulletin Editorial Department
Ryûsei 2-5-10, District 1, Seireitei
119-0163

Attn: Monthly Seireitei Bulletin, Dec. Issue

(Cut here)

☆In the boxes, write the numbers of the three articles from the December issue of Monthly Seireitei Bulletin that you liked best.

1	2	3
17	17	19

1) New Section: "Teach Me, Shuhei Sensei!!"
2) Shigekuni Genryûsai Yamamoto's "Got a Minute?"
3) Soi Fon's "I'll Do Anything to Live"
4) Retsu Unohana's "'Tis the Season"
5) Byakuya Kuchiki's "All About Etiquette"
6) Sajin Komamura's "A Puppy's Feelings"
7) Shunsui Kyôraku's "The Rose-Colored Path"
8) Tôshirô Hitsugaya's "Beautiful Crystal"
9) Mayuri Kurotsuchi's "Medicine for the Brain"
10) Jûshirô Ukitake's "Warning of the Twin Fish!"
11) Izuru Kira's "I Want to Apologize to You"
12) Renji Abarai's "Let's Do Shikai!!"
13) Tetsuzaemon Iba and Ikkaku Madarame's "Men's Section"
14) Nanao Ise's "Don't Get Carried Away"
15) Yumichika Ayasegawa's "Are You Okay with That?"
16) The Seireitei's Ranking of Everything
17) The Uncut Pages: Rangiku Matsumoto's "The Many Faces of a Wet Cat"
18) Cover
19) Bonus: Society of Female Soul Reapers Special Trading Card, "Tôshirô Hitsugaya Sleeping" (Extremely Rare)

*Monthly Seireitei Bulletin's Editorial Department does not conduct surveys using Hell Butterflies. This postcard will be used for the features published in Monthly Seireitei Bulletin.

*The authors of "Sôsuke Aizen's 'The Yin of the Pine Needle,'" "Kaname Tôsen's 'The Path of Justice'" and "Gin Ichimaru's 'That's Absurd'" are taking a little personal leave. The columns will appear in a future issue.

Address
4-6-16 Chidoribashi, District 10, Seireitei
801 Ibanarô Chidoribashi

Name
Rangiku Matsumoto

Male
Female (circled)

Age

This postcard is modeled on the reader surveys used by *Weekly Shonen Jump* magazine in Japan.

THE BACK OF THE POSTCARD

(Cut here)

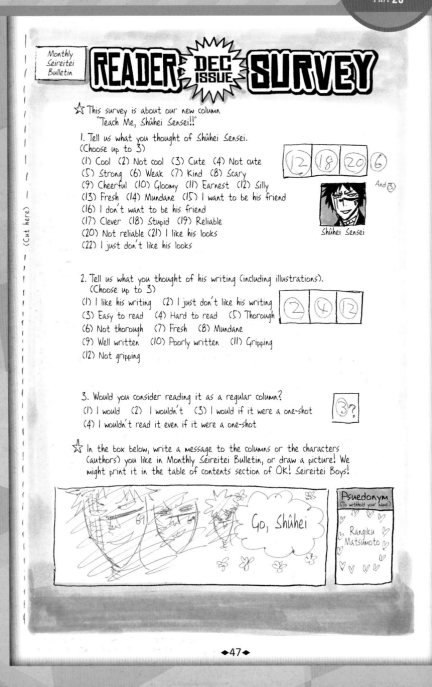

Monthly Seireitei Bulletin

READER DEC ISSUE SURVEY

☆ This survey is about our new column "Teach Me, Shûhei Sensei!!"

1. Tell us what you thought of Shûhei Sensei. (Choose up to 3)
(1) Cool (2) Not cool (3) Cute (4) Not cute
(5) Strong (6) Weak (7) Kind (8) Scary
(9) Cheerful (10) Gloomy (11) Earnest (12) Silly
(13) Fresh (14) Mundane (15) I want to be his friend
(16) I don't want to be his friend
(17) Clever (18) Stupid (19) Reliable
(20) Not reliable (21) I like his looks
(22) I just don't like his looks

12	18	20	6

And 3.

Shûhei Sensei

2. Tell us what you thought of his writing (including illustrations). (Choose up to 3)
(1) I like his writing (2) I just don't like his writing
(3) Easy to read (4) Hard to read (5) Thorough
(6) Not thorough (7) Fresh (8) Mundane
(9) Well written (10) Poorly written (11) Gripping
(12) Not gripping

2	4	12

3. Would you consider reading it as a regular column?
(1) I would (2) I wouldn't (3) I would if it were a one-shot
(4) I wouldn't read it even if it were a one-shot

3?

☆ In the box below, write a message to the columns or the characters (authors) you like in Monthly Seireitei Bulletin, or draw a picture! We might print it in the table of contents section of OK! Seireitei Boys!

Go, Shûhei

Psuedonym
(To withhold your name)

Rangiku Matsumoto

NEW YEAR'S AT THE SHIBAS'

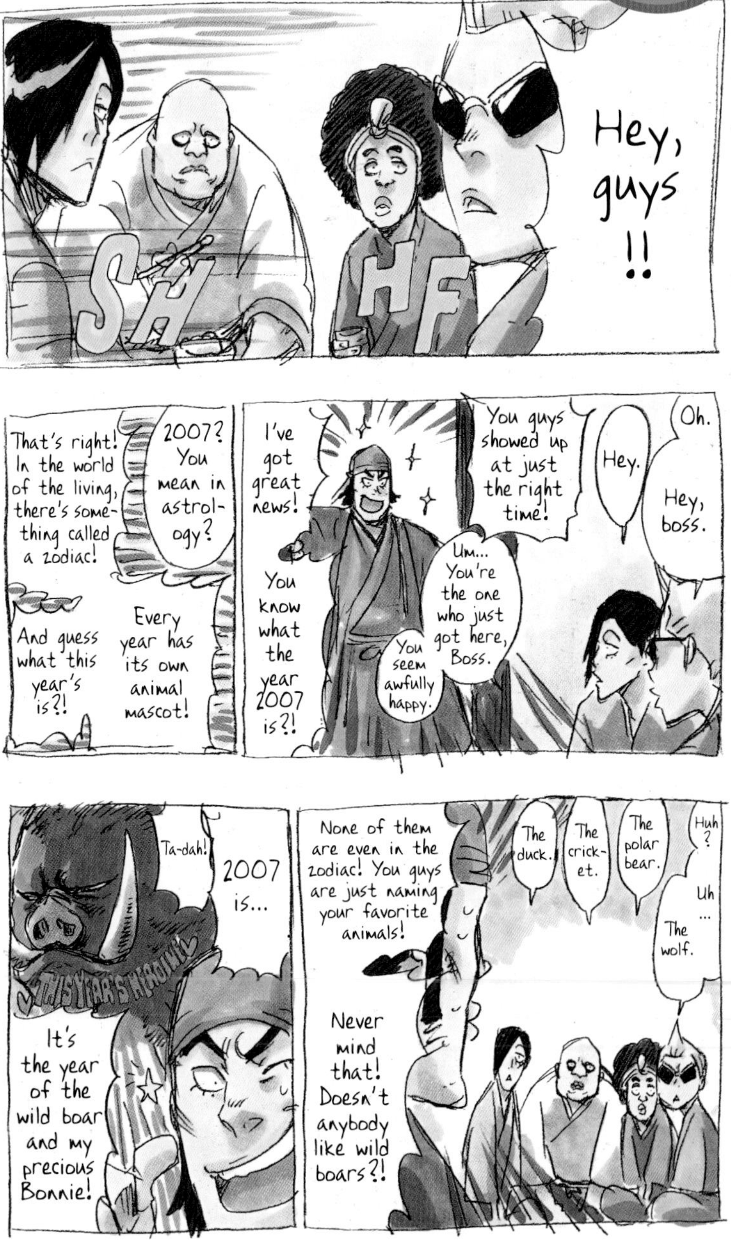
Hey, guys!!
SH
HF
Oh.
Hey.
Hey, boss.
You guys showed up at just the right time!
I've got great news!
Um... You're the one who just got here, Boss.
You seem awfully happy.
You know what the year 2007 is?!
2007? You mean in astrology?
That's right! In the world of the living, there's something called a zodiac!
Every year has its own animal mascot!
And guess what this year's is?!
Huh?
The polar bear.
The crick-et.
The duck.
Uh... The wolf.
None of them are even in the zodiac! You guys are just naming your favorite animals!
Never mind that! Doesn't anybody like wild boars?!
Ta-dah!
2007 is...
THIS YEAR'S HEROINE
It's the year of the wild boar and my precious Bonnie!

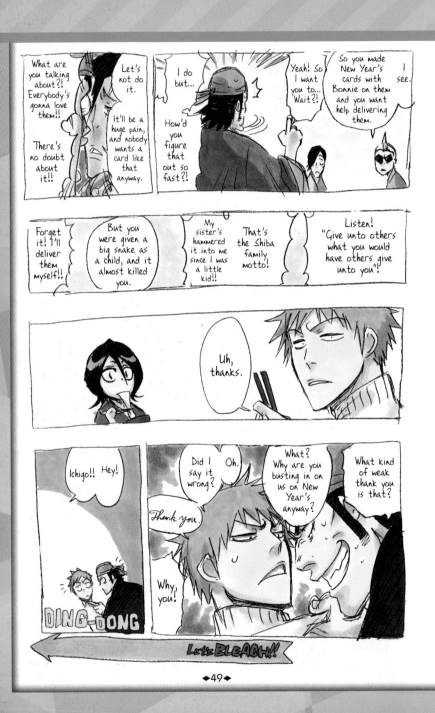

I see.
So you made New Year's cards with Bonnie on them and you want help delivering them.
Yeah! So I want you to... Wait?!
I do but...
How'd you figure that out so fast?!
Let's not do it.
It'll be a huge pain, and nobody wants a card like that anyway.
What are you talking about?! Everybody's gonna love them!!
There's no doubt about it!!
Listen! "Give unto others what you would have others give unto you"!
That's the Shiba family motto!
My sister's hammered it into me since I was a little kid!!
But you were given a big snake as a child, and it almost killed you.
Forget it! I'll deliver them myself!!
Uh, thanks.
What kind of weak thank you is that?
What? Why are you busting in on us on New Year's anyway?
Oh.
Did I say it wrong?
Thank you.
Why, you!
Hey!
Ichigo!!
DING-DONG

NEW YEAR'S AT THE KUROSAKIS'

ILLUSTRATED MANUSCRIPT OF DAILY IDLENESS Part 27

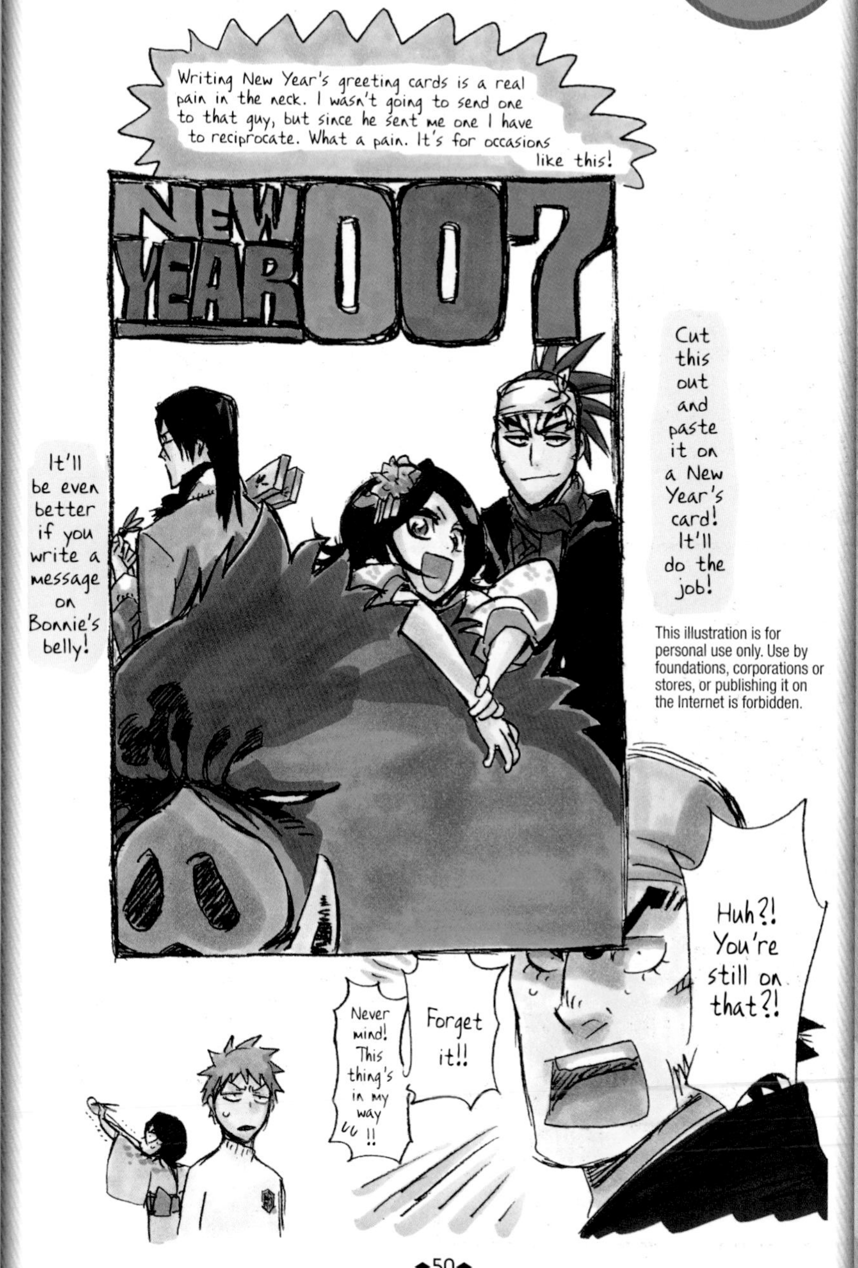
Writing New Year's greeting cards is a real pain in the neck. I wasn't going to send one to that guy, but since he sent me one I have to reciprocate. What a pain. It's for occasions like this!
NEW YEAR 007
Cut this out and paste it on a New Year's card! It'll do the job!
It'll be even better if you write a message on Bonnie's belly!
This illustration is for personal use only. Use by foundations, corporations or stores, or publishing it on the Internet is forbidden.
Huh?! You're still on that?!
Forget it!!
Never mind! This thing's in my way!!

THE SOCIETY OF FEMALE SOUL REAPERS OUTING

The Society of Female Soul Reapers was established for the advancement of the fairer members of the Seireitei. They've been sent on a trip to the beach for some R&R in appreciation of their hard work. (Really?)

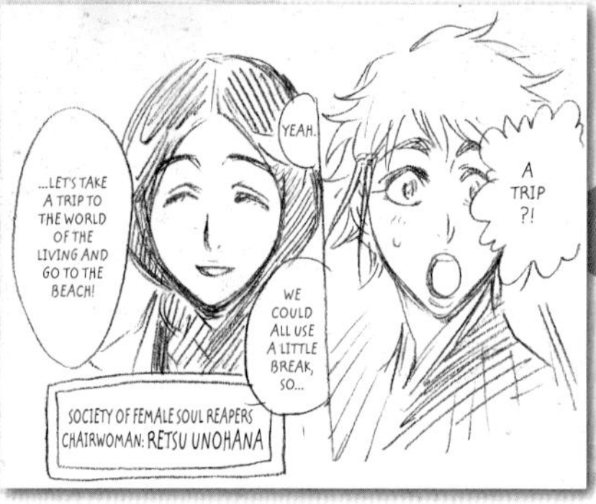
...LET'S TAKE A TRIP TO THE WORLD OF THE LIVING AND GO TO THE BEACH!
SOCIETY OF FEMALE SOUL REAPERS CHAIRWOMAN: RETSU UNOHANA
A TRIP ?!
YEAH.
WE COULD ALL USE A LITTLE BREAK, SO...

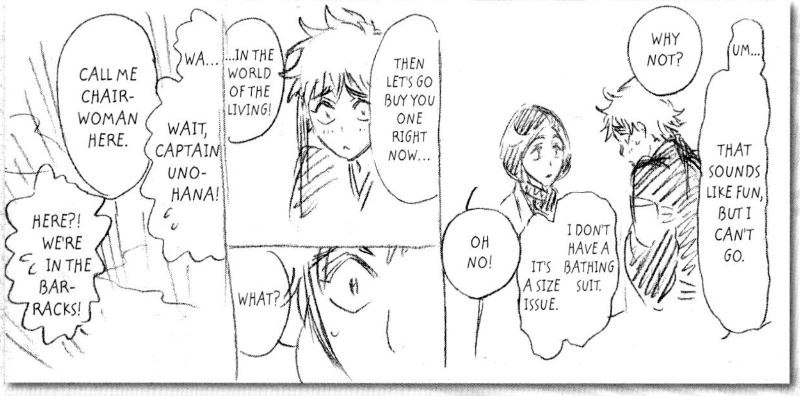
WHY NOT?
UM...
THAT SOUNDS LIKE FUN, BUT I CAN'T GO.
I DON'T HAVE A BATHING SUIT.
IT'S A SIZE ISSUE.
OH NO!
THEN LET'S GO BUY YOU ONE RIGHT NOW...
...IN THE WORLD OF THE LIVING!
WHAT?
WA...
WAIT, CAPTAIN UNO-HANA!
CALL ME CHAIR-WOMAN HERE.
HERE?! WE'RE IN THE BAR-RACKS!

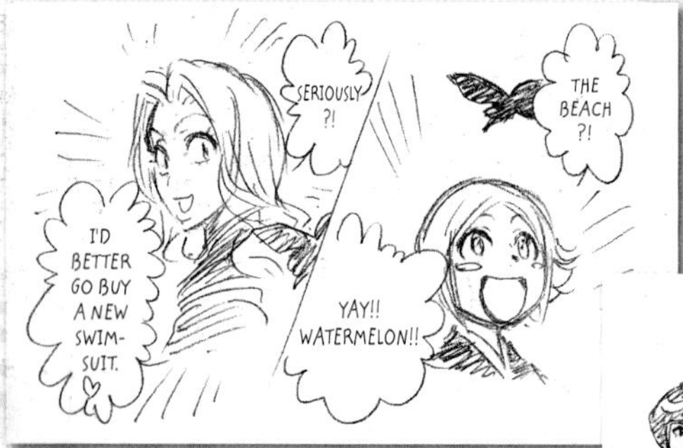
THE BEACH ?!
YAY!! WATERMELON!!
SERIOUSLY ?!
I'D BETTER GO BUY A NEW SWIM-SUIT.

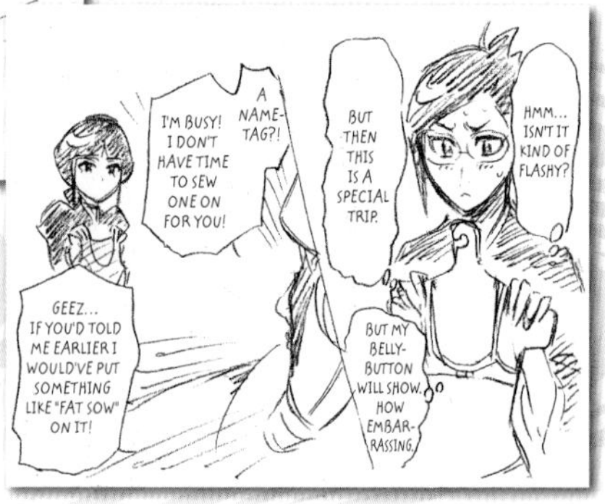
HMM... ISN'T IT KIND OF FLASHY?
BUT THEN THIS IS A SPECIAL TRIP.
BUT MY BELLY-BUTTON WILL SHOW. HOW EMBAR-RASSING.
A NAME-TAG?!
I'M BUSY! I DON'T HAVE TIME TO SEW ONE ON FOR YOU!
GEEZ... IF YOU'D TOLD ME EARLIER I WOULD'VE PUT SOMETHING LIKE "FAT SOW" ON IT!

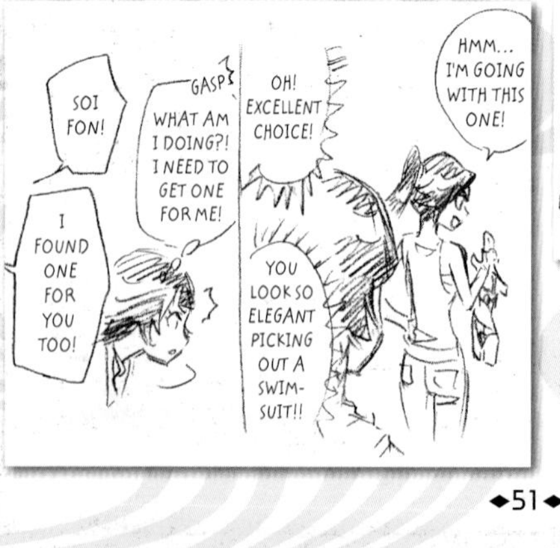
HMM... I'M GOING WITH THIS ONE!
OH! EXCELLENT CHOICE!
YOU LOOK SO ELEGANT PICKING OUT A SWIM-SUIT!!
GASP
WHAT AM I DOING?! I NEED TO GET ONE FOR ME!
SOI FON!
I FOUND ONE FOR YOU TOO!

COLOR BLEACH

THE SOCIETY OF FEMALE SOUL REAPERS MYSTERY

ILLUSTRATED MANUSCRIPT OF DAILY IDLENESS
Part 28

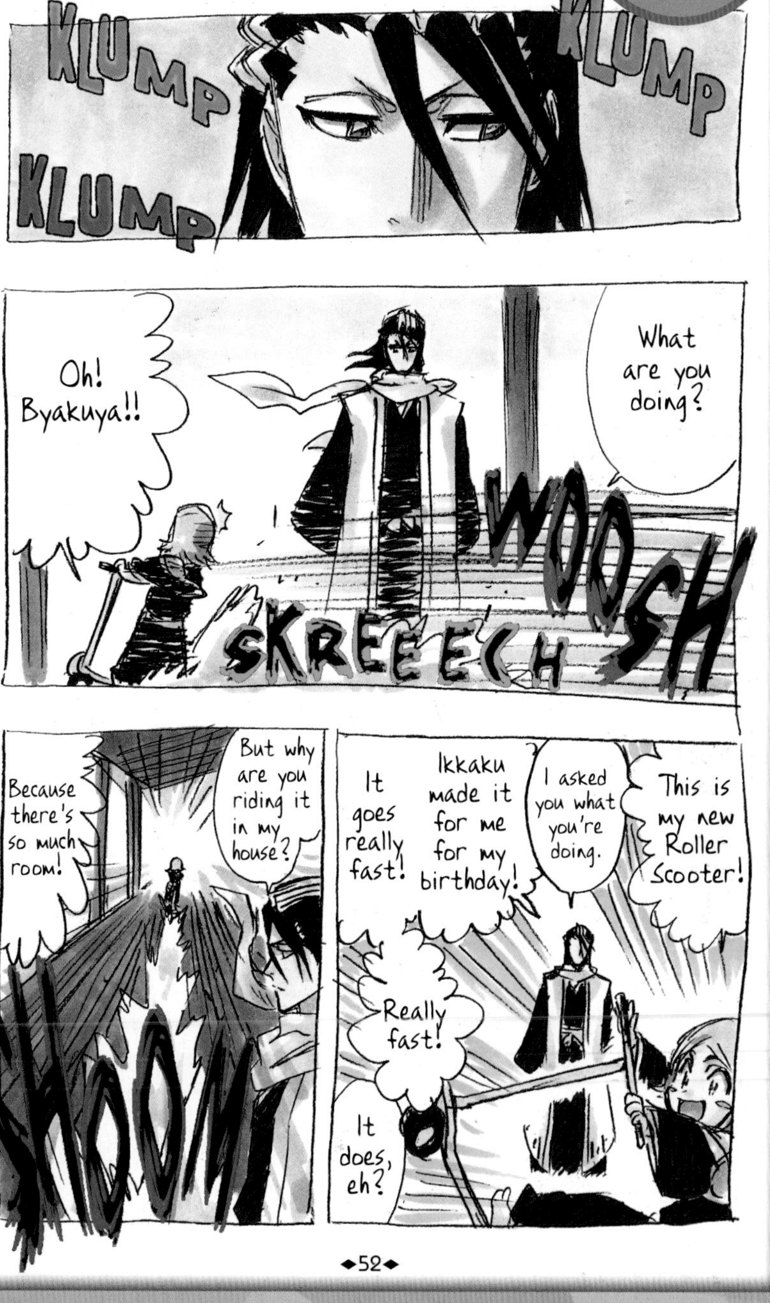
KLUMP
KLUMP
KLUMP
What are you doing?
Oh! Byakuya!!
WOOSH
SKREEECH
This is my new Roller Scooter!
I asked you what you're doing.
Ikkaku made it for me for my birthday!
It goes really fast!
Really fast!
It does, eh?
But why are you riding it in my house?
Because there's so much room!
SHOOM

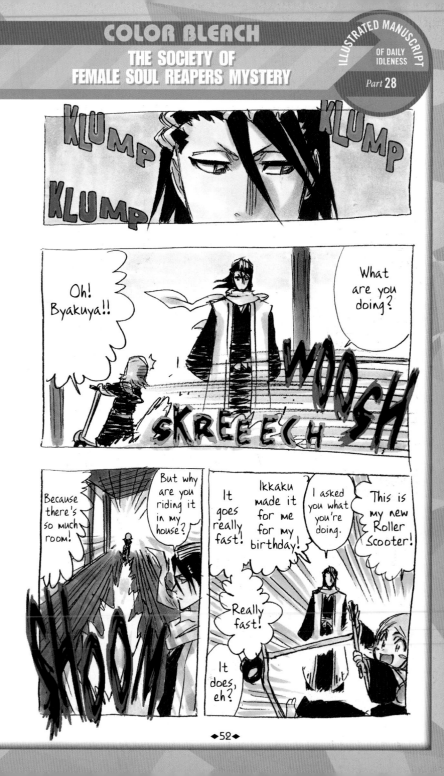

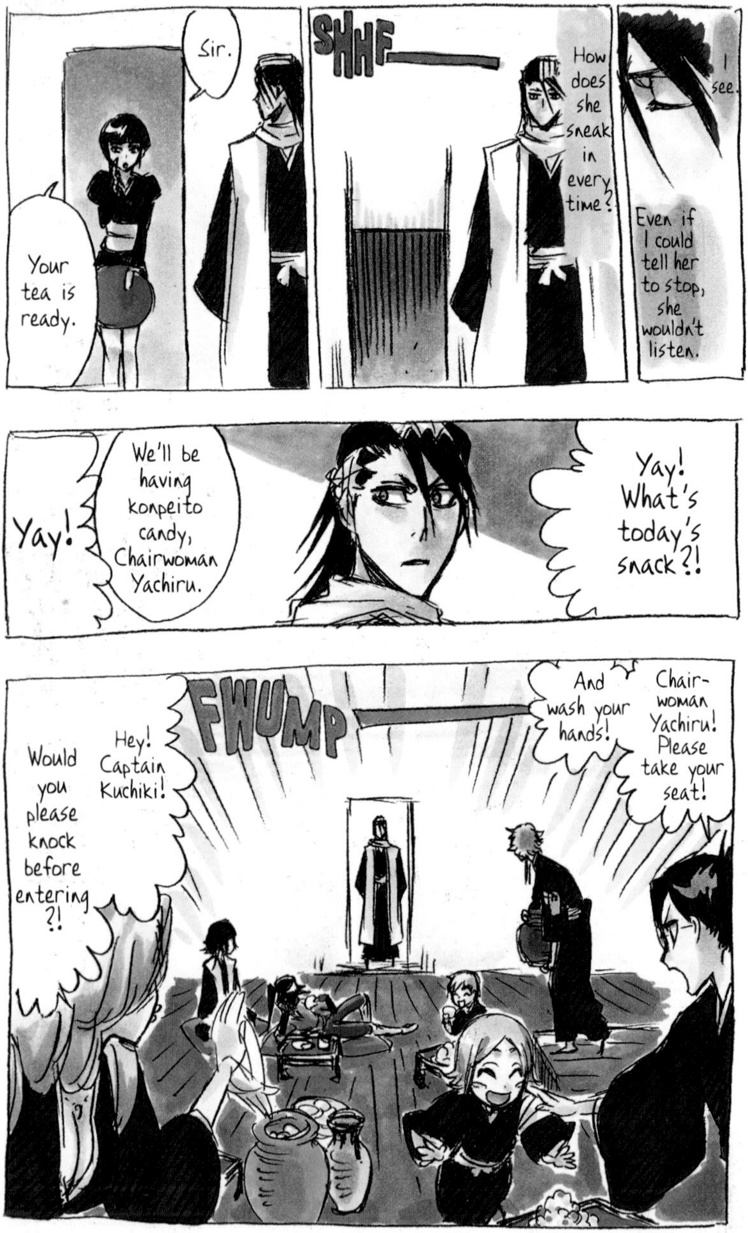
I see.
Even if I could tell her to stop, she wouldn't listen.
SHHF
How does she sneak in every time?
Sir.
Your tea is ready.
Yay! What's today's snack?!
We'll be having konpeito candy, Chairwoman Yachiru.
Yay!
Chair-woman Yachiru! Please take your seat!
And wash your hands!
FWUMP
Hey! Captain Kuchiki!
Would you please knock before entering?!

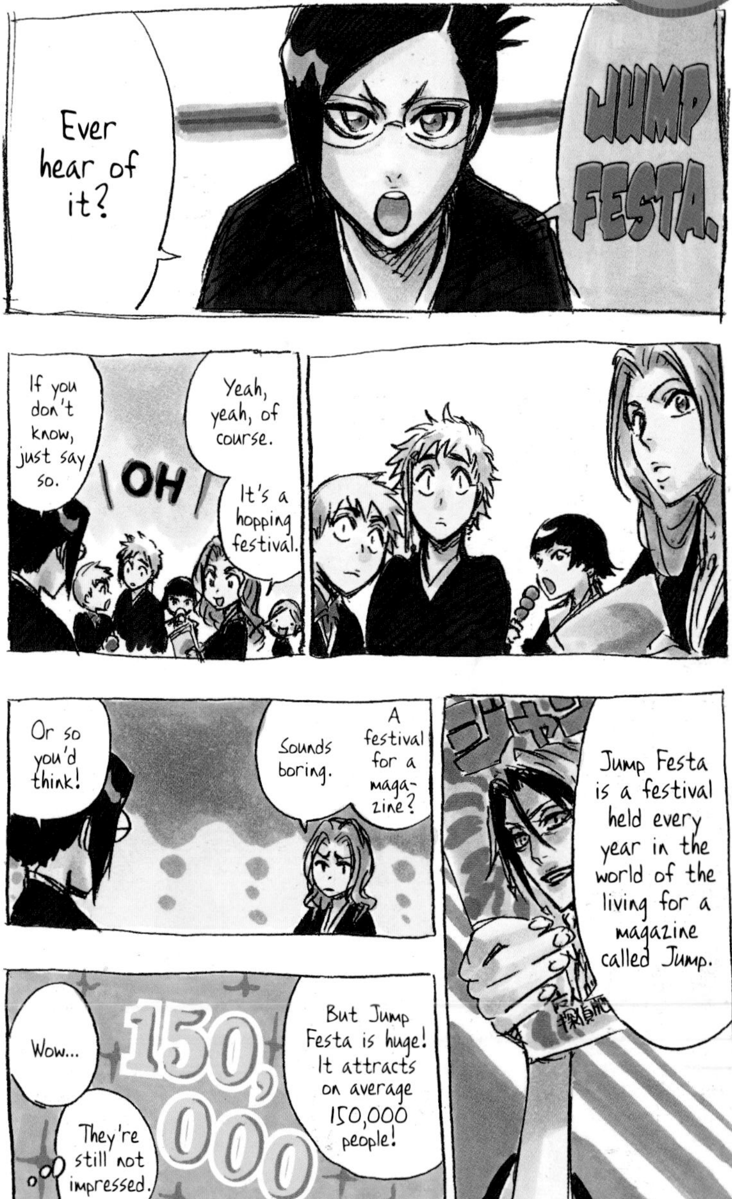

JUMP FESTA.
Ever hear of it?
Yeah, yeah, of course.
It's a hopping festival.
OH
If you don't know, just say so.
Jump Festa is a festival held every year in the world of the living for a magazine called Jump.
A festival for a magazine?
Sounds boring.
Or so you'd think!
But Jump Festa is huge! It attracts on average 150,000 people!
150,000
Wow...
They're still not impressed.

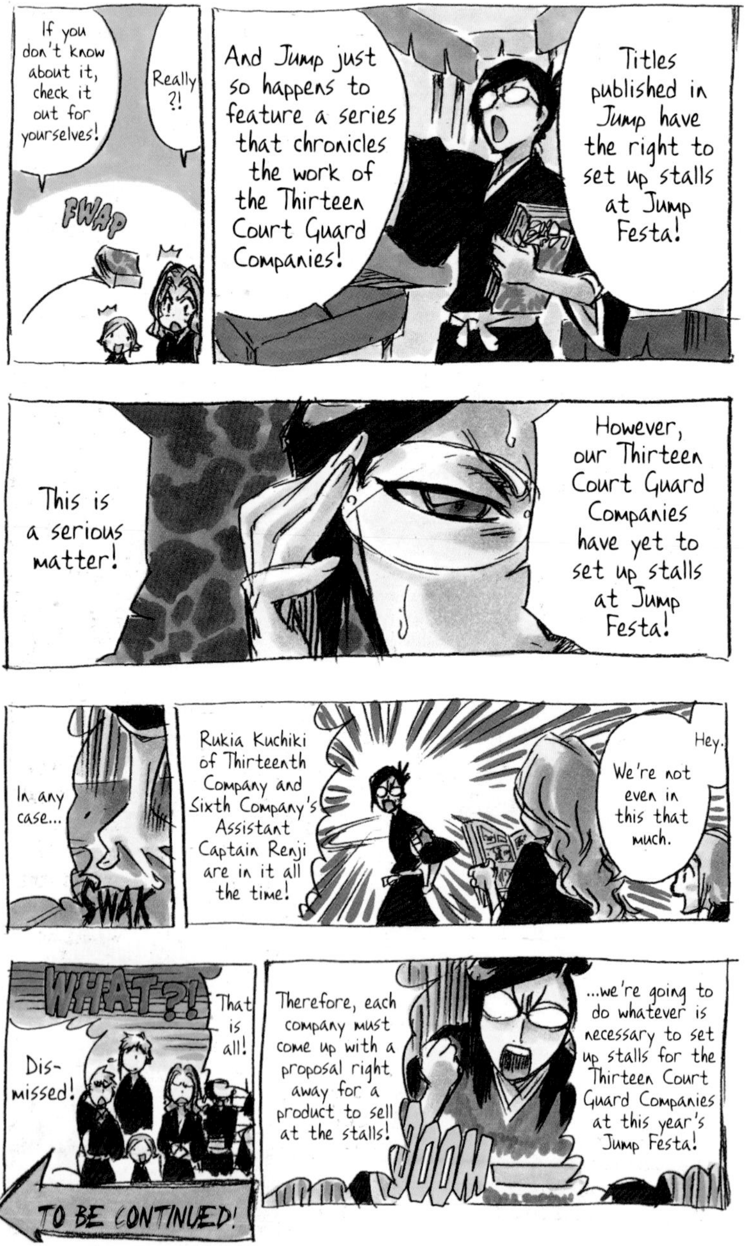

Titles published in Jump have the right to set up stalls at Jump Festa!
And Jump just so happens to feature a series that chronicles the work of the Thirteen Court Guard Companies!
Really?!
If you don't know about it, check it out for yourselves!
FWAP
However, our Thirteen Court Guard Companies have yet to set up stalls at Jump Festa!
This is a serious matter!
Hey.
We're not even in this that much.
Rukia Kuchiki of Thirteenth Company and Sixth Company's Assistant Captain Renji are in it all the time!
In any case...
SWAK
...we're going to do whatever is necessary to set up stalls for the Thirteen Court Guard Companies at this year's Jump Festa!
Therefore, each company must come up with a proposal right away for a product to sell at the stalls!
BOOM
That is all!
Dis-missed!
WHAT?!
TO BE CONTINUED!

COLOR BLEACH

OPERATION THIRTEEN COURT GUARD COMPANIES STALLS 1, 2 & 3!

ILLUSTRATED MANUSCRIPT OF DAILY IDLENESS

Part 30

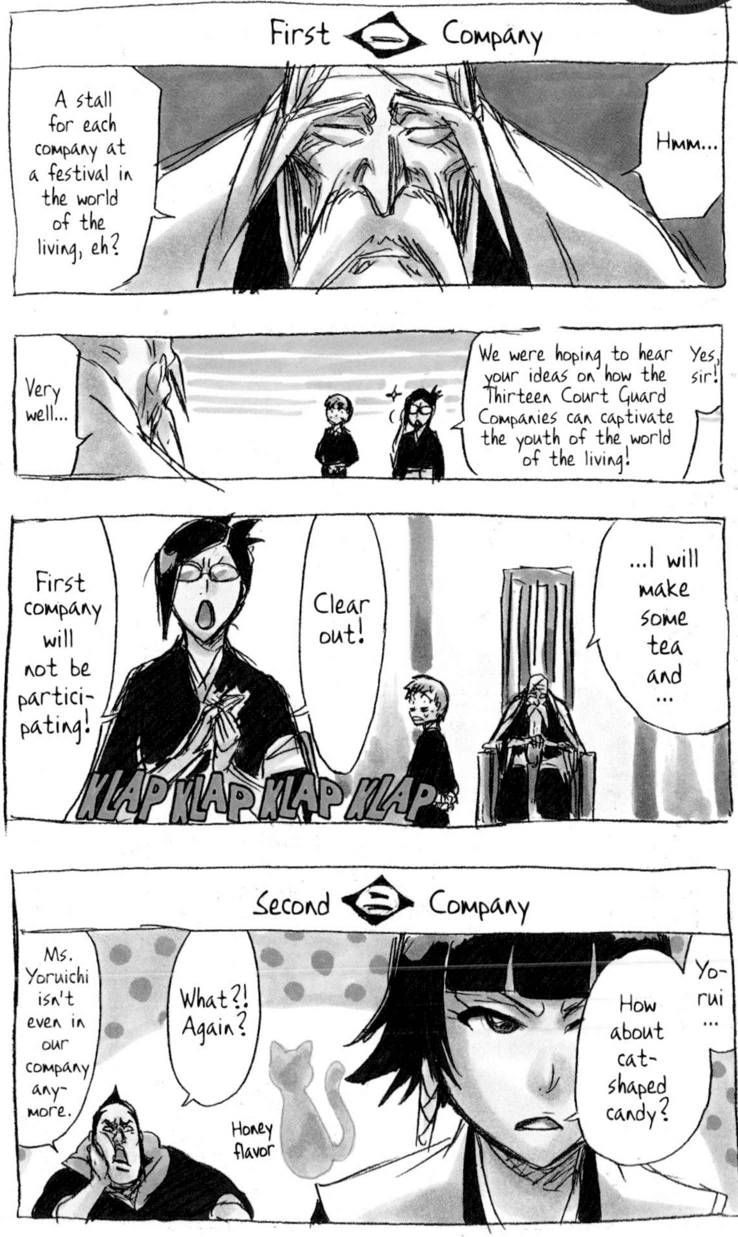
First Company
Hmm...
A stall for each company at a festival in the world of the living, eh?
Yes, sir!
We were hoping to hear your ideas on how the Thirteen Court Guard Companies can captivate the youth of the world of the living!
Very well...
...I will make some tea and ...
Clear out!
First company will not be partici-pating!
KLAP KLAP KLAP KLAP
Second Company
Yo-rui ...
How about cat-shaped candy?
Honey flavor
What?! Again?
Ms. Yoruichi isn't even in our company any-more.

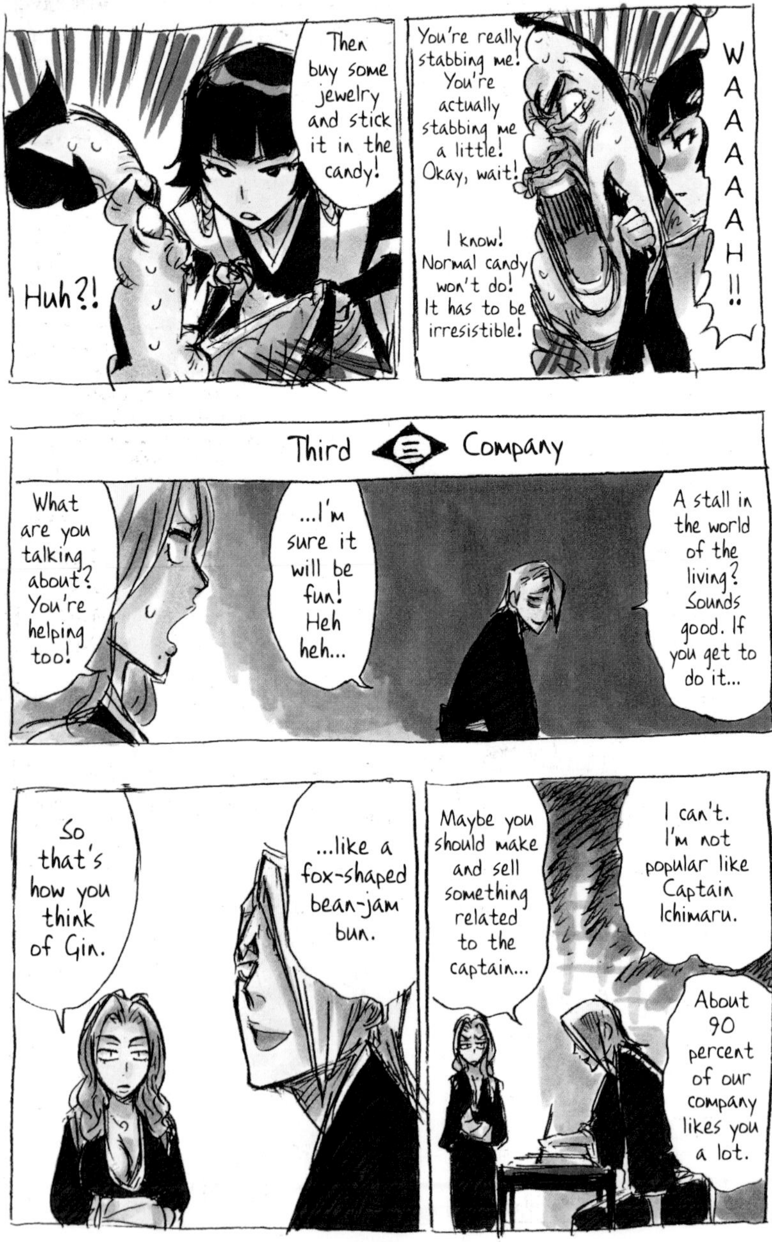
WAAAAAAH!!
You're really stabbing me! You're actually stabbing me a little! Okay, wait!
I know! Normal candy won't do! It has to be irresistible!
Then buy some jewelry and stick it in the candy!
Huh?!
Third Company
A stall in the world of the living? Sounds good. If you get to do it...
...I'm sure it will be fun! Heh heh...
What are you talking about? You're helping too!
I can't. I'm not popular like Captain Ichimaru.
Maybe you should make and sell something related to the captain...
About 90 percent of our company likes you a lot.
...like a fox-shaped bean-jam bun.
So that's how you think of Gin.

COLOR BLEACH

OPERATION THIRTEEN COURT GUARD COMPANIES STALLS 4 & 5!

ILLUSTRATED MANUSCRIPT OF DAILY IDLENESS

Part 31

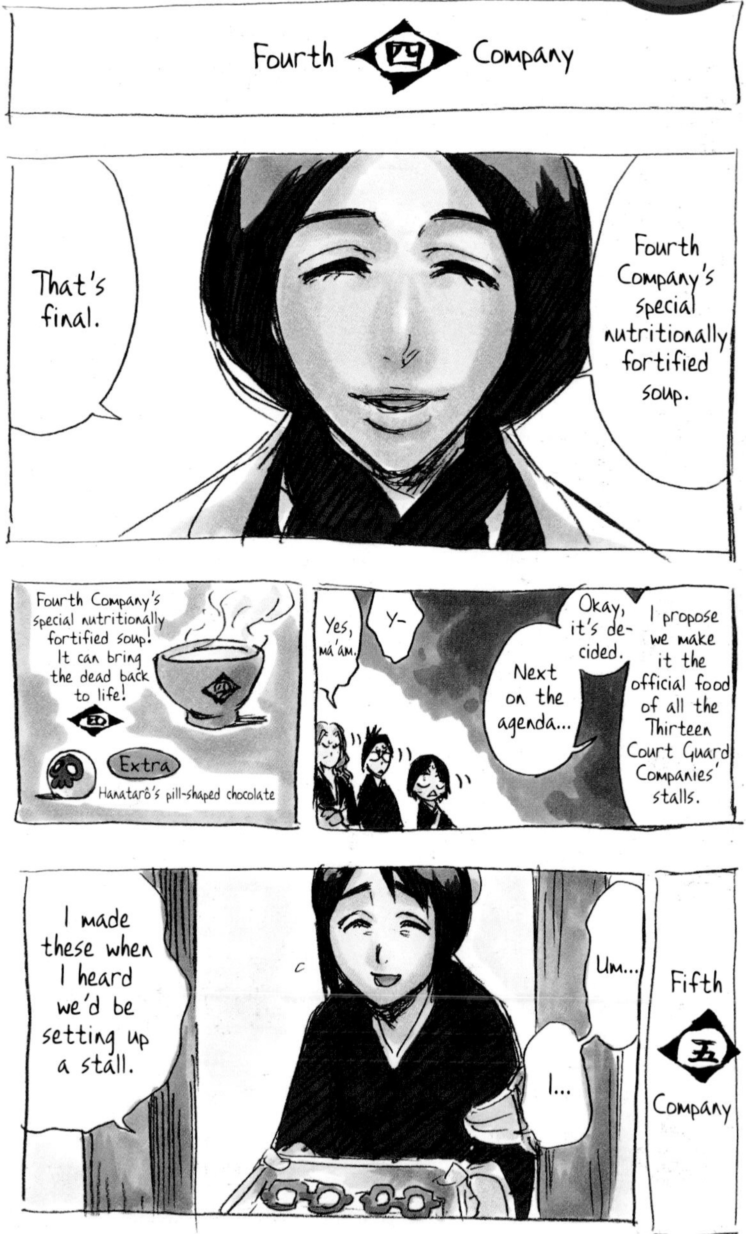

Fourth Company
Fourth Company's special nutritionally fortified soup.
That's final.
I propose we make it the official food of all the Thirteen Court Guard Companies' stalls.
Okay, it's decided.
Next on the agenda...
Y-
Yes, ma'am.
Fourth Company's special nutritionally fortified soup! It can bring the dead back to life!
Extra
Hanatarô's pill-shaped chocolate
Fifth Company
Um...
I...
I made these when I heard we'd be setting up a stall.

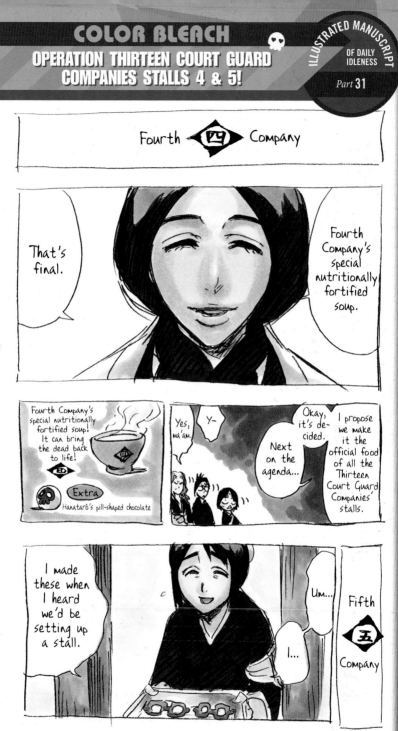

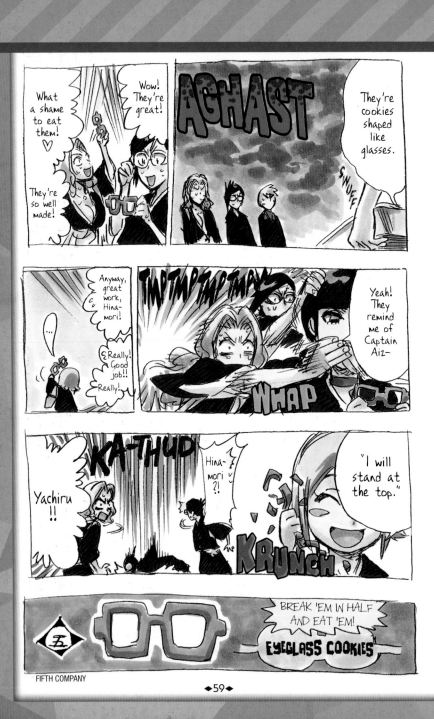

They're cookies shaped like glasses.
SNUFF
AGHAST
Wow! They're great!
What a shame to eat them! ♡
They're so well made!
Yeah! They remind me of Captain Aiz-
TMP TMP TMP TMP
WHAP
Anyway, great work, Hinamori!
Really! Good job!!
Really!
...
"I will stand at the top."
KRUNCH
Hinamori ?!
KA-THUD
Yachiru !!
BREAK 'EM IN HALF AND EAT 'EM!
EYEGLASS COOKIES

FIFTH COMPANY

COLOR BLEACH

OPERATION THIRTEEN COURT GUARD COMPANIES STALLS 6 & 7!

ILLUSTRATED MANUSCRIPT OF DAILY IDLENESS Part 32

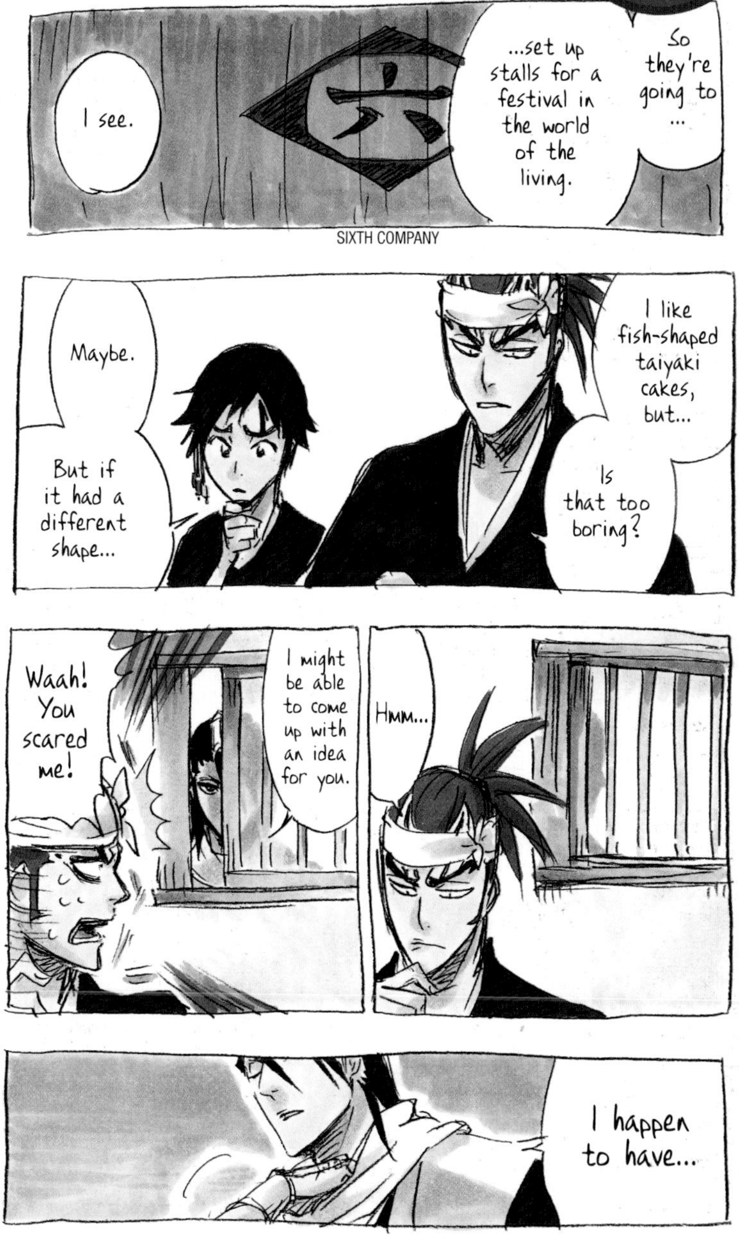
So they're going to ...
...set up stalls for a festival in the world of the living.
I see.
SIXTH COMPANY
I like fish-shaped taiyaki cakes, but...
Is that too boring?
Maybe.
But if it had a different shape...
Hmm...
I might be able to come up with an idea for you.
Waah! You scared me!
I happen to have...

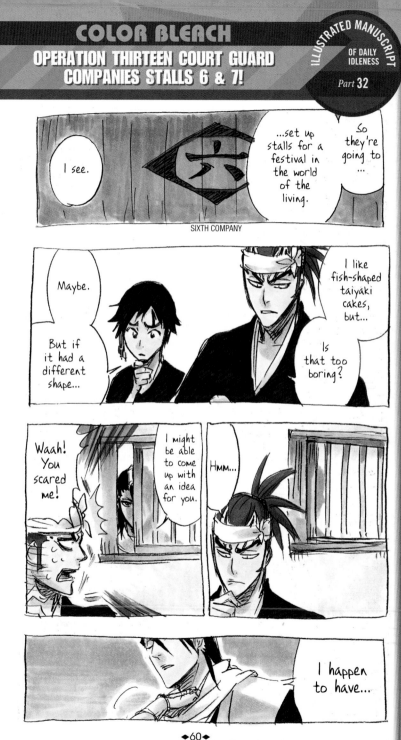

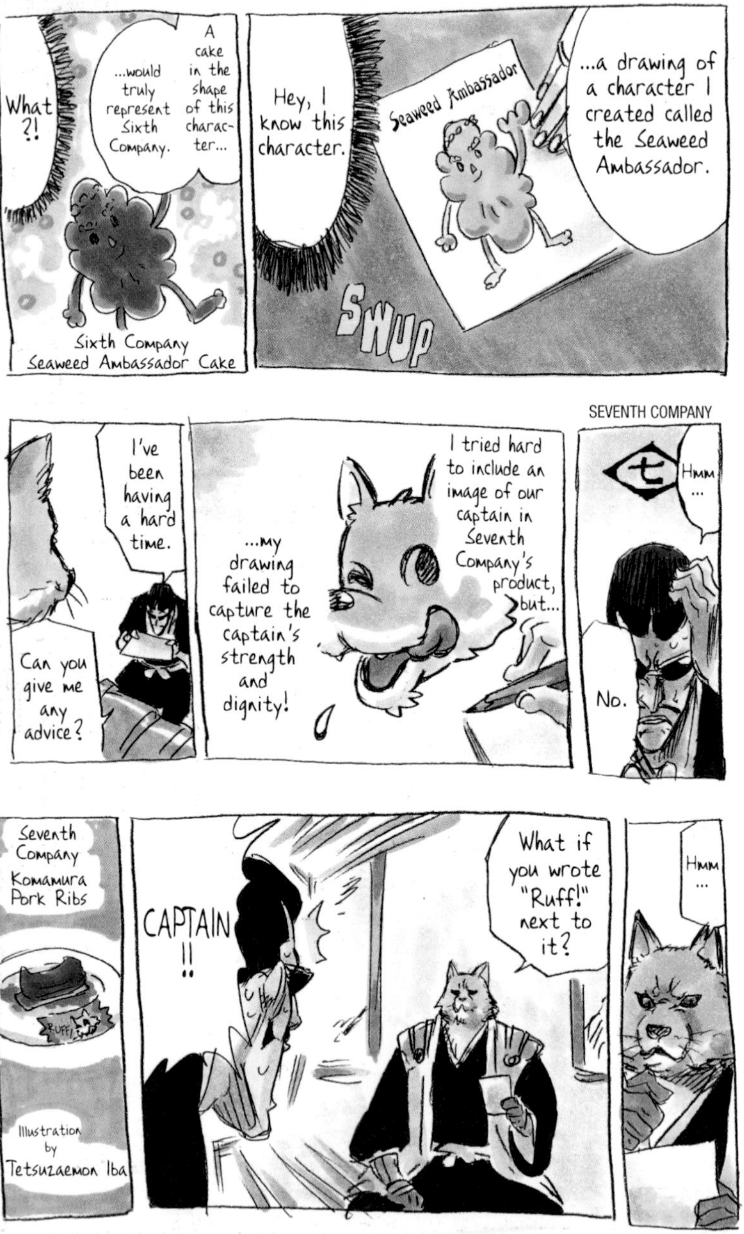
...a drawing of a character I created called the Seaweed Ambassador.
Seaweed Ambassador
Hey, I know this character.
SWUP
A cake in the shape of this character...
...would truly represent Sixth Company.
What?!
Sixth Company Seaweed Ambassador Cake
SEVENTH COMPANY
Hmm...
No.
I tried hard to include an image of our captain in Seventh Company's product, but...
...my drawing failed to capture the captain's strength and dignity!
I've been having a hard time.
Can you give me any advice?
Hmm...
What if you wrote "Ruff!" next to it?
CAPTAIN!!
Seventh Company Komamura Pork Ribs
RUFF!
Illustration by Tetsuzaemon Iba

COLOR BLEACH

OPERATION THIRTEEN COURT GUARD COMPANIES STALLS 8 & 9!

ILLUSTRATED MANUSCRIPT OF DAILY IDLENESS
Part 33

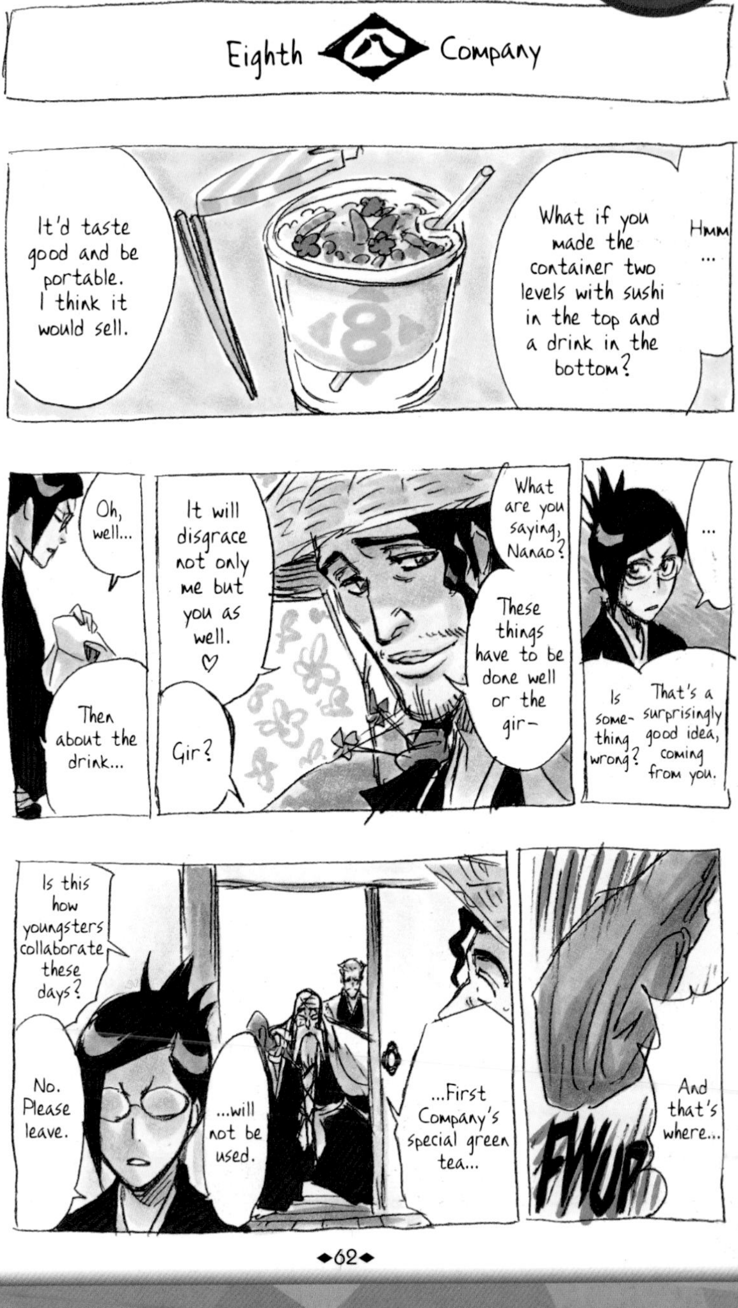
Eighth Company
Hmm...
What if you made the container two levels with sushi in the top and a drink in the bottom?
It'd taste good and be portable. I think it would sell.
...
That's a surprisingly good idea, coming from you.
Is something wrong?
What are you saying, Nanao?
These things have to be done well or the gir–
It will disgrace not only me but you as well. ♡
Gir?
Oh, well...
Then about the drink...
And that's where...
FWUP
...First Company's special green tea...
...will not be used.
Is this how youngsters collaborate these days?
No. Please leave.

Ninth Company

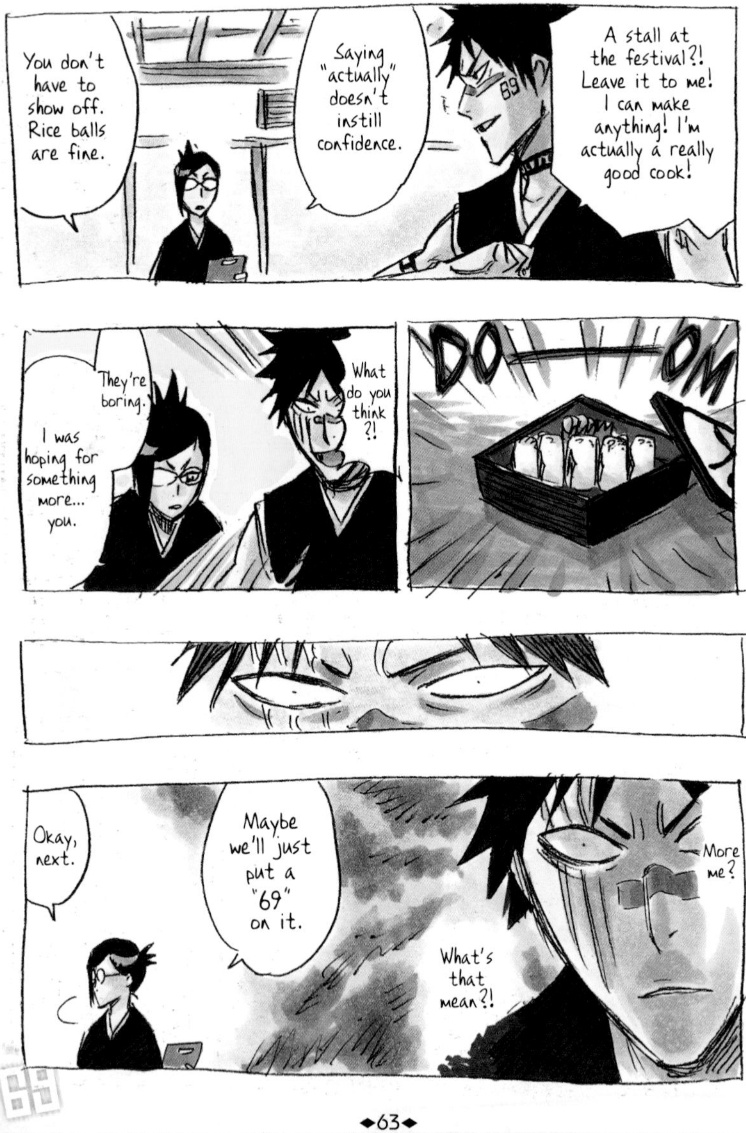
A stall at the festival?! Leave it to me! I can make anything! I'm actually a really good cook!
Saying "actually" doesn't instill confidence.
You don't have to show off. Rice balls are fine.
DO—OM
What do you think?!
They're boring.
I was hoping for something more... you.
More me?
Maybe we'll just put a "69" on it.
What's that mean?!
Okay, next.

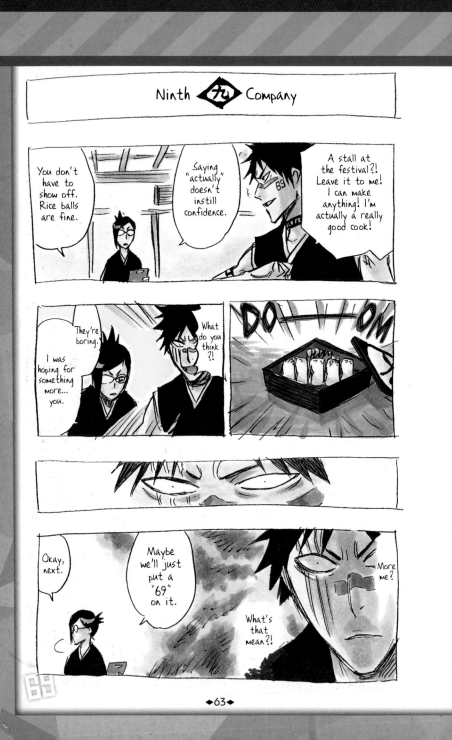

OPERATION THIRTEEN COURT GUARD COMPANIES STALLS 10 & 11!

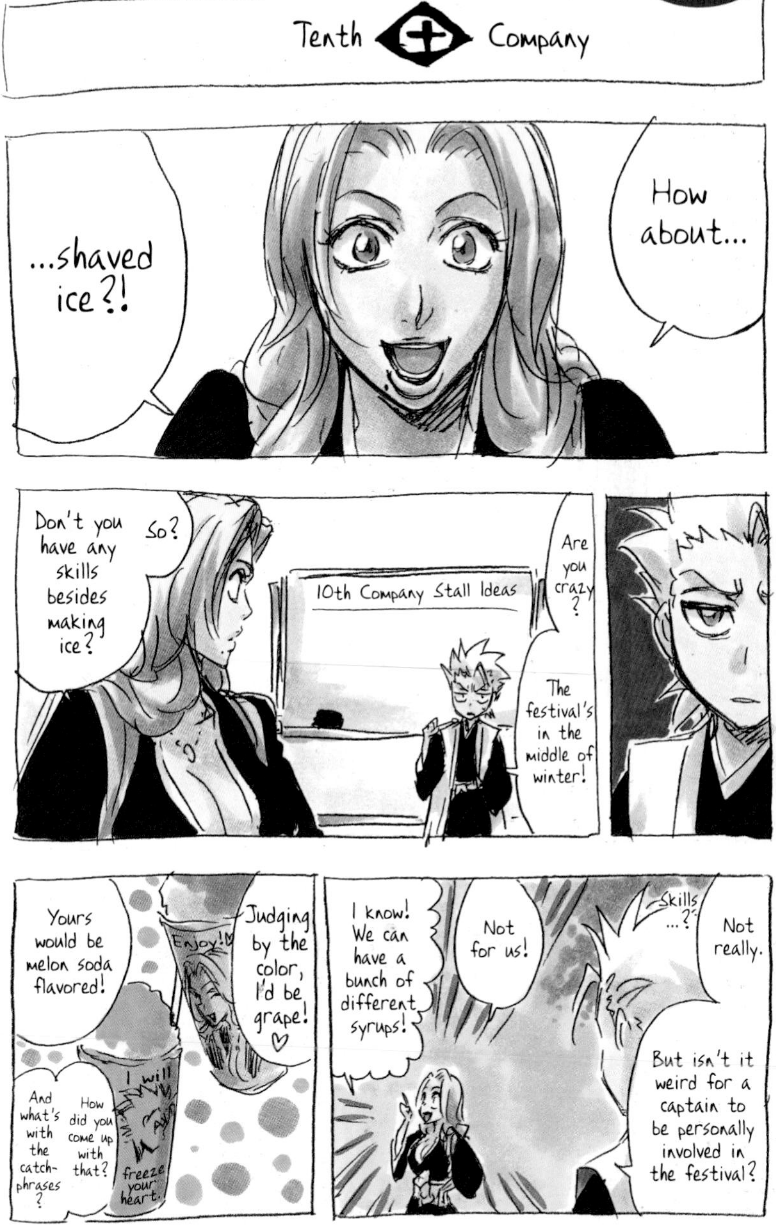
Tenth Company
How about...
...shaved ice?!
Are you crazy?
The festival's in the middle of winter!
10th Company Stall Ideas
So?
Don't you have any skills besides making ice?
Skills...?
Not really.
But isn't it weird for a captain to be personally involved in the festival?
Not for us!
I know! We can have a bunch of different syrups!
Judging by the color, I'd be grape!
Enjoy!
Yours would be melon soda flavored!
I will freeze your heart.
How did you come up with that?
And what's with the catch-phrases?

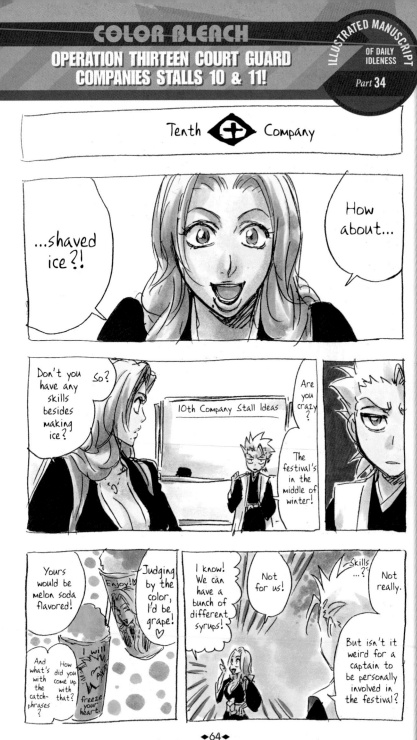

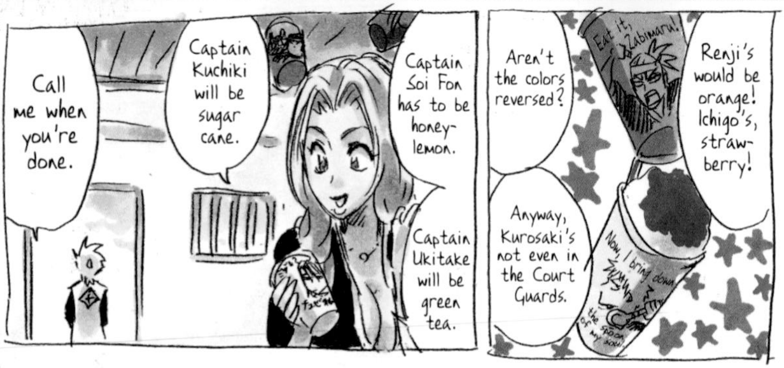
Renji's would be orange! Ichigo's, straw-berry!
Eat it, Zabimaru!
Aren't the colors reversed?
Now, I bring down the spoon of my soul!
Anyway, Kurosaki's not even in the Court Guards.
Captain Soi Fon has to be honey-lemon.
Captain Ukitake will be green tea.
Captain Kuchiki will be sugar cane.
Call me when you're done.

Eleventh Company

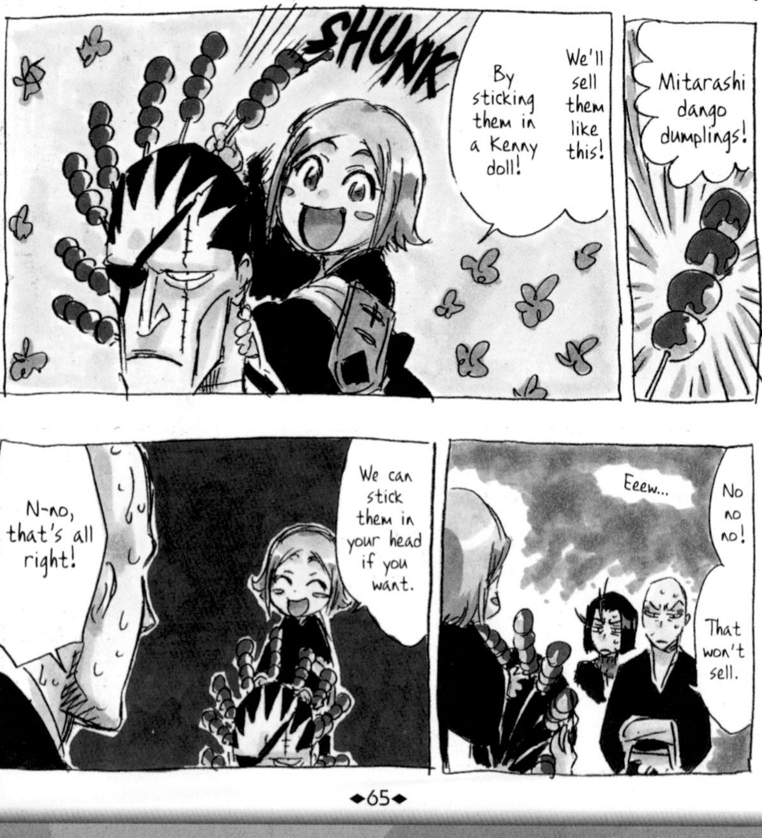
Mitarashi dango dumplings!
SHUNK
We'll sell them like this!
By sticking them in a Kenny doll!
No no no!
That won't sell.
Eeew...
We can stick them in your head if you want.
N-no, that's all right!

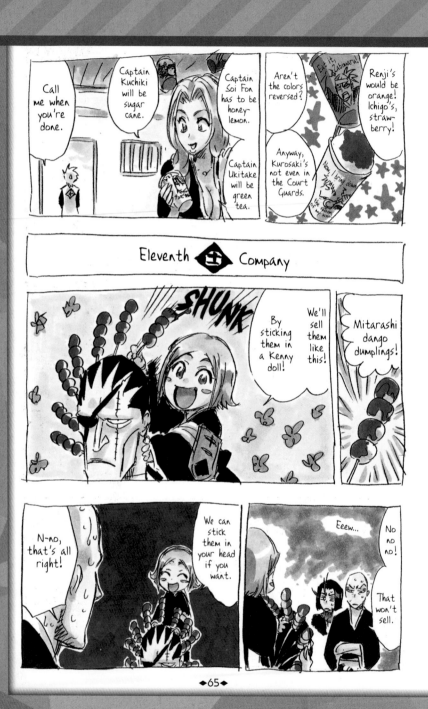

COLOR BLEACH

OPERATION THIRTEEN COURT GUARD COMPANIES STALLS 12 & 13!

ILLUSTRATED MANUSCRIPT OF DAILY IDLENESS

Part 35

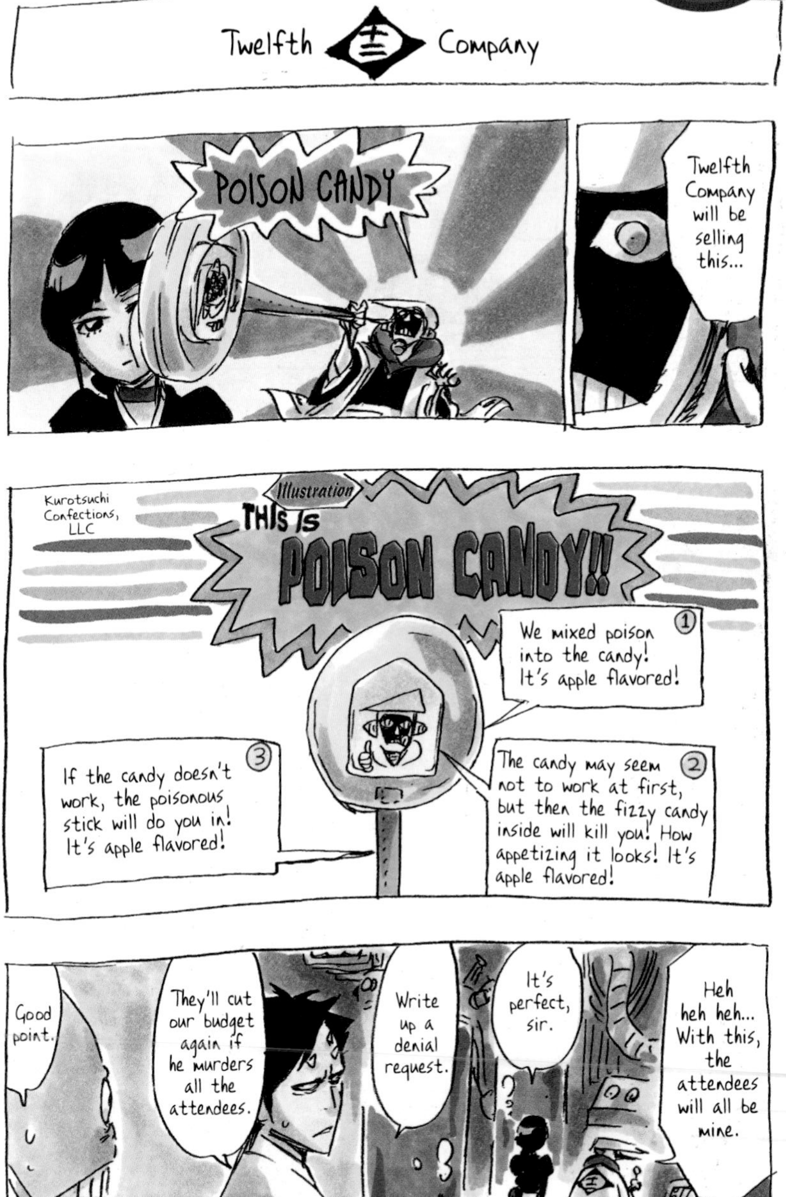
Twelfth Company
Twelfth Company will be selling this...
POISON CANDY
Illustration
Kurotsuchi Confections, LLC
THIS IS POISON CANDY!!
① We mixed poison into the candy! It's apple flavored!
② The candy may seem not to work at first, but then the fizzy candy inside will kill you! How appetizing it looks! It's apple flavored!
③ If the candy doesn't work, the poisonous stick will do you in! It's apple flavored!
Heh heh heh... With this, the attendees will all be mine.
It's perfect, sir.
Write up a denial request.
They'll cut our budget again if he murders all the attendees.
Good point.

Thirteenth Company

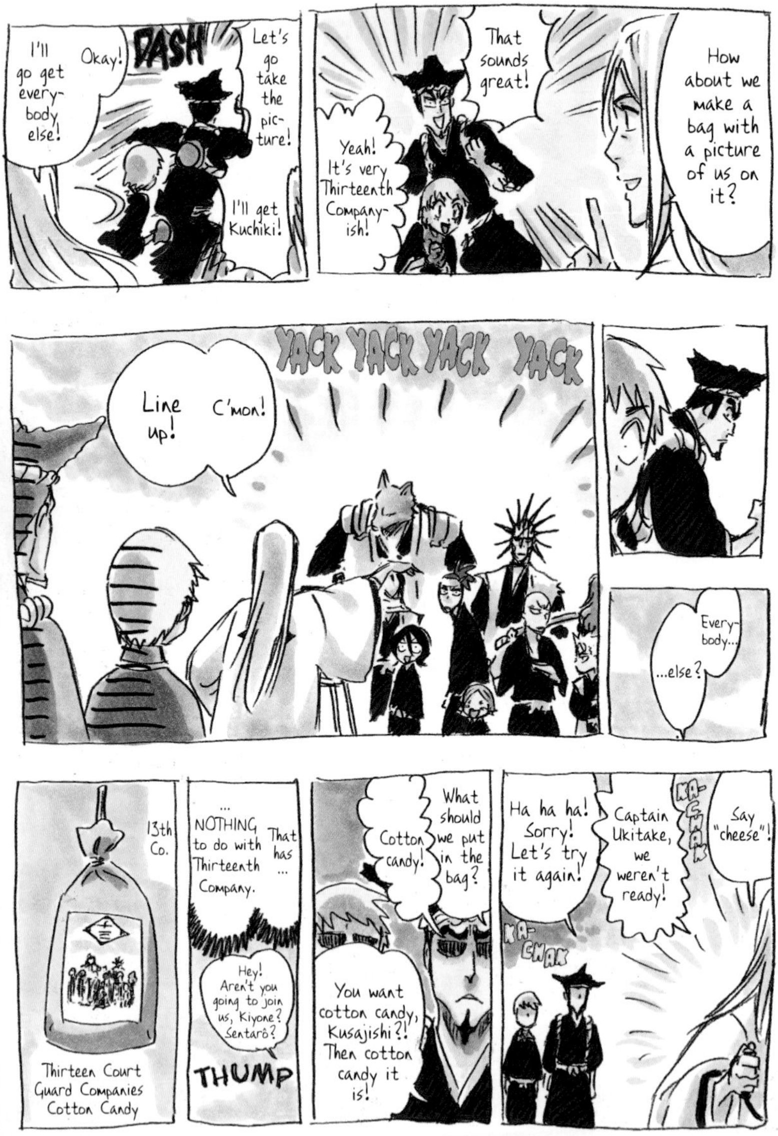
How about we make a bag with a picture of us on it?
That sounds great!
Yeah! It's very Thirteenth Company-ish!
Let's go take the picture!
Okay!
DASH
I'll get Kuchiki!
I'll go get every-body else!
Every-body...
...else?
YACK YACK YACK YACK
C'mon!
Line up!
Say "cheese"!
KA-CHAK
Captain Ukitake, we weren't ready!
Ha ha ha! Sorry! Let's try it again!
KA-CHAK
What should we put in the bag?
Cotton candy!
You want cotton candy, Kusajishi?! Then cotton candy it is!
That has...
...NOTHING to do with Thirteenth Company.
Hey! Aren't you going to join us, Kiyone? Sentarō?
THUMP
13th Co.
Thirteen Court Guard Companies Cotton Candy

COLOR BLEACH

THE SECRET PLOT OF THE SOCIETY OF MALE SOUL REAPERS, PART 1

ILLUSTRATED MANUSCRIPT OF DAILY IDLENESS
Part 36

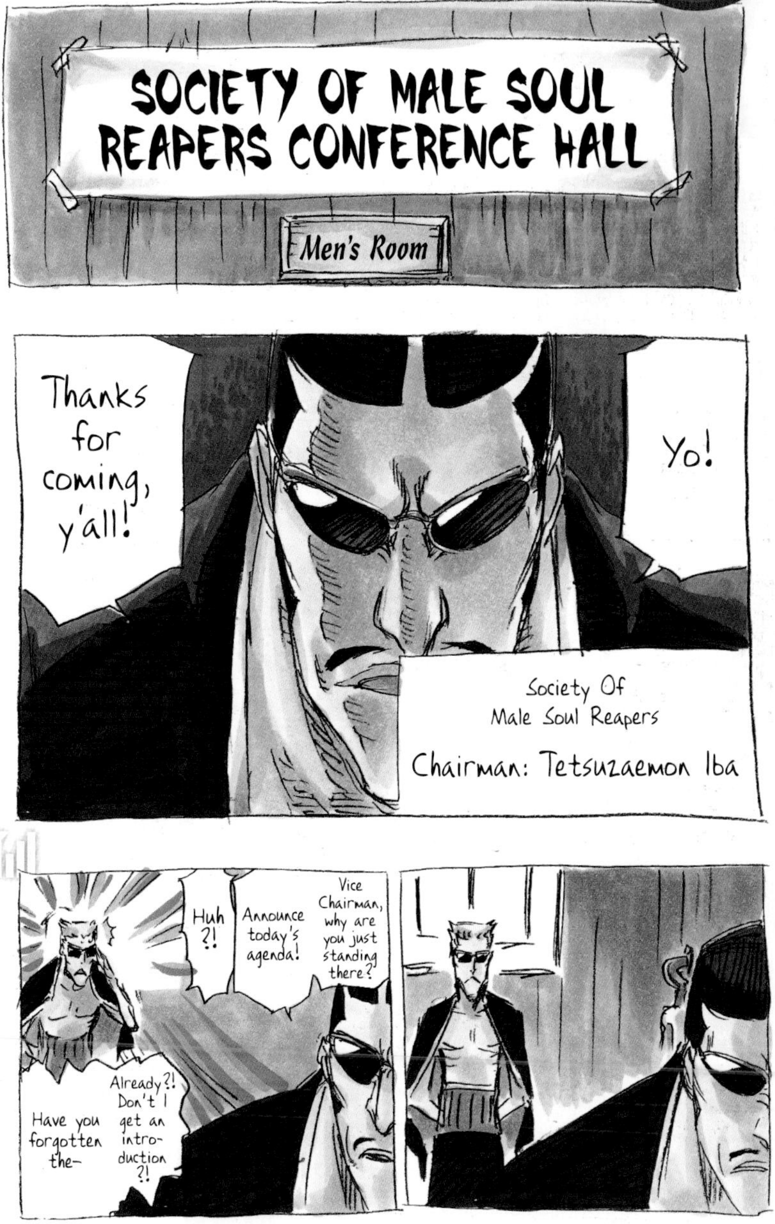
SOCIETY OF MALE SOUL REAPERS CONFERENCE HALL
Men's Room
Yo!
Thanks for coming, y'all!
Society Of Male Soul Reapers
Chairman: Tetsuzaemon Iba
Vice Chairman, why are you just standing there?
Announce today's agenda!
Huh?!
Already?! Don't I get an introduction?!
Have you forgotten the–

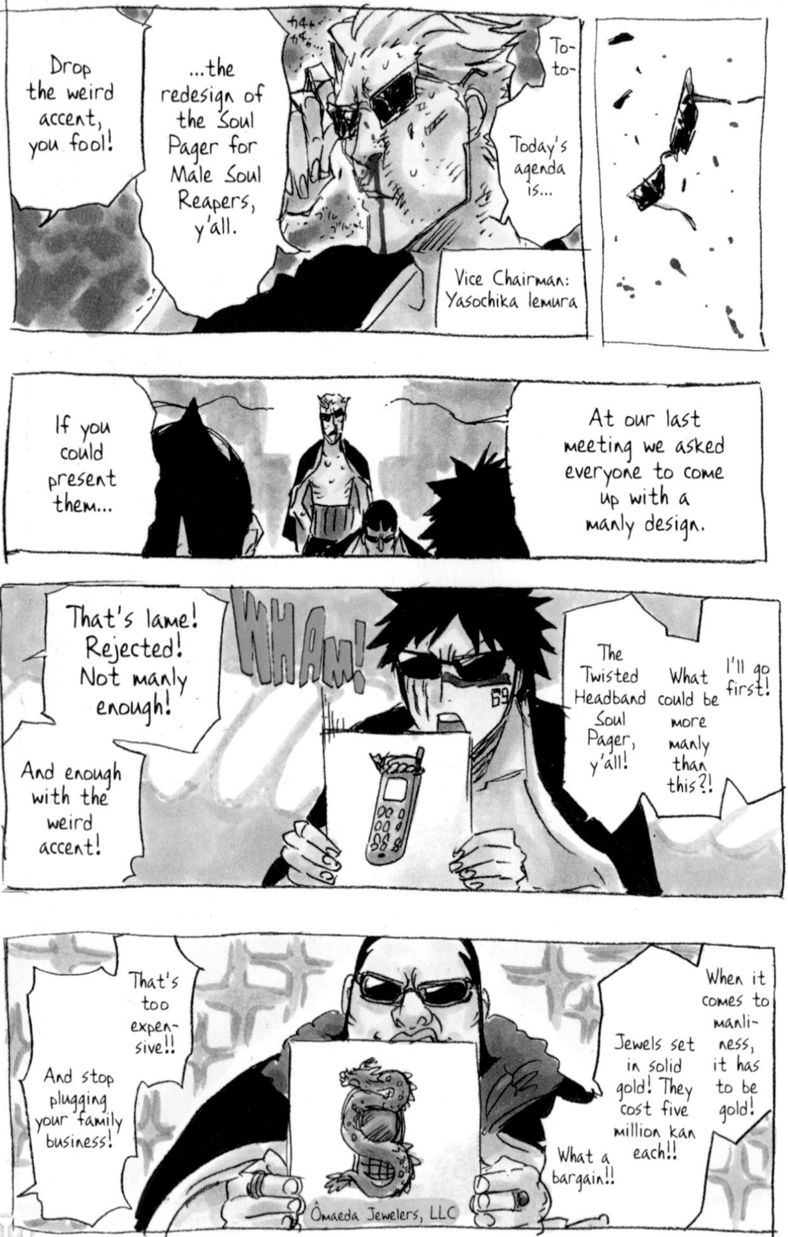
To- to-
Today's agenda is...
Vice Chairman: Yasochika Iemura
...the redesign of the Soul Pager for Male Soul Reapers, y'all.
Drop the weird accent, you fool!
At our last meeting we asked everyone to come up with a manly design.
If you could present them...
I'll go first!
What could be more manly than this?!
The Twisted Headband Soul Pager, y'all!
WHAM!
That's lame! Rejected! Not manly enough!
And enough with the weird accent!
When it comes to manliness, it has to be gold!
Jewels set in solid gold! They cost five million kan each!!
What a bargain!!
Ômaeda Jewelers, LLC
That's too expensive!!
And stop plugging your family business!

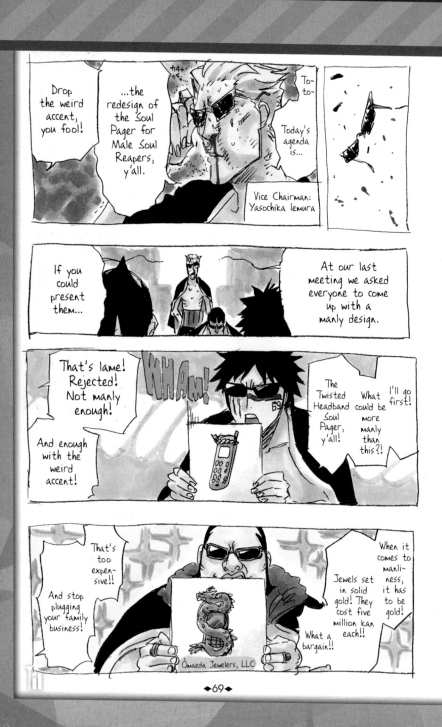

COLOR BLEACH

THE SECRET PLOT OF THE SOCIETY OF MALE SOUL REAPERS, PART 2

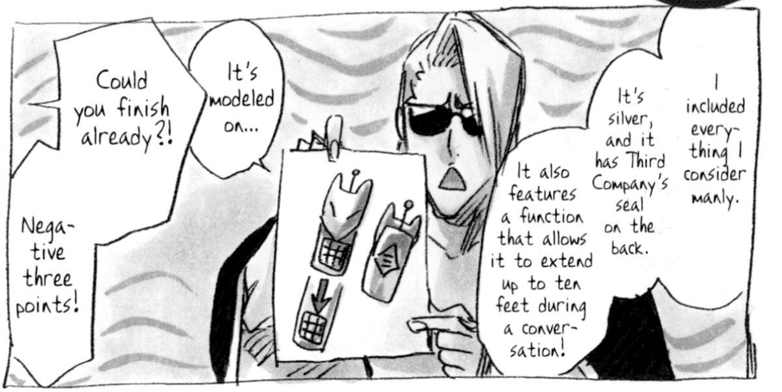
I included everything I consider manly.
It's silver, and it has Third Company's seal on the back.
It also features a function that allows it to extend up to ten feet during a conversation!
It's modeled on...
Could you finish already?!
Negative three points!

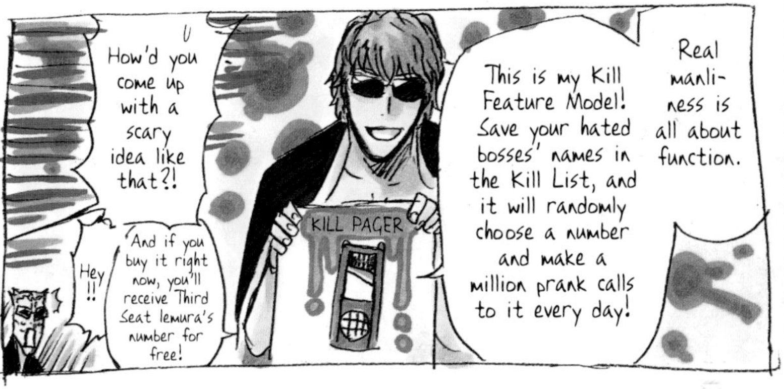
Real manliness is all about function.
This is my Kill Feature Model! Save your hated bosses' names in the Kill List, and it will randomly choose a number and make a million prank calls to it every day!
KILL PAGER
How'd you come up with a scary idea like that?!
And if you buy it right now, you'll receive Third Seat Iemura's number for free!
Hey!!

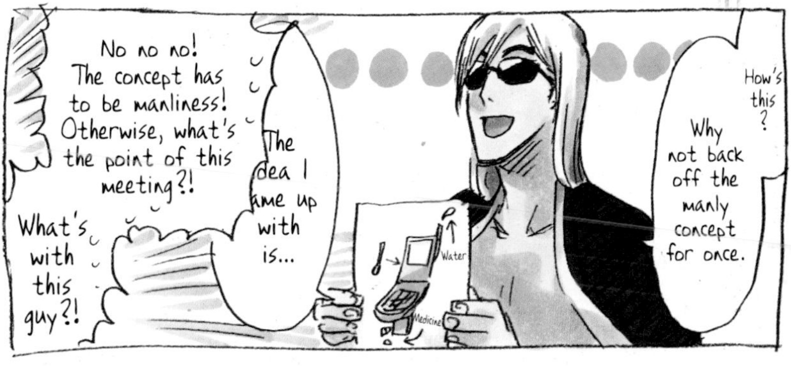
How's this?
Why not back off the manly concept for once.
Water
Medicine
The dea I ame up with is...
No no no! The concept has to be manliness! Otherwise, what's the point of this meeting?!
What's with this guy?!

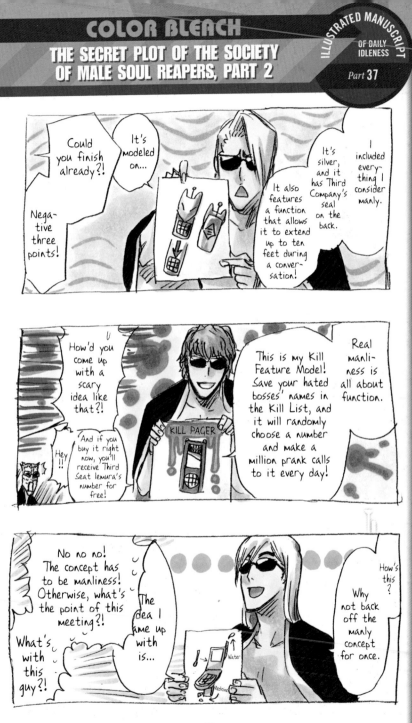

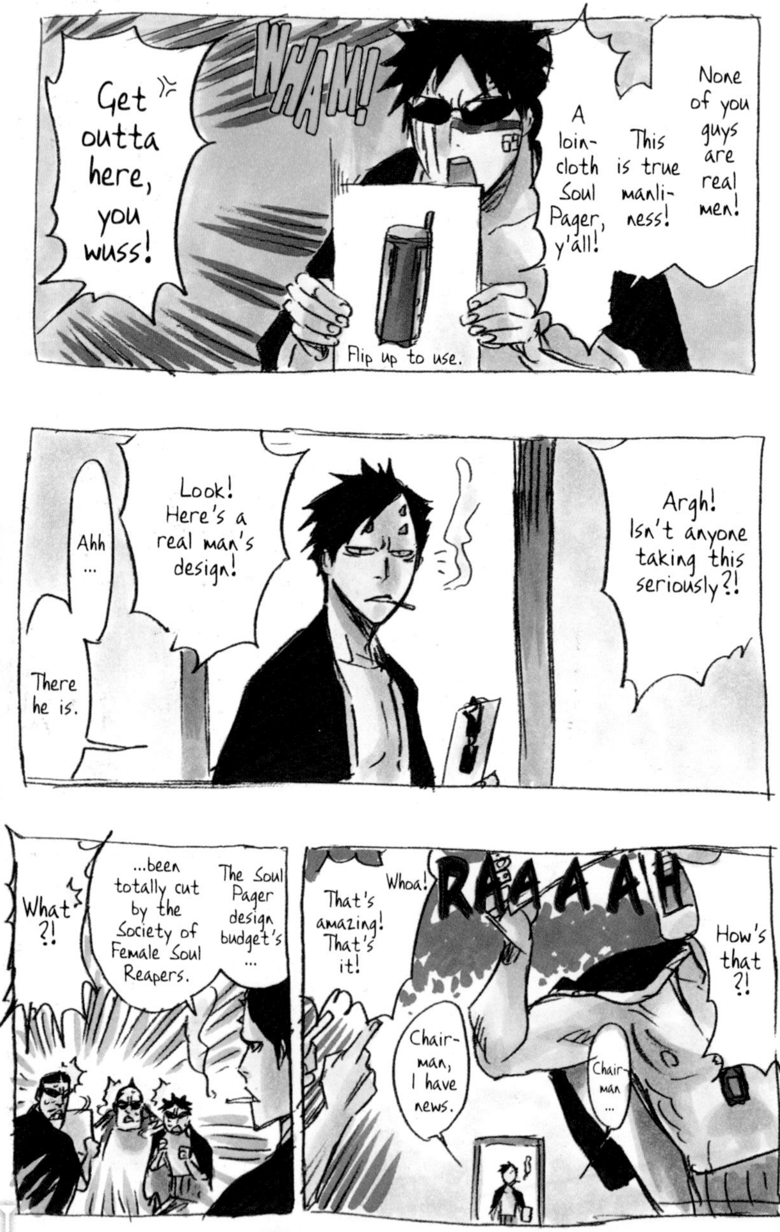
None of you guys are real men!
This is true manliness!
A loincloth Soul Pager, y'all!
WHAM!
Get outta here, you wuss!
Flip up to use.
Argh! Isn't anyone taking this seriously?!
Look! Here's a real man's design!
Ahh...
There he is.
How's that?!
RAAAAH
Whoa!
That's amazing! That's it!
Chairman...
Chairman, I have news.
The Soul Pager design budget's...
...been totally cut by the Society of Female Soul Reapers.
What?!

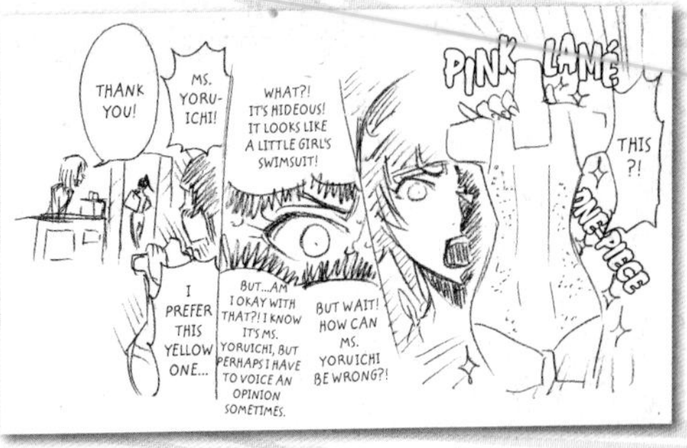
PINK LAMÉ
THIS?!
ONE-PIECE
BUT WAIT! HOW CAN MS. YORUICHI BE WRONG?!
WHAT?! IT'S HIDEOUS! IT LOOKS LIKE A LITTLE GIRL'S SWIMSUIT!
BUT...AM I OKAY WITH THAT?! I KNOW IT'S MS. YORUICHI, BUT PERHAPS I HAVE TO VOICE AN OPINION SOMETIMES.
MS. YORUICHI!
THANK YOU!
I PREFER THIS YELLOW ONE...

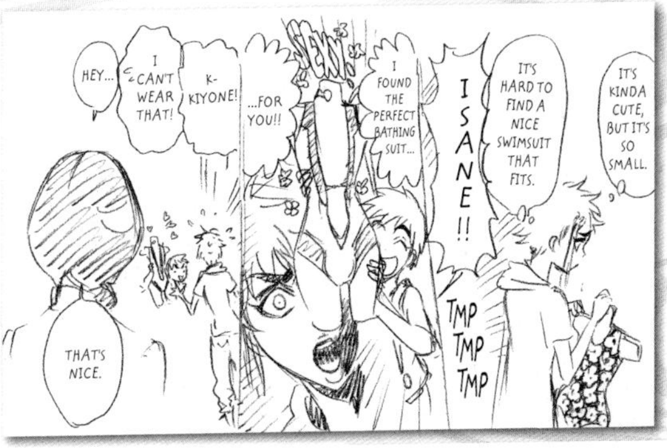
IT'S KINDA CUTE, BUT IT'S SO SMALL.
IT'S HARD TO FIND A NICE SWIMSUIT THAT FITS.
ISANE!!
TMP TMP TMP
I FOUND THE PERFECT BATHING SUIT...
...FOR YOU!!
K-KIYONE!
I CAN'T WEAR THAT!
HEY...
THAT'S NICE.

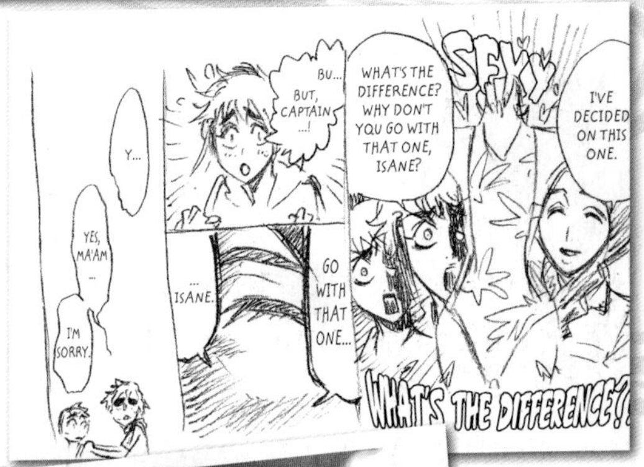
I'VE DECIDED ON THIS ONE.
WHAT'S THE DIFFERENCE? WHY DON'T YOU GO WITH THAT ONE, ISANE?
BU... BUT, CAPTAIN ...!
WHAT'S THE DIFFERENCE?!
GO WITH THAT ONE...
...ISANE.
Y...
YES, MA'AM ...
I'M SORRY.

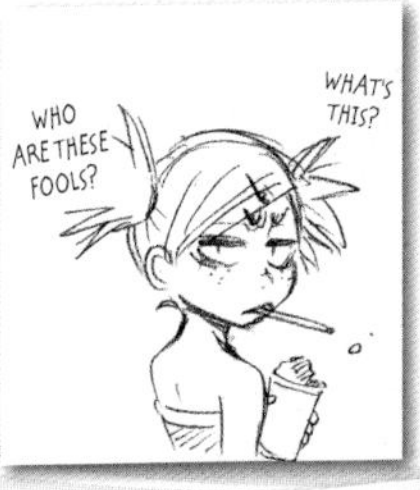
WHAT'S THIS?
WHO ARE THESE FOOLS?

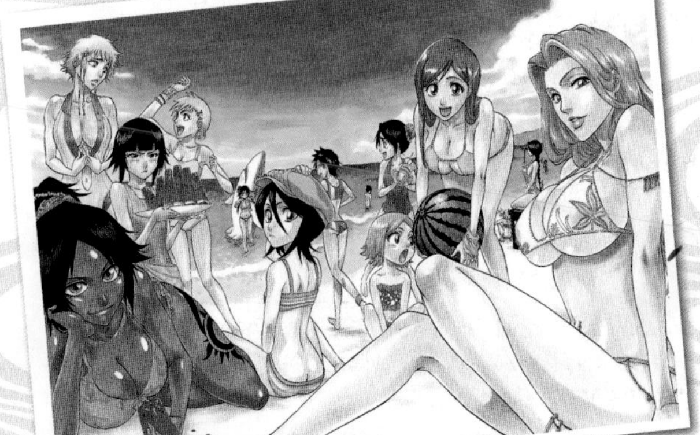

ONE SHOULD LISTEN TO ONE'S ELDERS.

...SPECIAL ISSUE.

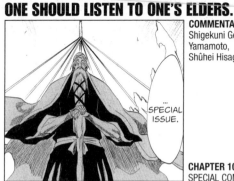

COMMENTATORS/
Shigekuni Genryûsai Yamamoto,
Shûhei Hisagi

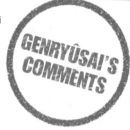

GENRYÛSAI'S COMMENTS

CHAPTER 10,526
SPECIAL COMMEMORATIVE ISSUE

To all young people who aspire to become Soul Reapers: Pound on the gates of Soul Reaper Academy, and the way will open to you.

I am filled with joy by the publication of this special issue of *Seireitei Bulletin*. This magazine, which was founded to raise morale and build solidarity among Soul Reapers, has been published continuously for more than a thousand years. Looking back, we've had to overcome many hardships. We didn't have today's technology. We used to use a gariban (mimeograph machine). I'm sure many young people won't even know what that is. Special stencils were made from wax paper, and ink drums were used to print the copies. The drum made the sound "gari-gari," hence the name gariban. I must admit, the world has become a convenient place since those days.

Messenger services are common today, but we had nothing as handy back then. The only modes of communication were the Secret Remote Unit or the Hell Butterfly. It wasn't easy to contact anyone far away. Hmm… I think I'm going off the subject.

This special issue is meant to open the way for young people who seek to become Soul Reaper candidates. The magazine contains detailed information about the Thirteen Court Guard Companies, their areas of expertise and the nature of their work. I hope this magazine will deepen the reader's commitment, and that he or she will strive, with renewed enthusiasm, to become a member of one of the Thirteen Court Guard Companies.

I look forward to seeing your rapid progress.

YES.
BUT STILL, THEY WERE AMAZING.
DO YOU THINK...
...WE COULD EVER BE LIKE THEM?

SHÛHEI'S COMMENTS

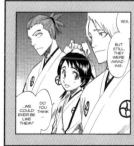

A BOUNDLESS FUTURE LIES BEFORE YOU.

I'm Shûhei Hisagi, standing in for the editor in chief. Attention, Soul Reaper wannabes. This special issue explains everything you need to know about the job of the Soul Reapers. In front of you is a blank canvas. What you draw on it is up to each of you. Get out there and draw something extraordinary!

COMPLETE GUIDE

THIRTEEN COURT GUARD COMPANIES

The Thirteen Court Guard Companies
are the fighting squads that protect
the Seireitei. Each company is
introduced here in great detail.

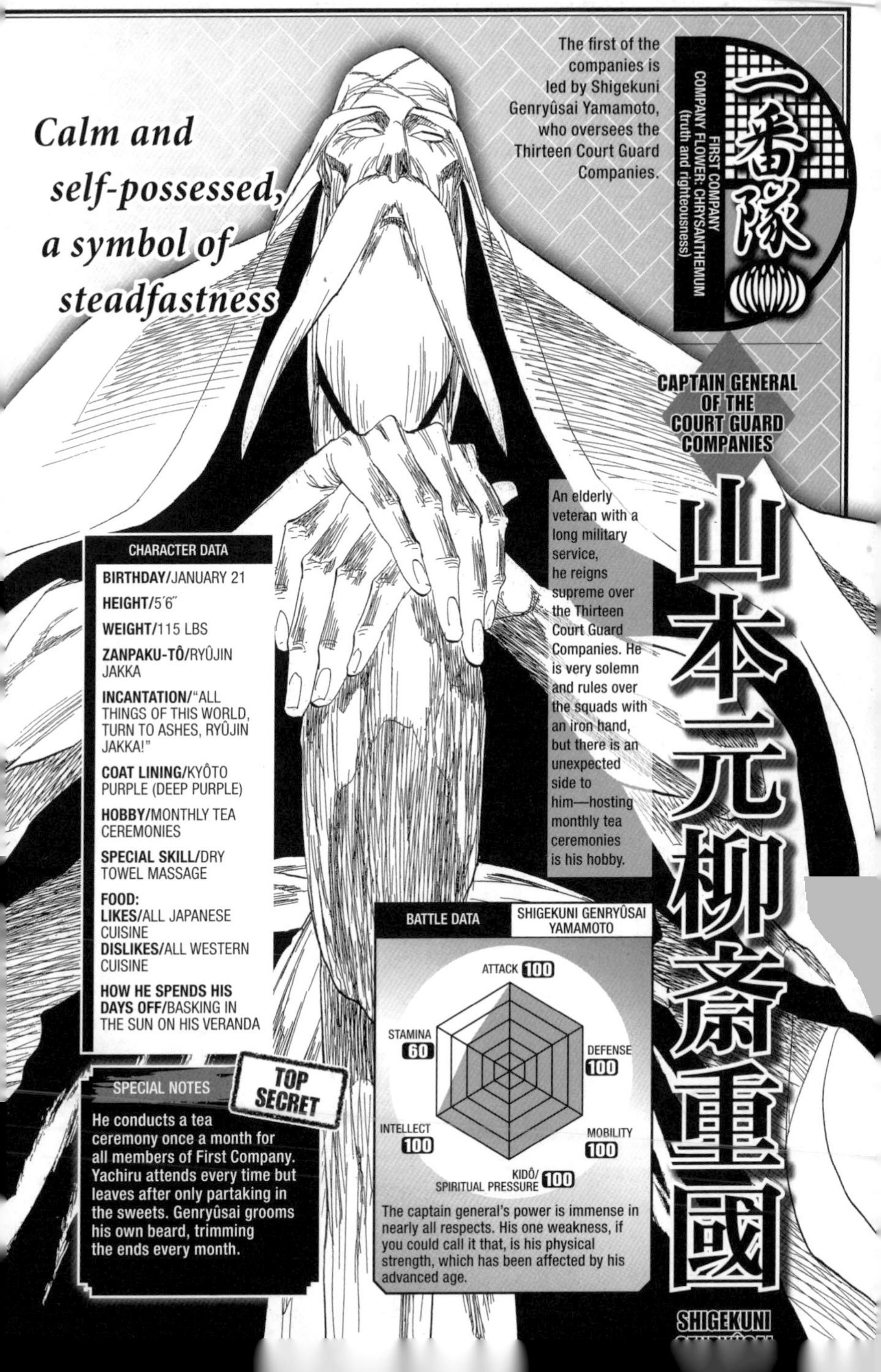

Calm and self-possessed, a symbol of steadfastness

一番隊

FIRST COMPANY
COMPANY FLOWER: CHRYSANTHEMUM
(truth and righteousness)

The first of the companies is led by Shigekuni Genryûsai Yamamoto, who oversees the Thirteen Court Guard Companies.

CAPTAIN GENERAL OF THE COURT GUARD COMPANIES

山本元柳斎重國

SHIGEKUNI

An elderly veteran with a long military service, he reigns supreme over the Thirteen Court Guard Companies. He is very solemn and rules over the squads with an iron hand, but there is an unexpected side to him—hosting monthly tea ceremonies is his hobby.

CHARACTER DATA

BIRTHDAY/JANUARY 21

HEIGHT/5´6″

WEIGHT/115 LBS

ZANPAKU-TÔ/RYÛJIN JAKKA

INCANTATION/“ALL THINGS OF THIS WORLD, TURN TO ASHES, RYÛJIN JAKKA!”

COAT LINING/KYÔTO PURPLE (DEEP PURPLE)

HOBBY/MONTHLY TEA CEREMONIES

SPECIAL SKILL/DRY TOWEL MASSAGE

FOOD:
LIKES/ALL JAPANESE CUISINE
DISLIKES/ALL WESTERN CUISINE

HOW HE SPENDS HIS DAYS OFF/BASKING IN THE SUN ON HIS VERANDA

SPECIAL NOTES — TOP SECRET

He conducts a tea ceremony once a month for all members of First Company. Yachiru attends every time but leaves after only partaking in the sweets. Genryûsai grooms his own beard, trimming the ends every month.

BATTLE DATA — SHIGEKUNI GENRYÛSAI YAMAMOTO

ATTACK 100
DEFENSE 100
MOBILITY 100
KIDÔ/SPIRITUAL PRESSURE 100
INTELLECT 100
STAMINA 60

The captain general's power is immense in nearly all respects. His one weakness, if you could call it that, is his physical strength, which has been affected by his advanced age.

During the recent rebellion in the Soul Society, rumor had it that captains Ukitake and Kyôraku obstructed the execution of Rukia Kuchiki of Thirteenth Company. The captain general was angry with the pair, whom he trusted implicitly… Knock on wood that this doesn't happen again.

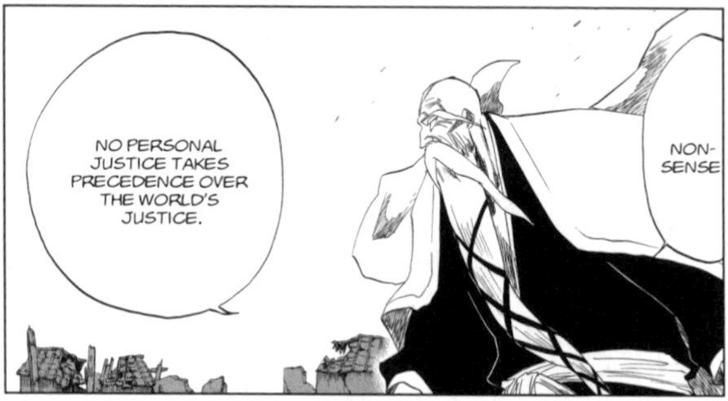
NON-SENSE
NO PERSONAL JUSTICE TAKES PRECEDENCE OVER THE WORLD'S JUSTICE.

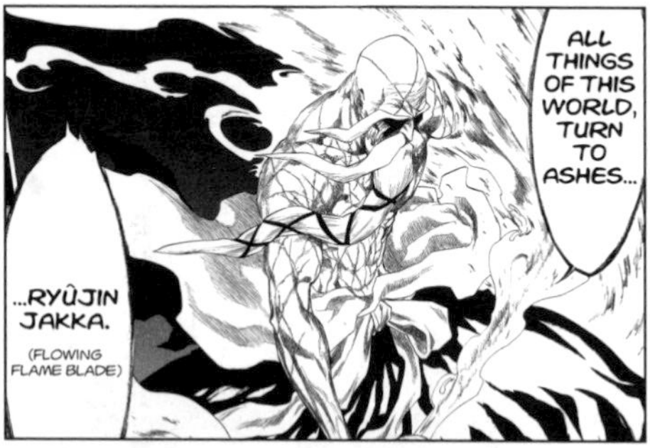
ALL THINGS OF THIS WORLD, TURN TO ASHES...
...RYÛJIN JAKKA.
(FLOWING FLAME BLADE)

"I'LL ALLOW NO ONE TO DISRUPT THE PEACE."

The captain general has always believed strongly in justice. Justice, for him, takes precedence over all other matters and must be served. A punishment that defies the imagination awaits anyone who goes against this principle.

ASSISTANT CAPTAIN

雀部長次郎

CHÔJIRO SASAKIBE

CHARACTER DATA

BIRTHDAY/NOVEMBER 4

HEIGHT/5′10″

WEIGHT/146 LBS

ZANPAKU-TÔ/GONRYÔMARU

INCANTATION/"BITE, GONRYÔMARU!"

HOBBY/CULTIVATING BLACK TEA

SPECIAL SKILL/FENCING

FOOD:
LIKES/ALL WESTERN CUISINE
DISLIKES/ALL JAPANESE CUISINE

HOW HE SPENDS HIS DAYS OFF/TRYING TO EMBRACE WESTERN CULTURE

Assistant Captain Chôjiro Sasakibe is a man of few words who always defers to the captain general. The two are considered the finest duo in the Court Guard Companies, but when it comes to food they are not compatible at all…

SPECIAL NOTES

TOP SECRET

Long ago, the sight of British gentlemen in the world of the living had a profound impact on Chôjiro, and for several decades now he has secretly admired them. During that time, he has brought back black leaf tea whenever he goes to the human world, but to this day he hasn't been able to cultivate it. He wears a cloak over his shihakushô uniform that is modeled after the British gentlemen's attire of the time. Chôjiro made the cloak himself.

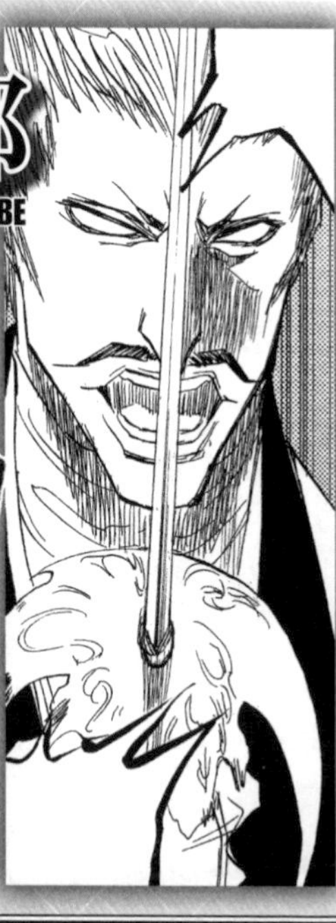

THE ELITE OF THE THIRTEEN COMPANIES

First Company, led by Captain General Yamamoto, ranks highest among the thirteen companies. Even subordinate members of First Company are recognized as model Reapers. To be assigned to First Company is a source of great pride.

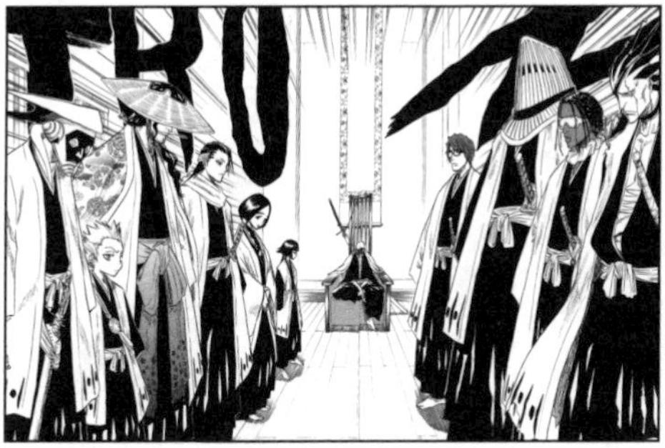

The captains of each company are lined up while the captain general sits calmly at the center. Every order issued by the captain general to the Thirteen Court Guard Companies is absolute and must be obeyed.

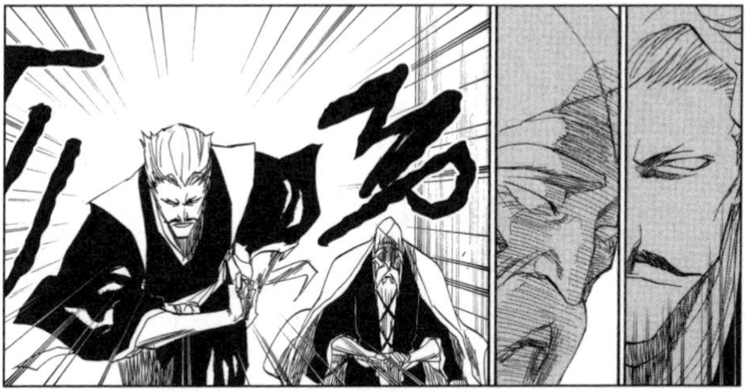

Emergencies must be dealt with swiftly; quick decisions and quick action are essential. The company is able to ascertain a situation and mobilize quickly even before an order is issued. That is the true value of First Company.

SOUL REAPER ACADEMY

SHINÔ-REIJUTSUIN

This is the Soul Reaper training facility that was founded 2,000 years ago by the captain general. Many have been born and trained here, and have gone on to serve in the Stealth Force, Kidô Corps and the Court Guard Companies. Once in a while, the place is called by its former name, Tôgakuin.

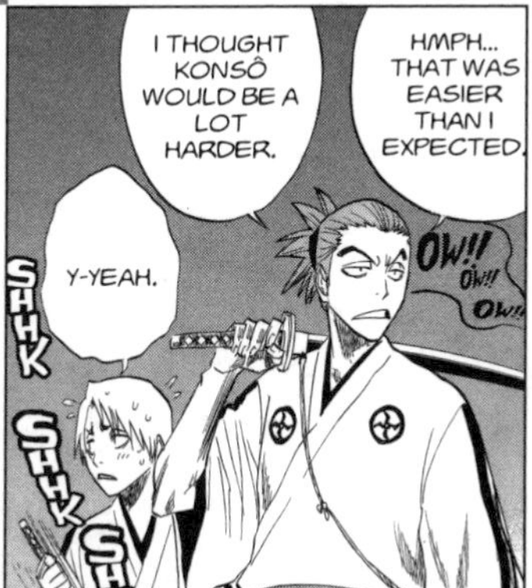
HMPH... THAT WAS EASIER THAN I EXPECTED.
I THOUGHT KONSÔ WOULD BE A LOT HARDER.
OW!! OW!! OW!!
Y-YEAH.
SHHK
SHHK
SHHK

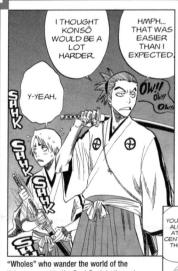

"Wholes" who wander the world of the living are sent to the Soul Society through the rite of konsô. The Soul Reaper Academy curriculum includes performing soul funerals.

THE TWO CAPTAINS

Ukitake and Kyôraku have the distinction of being the first Soul Academy graduates to reach the rank of captain.

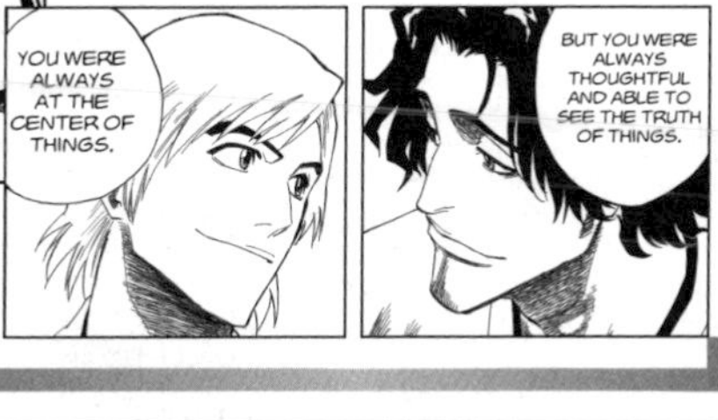
BUT YOU WERE ALWAYS THOUGHTFUL AND ABLE TO SEE THE TRUTH OF THINGS.
YOU WERE ALWAYS AT THE CENTER OF THINGS.

Second Company Captain Soi Fon is also the Supreme Commander of the Secret Remote Squad. Perhaps because of this, many in Second Company specialize in stealth operations. It is a combat unit with exceptional fighting skills.

二番隊

SECOND COMPANY
COMPANY FLOWER: OKINAGUSA
(desire nothing)

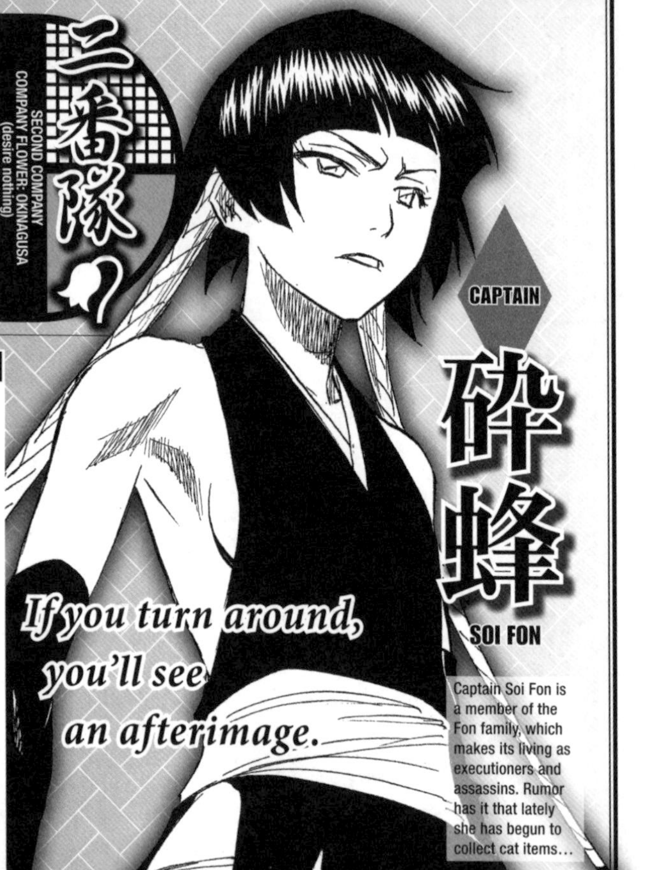

CAPTAIN

砕蜂

SOI FON

If you turn around, you'll see an afterimage.

Captain Soi Fon is a member of the Fon family, which makes its living as executioners and assassins. Rumor has it that lately she has begun to collect cat items…

CHARACTER DATA

BIRTHDAY/FEBRUARY 11

HEIGHT/4′11″

WEIGHT/84 LBS

ZANPAKU-TÔ/
SUZUMEBACHI

INCANTATION/"STING ALL ENEMIES TO DEATH, SUZUMEBACHI!"

COAT LINING/AMBER

HOBBY/COLLECTING CAT ITEMS

SPECIAL SKILL/
ASSASSINATION

FOOD:
LIKES/FISH
DISLIKES/MEAT

HOW SHE SPENDS HER DAYS OFF/PRACTICING HER SHUNKÔ (INSTANT WAR CRY) IN HOPES OF SOMEDAY BEING ABLE TO DUEL WITH YORUICHI

SPECIAL NOTES

TOP SECRET

She is calm and collected. The only time her personality suddenly changes is around Yoruichi, but luckily, this is not common knowledge among the company members. Many in the companies and the Secret Remote Squad admire Soi Fon, and she even has a fan club. After word spread about her hobby of collecting cat items, packages of cat-related goods have been delivered to the Second Company barracks from time to time.

BATTLE DATA — SOI FON

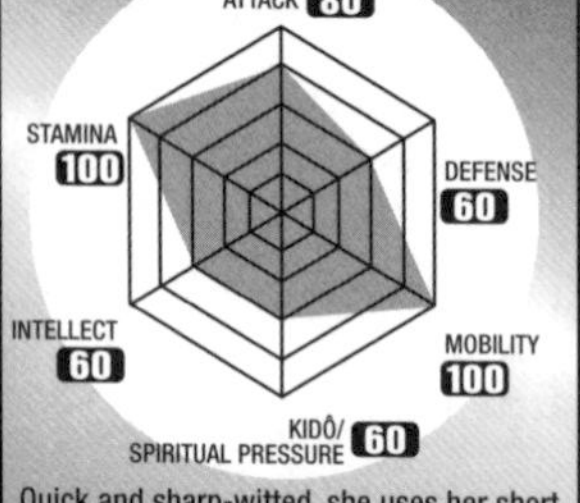
ATTACK 80
DEFENSE 60
MOBILITY 100
KIDÔ/ SPIRITUAL PRESSURE 60
INTELLECT 60
STAMINA 100

Quick and sharp-witted, she uses her short height to her advantage for kidô strength and attack power. Her physical strength is top class because of rigorous conditioning. Impressive.

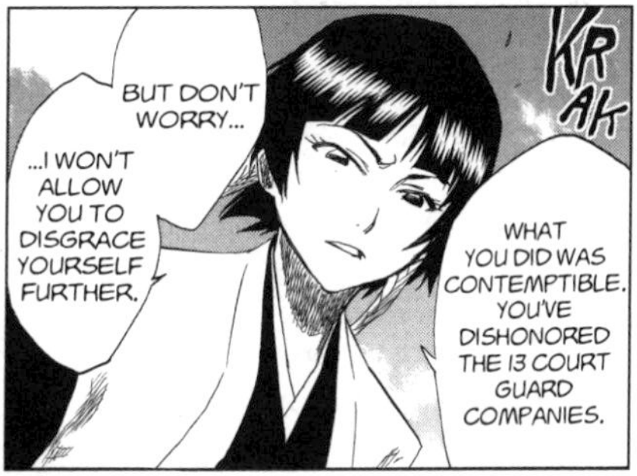
KRAK
WHAT YOU DID WAS CONTEMPTIBLE. YOU'VE DISHONORED THE 13 COURT GUARD COMPANIES.
BUT DON'T WORRY...
...I WON'T ALLOW YOU TO DISGRACE YOURSELF FURTHER.

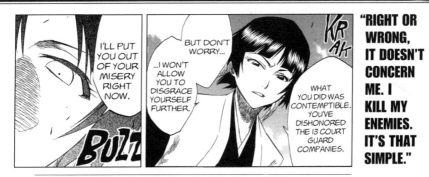

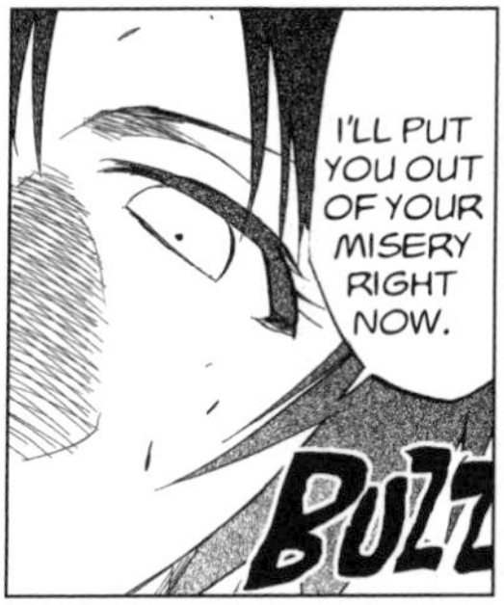
I'LL PUT YOU OUT OF YOUR MISERY RIGHT NOW.
BUZZ

"RIGHT OR WRONG, IT DOESN'T CONCERN ME. I KILL MY ENEMIES. IT'S THAT SIMPLE."

Upon release, Captain Soi Fon's zanpaku-tô, Suzumebachi, transforms into a needle mounted on her finger. When it strikes its target twice in the same spot, it always spells death.

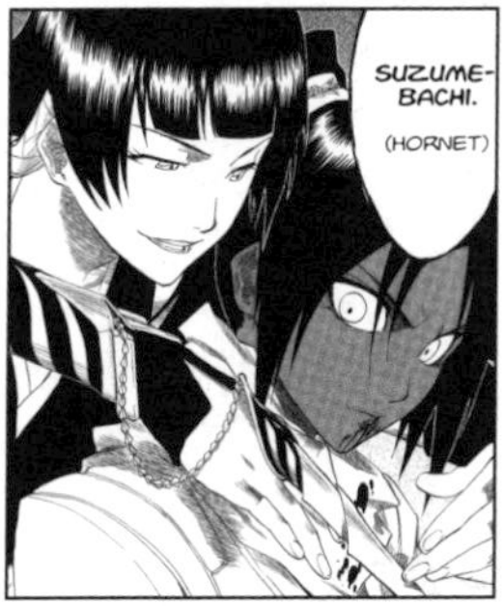
SUZUME-BACHI.
(HORNET)

Second Company Captain Soi Fon places utmost importance on completing her missions. She is merciless toward anyone who stands in the way of her duty, regardless of whether that person is a direct subordinate or a former superior. Using a cool head, she reads her enemies and moves to eliminate them. Company members should take heed.

ASSISTANT CAPTAIN 大前田希千代

MARECHIYO ÔMAEDA

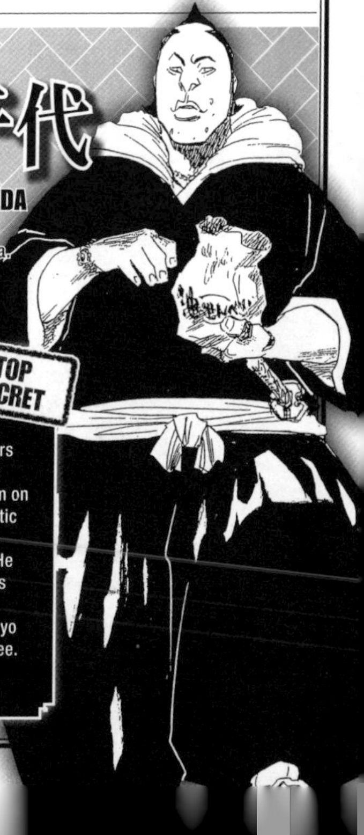

CHARACTER DATA

BIRTHDAY/MAY 5

HEIGHT/6′11″

WEIGHT/333 LBS

ZANPAKU-TÔ/GEGETSUBURI

INCANTATION/"CRUSH, GEGETSUBURI!"

HOBBY/MAKING BRACELETS

SPECIAL SKILL/MARECHIYO CHOP

FOOD:
LIKES/FRIED RICE CRACKERS, MEAT
DISLIKES/FISH

HOW HE SPENDS HIS DAYS OFF/INVITING COMMONERS TO HIS MANSION

His full name is Nikkôtarôemon Yoshiayamenosuke Marechiyo Ômaeda. He enjoys hosting commoners at his house on his days off. His younger sister is quite beautiful.

SPECIAL NOTES

TOP SECRET

His family is wealthy. Consequently, he has been renovating Second Company's quarters at his own expense. To accommodate Yoruichi any day, any time, every room on every level has heated floors, automatic doors and air conditioning. He uses gold for his hobby, bracelet-making. He made his own bracelet. Currently he is president of the Ômaeda Jewels and Precious Metals Factory. The Marechiyo Chop falls hard upon any lazy employee.

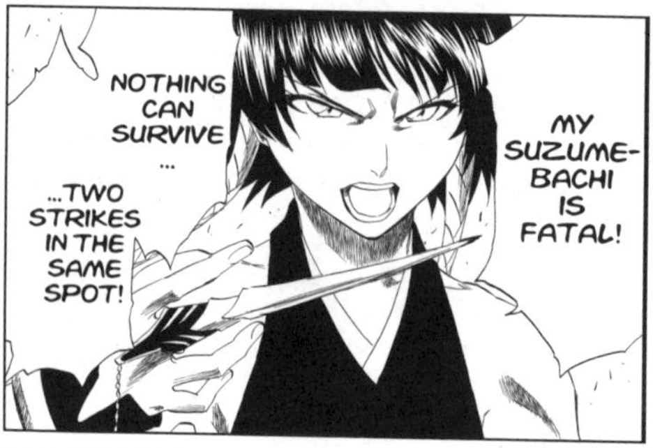
MY SUZUME-BACHI IS FATAL!
NOTHING CAN SURVIVE ...
...TWO STRIKES IN THE SAME SPOT!

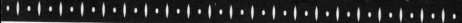

LIGHTNING FLASH! THE SWIFT HAKUDA CORPS

Hakuda is the general term for close-combat techniques that make use of one's own body as a weapon. High-speed taijutsu attacks are used to overwhelm the opponent. Captain Soi Fon is especially adept in this style, and Second Company members also use hakuda techniques.

Captain Soi Fon's battle with her former superior, Yoruichi Shihôin, during which she used this technique, is still a fresh memory. According to witnesses, they fought so swiftly, no one could make out the details... so it's said.

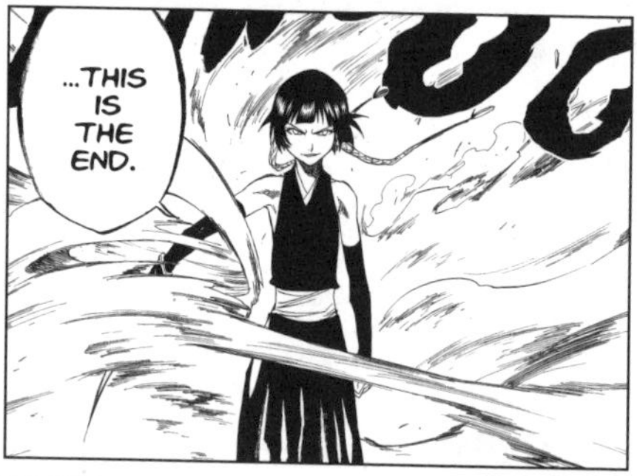
...THIS IS THE END.

ADVANCED BATTLE TECHNIQUE: SHUNKÔ

This secret style combines the grappling technique of hakuda and the incantation technique of kidô. It is an ultra-powerful technique in which one drives kidô into one's arms and legs. Shunkô is Captain Soi Fon's ultimate technique.

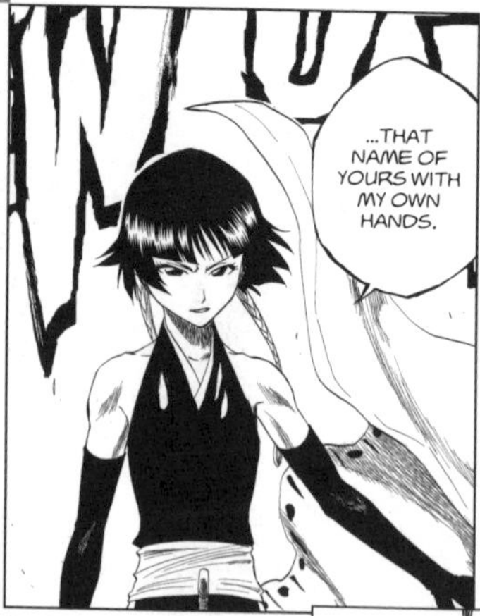
...THAT NAME OF YOURS WITH MY OWN HANDS.

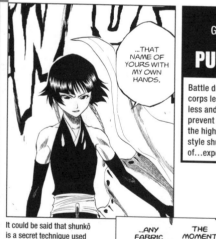

BATTLE UNIFORM OF THE GENERAL CORPS LEADER OF THE PUNISHMENT FORCE

PUNISHMENT ATTIRE

Battle dress approved solely for the general corps leader of the Punishment Force. Its back-less and sleeveless design is unique. This is to prevent the fabric from being ripped away by the high-density kidô produced by the fighting style shunkô, which explains the higher degree of...exposure.

The outfit was developed to be functional and therefore ogling is discouraged.

It could be said that shunkô is a secret technique used by the general corps leader of the Punishment Force. The uniform worn when punishment is carried out is specifically geared for shunkô.

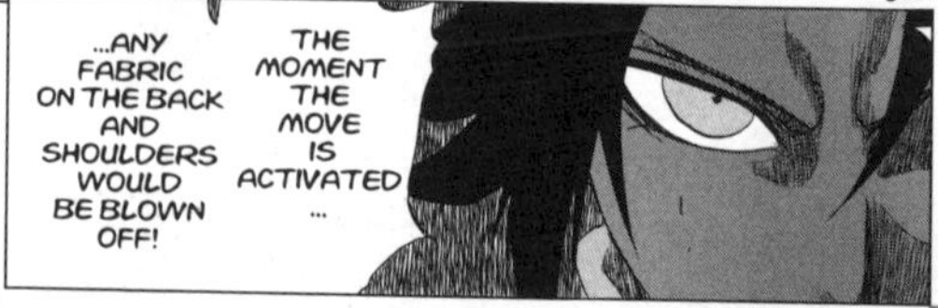
THE MOMENT THE MOVE IS ACTIVATED ...
...ANY FABRIC ON THE BACK AND SHOULDERS WOULD BE BLOWN OFF!

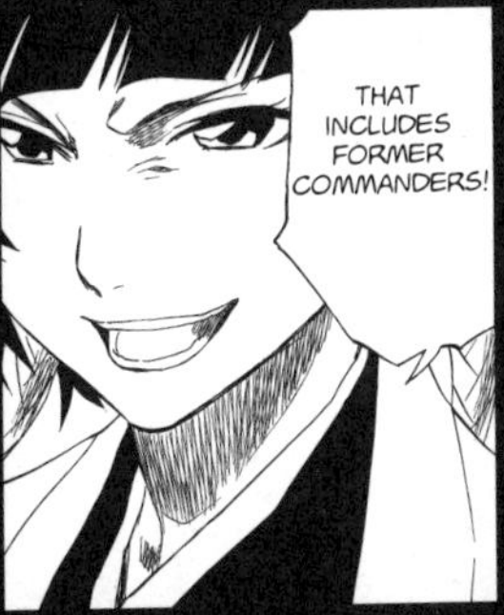
THAT INCLUDES FORMER COMMANDERS!

IT OPERATES UNDER A VEIL OF SECRECY
SECRET REMOTE SQUAD

One of the three major forces under the direct supervision of Central 46 (Thirteen Court Guard Companies, Kidô Corps, Secret Remote Squad). If the Thirteen Court Guard Companies operate openly, the Secret Remote Squad patrols and conducts surveillance in enemy territory and carries out top-secret operations, such as assassinations and the execution of Soul Reapers who have broken the law. Bizarre in their appearance, each one of its members is dressed in black from head to toe.

The entire squad under Captain Soi Fon's command races to join her. One can glimpse the efficient chain of command.

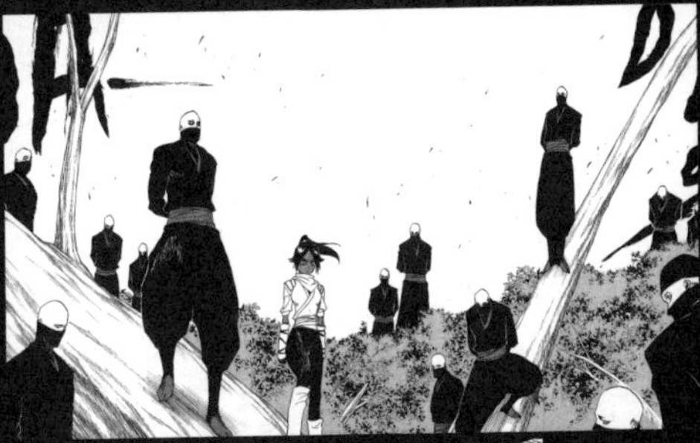

FORMER SUPREME COMMANDER OF THE SECRET REMOTE SQUAD

YORUICHI SHIHÔIN

四楓院夜一

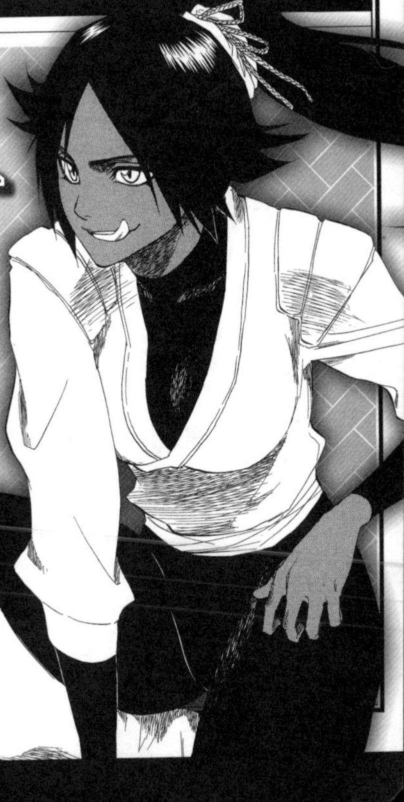

CHARACTER DATA

BIRTHDAY/JANUARY 1
HEIGHT/5′1″
WEIGHT/93 LBS

The 22nd head of the illustrious Shihôin family—caretakers of the hôgu (treasure) and bugu (weaponry) said to have been bestowed on them by the gods. Once the commander in chief of the Secret Remote Squad, she has given up her command to Soi Fon.

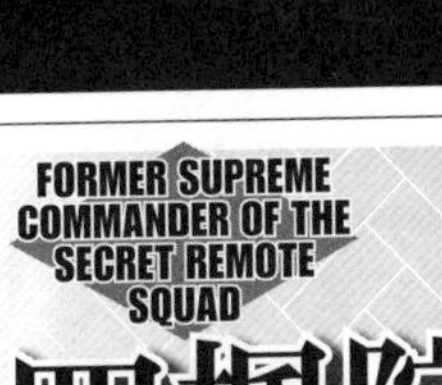

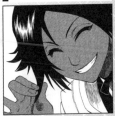

Yoruichi, when she was a commander. Her unpretentious personality won her the trust of her squad members.

ORGANIZATION CHART

SECRET REMOTE SQUAD

- **FIRST DIVISION:** PUNISHMENT FORCE
- **SECOND DIVISION:** SECURITY FORCE
- **THIRD DIVISION:** UNKNOWN
- **FOURTH DIVISION:** UNKNOWN
- **FIFTH DIVISION:** SECRET REMOTE UNIT

FIVE SQUADS MAKE UP THE SPECIAL OPERATIONS CORPS

There are five divisions under the Secret Remote Squad, with the First Division Punishment Force at the top. Each division is under the direct supervision of a corps leader, but the Supreme Commander of the Secret Remote Squad oversees the First Division Punishment Force as its General Corps Leader. Among the five divisions, the First Division Punishment Force carries out missions that involve combat; the Second Division Security Force is assigned mainly to the Seireitei area and gathers data on uprisings; and the Fifth Division Secret Remote Unit serves as the communication link for company members. While information about all three is widely available, little is known about the Third and Fourth Divisions, and they are shrouded in mystery to this day.

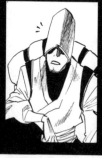

FIFTH DIVISION: SECRET REMOTE UNIT

A special ops unit that is mobilized whenever a mission is urgent and requires secrecy. Many of its members are masters of shun-po (flash step).

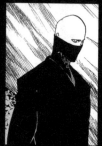

FIRST DIVISION: PUNISHMENT FORCE

A combat force under Soi Fon's command. It specializes in the unarmed combat technique known as hakuda and is able to operate silently and in secrecy.

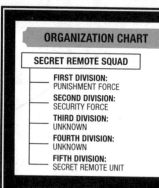

SOI FON & YORUICHI

Soi Fon and Yoruichi met more than a hundred years ago. Soi Fon was struck by Yoruichi's beauty and nobility, and swore her allegiance for life. While there has been discord between them at times, the bond they share is strong, and their love for one another remains unchanged.

TH...
THEN MAY I...
...AD-DRESS YOU...
...AS MS. YORUICHI?

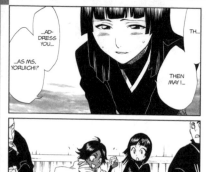

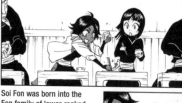

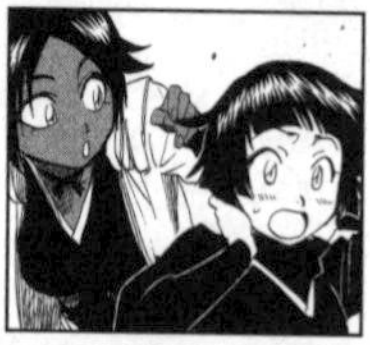

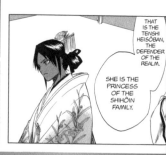

THAT IS THE TENSHI HEISÔBAN, THE DEFENDER OF THE REALM.
SHE IS THE PRINCESS OF THE SHIHÔIN FAMILY.

Soi Fon was born into the Fon family of lower-ranked nobles who have served in the Punishment Force for generations. Seven years after joining, she was assigned to lead the Court Guards and passed each day happily.

三番隊

THIRD COMPANY
COMPANY FLOWER: MARIGOLD
(despair)

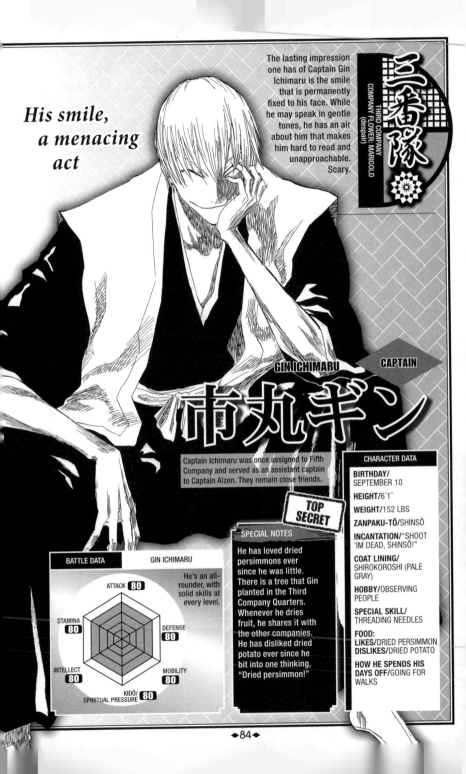

His smile, a menacing act

The lasting impression one has of Captain Gin Ichimaru is the smile that is permanently fixed to his face. While he may speak in gentle tones, he has an air about him that makes him hard to read and unapproachable. Scary.

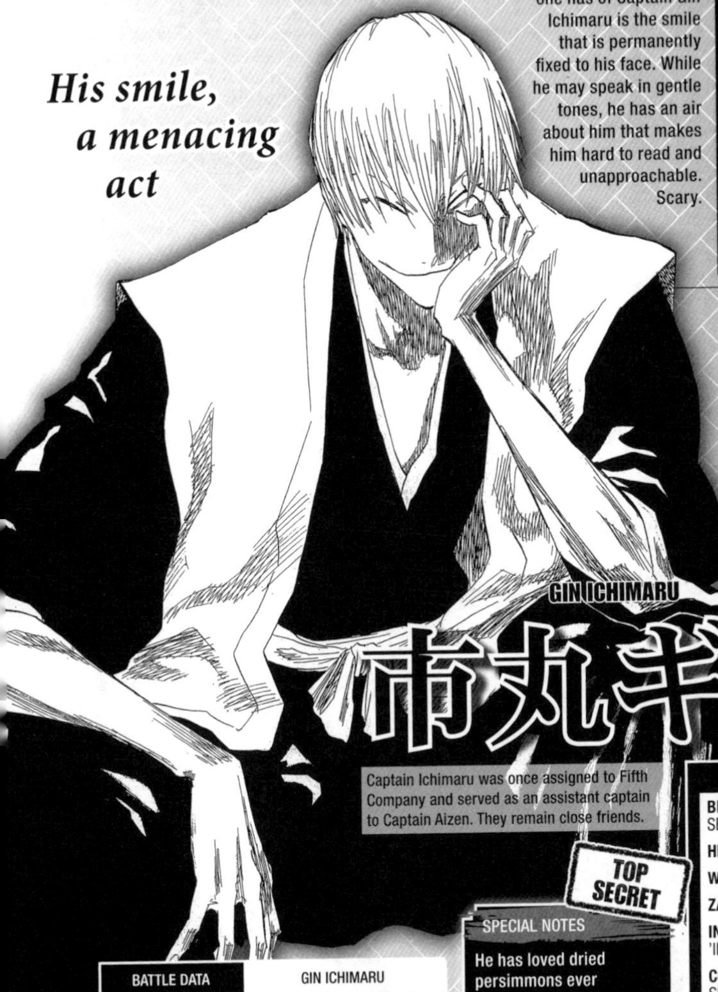

CAPTAIN

GIN ICHIMARU

市丸ギン

Captain Ichimaru was once assigned to Fifth Company and served as an assistant captain to Captain Aizen. They remain close friends.

TOP SECRET

BATTLE DATA — GIN ICHIMARU

He's an all-rounder, with solid skills at every level.

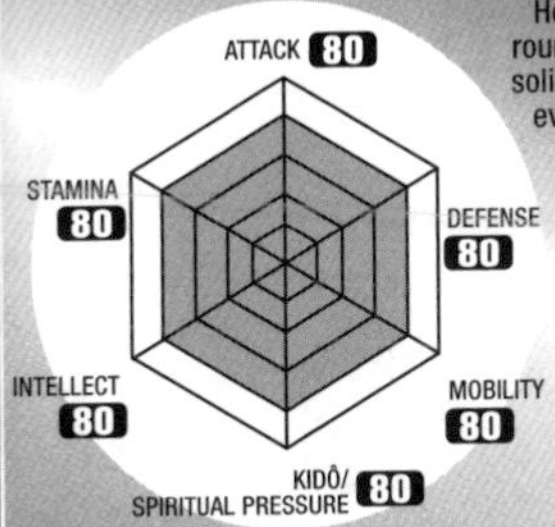
ATTACK 80
DEFENSE 80
MOBILITY 80
KIDÔ/ SPIRITUAL PRESSURE 80
INTELLECT 80
STAMINA 80

SPECIAL NOTES

He has loved dried persimmons ever since he was little. There is a tree that Gin planted in the Third Company Quarters. Whenever he dries fruit, he shares it with the other companies. He has disliked dried potato ever since he bit into one thinking, "Dried persimmon!"

CHARACTER DATA

BIRTHDAY/ SEPTEMBER 10

HEIGHT/ 6′1″

WEIGHT/ 152 LBS

ZANPAKU-TÔ/ SHINSÔ

INCANTATION/ "SHOOT 'IM DEAD, SHINSÔ!"

COAT LINING/ SHIROKOROSHI (PALE GRAY)

HOBBY/ OBSERVING PEOPLE

SPECIAL SKILL/ THREADING NEEDLES

FOOD:
LIKES/ DRIED PERSIMMON
DISLIKES/ DRIED POTATO

HOW HE SPENDS HIS DAYS OFF/ GOING FOR WALKS

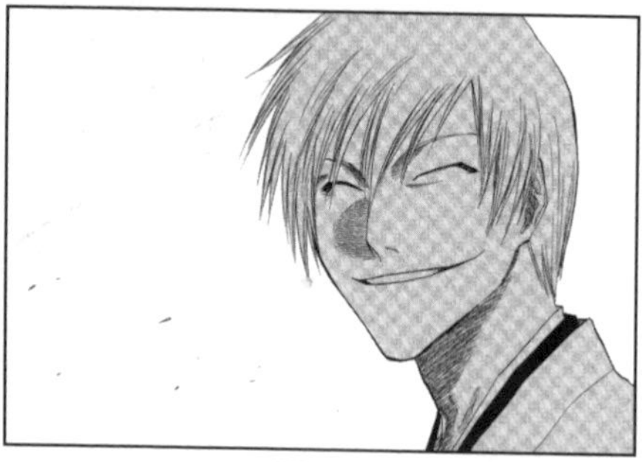

"I JUST THOUGHT I'D TAKE A WALK AND TEASE YOU A BIT."

On his days off, Captain Ichimaru enjoys taking walks around the Seireitei. Whenever he is engaged in his pastime—studying people—perhaps he is diligently looking for victims for his next prank. To members of Third Company: Let us be strong. Instead of fearing him, let us take delight in his mischievous nature.

Gin Ichimaru always has a wide grin on his face. No doubt he is planning something. Do beware of him.

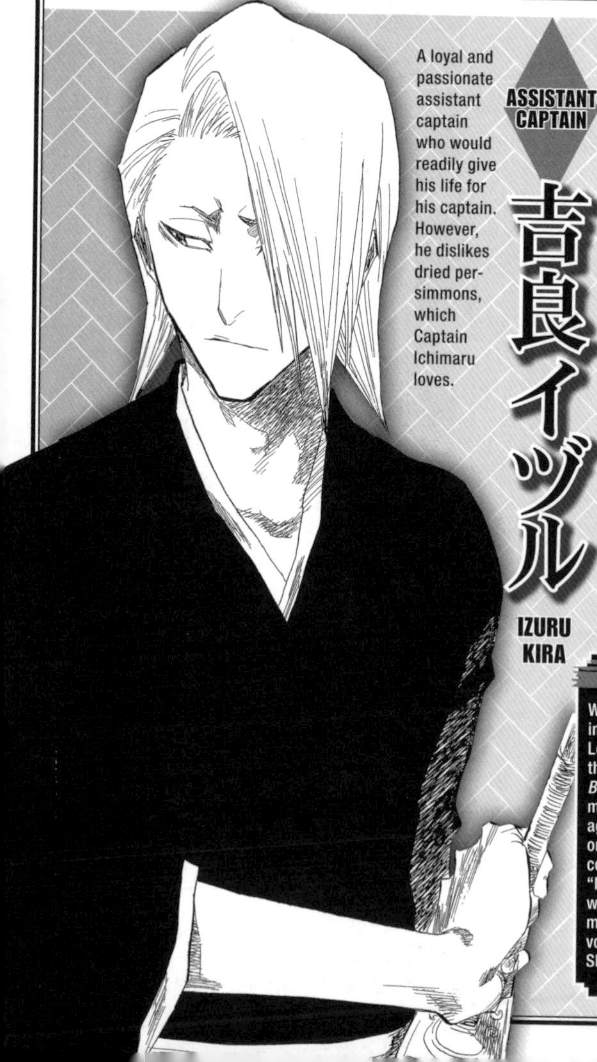

A loyal and passionate assistant captain who would readily give his life for his captain. However, he dislikes dried persimmons, which Captain Ichimaru loves.

ASSISTANT CAPTAIN

吉良イヅル

IZURU KIRA

CHARACTER DATA

BIRTHDAY/MARCH 27

HEIGHT/5′8″

WEIGHT/123 LBS

ZANPAKU-TÔ/WABISUKE

INCANTATION/"SHOW YOURSELF, WABISUKE!"

HOBBY/WRITING HAIKU POEMS

SPECIAL SKILL/PLAYING CAT'S CRADLE

FOOD:
LIKES/TOKOROTEN (GELATIN MADE FROM AGAR-AGAR)
DISLIKES/DRIED PERSIMMON

HOW HE SPENDS HIS DAYS OFF/PARTICIPATING IN THE HAIKU CLUB, TEACHING AS A SPECIAL INSTRUCTOR AT THE ACADEMY

SPECIAL NOTES **TOP SECRET**

Won top honors in the "Haiku by Mid-Level Management Category" in the September issue of *Seireitei Bulletin* with his poem, "Once more, persimmons. Oh, oh, oh, again this year. Persimmons once more." At present, he composes the opening haiku in "I Want to Apologize to You," which is serialized in the same magazine. He has published two volumes of haiku. Fellow poet Shûhei Hisagi is a close friend.

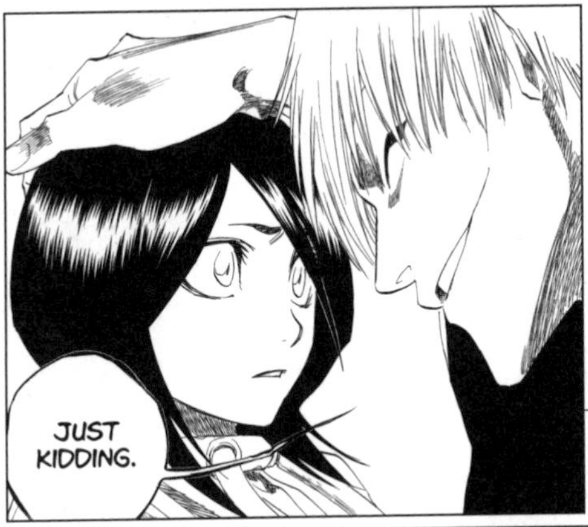
JUST KIDDING.

THE MYSTERIOUS COMPANY: A MIXTURE OF TRUTH AND LIES?!

Captain Ichimaru tends to be quite aloof, and he loves to perplex people with mysterious riddles. The members of Third Company who have fallen victim to his maliciousness are too many to count. It is probably wiser to listen to Assistant Captain Kira's instructions.

Captain Ichimaru has the uncanny ability to read a person's mind and pierce his or her heart with a few casually delivered words. How cruel.

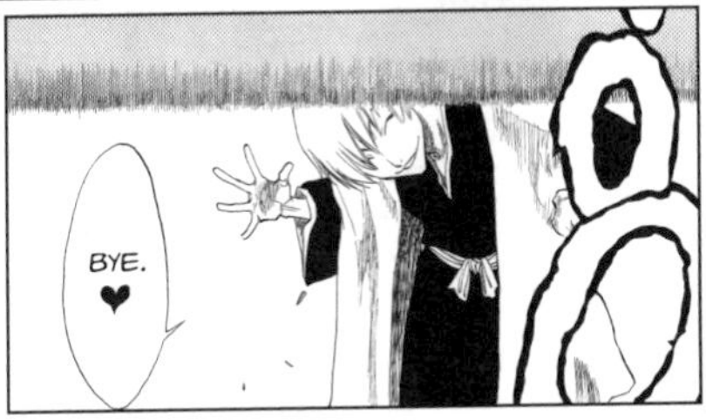
BYE. ♥

ONE CANNOT FATHOM HIS TRUE INTENTIONS

In the confusion resulting from the ryoka's incursion, Captain Ichimaru committed the grave error of letting them escape. A captain should have been able to crush the ryoka—if not capture them—with little effort...

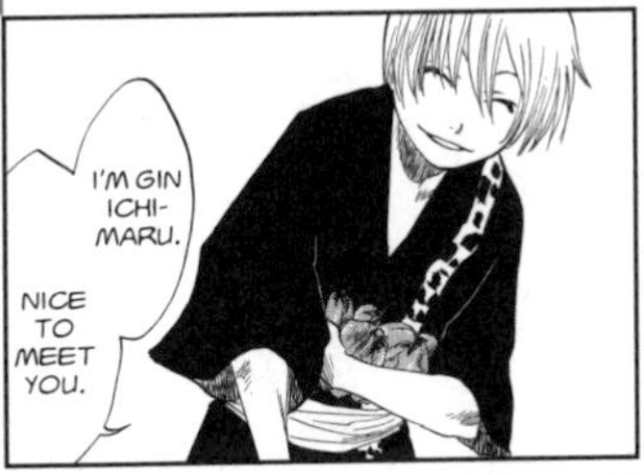
I'M GIN ICHI-MARU.
NICE TO MEET YOU.

TIME'S LONG PASSAGE

GIN AND RANGIKU

Captain Ichimaru and Tenth Company's Assistant Captain Matsumoto joined the Soul Reapers at the same time and are also close friends from childhood. When Matsumoto was on the verge of fainting from hunger, Captain Ichimaru quietly held out some dried persimmon to her. It is rumored that their fondness for dried persimmon stems from this incident.

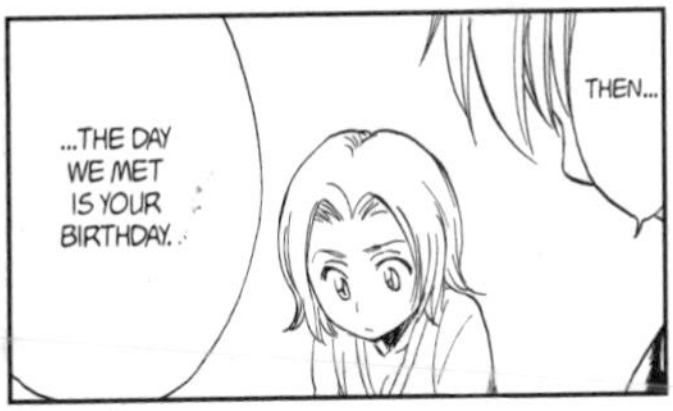
THEN...
...THE DAY WE MET IS YOUR BIRTHDAY.

FINAL APOLOGY

Captain Ichimaru's last words to Assistant Captain Rangiku before his disappearance were said to have been words of apology. What could have been the reason for them?

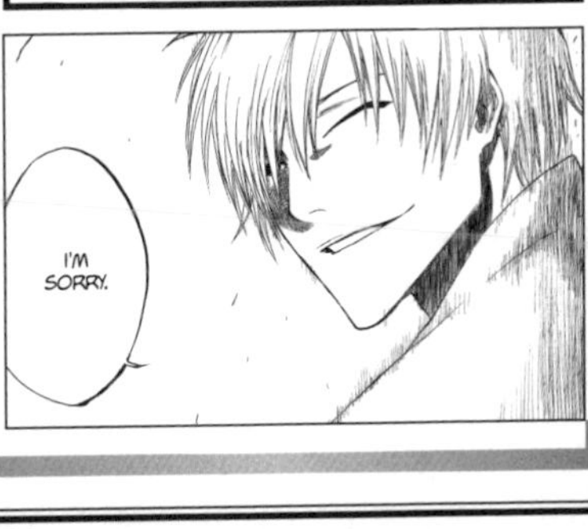
I'M SORRY.

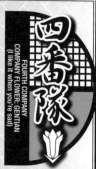

Fourth Company is the only squad among the accomplished Thirteen Court Guard Companies that specializes in medical assistance and provisions.

四番隊

FOURTH COMPANY
COMPANY FLOWER: GENTIAN
(I like it when you're sad)

Bona fide elegance

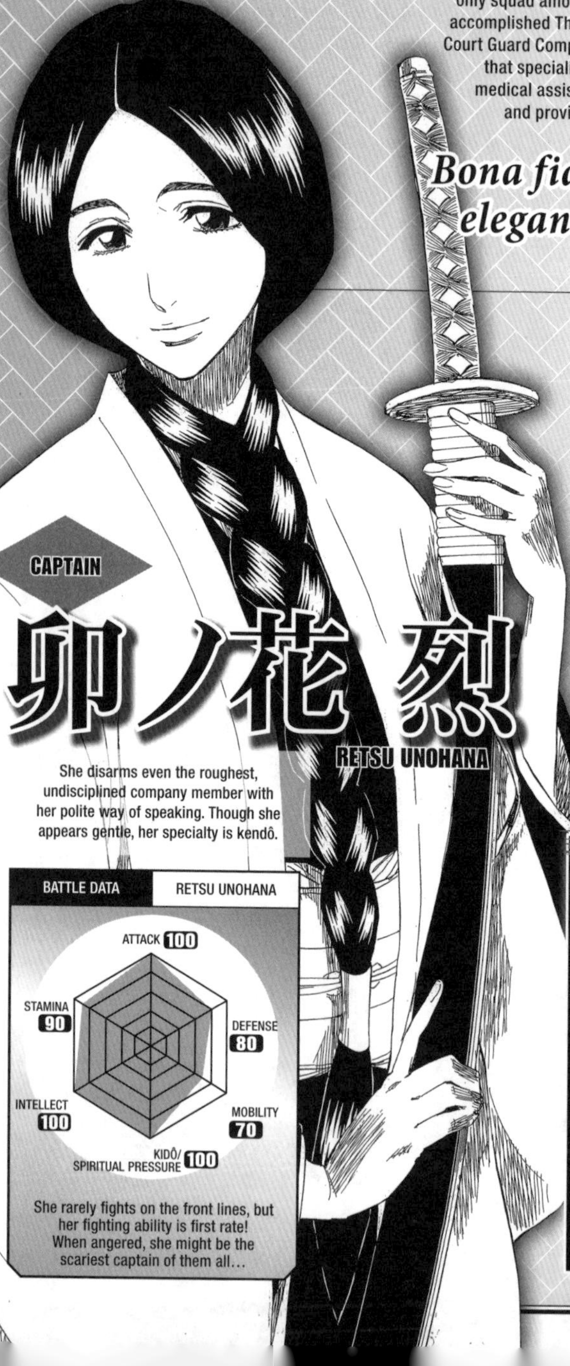

CAPTAIN

卯ノ花 烈

RETSU UNOHANA

She disarms even the roughest, undisciplined company member with her polite way of speaking. Though she appears gentle, her specialty is kendô.

CHARACTER DATA

BIRTHDAY/APRIL 21

HEIGHT/5′3″

WEIGHT/99 LBS

ZANPAKU-TÔ/MINAZUKI

COAT LINING/HAIZAKURA (DUSKY PINK)

HOBBY/FLOWER ARRANGING

SPECIAL SKILL/KENDÔ

FOOD:
LIKES/RICH FLAVORS
DISLIKES/BLAND FLAVORS

HOW SHE SPENDS HER DAYS OFF/LOOKING FOR MEDICINAL HERBS WHILE SHE IS MOUNTAINEERING

BATTLE DATA | RETSU UNOHANA

ATTACK 100
DEFENSE 80
MOBILITY 70
KIDÔ/ SPIRITUAL PRESSURE 100
INTELLECT 100
STAMINA 90

She rarely fights on the front lines, but her fighting ability is first rate! When angered, she might be the scariest captain of them all...

SPECIAL NOTES

TOP SECRET

On her days off, she climbs the mountains of Rukongai. It's hard to know if she actually climbs the mountains herself, as she has been seen riding Minazuki. She enjoys flower arranging and holds classes once a month for members of Fourth Company (not mandatory). Yachiru attends but leaves after partaking in the sweets served during the break.

When released, her zanpaku-tô Minazuki transforms into an enormous creature that one can ride. Minazuki also has the power to heal wounded people by swallowing them.

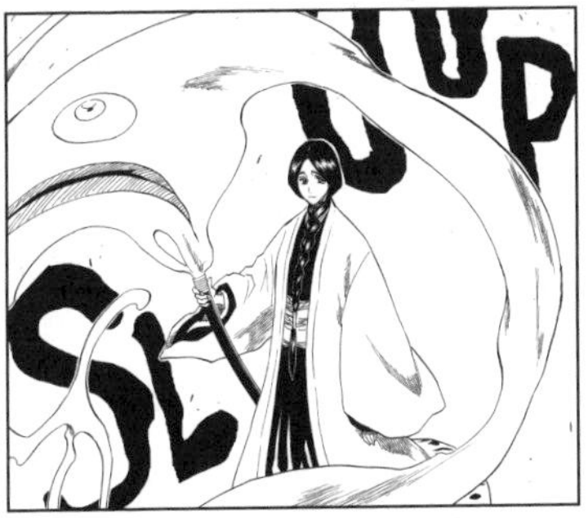
SLURP

"I'LL JOIN YOU SOON IN THE FIELD."

Captain Unohana is a talented woman who always makes competent decisions. Even during the recent ryoka incursion, she calmly analyzed the situation and gave her orders. She is a brave woman who is not afraid to engage the enemy.

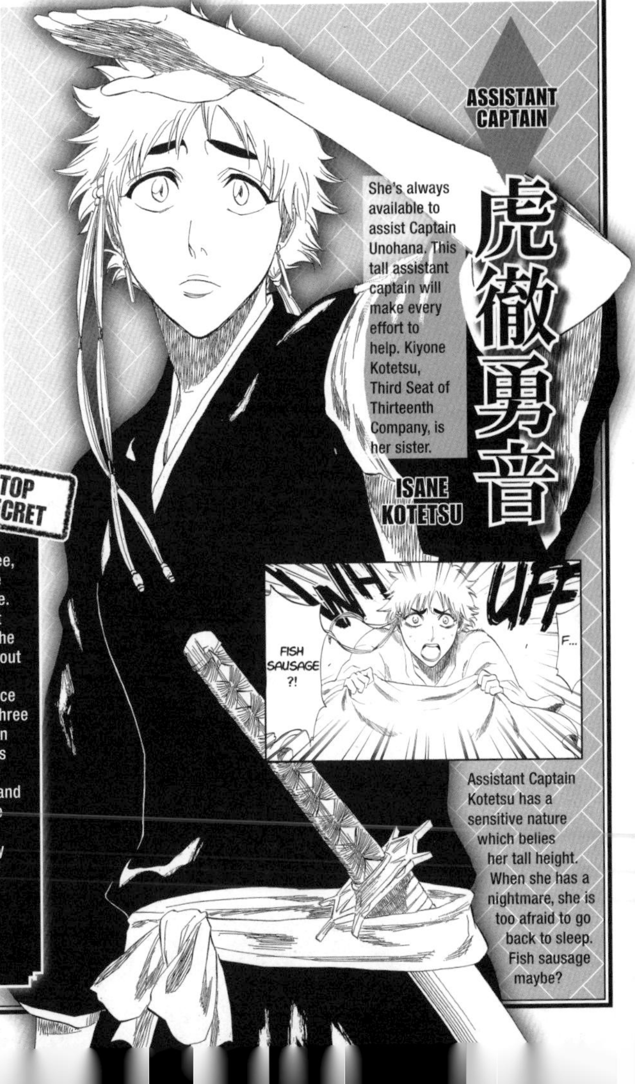
WH
UFF
F...
FISH SAUSAGE ?!

CHARACTER DATA

BIRTHDAY/AUGUST 2

HEIGHT/6′2″

WEIGHT/154 LBS

ZANPAKU-TÔ/ITEGUMO

INCANTATION/"RUN, ITEGUMO!"

HOBBY/FLOWER ARRANGING

SPECIAL SKILL/SEWING

FOOD:
LIKES/RICE PORRIDGE
DISLIKES/FISH SAUSAGE

HOW SHE SPENDS HER DAYS OFF/MEETING UP WITH KIYONE

ASSISTANT CAPTAIN

虎徹勇音

ISANE KOTETSU

She's always available to assist Captain Unohana. This tall assistant captain will make every effort to help. Kiyone Kotetsu, Third Seat of Thirteenth Company, is her sister.

SPECIAL NOTES

TOP SECRET

When Isane is free, she goes to see Kiyone. When Kiyone is free, she goes to see Isane. The sisters are extremely close. Lately, their favorite haunt is the Kuchiki residence, the location of the secret hideout of the Society of Female Soul Reapers. She loves rice porridge and could eat it three times a day. Actually, when she grew to 5 feet 7 inches tall, she declared, "I don't want to grow any taller!" and began eating rice porridge because it seemed like a no-nutrient dish. Currently she is 6 feet 2 inches tall.

Assistant Captain Kotetsu has a sensitive nature which belies her tall height. When she has a nightmare, she is too afraid to go back to sleep. Fish sausage maybe?

THEIR WOUNDS ARE SEVERE! SET UP A CHI-CLEANSING FORCE-FIELD AND TRANSPORT THEM TO THE GENERAL EMERGENCY RELIEF STATION FOR THE STAGE EIGHT TREATMENT!

Fourth Company administers emergency first aid to injured company members and transports them to the General Emergency Relief Station.

THE COMPANY THAT SHOULDERS THE RESPONSIBILITY OF PROVIDING AID TO THE SOUL REAPERS

Other company members use their spiritual power only for fighting. Members of Fourth Company possess spiritual power that is used to tend to wounds and provide relief. They use this special power and the benefits of their daily training to act with precision and speed to aid injured comrades.

...14TH ADVANCED RELIEF TEAM LEADER...

...HANATARÔ YAMADA?

AND

...4TH COMPANY, 7TH SEAT...

FOURTH COMPANY ENROLLMENT
KEY COMPANY MEMBERS AT A GLANCE

Fourth Company is scorned by Eleventh Company for the simple reason that they are "weak." Consequently, the poor members of Fourth Company are often ordered to do menial work like cleaning and running errands. Here, we introduce several senior members who refuse to give in to such adversity and continue to do their best.

CHARACTER DATA
BIRTHDAY/APRIL 1
HEIGHT/5´0˝
WEIGHT/99 LBS
ZANPAKU-TÔ/HISAGOMARU
INCANTATION/"FILL UP, HISAGOMARU!"

SEVENTH SEAT
山田花太郎
HANATARÔ YAMADA

He looks weak, but he possesses potent healing powers. He handles shinten, a spiritual tranquilizer, with ease.

I'LL HEAL HIM...

...IN ONE NIGHT.

TMP

EIGHTH SEAT
荻堂春信
HARUNOBU OGIDÔ

CHARACTER DATA
BIRTHDAY/APRIL 14
HEIGHT/5´9˝
WEIGHT/132 LBS

Fourth Company's most popular member. His good looks and easygoing nature have endeared him to female members of other companies.

THIRD SEAT
伊江村八十千和
YASOCHIKA IEMURA

CHARACTER DATA
BIRTHDAY/FEBRUARY 29
HEIGHT/5´10˝
WEIGHT/154 LBS

The Third Seat of Fourth Company is a squad leader who takes direct command at the scene. His speed in rendering aid rivals that of Assistant Captain Isane Kotetsu.

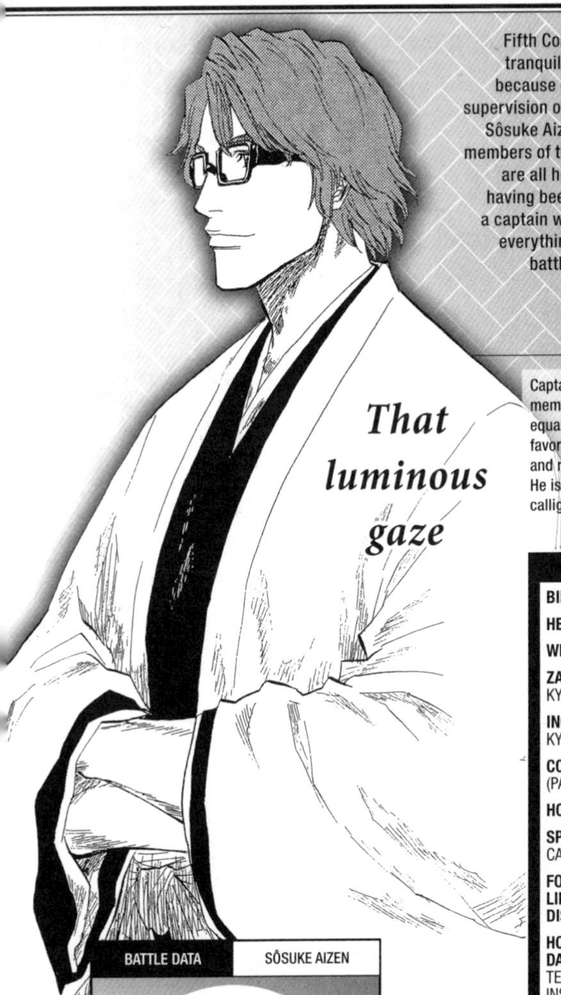
That luminous gaze

五番隊

FIFTH COMPANY
COMPANY FLOWER: ASHIBI
SACRIFICE • DANGER • PURE LOVE
(Let us take a journey together)

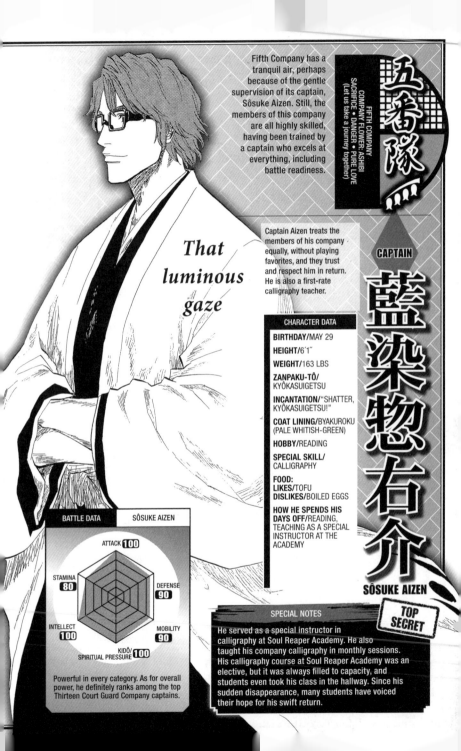

Fifth Company has a tranquil air, perhaps because of the gentle supervision of its captain, Sôsuke Aizen. Still, the members of this company are all highly skilled, having been trained by a captain who excels at everything, including battle readiness.

CAPTAIN

藍染惣右介

SÔSUKE AIZEN

Captain Aizen treats the members of his company equally, without playing favorites, and they trust and respect him in return. He is also a first-rate calligraphy teacher.

CHARACTER DATA

BIRTHDAY/MAY 29

HEIGHT/6′1″

WEIGHT/163 LBS

ZANPAKU-TÔ/
KYÔKASUIGETSU

INCANTATION/"SHATTER, KYÔKASUIGETSU!"

COAT LINING/BYAKUROKU (PALE WHITISH-GREEN)

HOBBY/READING

SPECIAL SKILL/
CALLIGRAPHY

FOOD:
LIKES/TOFU
DISLIKES/BOILED EGGS

HOW HE SPENDS HIS DAYS OFF/READING, TEACHING AS A SPECIAL INSTRUCTOR AT THE ACADEMY

BATTLE DATA | SÔSUKE AIZEN

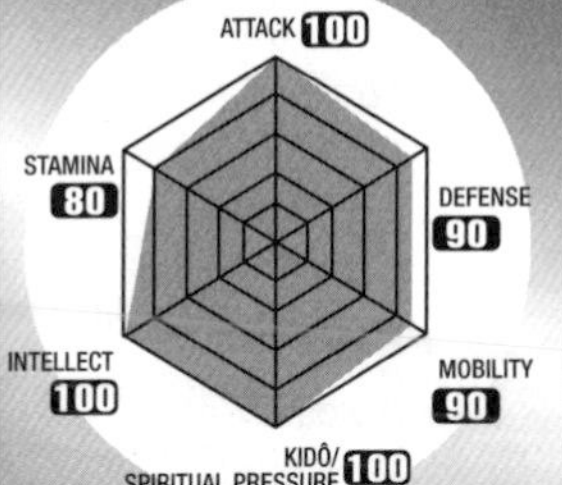
ATTACK 100
DEFENSE 90
MOBILITY 90
KIDÔ/ SPIRITUAL PRESSURE 100
INTELLECT 100
STAMINA 80

Powerful in every category. As for overall power, he definitely ranks among the top Thirteen Court Guard Company captains.

SPECIAL NOTES

TOP SECRET

He served as a special instructor in calligraphy at Soul Reaper Academy. He also taught his company calligraphy in monthly sessions. His calligraphy course at Soul Reaper Academy was an elective, but it was always filled to capacity, and students even took his class in the hallway. Since his sudden disappearance, many students have voiced their hope for his swift return.

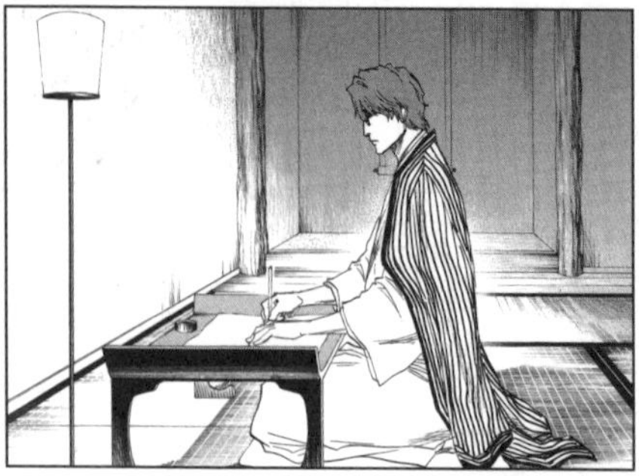

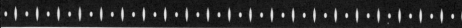

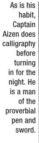

As is his habit, Captain Aizen does calligraphy before turning in for the night. He is a man of the proverbial pen and sword.

"YOU'D BE WISE NOT TO UNDERESTIMATE ME."

Captain Aizen is usually very calm, but he becomes alert and quick-witted during an emergency in the Soul Society. Hidden inside him is an iron will that has won him his company's complete trust.

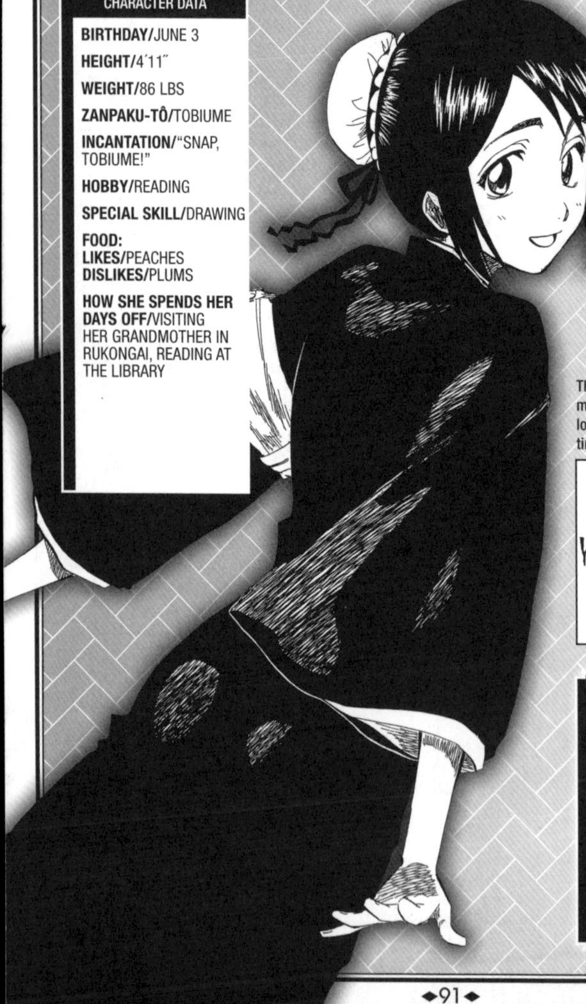

ASSISTANT CAPTAIN

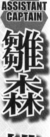

雛森桃

MOMO HINAMORI

This cute assistant captain loves and respects her captain completely. Naturally, she is popular with members of other companies. It's understandable.

CHARACTER DATA

BIRTHDAY/JUNE 3

HEIGHT/4′11″

WEIGHT/86 LBS

ZANPAKU-TÔ/TOBIUME

INCANTATION/"SNAP, TOBIUME!"

HOBBY/READING

SPECIAL SKILL/DRAWING

FOOD:
LIKES/PEACHES
DISLIKES/PLUMS

HOW SHE SPENDS HER DAYS OFF/VISITING HER GRANDMOTHER IN RUKONGAI, READING AT THE LIBRARY

This assistant captain is a master of kidô. The stern look that she puts on at times is quite appealing.

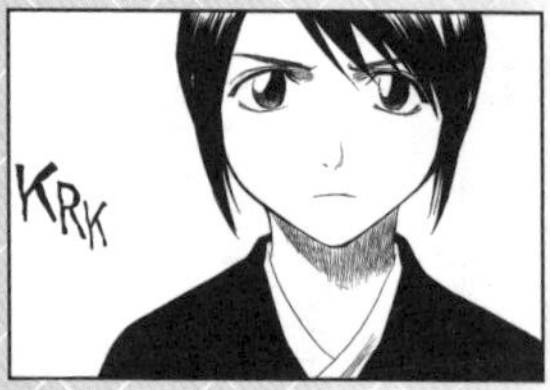
KRK

SPECIAL NOTES

TOP SECRET

Reading is her hobby. She grew to love reading from borrowing books that Aizen had finished. She enjoys it so much now that she goes to the library to read on her days off. She is good at drawing and has overseen work on book illustrations at Soul Reaper Academy. She also attends flower-arranging classes held by Fourth Company.

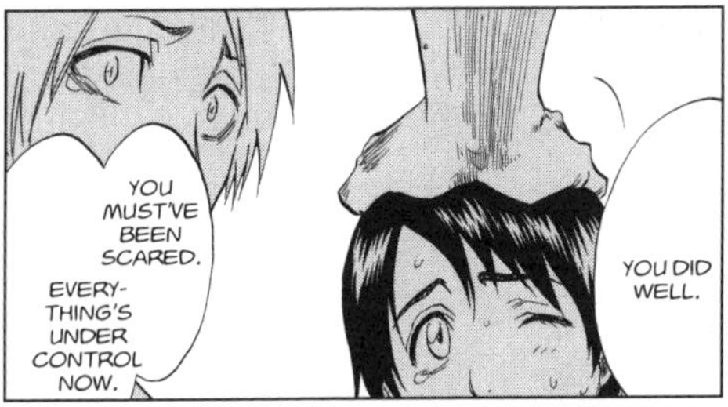
YOU DID WELL.
YOU MUST'VE BEEN SCARED.
EVERY-THING'S UNDER CONTROL NOW.

Captain Aizen is said to have come to the assistant captain's rescue when she was confronted by an emergency during training at Soul Reaper Academy. It is a heartwarming story.

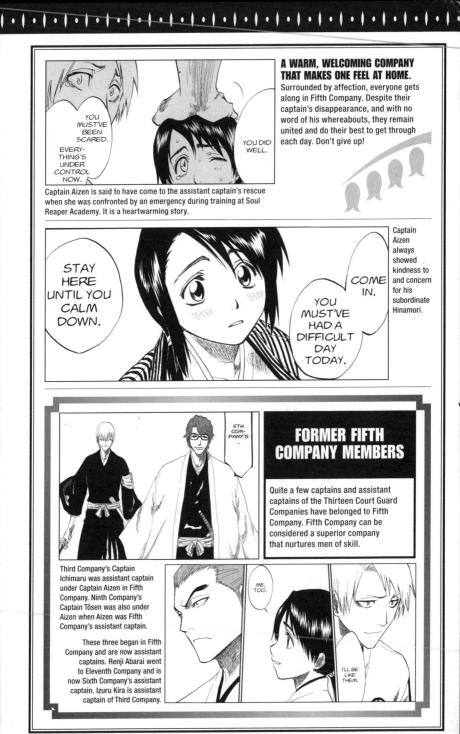

A WARM, WELCOMING COMPANY THAT MAKES ONE FEEL AT HOME.

Surrounded by affection, everyone gets along in Fifth Company. Despite their captain's disappearance, and with no word of his whereabouts, they remain united and do their best to get through each day. Don't give up!

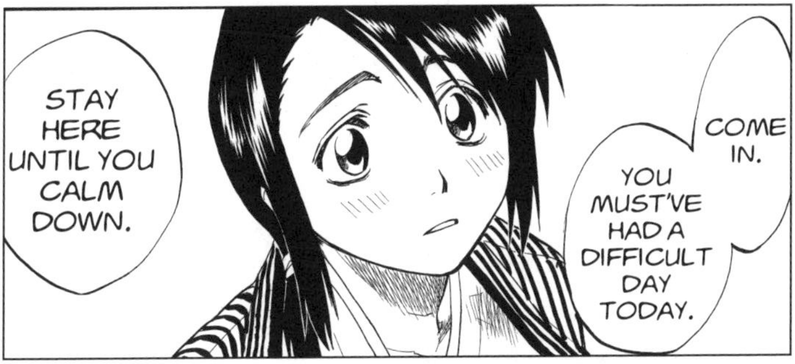
COME IN.
YOU MUST'VE HAD A DIFFICULT DAY TODAY.
STAY HERE UNTIL YOU CALM DOWN.

Captain Aizen always showed kindness to and concern for his subordinate Hinamori.

FORMER FIFTH COMPANY MEMBERS

Quite a few captains and assistant captains of the Thirteen Court Guard Companies have belonged to Fifth Company. Fifth Company can be considered a superior company that nurtures men of skill.

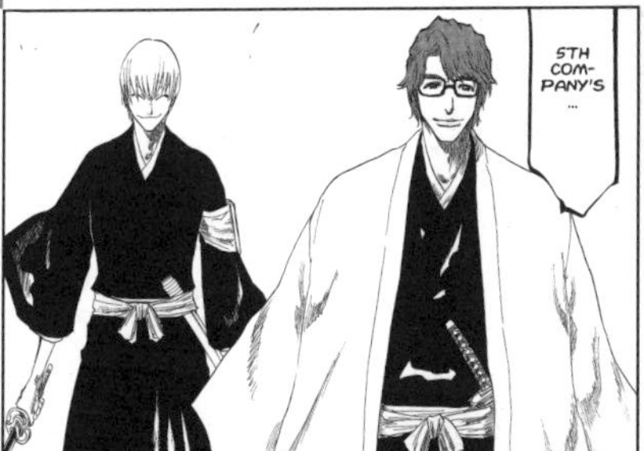
5TH COM-PANY'S ...

Third Company's Captain Ichimaru was assistant captain under Captain Aizen in Fifth Company. Ninth Company's Captain Tôsen was also under Aizen when Aizen was Fifth Company's assistant captain.

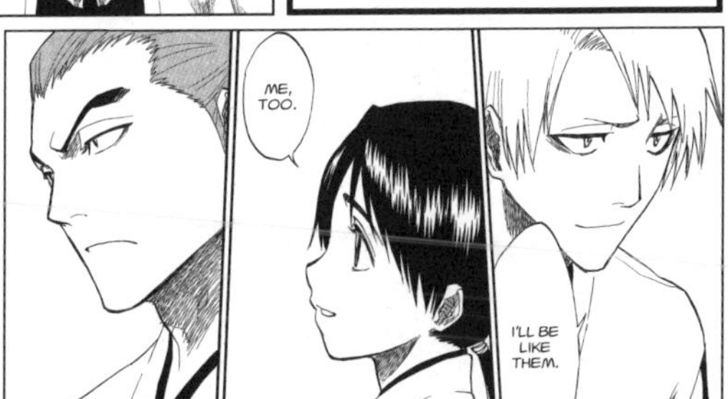
I'LL BE LIKE THEM.
ME, TOO.

These three began in Fifth Company and are now assistant captains. Renji Abarai went to Eleventh Company and is now Sixth Company's assistant captain. Izuru Kira is assistant captain of Third Company.

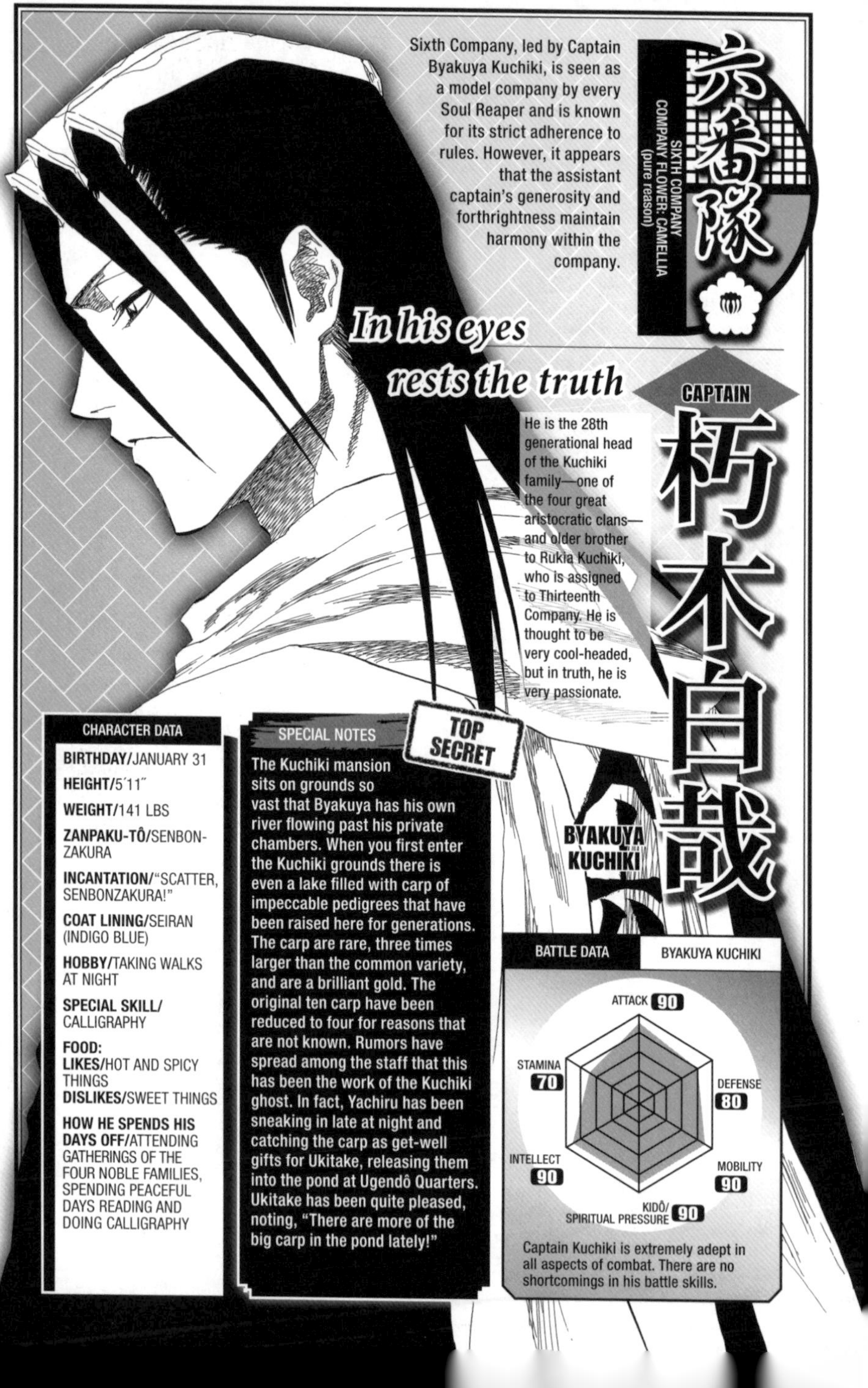

Sixth Company, led by Captain Byakuya Kuchiki, is seen as a model company by every Soul Reaper and is known for its strict adherence to rules. However, it appears that the assistant captain's generosity and forthrightness maintain harmony within the company.

六番隊

SIXTH COMPANY
COMPANY FLOWER: CAMELLIA
(pure reason)

In his eyes rests the truth

CAPTAIN

朽木白哉

BYAKUYA KUCHIKI

He is the 28th generational head of the Kuchiki family—one of the four great aristocratic clans—and older brother to Rukia Kuchiki, who is assigned to Thirteenth Company. He is thought to be very cool-headed, but in truth, he is very passionate.

CHARACTER DATA

BIRTHDAY/JANUARY 31

HEIGHT/5′11″

WEIGHT/141 LBS

ZANPAKU-TÔ/SENBON-ZAKURA

INCANTATION/"SCATTER, SENBONZAKURA!"

COAT LINING/SEIRAN (INDIGO BLUE)

HOBBY/TAKING WALKS AT NIGHT

SPECIAL SKILL/ CALLIGRAPHY

FOOD:
LIKES/HOT AND SPICY THINGS
DISLIKES/SWEET THINGS

HOW HE SPENDS HIS DAYS OFF/ATTENDING GATHERINGS OF THE FOUR NOBLE FAMILIES, SPENDING PEACEFUL DAYS READING AND DOING CALLIGRAPHY

SPECIAL NOTES

TOP SECRET

The Kuchiki mansion sits on grounds so vast that Byakuya has his own river flowing past his private chambers. When you first enter the Kuchiki grounds there is even a lake filled with carp of impeccable pedigrees that have been raised here for generations. The carp are rare, three times larger than the common variety, and are a brilliant gold. The original ten carp have been reduced to four for reasons that are not known. Rumors have spread among the staff that this has been the work of the Kuchiki ghost. In fact, Yachiru has been sneaking in late at night and catching the carp as get-well gifts for Ukitake, releasing them into the pond at Ugendô Quarters. Ukitake has been quite pleased, noting, "There are more of the big carp in the pond lately!"

BATTLE DATA | BYAKUYA KUCHIKI

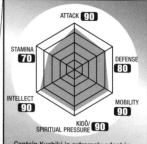

ATTACK **90**
STAMINA **70**
DEFENSE **80**
INTELLECT **90**
MOBILITY **90**
KIDÔ/ SPIRITUAL PRESSURE **90**

Captain Kuchiki is extremely adept in all aspects of combat. There are no shortcomings in his battle skills.

Captain Kuchiki prevented the sentence from being carried out in the end. Many company members praised his action.

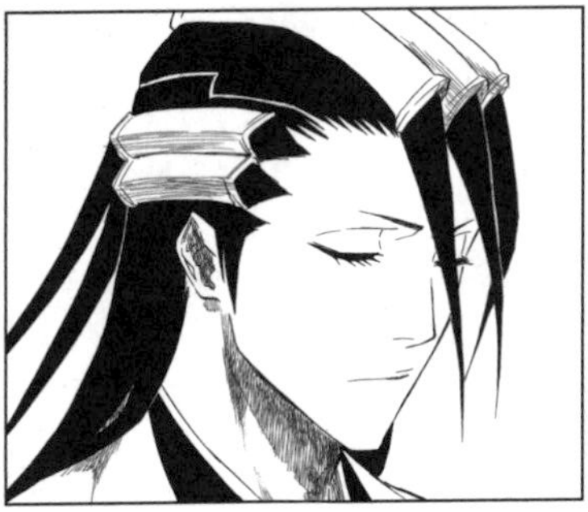

"IF WE DO NOT UPHOLD THE LAW, WHO WILL?"

Captain Kuchiki may seem aloof, given that he is an aristocrat, but he truly believes in sticking to the law. He didn't waver from his belief even when his sister-in-law Rukia was sentenced to death.

ASSISTANT CAPTAIN

阿散井恋次

RENJI ABARAI

This assistant captain is hot-blooded and openly expresses his emotions—the complete opposite of Captain Kuchiki. Renji isn't all that refined, perhaps because he comes from Rukongai, but he is compassionate and brotherly. He is Rukia Kuchiki's childhood friend.

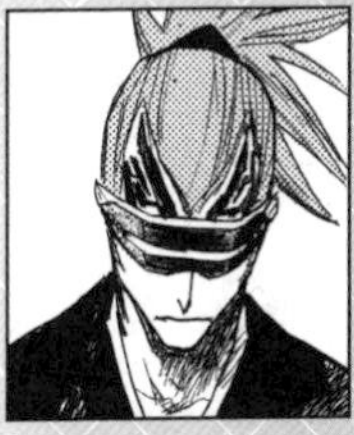

The goggles he collects are among his fashion accessories.

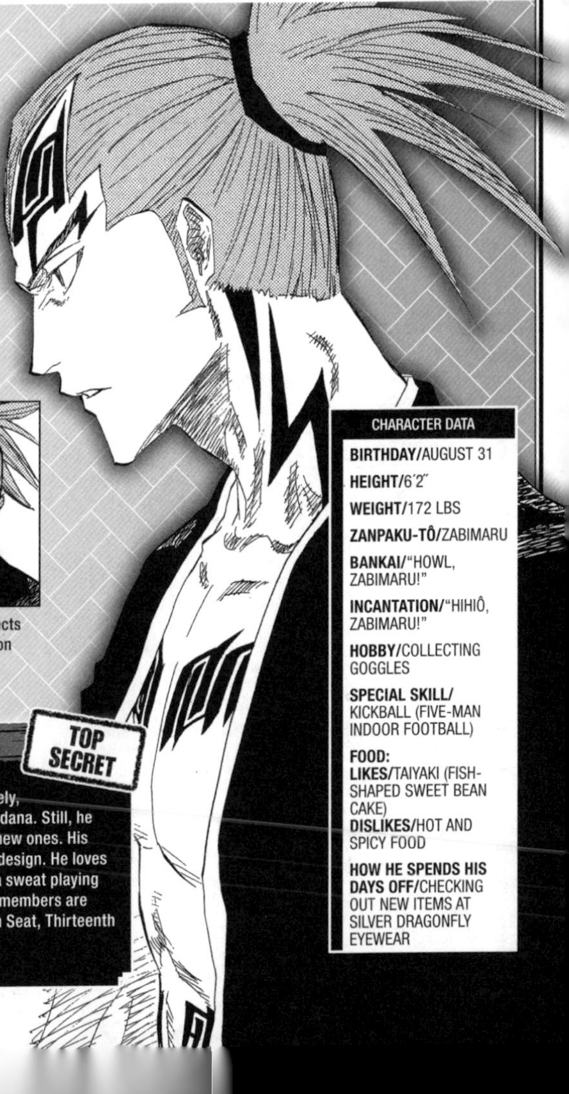

SPECIAL NOTES

All of his goggles are broken, and he hasn't been able to buy new ones lately, so he has been making do with a bandana. Still, he never misses a chance to check out new ones. His dream is to wear goggles of his own design. He loves playing kickball and often works up a sweat playing with Sixth Company's team. The key members are Renji, Rikichi, the Fourth Seat, Eighth Seat, Thirteenth Seat and Twentieth Seat.

TOP SECRET

CHARACTER DATA

BIRTHDAY/AUGUST 31

HEIGHT/6′2″

WEIGHT/172 LBS

ZANPAKU-TÔ/ZABIMARU

BANKAI/"HOWL, ZABIMARU!"

INCANTATION/"HIHIÔ, ZABIMARU!"

HOBBY/COLLECTING GOGGLES

SPECIAL SKILL/ KICKBALL (FIVE-MAN INDOOR FOOTBALL)

FOOD:
LIKES/TAIYAKI (FISH-SHAPED SWEET BEAN CAKE)
DISLIKES/HOT AND SPICY FOOD

HOW HE SPENDS HIS DAYS OFF/CHECKING OUT NEW ITEMS AT SILVER DRAGONFLY EYEWEAR

Renji appears in his sleepwear. This common occurrence doesn't seem to faze the female company members.

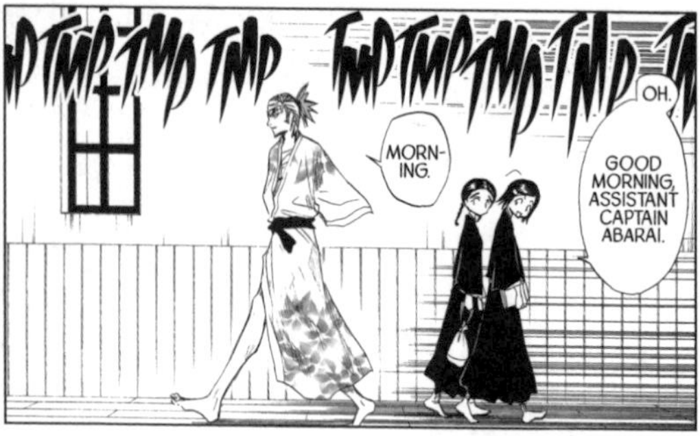
TMP TMP TMP TMP
OH.
GOOD MORNING, ASSISTANT CAPTAIN ABARAI.
MORN-ING.

AN EVERYDAY SCENE

When all is said and done, greetings are fundamental for human relationships. As such, being unable to greet people appropriately means one's failure as a Soul Reaper. Sixth Company encourages proper salutations.

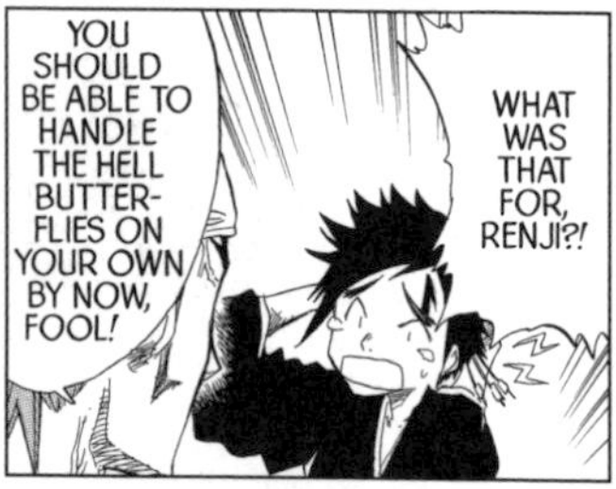
WHAT WAS THAT FOR, RENJI?!
YOU SHOULD BE ABLE TO HANDLE THE HELL BUTTER-FLIES ON YOUR OWN BY NOW, FOOL!

Rikichi is always bungling things, such as letting a Hell Butterfly get away. Renji is constantly scolding him.

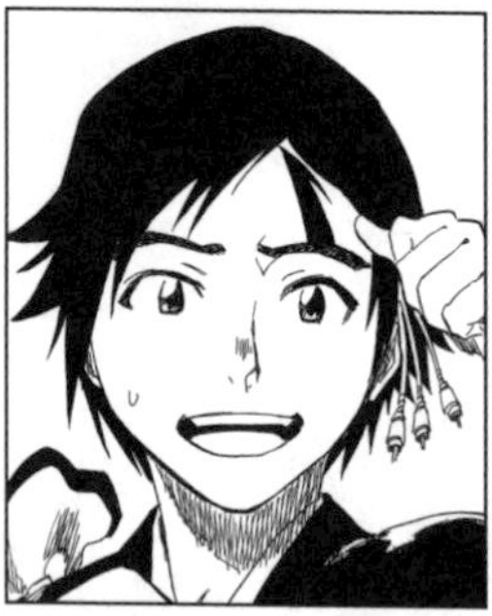

RIKICHI, A MEMBER OF SIXTH COMPANY

This new member admires the assistant captain and tries to emulate him as much as possible. This explains the tattoo identical to one of Renji's on the left side of Rikichi's forehead. During the ryoka's incursion, Rikichi rescued Renji, who was injured, and cheered him up.

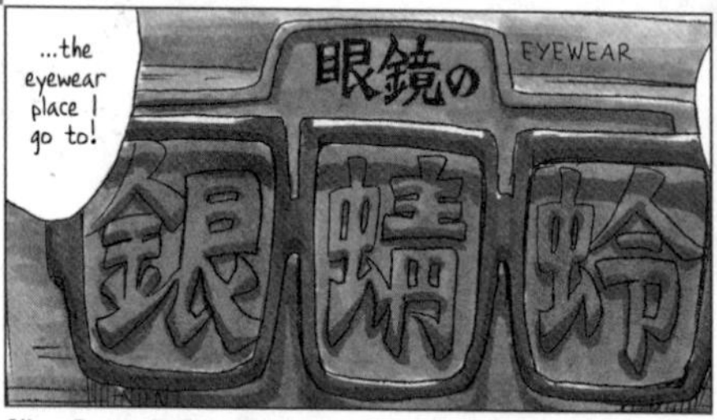
...the eyewear place I go to!
眼鏡の
EYEWEAR
銀蜻蛉

Silver Dragonfly Eyewear, purveyor to the Court Guard Companies, also supplies sunglasses to the Society of Male Soul Reapers.

PURVEYOR TO THE COMPANIES

SILVER DRAGONFLY EYEWEAR

The shop that carries Renji's goggles is the most popular of its kind. Renji goes there regularly, but due to the high prices, he's there mostly just to window shop.

SPECIAL NOTES

TOP SECRET

Before Renji, the assistant captain of Sixth Company was Ginjirô Shirogane. He is currently the owner of Silver Dragonfly Eyewear. Ginjirô stepped down as assistant captain to become a merchant when his side business of selling eyeglasses became successful. Whenever Renji, who filled the open position, visits the shop, Ginjirô greets him with, "Well, if it isn't my replacement!" and offers him a discount on purchases. Even so, Renji can't buy goggles often even with a discount because the selling price is still high. Members of the Society of Male Soul Reapers get their sunglasses from this shop. Ginjirô's daughter is named Mihane. He has sent goggles to Byakuya, his old boss, but they've been returned with the note "No, thank you." Ginjirô isn't offended whatsoever and continues to send goggles to Sixth Company barracks.

七番隊
SEVENTH COMPANY
COMPANY FLOWER: IRIS
(courage)

Captain Sajin Komamura is a man who lives for and has absolute faith in loyalty. His company is made up of sincere, unpretentious people who live life with gusto.

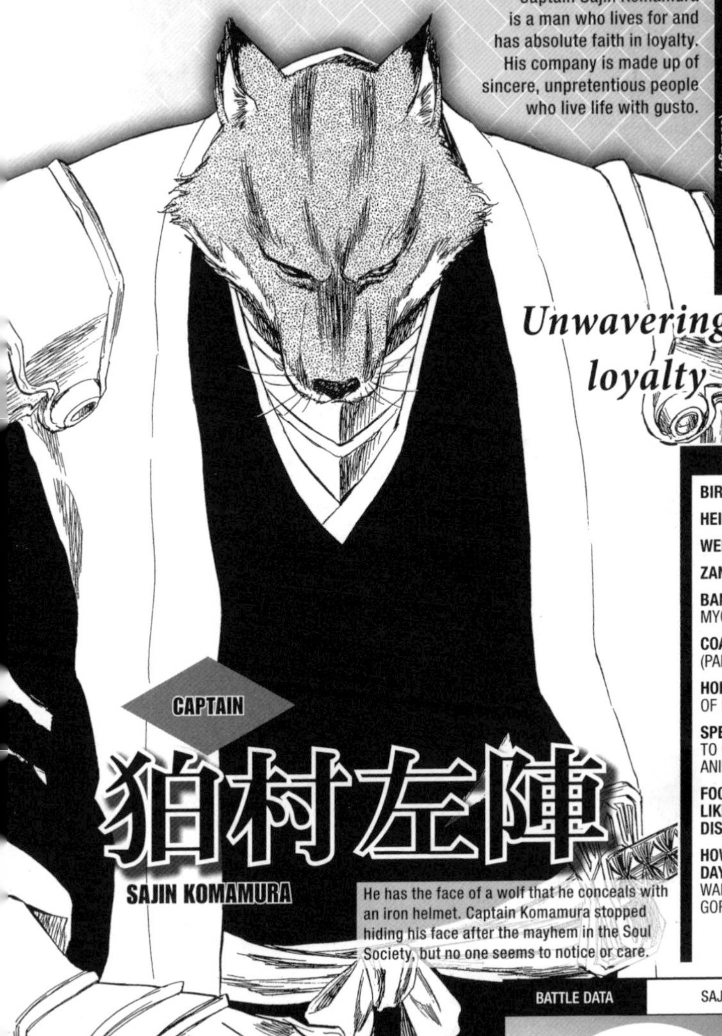

Unwavering loyalty

CAPTAIN

狛村左陣

SAJIN KOMAMURA

He has the face of a wolf that he conceals with an iron helmet. Captain Komamura stopped hiding his face after the mayhem in the Soul Society, but no one seems to notice or care.

CHARACTER DATA

BIRTHDAY/AUGUST 23

HEIGHT/9′5″

WEIGHT/664 LBS

ZANPAKU-TÔ/TENKEN

BANKAI/KOKUJÔ TENGEN MYÔ-OH!

COAT LINING/RIKANCHA (PALE OLIVE GREEN)

HOBBY/TAKING CARE OF DOGS

SPECIAL SKILL/ABLE TO COMMUNICATE WITH ANIMALS

FOOD:
LIKES/MEAT
DISLIKES/CARROTS

HOW HE SPENDS HIS DAYS OFF/GOING FOR WALKS WITH HIS DOG, GORÔ

BATTLE DATA

SAJIN KOMAMURA

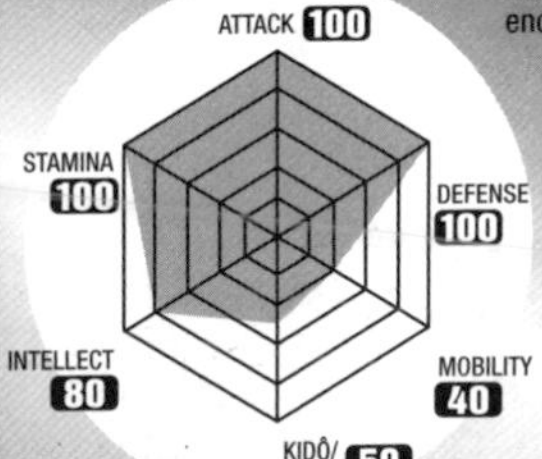

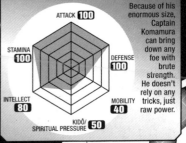

ATTACK 100
DEFENSE 100
MOBILITY 40
KIDÔ/ SPIRITUAL PRESSURE 50
INTELLECT 80
STAMINA 100

Because of his enormous size, Captain Komamura can bring down any foe with brute strength. He doesn't rely on any tricks, just raw power.

SPECIAL NOTES

TOP SECRET

People often think he is a dog, but in truth, he is a wolf. He loves dogs and keeps a pet dog, Gorô, behind the company's barracks. Gorô seems to be closest to Komamura, perhaps because the two can communicate. Komamura came to dislike carrots long ago when his father instructed, "This isn't something we eat." Komamura hasn't tasted carrots since.

Central to the captain general's character is his ability to ascertain a person's nature. He values Captain Komamura's sense of honor and loyalty.

"SHOULD HE EVER NEED MY LIFE, HE SHALL HAVE IT."

Captain General Yamamoto accepted Komamura when others shunned him because of his appearance. Captain Komamura therefore feels deeply grateful to the captain general. Komamura would gladly give his life to repay the captain general for his kindness.

ASSISTANT CAPTAIN

射場鉄左衛門

TETSUZAEMON IBA

Sunglasses and a Hiroshima dialect are this assistant captain's trademarks. He loves Hiroshima with all his being and eats only Hiroshima-style cuisine.

He believes that worldly success is the true measure of a man, but it seems he does it all to keep his mother in comfort.

A MAN SHOULD AIM FOR THE STARS.
AND IT IS FUN.

CHARACTER DATA

BIRTHDAY/JULY 18

HEIGHT/6′0″

WEIGHT/150 LBS

HOBBY/COLLECTING SUNGLASSES

SPECIAL SKILL/BEING MACHO

FOOD:
LIKES/HIROSHIMA-STYLE OKONOMIYAKI GRIDDLECAKE
DISLIKES/OSAKA-STYLE OKONOMIYAKI GRIDDLECAKE

HOW HE SPENDS HIS DAYS OFF/CHECKING OUT NEW ITEMS AT SILVER DRAGONFLY EYEWEAR

SPECIAL NOTES

TOP SECRET

Chairman of the Society of Male Soul Reapers. To spread the use of the Hiroshima dialect, Komamura offered a course at his own expense but was forced to cancel it when no one signed up. He currently writes for *Seireitei Bulletin*, contributing to the column "Lessons in the Macho Dialect of Hiroshima" in the "Men's Section."

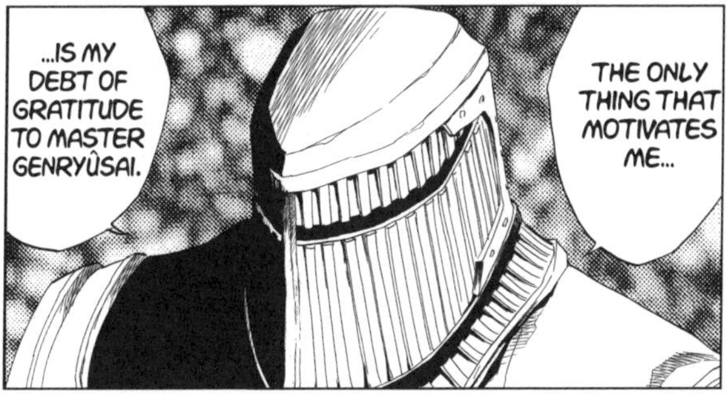
THE ONLY THING THAT MOTIVATES ME...
...IS MY DEBT OF GRATITUDE TO MASTER GENRYÛSAI.

THE CODES OF MORAL OBLIGATION AND COMPASSION

Both captain and assistant captain believe strongly in moral obligation and compassion. This ethos has been passed down through the ranks of Seventh Company.

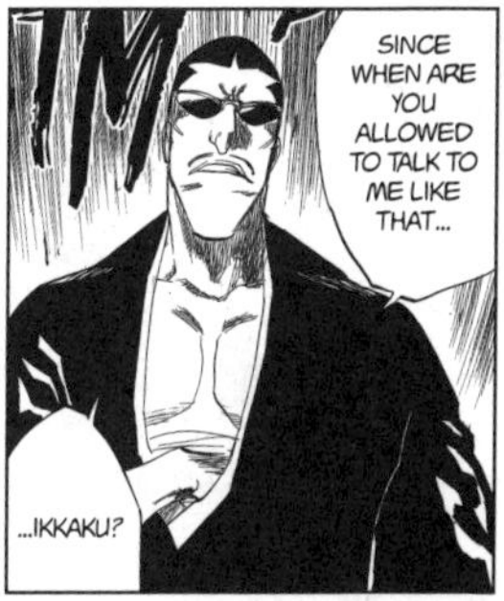
SINCE WHEN ARE YOU ALLOWED TO TALK TO ME LIKE THAT...
...IKKAKU?

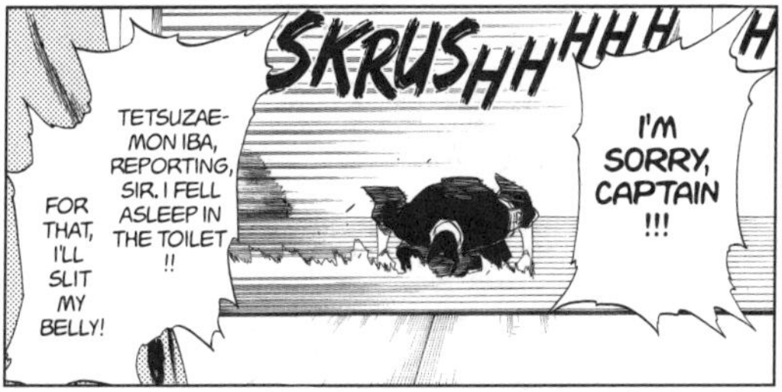
SKRUSHHHHH H
I'M SORRY, CAPTAIN !!!
TETSUZAEMON IBA, REPORTING, SIR. I FELL ASLEEP IN THE TOILET !!
FOR THAT, I'LL SLIT MY BELLY!

Honor is most important of all to these men of chivalry. They will raise their swords and employ any means necessary to defend their honor.

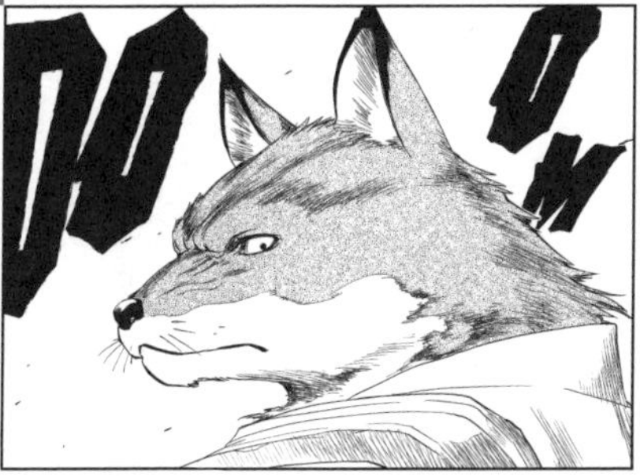

HIS FACE, HIDDEN UNDER AN IRON HELMET

Until the ryoka's incursion, Captain Komamura had kept his face concealed under an iron helmet. He is often mistaken for a dog, but he is in fact a wolf. Surprisingly, he loves little animals, like dogs and cats.

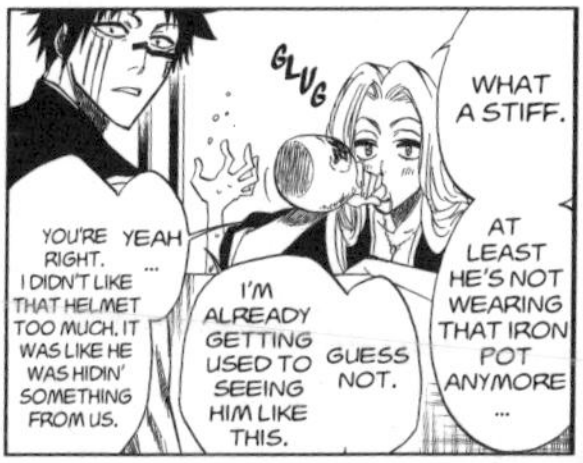
WHAT A STIFF.
GLUG
AT LEAST HE'S NOT WEARING THAT IRON POT ANYMORE ...
GUESS NOT.
I'M ALREADY GETTING USED TO SEEING HIM LIKE THIS.
YEAH ...
YOU'RE RIGHT. I DIDN'T LIKE THAT HELMET TOO MUCH. IT WAS LIKE HE WAS HIDIN' SOMETHING FROM US.

The reaction to Komamura's uncovered face has been more favorable than expected.

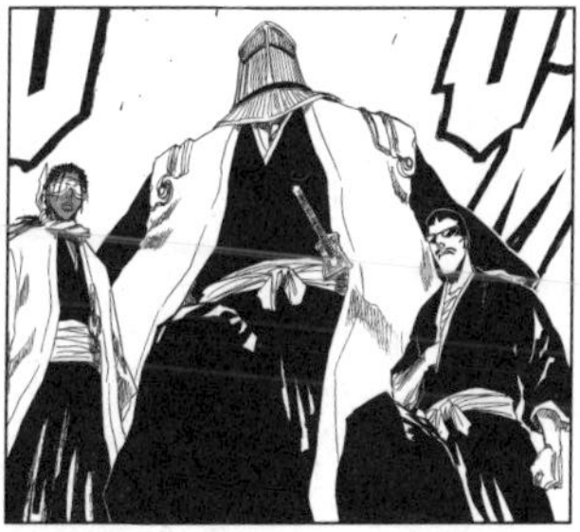

During the chaos of the ryoka's incursion into the Soul Society, Komamura wore an iron helmet that covered his entire head. His enormous size and the iron helmet made him an intimidating sight to his foes.

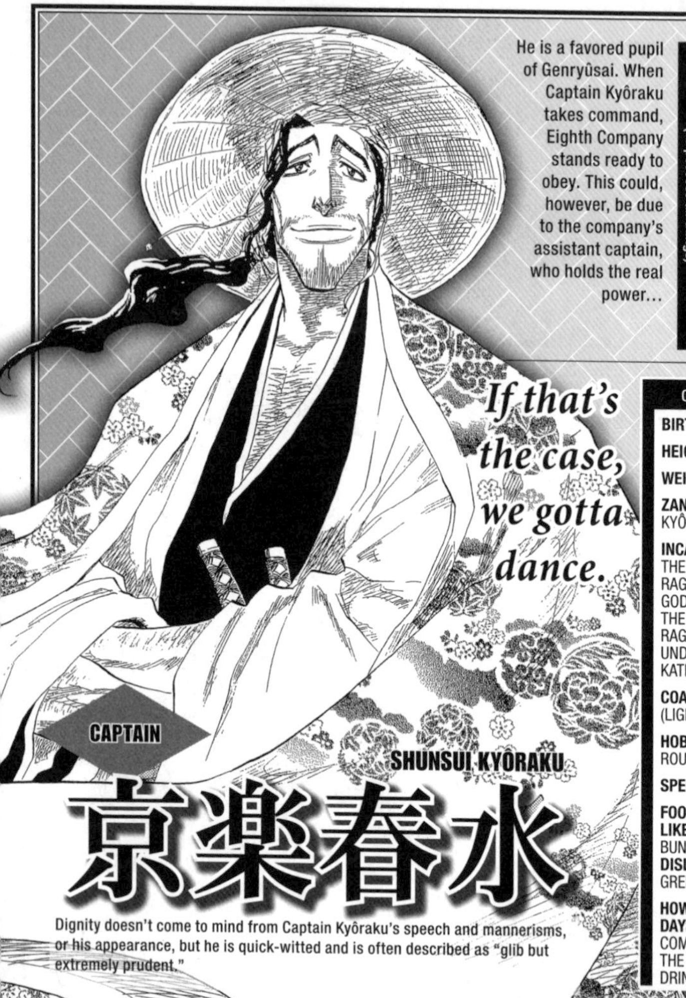

八番隊

EIGHTH COMPANY
COMPANY FLOWER: BIRD OF PARADISE
(To possess all things)

He is a favored pupil of Genryûsai. When Captain Kyôraku takes command, Eighth Company stands ready to obey. This could, however, be due to the company's assistant captain, who holds the real power…

If that's the case, we gotta dance.

CAPTAIN

SHUNSUI KYÔRAKU

京楽春水

Dignity doesn't come to mind from Captain Kyôraku's speech and mannerisms, or his appearance, but he is quick-witted and is often described as "glib but extremely prudent."

CHARACTER DATA

BIRTHDAY/JULY 11

HEIGHT/6´4˝

WEIGHT/192 LBS

ZANPAKU-TÔ/KATEN KYÔKOTSU

INCANTATION/"WHEN THE FLOWER WIND RAGES, THE FLOWER GOD ROARS. WHEN THE WIND OF HEAVEN RAGES, THE GOD OF THE UNDERWORLD SNEERS… KATEN KYÔKOTSU!"

COAT LINING/SUÔIRO (LIGHT MAGENTA)

HOBBY/MAKING THE ROUNDS OF THE PUBS

SPECIAL SKILL/NAPPING

FOOD:
LIKES/STEAMED SAKE BUNS
DISLIKES/POWDERED GREEN TEA

HOW HE SPENDS HIS DAYS OFF/TAKING COMRADES WHO HAVE THE SAME DAY OFF OUT DRINKING

BATTLE DATA | SHUNSUI KYÔRAKU

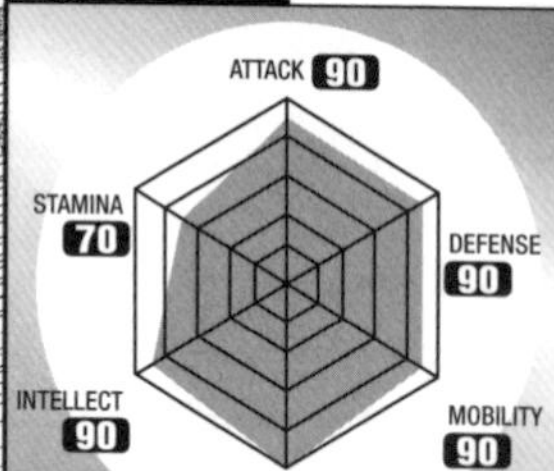
ATTACK 90
DEFENSE 90
MOBILITY 90
KIDÔ/ SPIRITUAL PRESSURE 100
INTELLECT 90
STAMINA 70

His skill and power rank are at the captain level, but his one shortcoming is his tendency to walk away from battles that he isn't concerned about.

SPECIAL NOTES — TOP SECRET

He is the author of the romance novel *The Rose-Colored Path*, which may be published in *Seireitei Bulletin* but isn't popular at all. He receives no fan letters, and not one present was delivered to him on his birthday. However, his photo collection "Cuddly Pillow" was so popular it sold out. He says, "My kittens are very shy," and he doesn't seem concerned at all that his serial novel ranks dead last in popularity. Incidentally, there were fewer copies of the first edition of "Cuddly Pillow" than the photo collections of other captains. To this day, the book has not gone into reprint, which he is unaware of.

Captain Kyôraku was very reluctant to obey the captain general's orders to fight the ryoka. Instead, he drank and indulged in a nap. He isn't one to act on something he finds disagreeable.

AW...
HERE ALREADY?

"I'LL BE OVER SOON. IT'S JUST FUN AND GAMES."

Captain Kyôraku hides his true intentions behind his lightheartedness, and he is never one to say how he feels. And yet he and Captain Ukitake of Thirteenth Company are stalwart men who have demonstrated abilities that are unmatched. Their confidence remained unshaken even though it was only the day before that the ryoka infiltrated the Seireitei. Just how serious is Captain Kyôraku?!

ASSISTANT CAPTAIN

伊勢七緒

NANAO ISE

IF MY NANAO WENT OUT TO BATTLE...
...AND BECAME DAMAGED GOODS, I DON'T KNOW WHAT I'D DO.♡
SWAK
WHO'S "YOUR" NANAO?

A master of clerical duties, she fills in for her captain, who rarely pays any attention to day-to-day matters.

CHARACTER DATA

BIRTHDAY/JULY 7

HEIGHT/5′5″

WEIGHT/106 LBS

HOBBY/READING

SPECIAL SKILL/ MATHEMATICS

FOOD:
LIKES/SWEET BEAN JELLY
DISLIKES/POWDERED GREEN TEA

HOW SHE SPENDS HER DAYS OFF/GOING TO THE LIBRARY, SHOPPING (CURRENTLY LOOKING FOR A NEW HAIRPIN)

SPECIAL NOTES

TOP SECRET

The vice chairwoman of the Society of Female Soul Reapers. She often meets her reading partner Hinamori at the library. They enjoy exchanging good books and reviewing them together. When Hinamori was hospitalized, Nanao visited often and brought her books to read. Nanao's own column, "Don't Get Carried Away," which is serialized in *Seireitei Bulletin*, is one of the top three most popular columns. She gets fan letters as well as presents on her birthday. "Don't Get Carried Away" is a column that resounds with readers' problems and complaints. It's very popular with male readers.

The extent of her combat abilities is not known as she rarely goes out to the front lines. Whether or not this is Captain Kyôraku's wish is unclear.

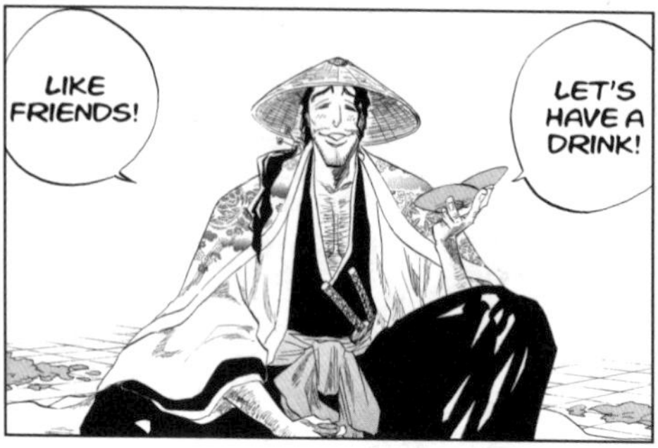
LET'S HAVE A DRINK!
LIKE FRIENDS!

ENJOY SPRING IN THE FLOATING WORLD!

Captain Kyôraku's motto for living is simple: Enjoy. Although he invites Eighth Company members to go drinking once a week, male members are prohibited, and he parties only with the female members. This is only a rumor.

DRINKING BUDDIES

On his days off, he goes drinking with Eighth Company members as well as Rangiku and others. His circle of friends appears quite large.

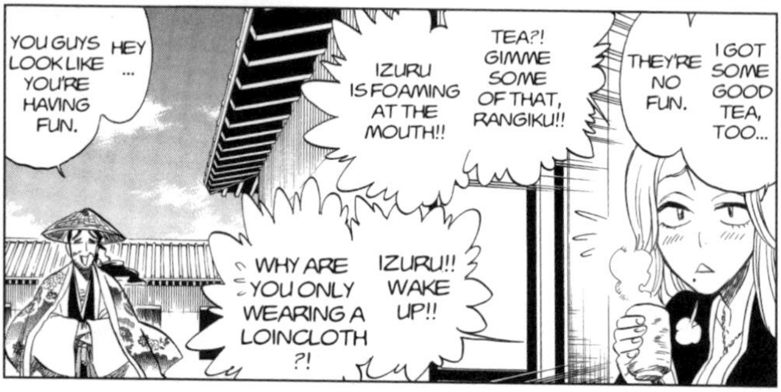
I GOT SOME GOOD TEA, TOO...
THEY'RE NO FUN.
TEA?! GIMME SOME OF THAT, RANGIKU!!
IZURU IS FOAMING AT THE MOUTH!!
IZURU!! WAKE UP!!
WHY ARE YOU ONLY WEARING A LOINCLOTH ?!
HEY ...
YOU GUYS LOOK LIKE YOU'RE HAVING FUN.

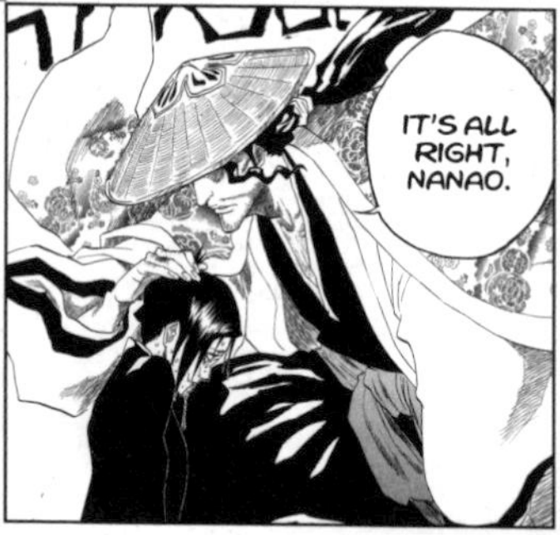
IT'S ALL RIGHT, NANAO.

NANAO AND SHUNSUI

COULD THESE TWO BE...?

Captain Kyôraku is very attentive toward his assistant captain. Consider the time he protected Nanao when she lost consciousness under the captain general's spiritual pressure, or the time he carried her to safety from the battlefield. Perhaps the two have gone slightly beyond a superior and subordinate's relationship... in a manner of speaking, that is.

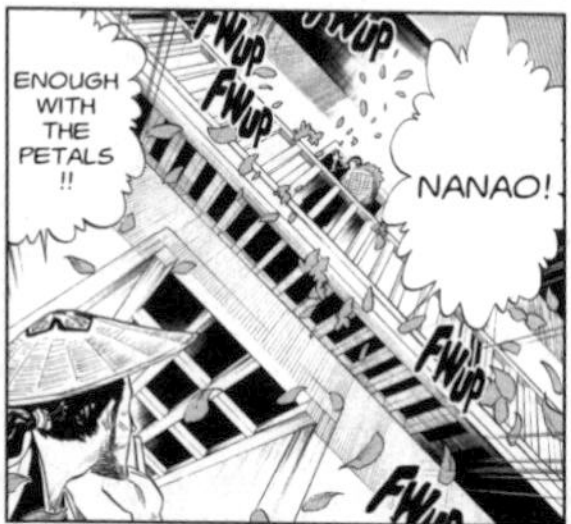
NANAO!
FWUP
FWUP
ENOUGH WITH THE PETALS !!
FWUP
FWUP

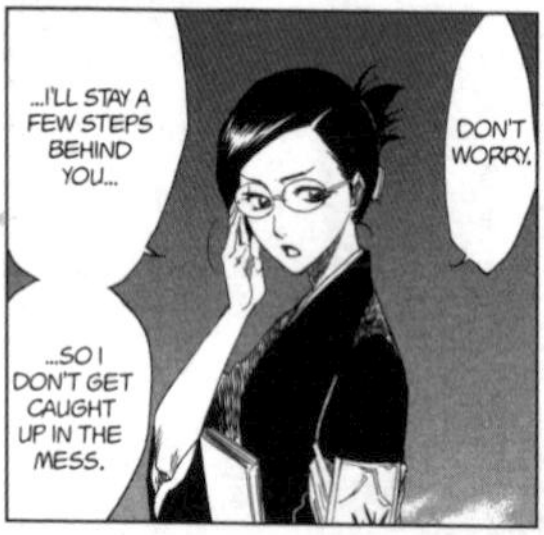
DON'T WORRY.
...I'LL STAY A FEW STEPS BEHIND YOU...
...SO I DON'T GET CAUGHT UP IN THE MESS.

On the other hand, Nanao coldly brushes off Kyôraku, who constantly pushes work onto her and harasses her. But deep down, she seems to really care about his safety and welfare.

Shut away in the dark, a ray of light

九番隊

NINTH COMPANY
COMPANY FLOWER: WHITE POPPY
(oblivion))

The mission of Ninth Company is to protect the Seireitei. It also oversees the editing of *Seireitei Bulletin.* At present, Assistant Captain Shûhei Hisagi has taken over all responsibilities because Captain Tôsen's whereabouts are not known.

CHARACTER DATA

BIRTHDAY/NOVEMBER 13

HEIGHT/5′9″

WEIGHT/134 LBS

ZANPAKU-TÔ/ SUZUMUSHI

INCANTATION/"CRY, SUZUMUSHI!"

COAT LINING/ KARETAKEIRO (YELLOWISH BROWN)

HOBBY/COOKING

SPECIAL SKILL/COOKING

FOOD:
LIKES/CHIKUZENNI (CHICKEN SIMMERED WITH VEGETABLES)
DISLIKES/VINEGAR-FLAVORED DISHES

HOW HE SPENDS HIS DAYS OFF/WORKING AS AN EDITOR FOR *SEIREITEI BULLETIN*

CAPTAIN

KANAME TÔSEN

東仙 要

A truly decent man who despises war and fighting, he wishes for nothing but world peace and harmony. He will not go easy on anyone who disturbs the peace.

TOP SECRET

SPECIAL NOTES

Traditionally, Ninth Company has overseen arts and culture. For this reason, it publishes *Seireitei Bulletin*, and Tôsen is its editor in chief. Tôsen has his own column, "The Path of Justice." Owing to his position, the column has never been cancelled; popularity isn't an issue. The column has focused until now on themes like "What is justice?" However, it has explored other ideas recently, such as "Recipe for Justice," which contains cooking recipes. The column has been steadily growing in popularity, sparking interest among female Soul Reaper readers.

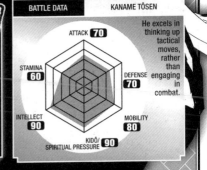

BATTLE DATA — KANAME TÔSEN

ATTACK 70
DEFENSE 70
MOBILITY 80
KIDÔ/ SPIRITUAL PRESSURE 90
INTELLECT 90
STAMINA 60

He excels in thinking up tactical moves, rather than engaging in combat.

Captain Tôsen is devoted to peace above all else, and the only time he will raise his sword is to uphold justice—something he passionately believes in.

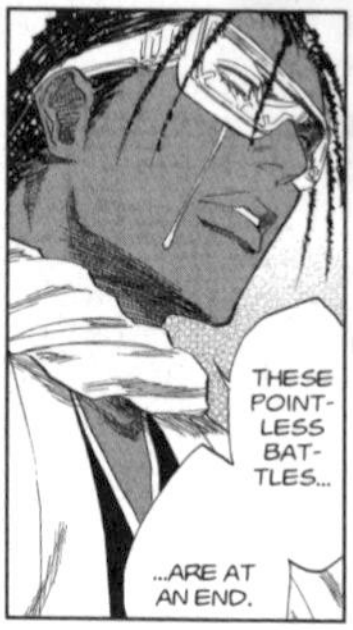
THESE POINTLESS BATTLES...
...ARE AT AN END.

"THIS ISN'T PERSONAL BUT... I MUST ELIMINATE YOU TO RESTORE THE PEACE."

Captain Tôsen bears the heavy responsibility of this elite company, which is always on standby for combat because it is the security force of the Court Guard Companies. However, he dislikes fighting and puts world peace and stability first. Captain Tôsen is the polar opposite of Eleventh Company Captain Zaraki. As a result the two aren't close, much like a cat and dog.

CHARACTER DATA

BIRTHDAY/AUGUST 14

HEIGHT/5′11″

WEIGHT/148 LBS

HOBBY/MUSIC

SPECIAL SKILL/COOKING

FOOD:
LIKES/FRANKFURTERS
DISLIKES/SEA URCHIN

HOW HE SPENDS HIS DAYS OFF/PRACTICING THE GUITAR, WORKING AS AN EDITOR

He is extremely busy attending to his daily duties, editing the magazine and practicing the guitar, but he is a supportive young man relied on by Ninth Company.

檜佐木修兵

ASSISTANT CAPTAIN

SHÛHEI HISAGI

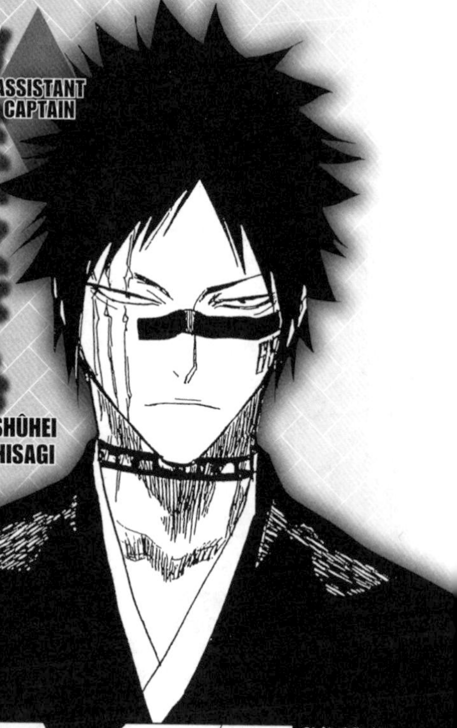

SPECIAL NOTES

TOP SECRET

After graduating from Soul Reaper Academy, he was assigned a seat in the company. During that time he was sent to the world of the living, where he discovered the guitar. Although he brought one back with him and practiced diligently, he couldn't play. When everyone told him to stop making such a racket, he went to practice in the mountains of Rukongai. He learned that among the ryoka, Yasutora Sado played the guitar, and he took lessons from him. Now Shûhei can play a little. In editor Tôsen's absence, he's been filling in at the magazine and has no time to practice. And yet he still has plans to form a band someday and perform in front of everyone (that is, Rangiku). By the way, his new serial, "Teach Me, Shûhei Sensei!!" had a dreadful debut, coming in third to last in popularity. It's said that he didn't leave the editorial office for three days after he discovered the postcard that Rangiku had sent in for the reader survey.

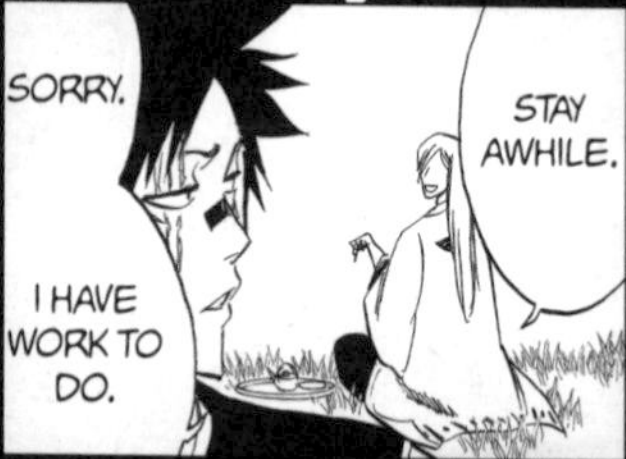
STAY AWHILE.
SORRY.
I HAVE WORK TO DO.

Shûhei finds his days to be extremely hectic, filling in as both captain and editor. If it weren't for Shûhei, we couldn't discuss Ninth Company!

THE PATH OF JUSTICE FORGES AHEAD WITH FERVOR

Captain Tôsen believes in action that is founded on justice—of bringing about world peace without meaningless fighting. He has passed on this belief to the rest of Ninth Company, and as a result, unnecessary bloodshed is strictly forbidden.

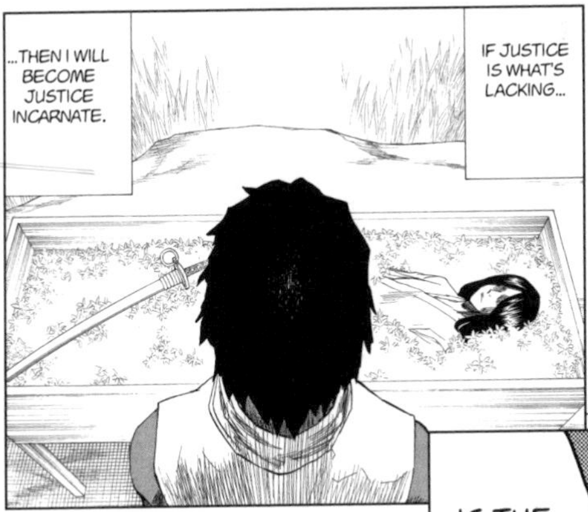
IF JUSTICE IS WHAT'S LACKING...
...THEN I WILL BECOME JUSTICE INCARNATE.

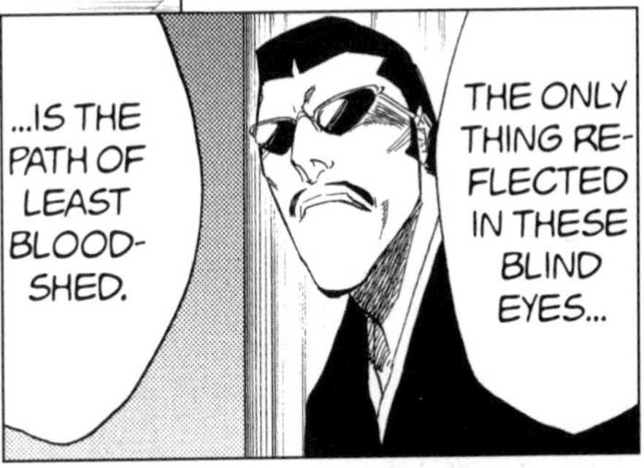
THE ONLY THING REFLECTED IN THESE BLIND EYES...
...IS THE PATH OF LEAST BLOODSHED.

STAUNCH CONVICTION

Behind Captain Tôsen's determination to live for peace is the memory of a close friend who passed away. She died fervently wishing for world peace. The captain swore at her grave that he would walk the path of justice.

AN ALL-ROUNDER WITH LITERARY AND MILITARY SKILLS
SHÛHEI HISAGI

Shûhei was recognized for his abilities from the time he attended Soul Reaper Academy, and quickly rose to assistant captain after joining the Thirteen Court Guards. Having cornered combat expert Yumichika Ayasegawa of Eleventh Company, Shûhei is an outstanding member who represents the promise of the next generation of Court Guards.

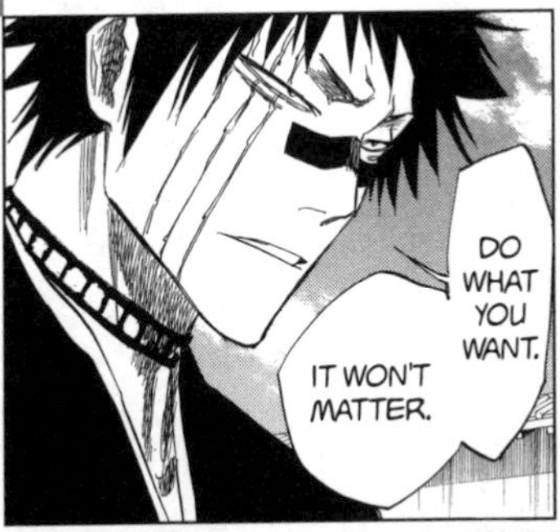
DO WHAT YOU WANT.
IT WON'T MATTER.

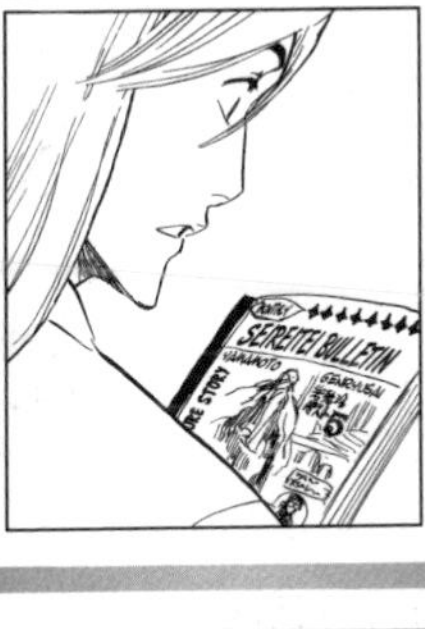
SEIREITEI BULLETIN

Shûhei has superior fighting skills, but he is also a genius at editing *Seireitei Bulletin*. It would be difficult to find anyone as capable among the Court Guard Companies.

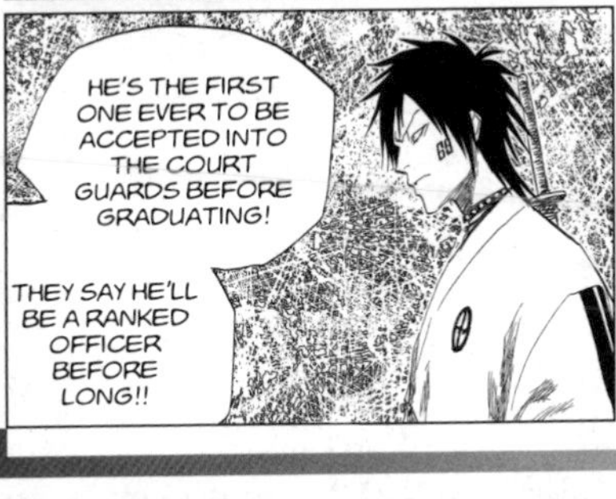
HE'S THE FIRST ONE EVER TO BE ACCEPTED INTO THE COURT GUARDS BEFORE GRADUATING!
THEY SAY HE'LL BE A RANKED OFFICER BEFORE LONG!!

Tenth Company is led by boy genius Tôshirô Hitsugaya. He is meticulous about guiding each and every member. Consequently, everyone in Tenth Company works hard (except the assistant captain).

十番隊

TENTH COMPANY
COMPANY FLOWER: NARCISSUS (occultism and egoism)

Bone-chilling passion

CHARACTER DATA

BIRTHDAY/DECEMBER 20

HEIGHT/4´4˝

WEIGHT/62 LBS

ZANPAKU-TÔ/HYÔRINMARU

INCANTATION/"REIGN OVER THE FROSTED HEAVENS, HYÔRINMARU!"

BANKAI/DAIGUREN HYÔRINMARU!

COAT LINING/CHITOSE MIDORI (GREEN)

HOBBY/NAPPING

SPECIAL SKILL/SPINNING TOPS

FOOD:
LIKES/SUGARED BEANS
DISLIKES/DRIED PERSIMMON

HOW HE SPENDS HIS DAYS OFF/GOING TO HIS GRANDMOTHER'S HOUSE IN RUKONGAI, VISITING JIDANBÔ

CAPTAIN

TÔSHIRÔ HITSUGAYA

日番谷冬獅郎

He is a prodigy and the youngest-ever captain in the Court Guards. His fighting ability goes without saying, but he is also an efficient administrator. The only thing that distresses him is his height.

BATTLE DATA

TÔSHIRÔ HITSUGAYA

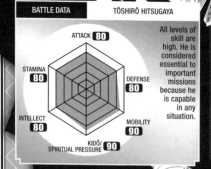

ATTACK 80
STAMINA 80
DEFENSE 80
INTELLECT 80
MOBILITY 90
KIDÔ/SPIRITUAL PRESSURE 90

All levels of skill are high. He is considered essential to important missions because he is capable in any situation.

SPECIAL NOTES

TOP SECRET

His grandmother, who lives in Rukongai, counts sweet fermented soybeans among her favorite foods. Tôshirô acquired his taste for them from her and still craves them. She sends him some from time to time. He remains friends with Jidanbô. He is adept at spinning tops and is proud to have been undefeated as a child when he lived in West Rukon District 1 in Junrinan. He works quickly and efficiently so that he can return to his quarters to nap. He believes in his grandmother's motto, "Children who sleep will grow." He's a real grandma's boy.

Usually he seems uninterested in anything that happens, but Captain Hitsugaya changes when it comes to Assistant Captain Hinamori. If anyone hurts her, he shows no mercy at all.

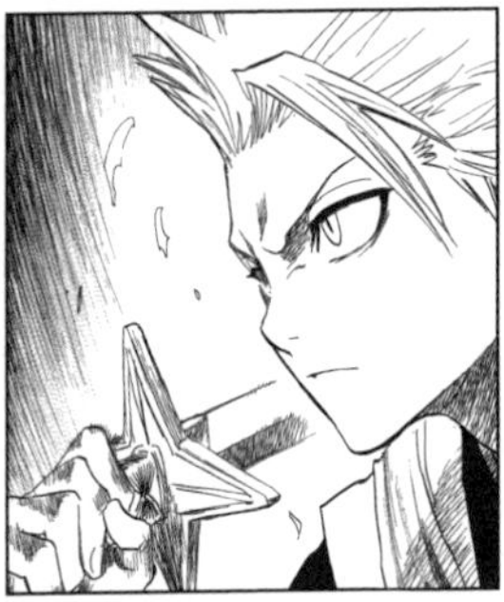

"IF YOU MADE HER BLEED, I'LL KILL YOU!!!"

The extremely insightful Captain Hitsugaya takes action calmly and thoughtfully. During the ryoka incident, he personally conducted an in-depth investigation to get to the truth. The only time his fury surfaces is when his childhood friend Assistant Captain Hinamori is in danger.

CHARACTER DATA

BIRTHDAY/SEPTEMBER 29

HEIGHT/5′8″

WEIGHT/126 LBS

ZANPAKU-TÔ/HAINEKO

INCANTATION/"ROAR, HAINEKO!"

HOBBY/NAPPING

SPECIAL SKILL/JAPANESE CLASSICAL DANCING

FOOD:
LIKES/DRIED PERSIMMON
DISLIKES/BAMBOO SHOOTS

HOW SHE SPENDS HER DAYS OFF/LOOKING FOR PEOPLE WHO AREN'T DOING ANYTHING AND GETTING THEM TO GO DRINKING WITH HER, PEEKING INTO KIMONO SHOPS

The sexiest and most voluptuous woman in the Thirteen Court Guards. She is quite broadminded, and there is probably no man in the Thirteen Court Guards who is able to... to defy her.

松本乱菊

ASSISTANT CAPTAIN

RANGIKU MATSUMOTO

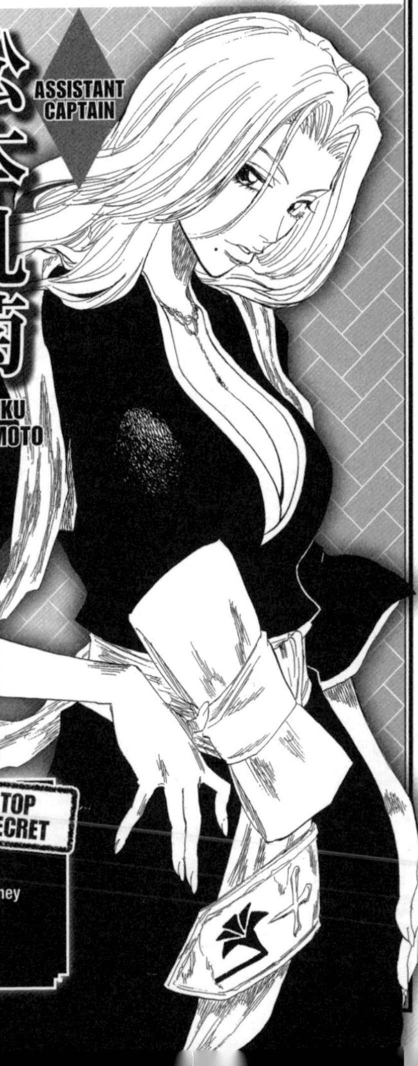

She loves drinking parties. On her days off, she is known to grab members to go drinking, and will drink all day.

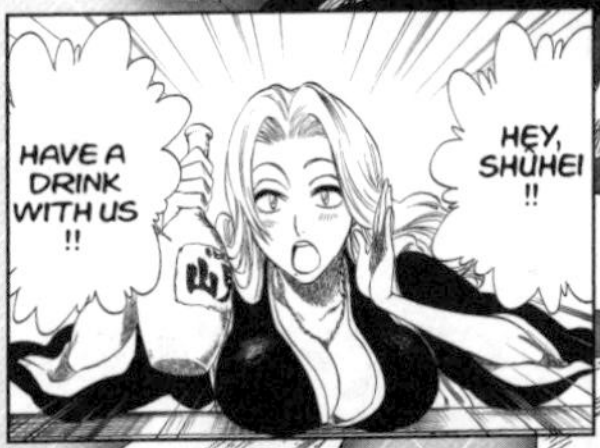
HEY, SHÛHEI !!
HAVE A DRINK WITH US !!

SPECIAL NOTES

TOP SECRET

She dislikes bamboo shoots because they give her a rash. She enjoys Japanese classical dancing and has specially made kimono besides her Soul Reaper uniform. Because it costs money to go drinking, she invites others and makes them pay the tab. Her drinking buddies are Shûhei and Shunsui.

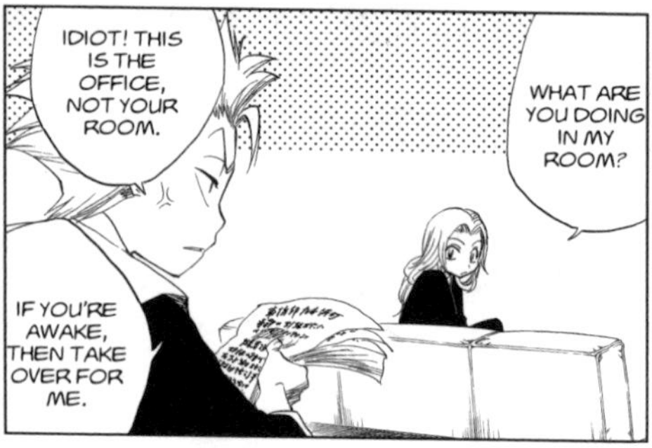
WHAT ARE YOU DOING IN MY ROOM?
IDIOT! THIS IS THE OFFICE, NOT YOUR ROOM.
IF YOU'RE AWAKE, THEN TAKE OVER FOR ME.

ADD TOGETHER, THEN DIVIDE?!: THE PERFECT BALANCE OF POWER

Those in charge of Tenth Company are the workaholic captain and the assistant captain who deftly pushes work onto the captain. For some reason, this arrangement works well for them. This duo is well liked in the company, and things run smoothly as a result.

LIKE OIL AND WATER, AN UNLIKELY COMBO

These two often spend time together during their off-hours. Their hobbies and interests are totally contrary. Captain Hitsugaya views Rangiku's carousing with disdain… but this is a typical scene between them.

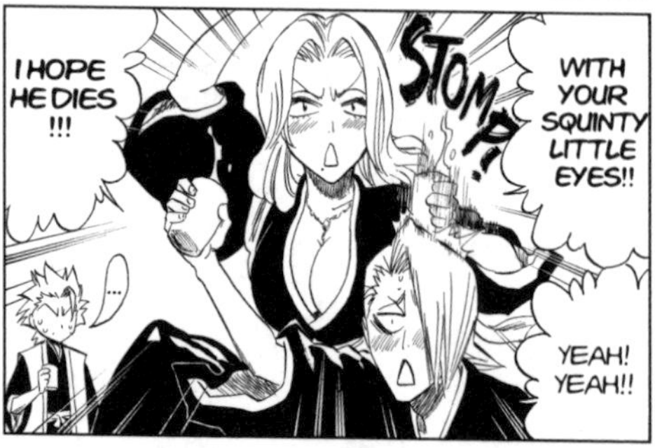
WITH YOUR SQUINTY LITTLE EYES!!
STOMP!
I HOPE HE DIES !!!
YEAH! YEAH!!
...

CHILDHOOD FRIENDS HITSUGAYA AND HINAMORI

Captain Hitsugaya and Assistant Captain Hinamori both hail from West Rukon District 1 in Junrinan. Friends from childhood, they used to call each other Bedwetter Momo and Shiro. Their bond remains strong to this day.

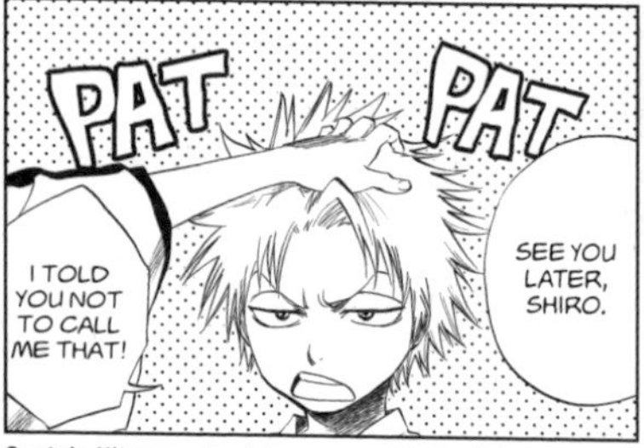
PAT PAT
SEE YOU LATER, SHIRO.
I TOLD YOU NOT TO CALL ME THAT!

Captain Hitsugaya's nickname used to be Shiro. He has to remind Hinamori constantly that she should address him as "Captain," but…

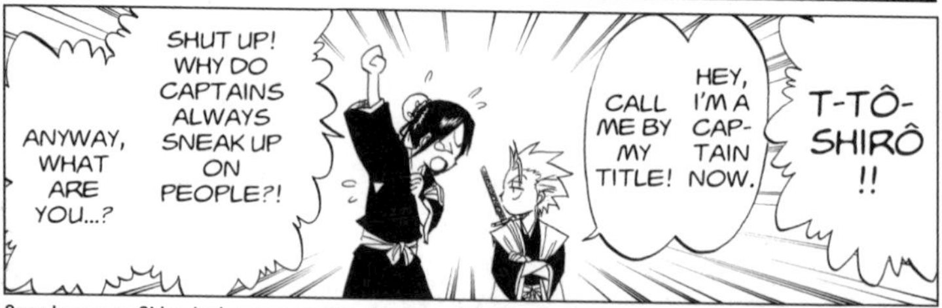
T-TÔ-SHIRÔ !!
HEY, I'M A CAP-TAIN NOW.
CALL ME BY MY TITLE!
SHUT UP! WHY DO CAPTAINS ALWAYS SNEAK UP ON PEOPLE?!
ANYWAY, WHAT ARE YOU...?

Once known as Shiro, he is now a captain. Even so, old habits die hard…

Eleventh Company probably has the best fighters among the Court Guards, being a rowdy bunch that idolizes Captain Kenpachi. They appear like a lawless gang at first glance, but Kenpachi has them unified and tightly under control.

十一番隊

ELEVENTH COMPANY
COMPANY FLOWER: YARROW (combat)

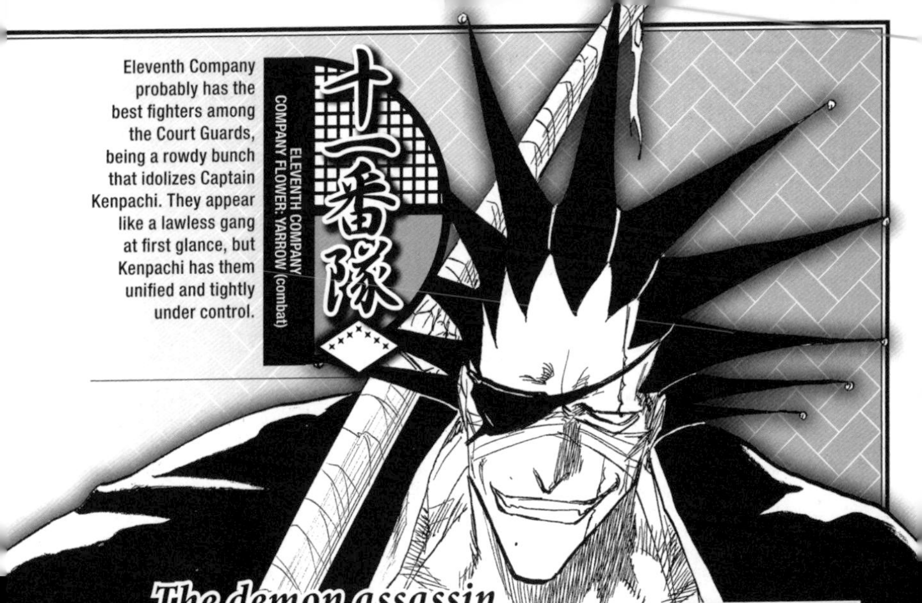

The demon assassin dagger that devours all

CAPTAIN

更木剣八

This sword demon lives only to fight. Without even passing the entrance exam, he defeated two hundred guards in a challenge, including the former Eleventh Company captain, and rose to captain.

KENPACHI ZARAKI

CHARACTER DATA

BIRTHDAY/NOVEMBER 19

HEIGHT/6′8″

WEIGHT/198 LBS

COAT LINING/KESHI MURASAKI (LAVENDER)

HOBBY/NAPPING

SPECIAL SKILL/DUELING

FOOD:
LIKES/HAS NO FAVORITES
DISLIKES/FERMENTED SOYBEANS

HOW HE SPENDS HIS DAYS OFF/NAPPING

SPECIAL NOTES

TOP SECRET

He always bathes before going to bed because he tends to perspire a lot. For that reason, he washes his hair every day. His hair is very stiff because he uses soap. He says his hair is easier to style this way and prefers this. Chôjiro Sasakibe once offered him conditioner at a communal bath. The next day, Kenpachi's hair was so smooth and silky that he couldn't style his hair, and his locks wouldn't stay in place. Now he only uses soap. He kind of dislikes Sasakibe as well.

BATTLE DATA

KENPACHI ZARAKI

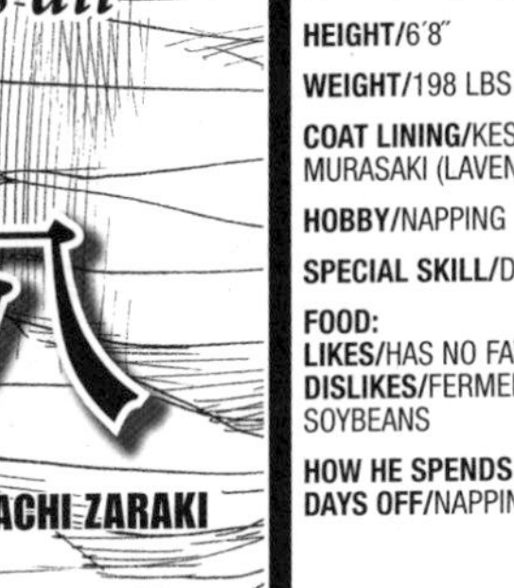
ATTACK 199
DEFENSE 80
MOBILITY 60
KIDÔ/ SPIRITUAL PRESSURE 0
INTELLECT 50
STAMINA 100

His physical prowess and fighting skills are beyond question, but he scores dead last among the captains in kidô readings.

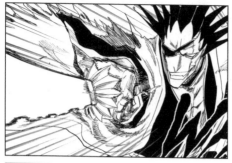

"THE STRONGEST ONE... WHICH ONE IS IT?!"

Kenpachi gets more satisfaction when facing a strong opponent than from anything else. In fact, combat to him is his reason for living. He couldn't care less about his duties as a captain in the face of such a thrill.

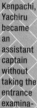

Like Kenpachi, Yachiru became an assistant captain without taking the entrance examination.

草鹿やちる

ASSISTANT CAPTAIN

YACHIRU KUSAJISHI

CHARACTER DATA

BIRTHDAY/FEBRUARY 12

HEIGHT/3′7″

WEIGHT/34 LBS

HOBBY/EATING CANDY

SPECIAL SKILL/INFILTRATION

FOOD:
LIKES/KONPEITO CANDY
DISLIKES/NONE

HOW SHE SPENDS HER DAYS OFF/HAVING FUN WITH MEMBERS OF THE SOCIETY OF FEMALE SOUL REAPERS

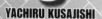

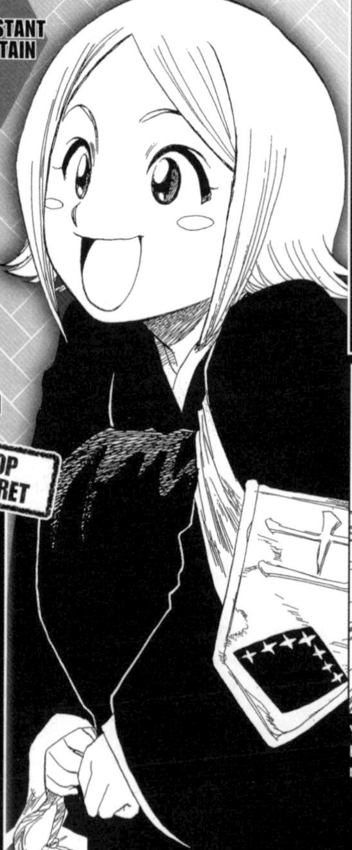

SPECIAL NOTES

TOP SECRET

She is chairwoman of the Society of Female Soul Reapers. Whenever Kenpachi takes a nap she has some free time, so she'll go out to play. She likes to visit the Kuchiki mansion, which offers spaciousness, beauty and everything that she could want. She loves to go shopping for toys and candy, which she buys with money from the Society of Female Soul Reapers. She stores her precious finds in an empty room at the Kuchiki mansion. This is kept a secret from Byakuya.

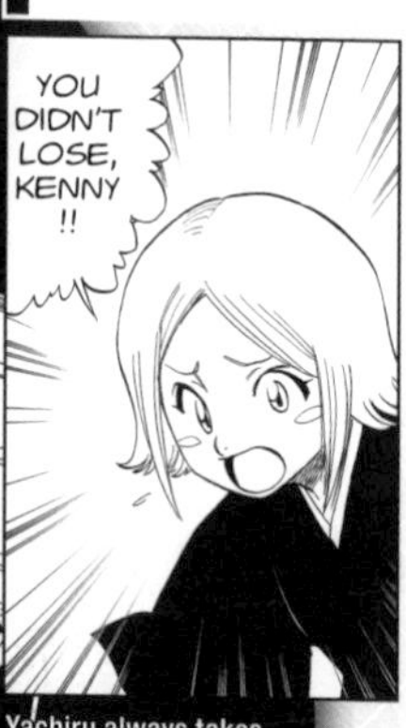

YOU DIDN'T LOSE, KENNY !!

Yachiru always takes Kenpachi's side, whatever the reason or occasion.

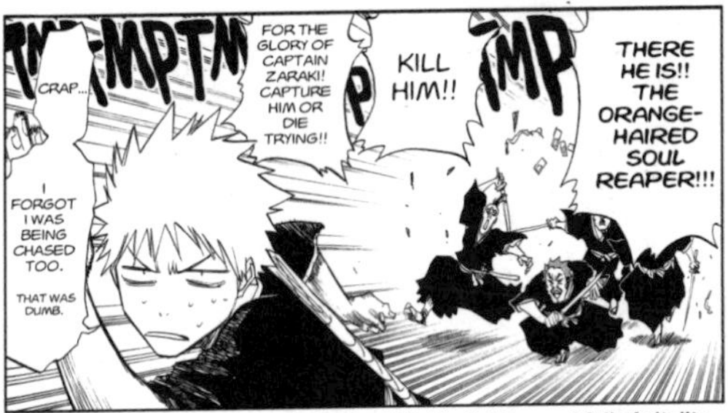
THERE HE IS!! THE ORANGE-HAIRED SOUL REAPER!!!
KILL HIM!!
FOR THE GLORY OF CAPTAIN ZARAKI! CAPTURE HIM OR DIE TRYING!!
CRAP...
I FORGOT I WAS BEING CHASED TOO.
THAT WAS DUMB.

Everyone in Zaraki's company is highly skilled in fighting and full of vitality. You don't want any of them for an enemy.

THE STRONGEST FIGHTING FORCE AMONG THE THIRTEEN COURT GUARD COMPANIES

The company's doctrine of dominating in battle is what appeals to its members; they believe that fighting is what makes life worth living. This is what separates Eleventh Company from the others and makes them the strongest squad.

EVERYONE LOVES FIGHTING EVEN MORE THAN THEIR THREE DAILY MEALS! ZARAKI'S COMPANY

Every member of Eleventh Company, nicknamed Zaraki's Company, is a strong fighter who believes that if you're going to die anyway, go down fighting gloriously. The men of Eleventh Company are more than qualified for the positions they occupy, and some, like Iba and Abarai, have moved on to become assistant captains of other companies.

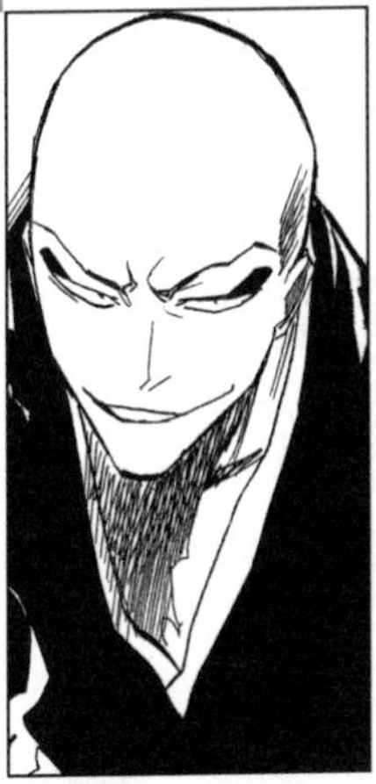

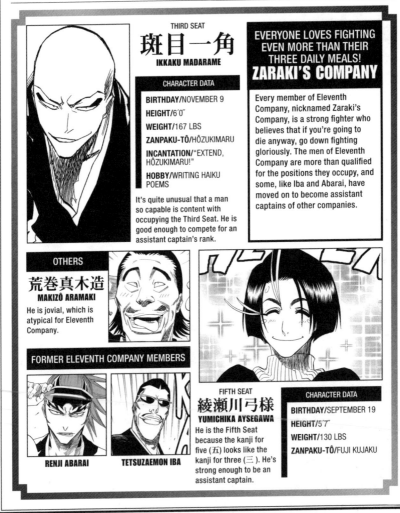

THIRD SEAT

斑目一角

IKKAKU MADARAME

CHARACTER DATA

BIRTHDAY/NOVEMBER 9

HEIGHT/6′0″

WEIGHT/167 LBS

ZANPAKU-TÔ/HÔZUKIMARU

INCANTATION/"EXTEND, HÔZUKIMARU!"

HOBBY/WRITING HAIKU POEMS

It's quite unusual that a man so capable is content with occupying the Third Seat. He is good enough to compete for an assistant captain's rank.

OTHERS

荒巻真木造

MAKIZÔ ARAMAKI

He is jovial, which is atypical for Eleventh Company.

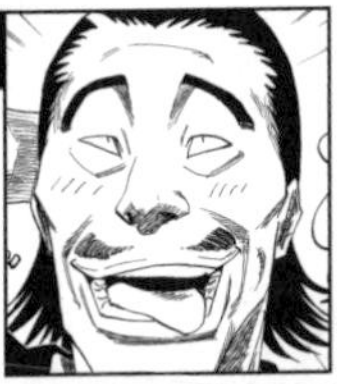

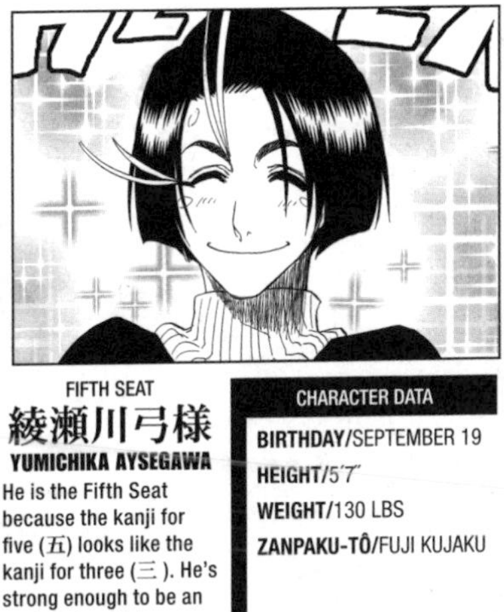

FIFTH SEAT

綾瀬川弓様

YUMICHIKA AYSEGAWA

He is the Fifth Seat because the kanji for five (五) looks like the kanji for three (三). He's strong enough to be an assistant captain.

CHARACTER DATA

BIRTHDAY/SEPTEMBER 19

HEIGHT/5′7″

WEIGHT/130 LBS

ZANPAKU-TÔ/FUJI KUJAKU

FORMER ELEVENTH COMPANY MEMBERS

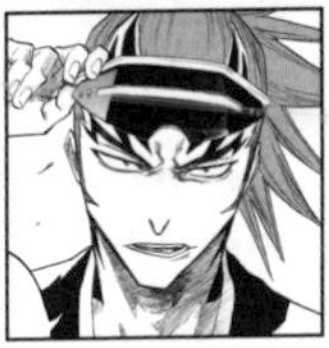

RENJI ABARAI

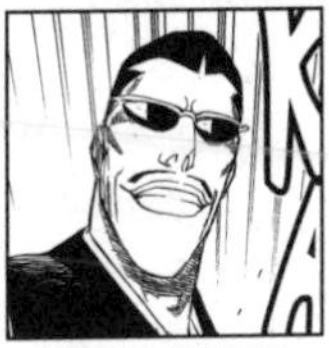

TETSUZAEMON IBA

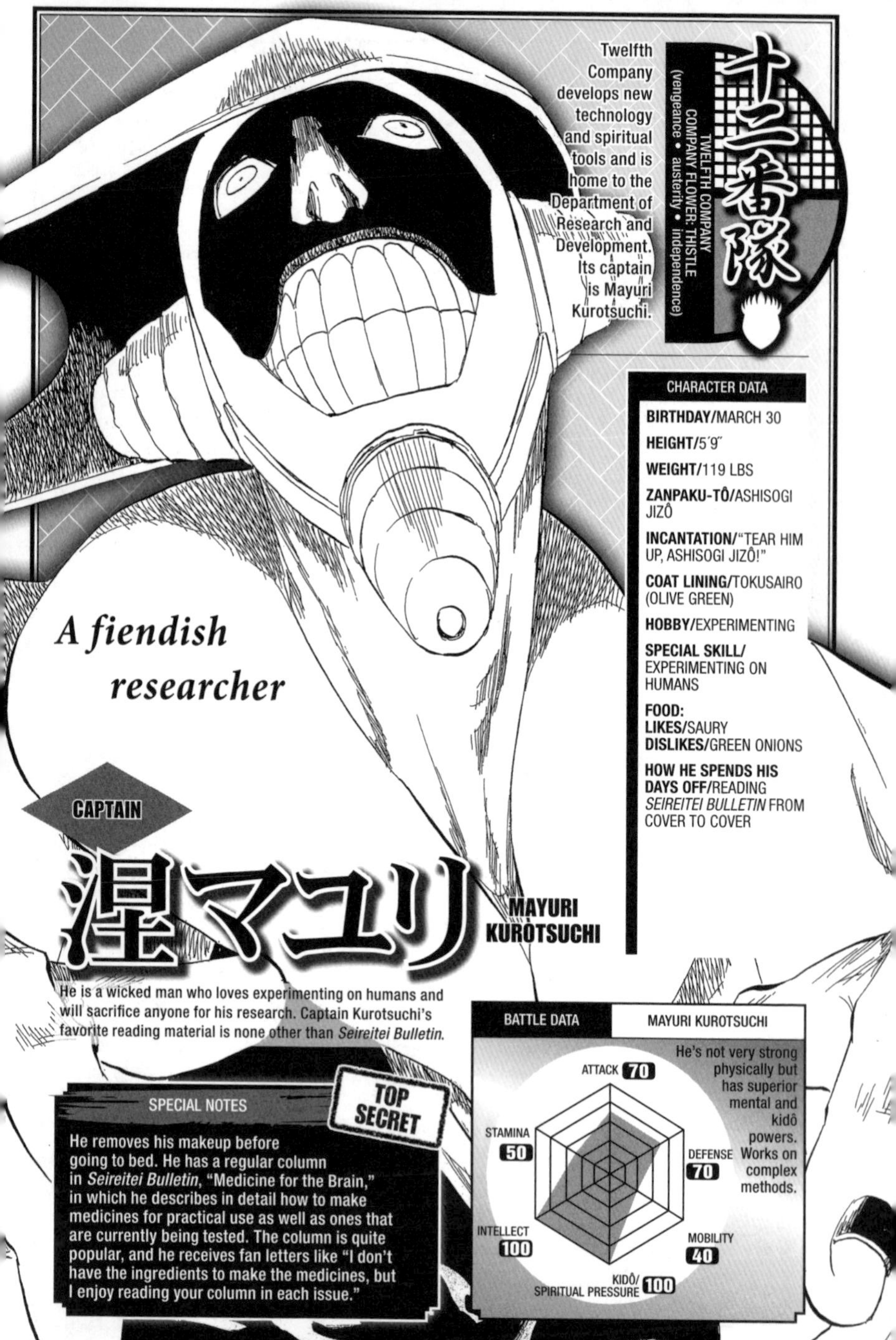

十二番隊

TWELFTH COMPANY
COMPANY FLOWER: THISTLE
(vengeance • austerity • independence)

Twelfth Company develops new technology and spiritual tools and is home to the Department of Research and Development. Its captain is Mayuri Kurotsuchi.

A fiendish researcher

CAPTAIN

涅マユリ

MAYURI KUROTSUCHI

He is a wicked man who loves experimenting on humans and will sacrifice anyone for his research. Captain Kurotsuchi's favorite reading material is none other than *Seireitei Bulletin*.

CHARACTER DATA

BIRTHDAY/MARCH 30

HEIGHT/5′9″

WEIGHT/119 LBS

ZANPAKU-TÔ/ASHISOGI JIZÔ

INCANTATION/"TEAR HIM UP, ASHISOGI JIZÔ!"

COAT LINING/TOKUSAIRO (OLIVE GREEN)

HOBBY/EXPERIMENTING

SPECIAL SKILL/ EXPERIMENTING ON HUMANS

FOOD:
LIKES/SAURY
DISLIKES/GREEN ONIONS

HOW HE SPENDS HIS DAYS OFF/READING *SEIREITEI BULLETIN* FROM COVER TO COVER

SPECIAL NOTES

TOP SECRET

He removes his makeup before going to bed. He has a regular column in *Seireitei Bulletin*, "Medicine for the Brain," in which he describes in detail how to make medicines for practical use as well as ones that are currently being tested. The column is quite popular, and he receives fan letters like "I don't have the ingredients to make the medicines, but I enjoy reading your column in each issue."

BATTLE DATA | **MAYURI KUROTSUCHI**

ATTACK	70
DEFENSE	70
MOBILITY	40
KIDÔ/SPIRITUAL PRESSURE	100
INTELLECT	100
STAMINA	50

He's not very strong physically but has superior mental and kidô powers. Works on complex methods.

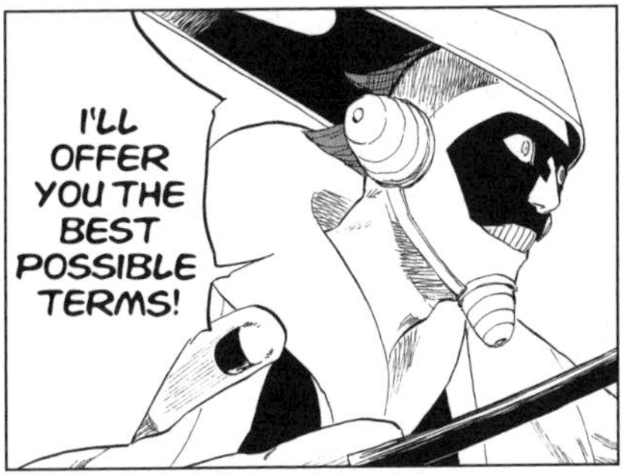
I'LL OFFER YOU THE BEST POSSIBLE TERMS!

"HOW WOULD YOU LIKE TO BE MY RESEARCH SUBJECT?"

Captain Kurotsuchi doesn't take much interest in the happenings in the Soul Society or in the Thirteen Court Guard Companies. Instead, all of his efforts go into researching and experimenting with new techniques. As for the ryoka that infiltrated the Soul Society, he fought them solely for the purpose of using them as test subjects. Could he be the model research scientist?!

SOLELY FOR RESEARCH

Captain Kurotsuchi, who is fascinated only by research, has a favorite motto: Listen, I'm really not interested in you. It can be extremely dangerous if he happens to take an interest in you, in which case you should flee immediately.

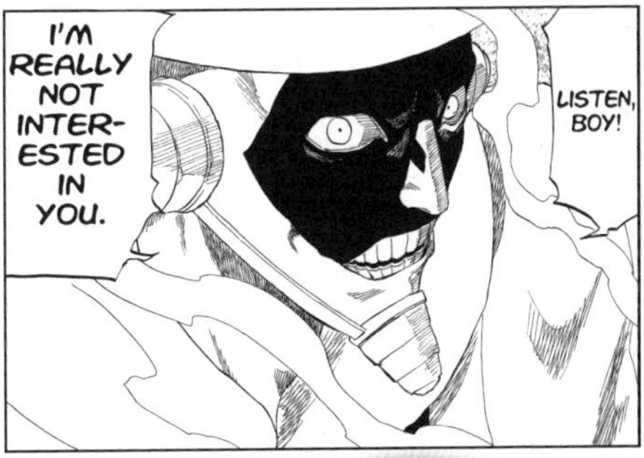
LISTEN, BOY!
I'M REALLY NOT INTERESTED IN YOU.

ASSISTANT CAPTAIN

涅ネム

NEMU KUROTSUCHI

Assistant Captain Nemu Kurotsuchi is a quasi-soul who was created through a combination of Captain Kurotsuchi's gigai technology and substitute soul technology. Perhaps because Captain Kurotsuchi's blood flows through her, Nemu has interests identical to the captain's and spends her days off in the same way he does.

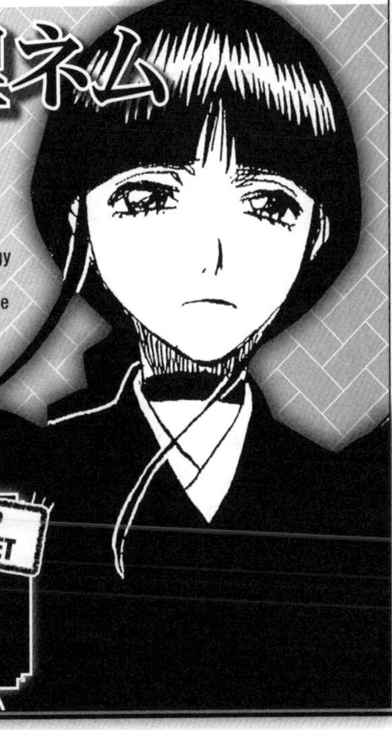

CHARACTER DATA

BIRTHDAY/MARCH 30

HEIGHT/5′6″

WEIGHT/115 LBS

HOBBY/EXPERIMENTING

SPECIAL SKILL/ EXPERIMENTING ON HUMANS

FOOD:
LIKES/SAURY
DISLIKES/GREEN ONIONS

HOW SHE SPENDS HER DAYS OFF/READING *SEIREITEI BULLETIN* FROM COVER TO COVER

SPECIAL NOTES

TOP SECRET

She is poised to become the next chairwoman of the Society of Female Soul Reapers. At Yachiru's request, Nemu built a secret meeting place in the Kuchiki mansion. Besides the hideout, the Kuchiki mansion has many hidden devices (like passageways under the tatami mats), which are unknown even to Byakuya.

JUST BE QUIET AND FOLLOW ME! A CAPRICIOUS AND DOMINEERING ONE-MAN COMPANY

Twelfth Company is a one-man company, with Mayuri Kurotsuchi having absolute authority. If one dares to utter an opinion, he could very well find himself reconstructed into a human bomb. The secret to longevity here is working quietly and without being noticed.

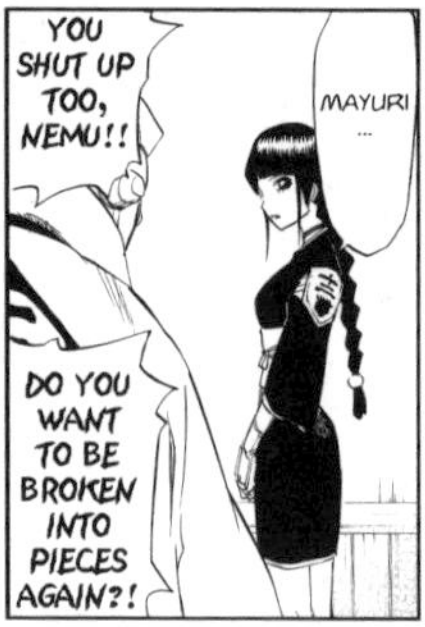
YOU SHUT UP TOO, NEMU!!
MAYURI ...
DO YOU WANT TO BE BROKEN INTO PIECES AGAIN?!

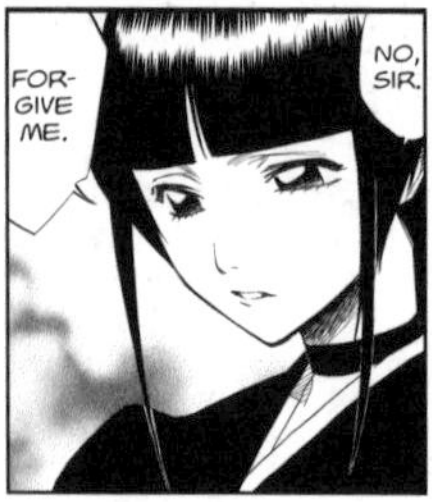
NO, SIR.
FOR-GIVE ME.

Company members, including even the assistant captain, are not allowed to voice an opinion.

A PERSONAL WAY OF SHOWING LOVE

Captain Kurotsuchi has a unique way of demonstrating his love; he emphatically refers to Assistant Captain Nemu as "my daughter." He selects everything to his personal taste, whether it's a birthday present, food or even his daily routine. Sometimes the physical contact is a bit extreme, but could that be the captain's way of expressing affection? The mystery deepens...

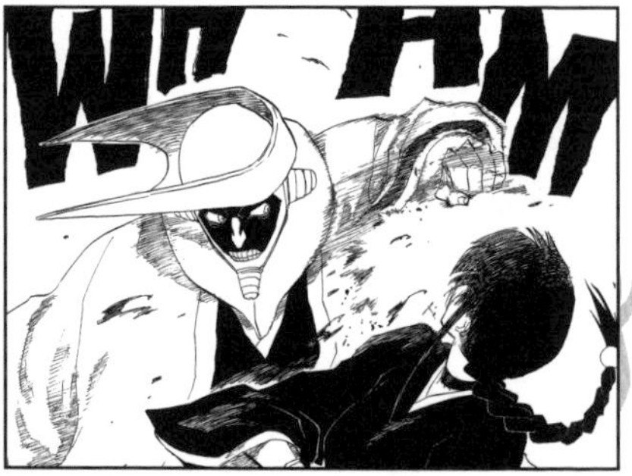

THE CULMINATION OF BODY MODIFICATION!

THE TRANSFORMATION OF MASTER MAYURI

Naturally, Captain Kurotsuchi doesn't limit his research to others and has conducted experiments on himself. Let us introduce you to his beautiful and brilliant transformations. Behold.

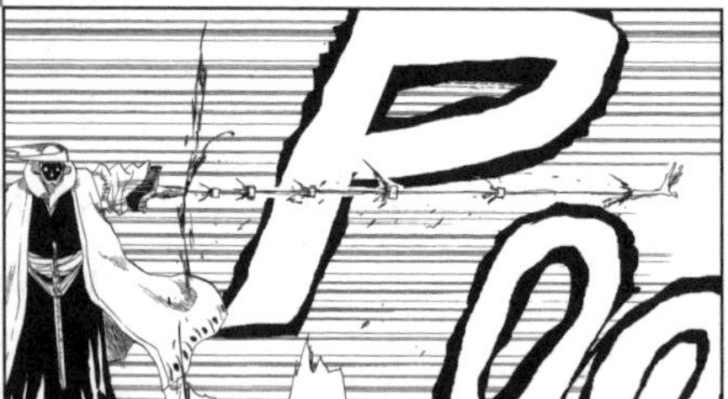

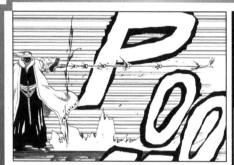

Arm extensions, regeneration, liquefaction... There is no limit to Captain Kurotsuchi's metamorphoses. Look forward to his new innovations!

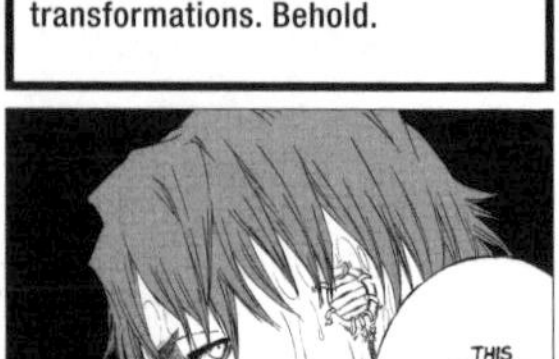
THIS DOESN'T INTEREST ME.

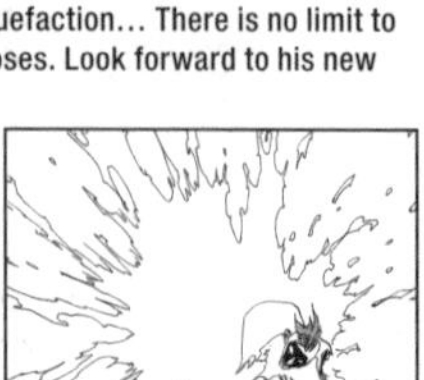

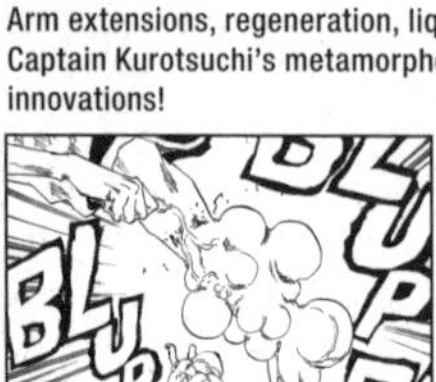
BLUP
BLUP
BLUP

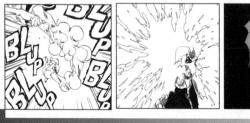

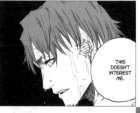

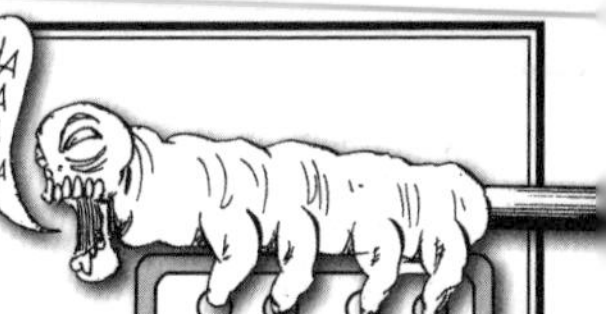
HA HA HA HA

The
SOUL SOCIETY'S TOP TECHNICIANS
技術開発局
DEPARTMENT OF RESEARCH AND DEVELOPMENT

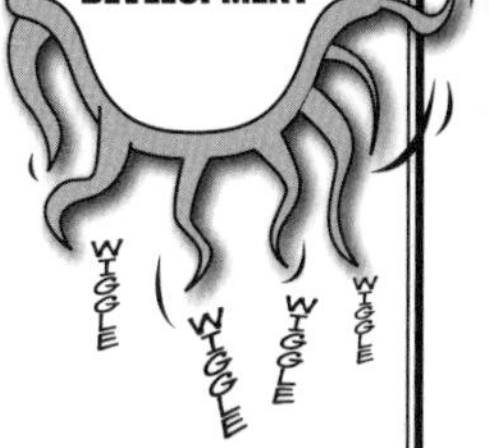
WIGGLE
WIGGLE
WIGGLE
WIGGLE

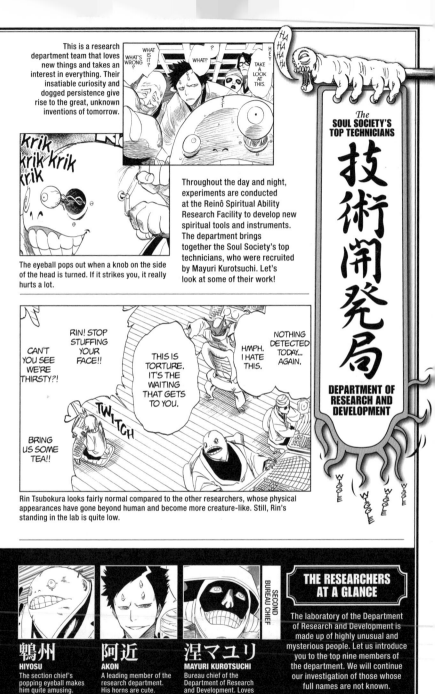

This is a research department team that loves new things and takes an interest in everything. Their insatiable curiosity and dogged persistence give rise to the great, unknown inventions of tomorrow.

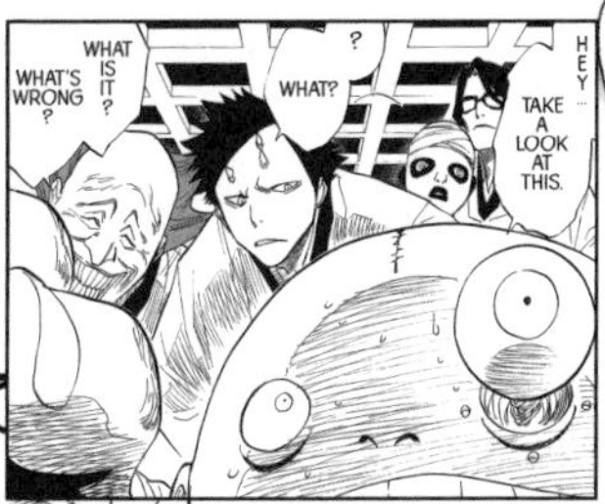
HEY... TAKE A LOOK AT THIS.
?
WHAT?
WHAT IS IT?
WHAT'S WRONG?

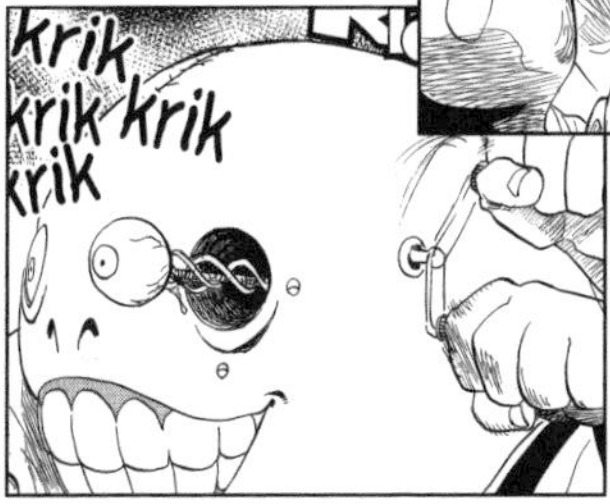
krik krik krik krik

The eyeball pops out when a knob on the side of the head is turned. If it strikes you, it really hurts a lot.

Throughout the day and night, experiments are conducted at the Reinô Spiritual Ability Research Facility to develop new spiritual tools and instruments. The department brings together the Soul Society's top technicians, who were recruited by Mayuri Kurotsuchi. Let's look at some of their work!

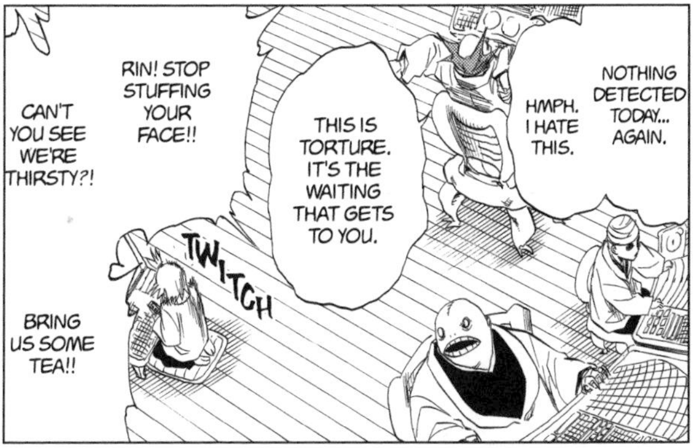
NOTHING DETECTED TODAY... AGAIN.
HMPH. I HATE THIS.
THIS IS TORTURE. IT'S THE WAITING THAT GETS TO YOU.
RIN! STOP STUFFING YOUR FACE!!
CAN'T YOU SEE WE'RE THIRSTY?!
TWITCH
BRING US SOME TEA!!

Rin Tsubokura looks fairly normal compared to the other researchers, whose physical appearances have gone beyond human and become more creature-like. Still, Rin's standing in the lab is quite low.

THE RESEARCHERS AT A GLANCE

The laboratory of the Department of Research and Development is made up of highly unusual and mysterious people. Let us introduce you to the top nine members of the department. We will continue our investigation of those whose full names are not known.

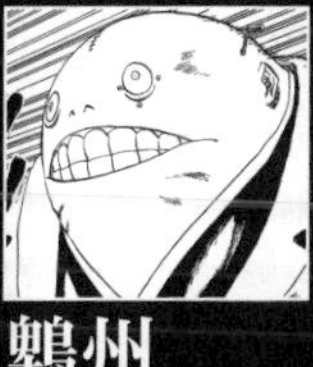

鵯州
HIYOSU
The section chief's popping eyeball makes him quite amusing.

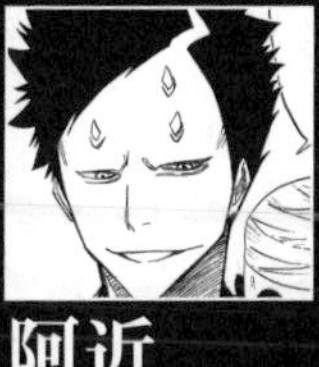

阿近
AKON
A leading member of the research department. His horns are cute.

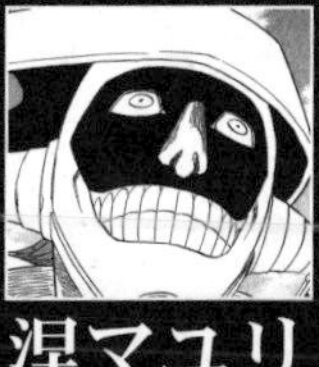

SECOND BUREAU CHIEF

涅マユリ
MAYURI KUROTSUCHI
Bureau chief of the Department of Research and Development. Loves to experiment on humans.

DUTY 1

TO RESEARCH AND DEVELOP NEW TECHNOLOGY AND SPIRITUAL TOOLS

This is the main function of the Department of Research and Development. They have invented countless items, including the gigai and Soul Candy. Incidentally, this department manufactured Captain Zaraki's eyepatch.

Tools like the gokon tekkô, which forcibly removes the soul from the body, and the Soul Pager are also this department's inventions. Other inventions are top secret.

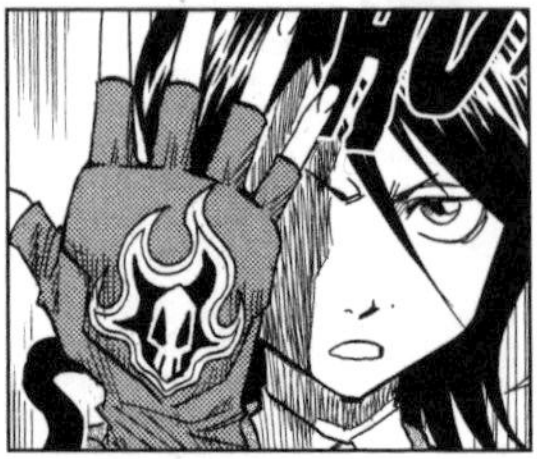

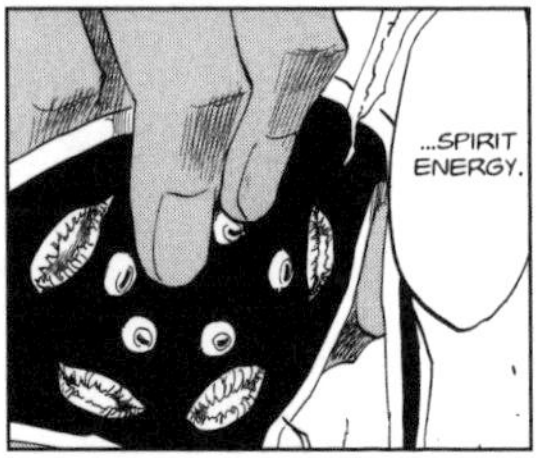
...SPIRIT ENERGY.

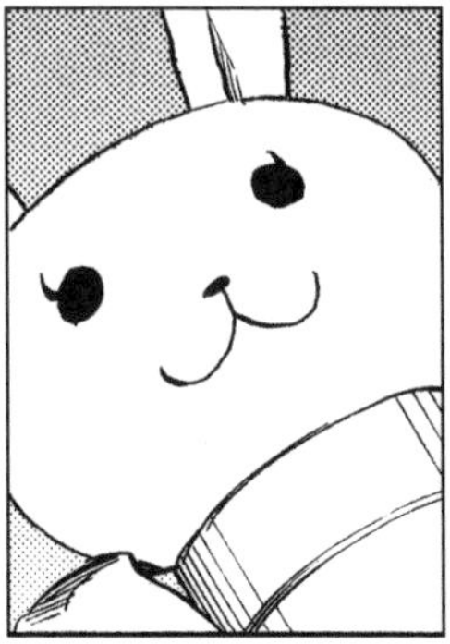

DUTY 2

TO MEASURE SPIRITUAL WAVES AND OVERSEE COMMUNICATIONS

The Spiritual Wave Measurement Lab closely monitors the world of the living to ensure spiritual stability. The Communication Research Section oversees transmissions between the human world and the Soul Society, carrying out this other important function of the department.
If an incident occurs, things become pretty hectic here, but otherwise, it's usually slow.

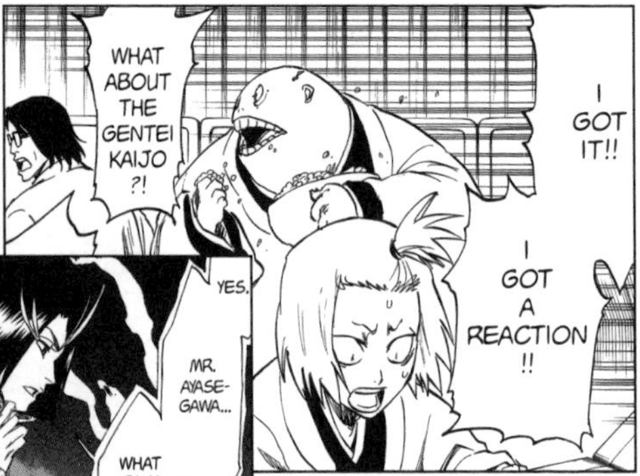
WHAT ABOUT THE GENTEI KAIJO ?!
I GOT IT!!
I GOT A REACTION !!

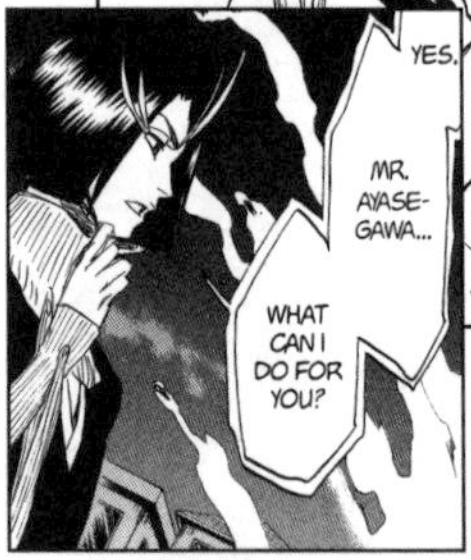
YES.
MR. AYASE-GAWA...
WHAT CAN I DO FOR YOU?

Low-ranking staff member Rin Tsubokura is the main operator. But more often than not, he has leftover bits of candy stuck to his mouth and displays considerable anxiety.

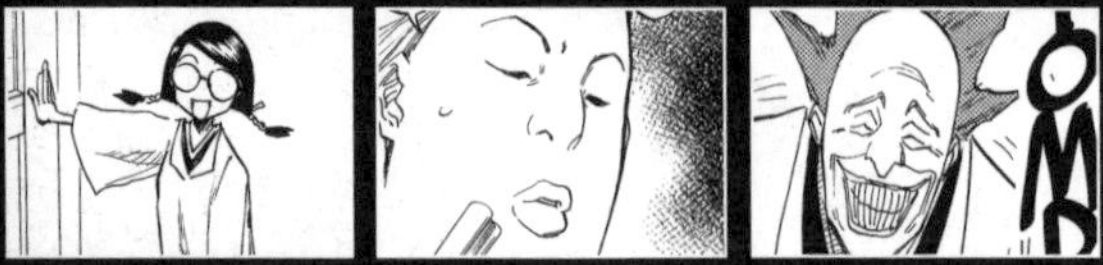

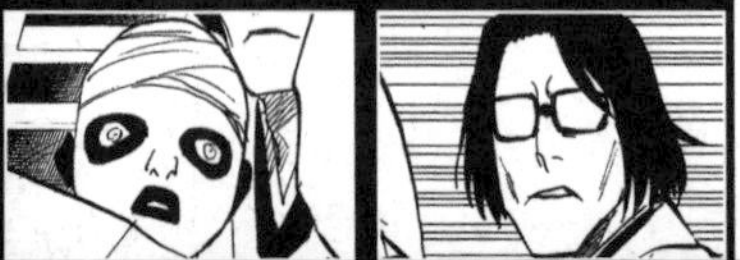

OTHER MEMBERS

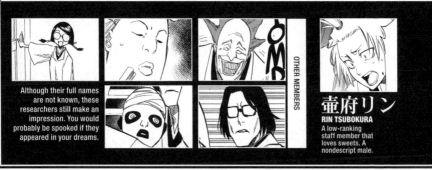

Although their full names are not known, these researchers still make an impression. You would probably be spooked if they appeared in your dreams.

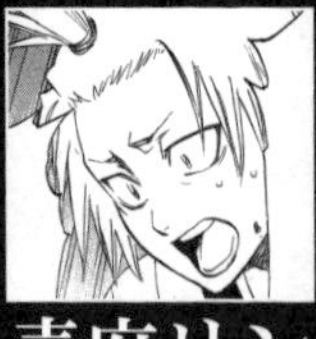

壷府リン
RIN TSUBOKURA
A low-ranking staff member that loves sweets. A nondescript male.

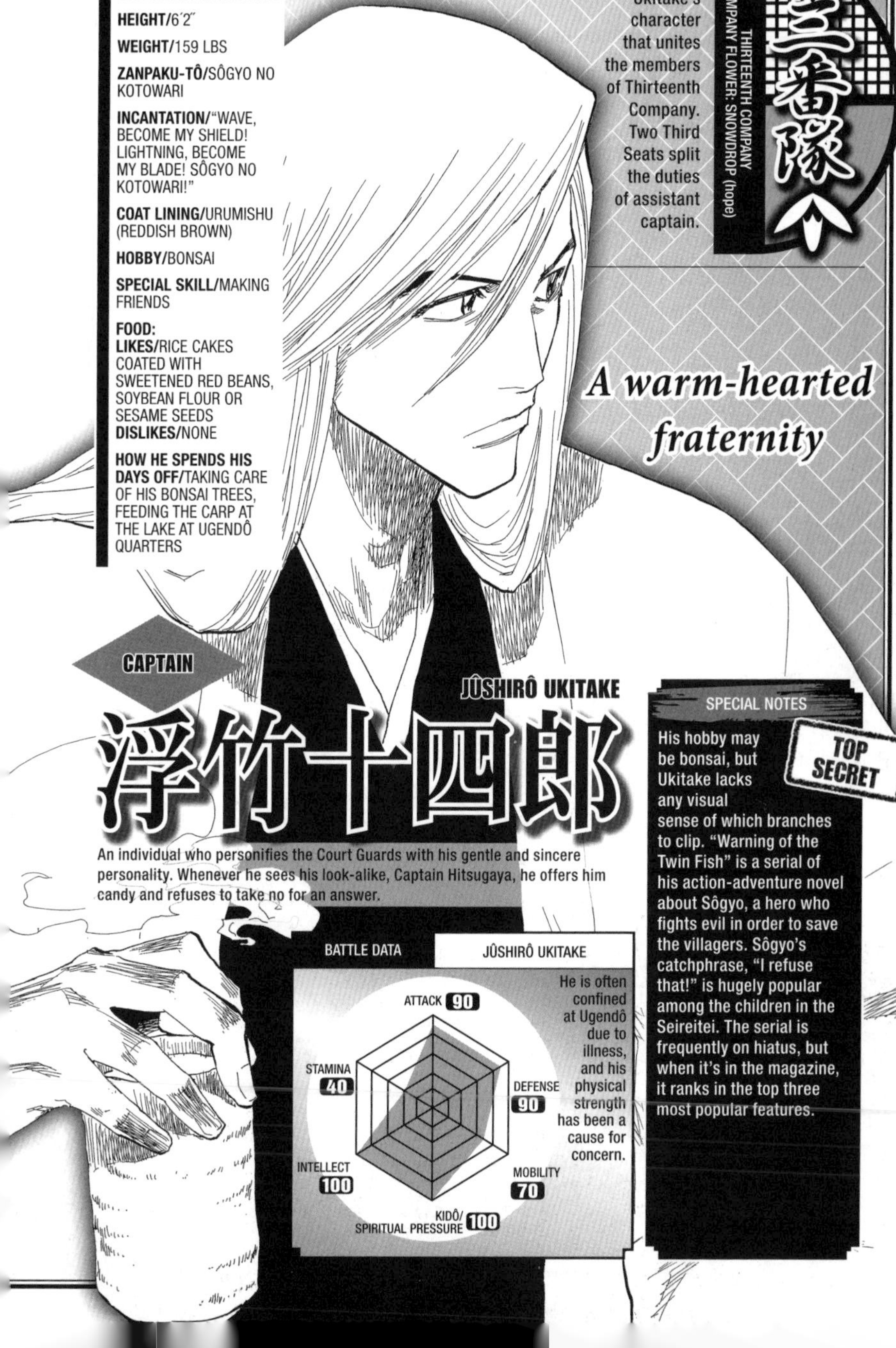

十三番隊

THIRTEENTH COMPANY
COMPANY FLOWER: SNOWDROP (hope)

Perhaps it is Captain Ukitake's character that unites the members of Thirteenth Company. Two Third Seats split the duties of assistant captain.

A warm-hearted fraternity

CHARACTER DATA

BIRTHDAY/DECEMBER 21

HEIGHT/6′2″

WEIGHT/159 LBS

ZANPAKU-TÔ/SÔGYO NO KOTOWARI

INCANTATION/"WAVE, BECOME MY SHIELD! LIGHTNING, BECOME MY BLADE! SÔGYO NO KOTOWARI!"

COAT LINING/URUMISHU (REDDISH BROWN)

HOBBY/BONSAI

SPECIAL SKILL/MAKING FRIENDS

FOOD:
LIKES/RICE CAKES COATED WITH SWEETENED RED BEANS, SOYBEAN FLOUR OR SESAME SEEDS
DISLIKES/NONE

HOW HE SPENDS HIS DAYS OFF/TAKING CARE OF HIS BONSAI TREES, FEEDING THE CARP AT THE LAKE AT UGENDÔ QUARTERS

CAPTAIN

JÛSHIRÔ UKITAKE

浮竹十四郎

An individual who personifies the Court Guards with his gentle and sincere personality. Whenever he sees his look-alike, Captain Hitsugaya, he offers him candy and refuses to take no for an answer.

SPECIAL NOTES

TOP SECRET

His hobby may be bonsai, but Ukitake lacks any visual sense of which branches to clip. "Warning of the Twin Fish" is a serial of his action-adventure novel about Sôgyo, a hero who fights evil in order to save the villagers. Sôgyo's catchphrase, "I refuse that!" is hugely popular among the children in the Seireitei. The serial is frequently on hiatus, but when it's in the magazine, it ranks in the top three most popular features.

BATTLE DATA | JÛSHIRÔ UKITAKE

ATTACK 90
DEFENSE 90
MOBILITY 70
KIDÔ/ SPIRITUAL PRESSURE 100
INTELLECT 100
STAMINA 40

He is often confined at Ugendô due to illness, and his physical strength has been a cause for concern.

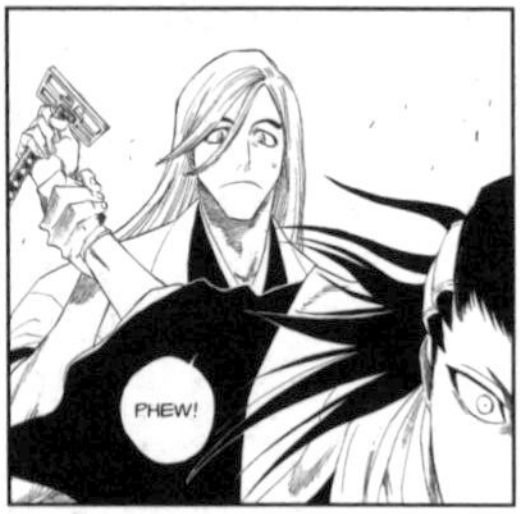
PHEW!

Captain Ukitake will step in to stop a pointless battle, even if it means confronting another captain.

"IF ONLY THIS FLEETING PEACE COULD LAST A LITTLE LONGER..."

Perhaps it was the battle with the Hollows in which he lost Assistant Captain Kaien, but ever since that incident Captain Ukitake has done his best to avoid violence. When his subordinate Rukia Kuchiki was sentenced to die by execution, he did everything in his power to overturn the conviction. It is this humane side of Captain Ukitake that creates the warm atmosphere in Thirteenth Company.

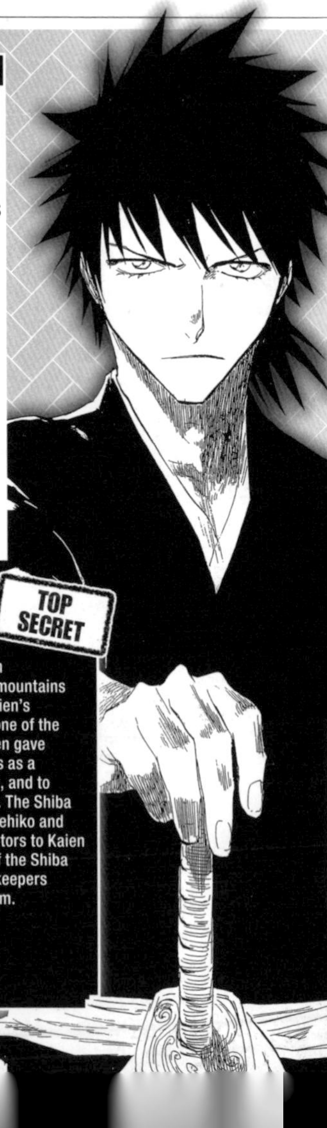

THE LATE ASSISTANT CAPTAIN

志波海燕

KAIEN SHIBA

This likable man often stood in for his ill captain. There is a rumor that a Soul Reaper resembling Kaien was among the ryoka who recently infiltrated the Seireitei.

CHARACTER DATA

BIRTHDAY/OCTOBER 27

HEIGHT/6′0″

WEIGHT/150 LBS

ZANPAKU-TÔ/NEJIBANA

INCANTATION/"RAGE ACROSS THE SEAS AND HEAVENS, NEJIBANA!"

HOBBY/NAPPING

SPECIAL SKILL/MAKING FRIENDS

FOOD:
LIKES/RICE CAKES COVERED WITH SWEETENED RED BEANS, SOYBEAN FLOUR OR SESAME SEEDS
DISLIKES/NONE

HOW HE SPENDS HIS DAYS OFF/TRAINING WITH HIS SUBORDINATES, RETURNING TO HIS HOME IN RUKONGAI

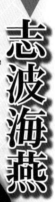

SPECIAL NOTES — **TOP SECRET**

Kaien found Ganju's cherished boar Bonnie when she was still a piglet in the mountains of Rukongai. At the time, Kaien's family, the Shiba, was still one of the Five Great Noble Clans. Kaien gave Bonnie the ribbon she wears as a present. Bonnie loved Kaien, and to this day isn't close to Ganju. The Shiba family's gatekeepers Koganehiko and Shiroganehiko were once tutors to Kaien and Kûkaku. After the fall of the Shiba family, only these two gatekeepers have continued to serve them.

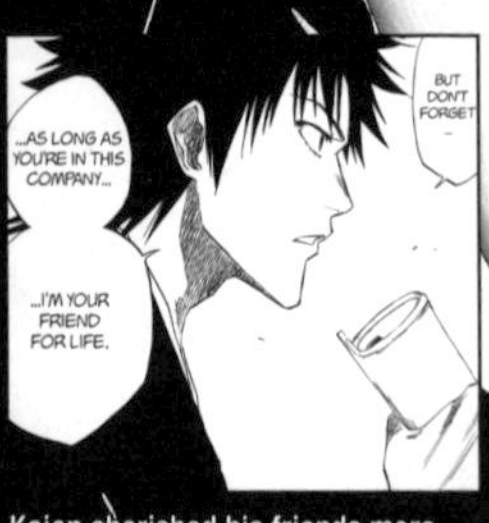
BUT DON'T FORGET
...AS LONG AS YOU'RE IN THIS COMPANY...
...I'M YOUR FRIEND FOR LIFE.

Kaien cherished his friends more than anything and loved them deeply. His spirit remains alive to this day.

THE BODY IS WEAK, BUT THE BOND IS STRONG! THE VIRTUES OF CAPTAIN UKITAKE

Captain Ukitake was born with a sickly constitution. Kotetsu and Kotsubaki are the Third Seats and are his reliable backups. Their devotion to the captain borders on rivalry, and they are often heard having heated arguments over who cares for the captain more. The two are very close.

THIRD SEAT
小椿仙太郎
SENTARÔ KOTSUBAKI

CHARACTER DATA
BIRTHDAY/SEPTEMBER 22
HEIGHT/6´0˝
WEIGHT/165 LBS

One always knows where he is by his loud voice. He has a stern look and a gruff voice, but he's warmhearted and thinks of his comrades. He respects Captain Ukitake just as much as Kiyone (his own words).

THIRD SEAT
虎徹清音
KIYONE KOTETSU

CHARACTER DATA
BIRTHDAY/SEPTEMBER 22
HEIGHT/5´1˝
WEIGHT/95 LBS

The younger sister of Assistant Captain Isane Kotetsu of Fourth Company. In contrast to her tall sister, Kiyone is small in stature. She definitely has as much respect for Captain Ukitake as Sentarô (her own words).

STAND-INS FOR ASSISTANT CAPTAIN
THE TWO THIRD SEATS

Instead of an assistant captain, Thirteenth Company has two Third Seats fulfilling the duties. They are the only squad among the Thirteen Court Guard Companies to have made such a radical change to its organization. But whatever the case, these two Third Seats make an excellent combination.

朽木ルキア

MEMBER

RUKIA KUCHIKI

Although she has no official rank, she has the power of a high-ranking Court Guard. Her situation can be explained by her connections to her brother-in-law, Byakuya Kuchiki. She was a childhood friend of Renji Abarai of Sixth Company.

CHARACTER DATA

BIRTHDAY/JANUARY 14

HEIGHT/4′9″

WEIGHT/73 LBS

ZANPAKU-TÔ/SODE NO SHIRAYUKI

INCANTATION/"DANCE, SODE NO SHIRAYUKI!"

HOBBY/CLIMBING HIGH PLACES

FOOD:
LIKES/CUCUMBERS AND DUMPLINGS
DISLIKES/NONE

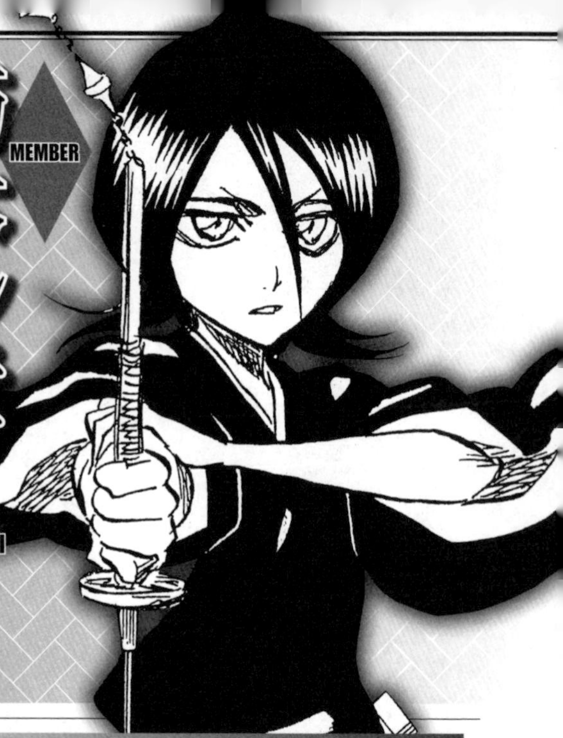

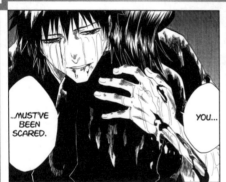

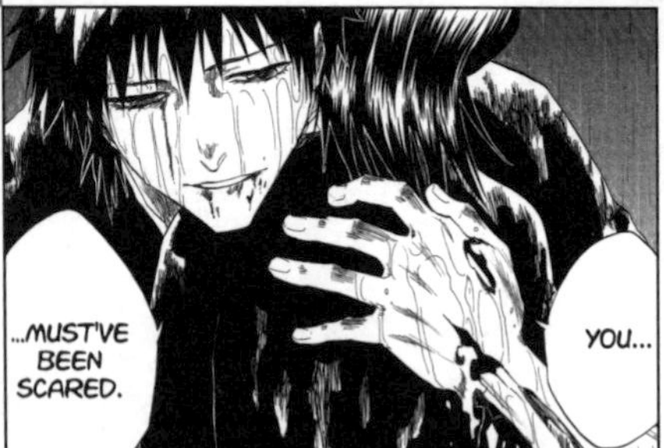
YOU...
...MUST'VE BEEN SCARED.

THE MYSTERY OF THIRTEENTH COMPANY

THE VACANT ASSISTANT CAPTAIN'S SEAT

This is the only company among the Thirteen Court Guard Companies without an assistant captain. It was their way of honoring the late Assistant Captain Kaien, whom they remember to this day. They have suffered an enormous loss.

ONE WHO IS IRREPLACEABLE

When Hollows killed his wife, Kaien swore to avenge her, but they stole his body instead. Rukia happened to be at the scene and thrust her sword into him. His parting words to her were, "Thank you. Now I can leave my heart behind." He then died, leaving behind a deep wound that could not be healed.

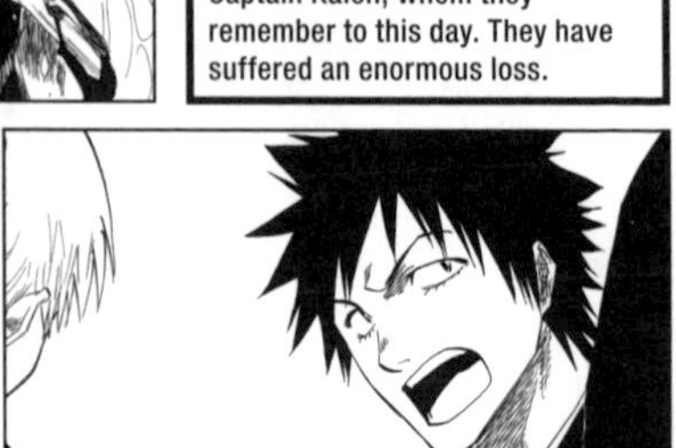

NEW MEMBERS WANTED

Come Forth, Thirteen Court Guard Companies!

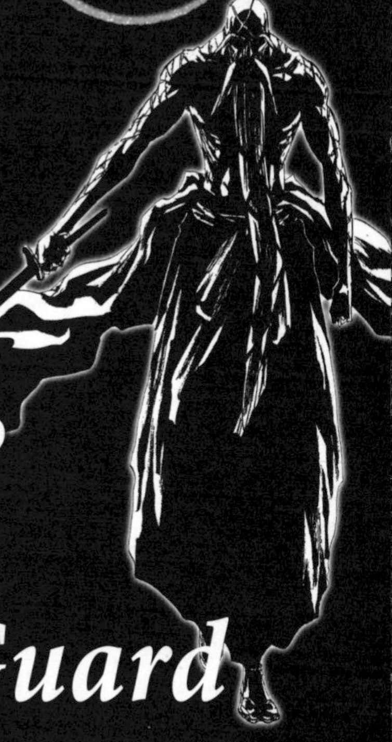

For all who aspire to become members of the Thirteen Court Guard Companies, I now present messages from every captain and assistant captain! Which company will you apply to? Think long and hard before deciding!

Includes messages to Soul Reaper candidates from

EVERY CAPTAIN AND ASSISTANT CAPTAIN!

CONTENTS

1. What kind of person do you seek?
2. What are the barracks and members like?
3. Any stipulations?
4. A word to the Soul Reaper candidate.

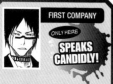

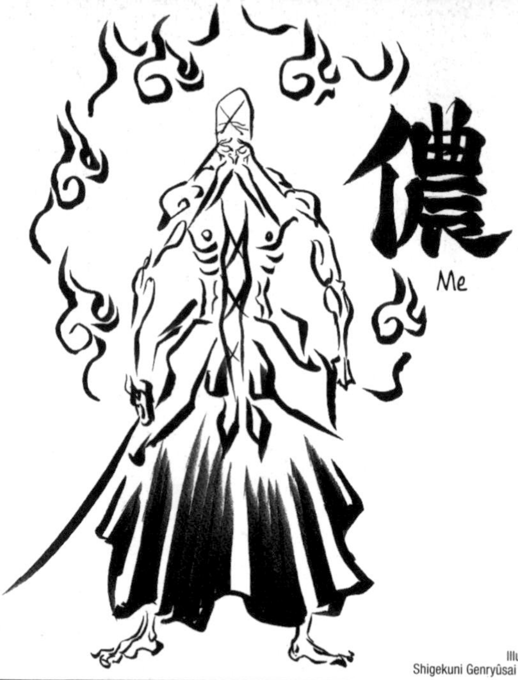

僕
Me

Illustrated by
Shigekuni Genryûsai Yamamoto

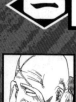

SHIGEKUNI GENRYÛSAI YAMAMOTO

1. Someone devoted, who believes in justice.
2. They are fine.
3. Nothing in particular.
4. I shall personally train you.

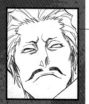

CHÔJIRÔ SASAKIBE

1. Someone young and capable of growing plants.
2. A mix of East meets West
3. Nothing in particular.
4. First Company is livelier than it looks. Apply! The captain general holds a tea ceremony once a month.

NEW MEMBERS WANTED

FIRST COMPANY

ONLY HERE

SPEAKS CANDIDLY!

NINTH COMPANY
ASSISTANT CAPTAIN
SHÛHEI HISAGI

First Company might seem stuffy at first, because Captain General Shigekuni Genryûsai Yamamoto is their captain. In fact, there's a lot going on because of things like the captain's monthly tea ceremonies and the assistant captain's English lessons! What's more, First Company's barracks are near a bathhouse and stone sauna that have also been featured in this magazine. This company is perfect for you if you want to get stronger and still want a place where you can relax and recuperate!

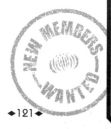

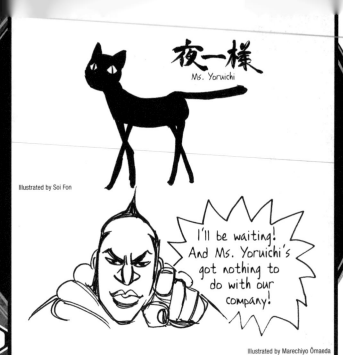

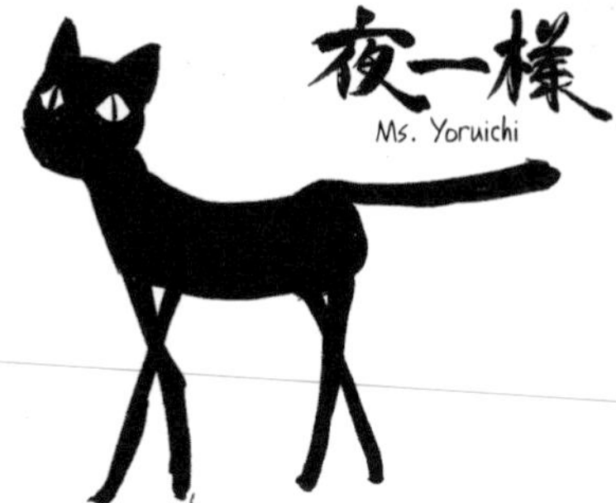
夜一様
Ms. Yoruichi

Illustrated by Soi Fon

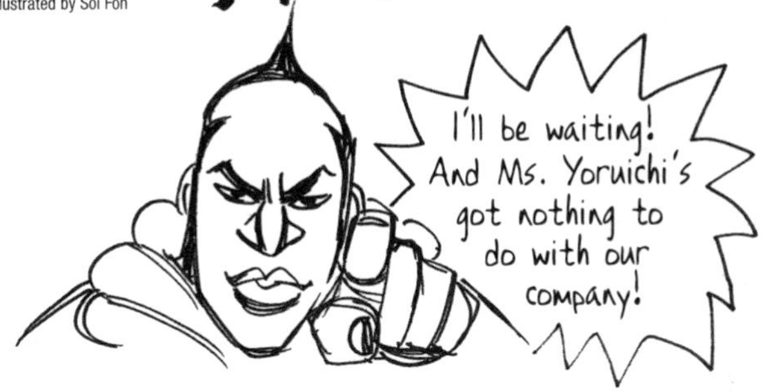
I'll be waiting! And Ms. Yoruichi's got nothing to do with our company!

Illustrated by Marechiyo Ômaeda

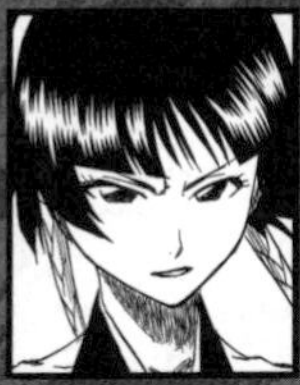

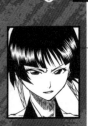

SOI FON

❶ No opinion.
❷ No opinion.
❸ No opinion.
❹ Only those willing to give their lives need apply.

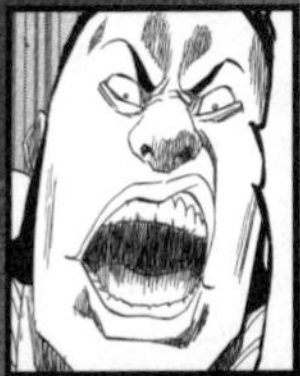

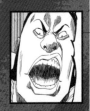

MARECHIYO ÔMAEDA

❶ Someone who will respect me.
❷ Thanks to me, our barracks are the only ones with floor heating in every room, automatic doors and air conditioning! How amazing is that?!
❸ Those who complain and can't work are no good.
❹ I'm willing to invite you to my mansion once in a while.

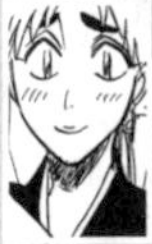

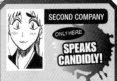

SECOND COMPANY

ONLY HERE **SPEAKS CANDIDLY!**

FOURTH COMPANY ASSISTANT CAPTAIN
ISANE KOTETSU

Second Company is famous for doing countless renovations that have made its barracks modern and luxurious. Word has it that there's been digging lately for an open-air spa in the rear training grounds. I really wish Fourth Company had one too.

NEW MEMBERS WANTED

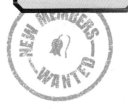

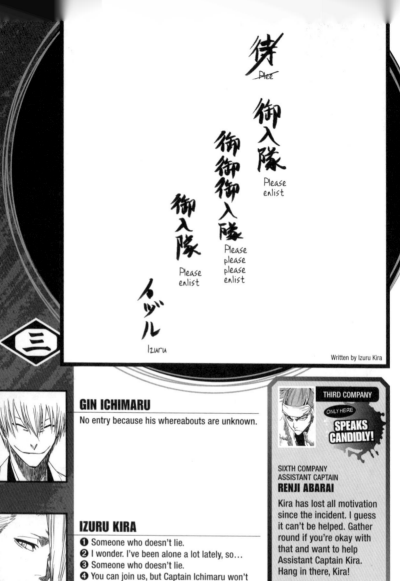

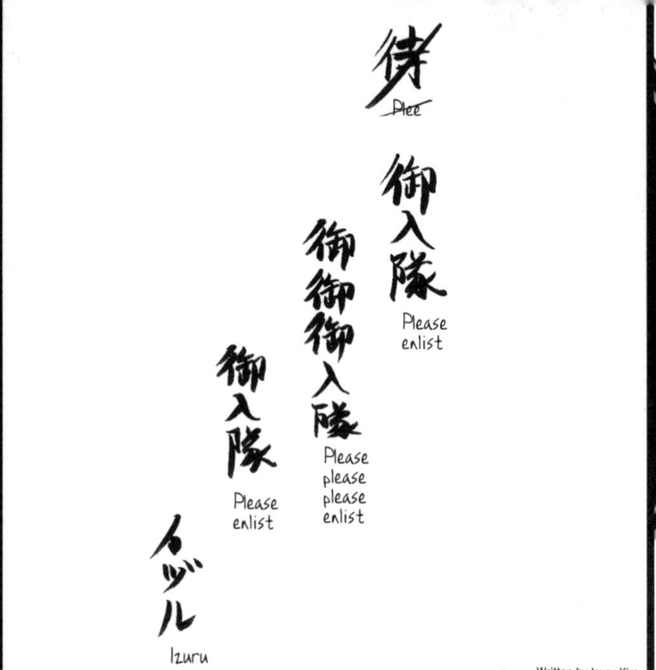
~~Plee~~
御入隊
Please enlist
御御御入隊
Please please please enlist
御入隊
Please enlist
イヅル
Izuru

Written by Izuru Kira

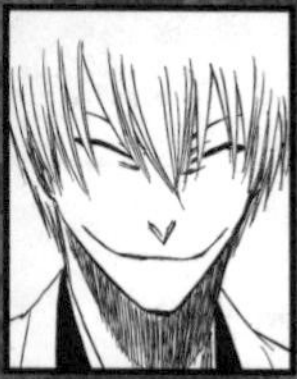

GIN ICHIMARU

No entry because his whereabouts are unknown.

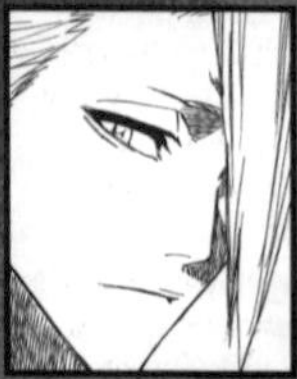

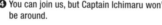

IZURU KIRA

1. Someone who doesn't lie.
2. I wonder. I've been alone a lot lately, so…
3. Someone who doesn't lie.
4. You can join us, but Captain Ichimaru won't be around.

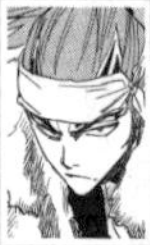

THIRD COMPANY

ONLY HERE **SPEAKS CANDIDLY!**

SIXTH COMPANY
ASSISTANT CAPTAIN
RENJI ABARAI

Kira has lost all motivation since the incident. I guess it can't be helped. Gather round if you're okay with that and want to help Assistant Captain Kira. Hang in there, Kira!

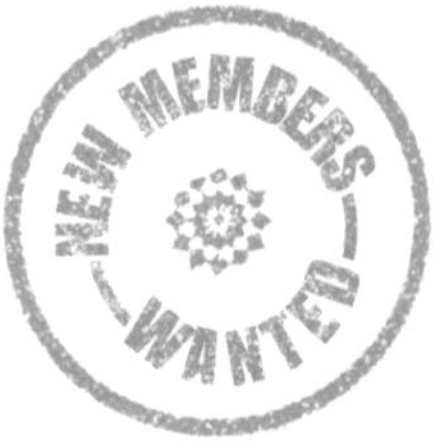
NEW MEMBERS
WANTED

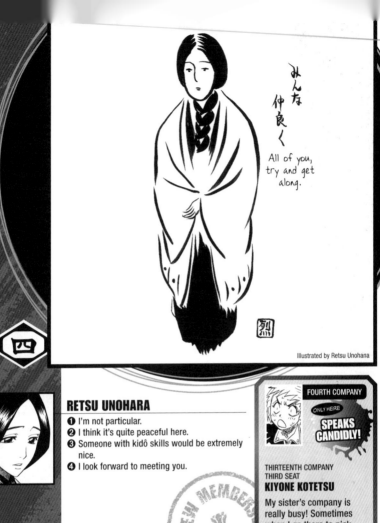

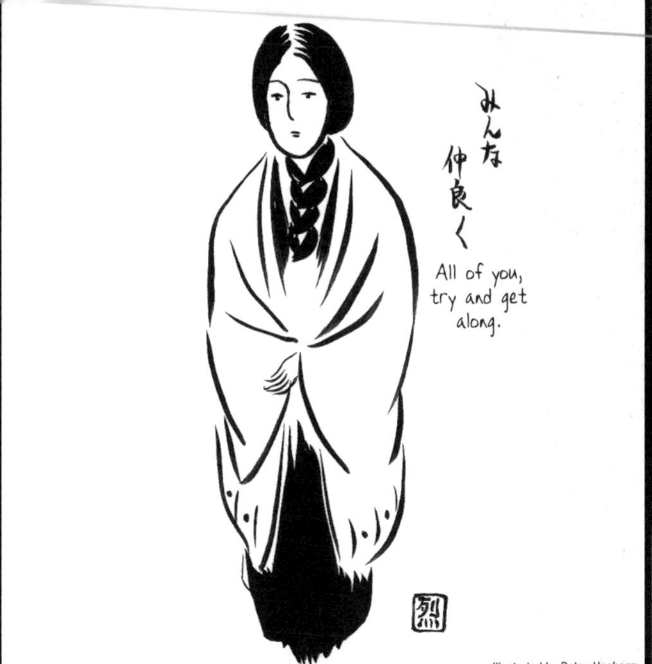
みんな仲良く
All of you, try and get along.

Illustrated by Retsu Unohana

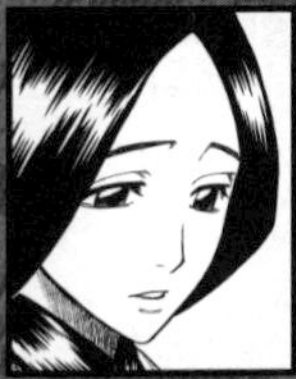

RETSU UNOHARA

❶ I'm not particular.
❷ I think it's quite peaceful here.
❸ Someone with kidô skills would be extremely nice.
❹ I look forward to meeting you.

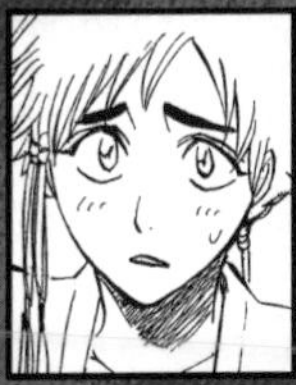

ISANE KOTETSU

❶ I'm not particular.
❷ We have a relief station where people recover and also seek treatment. The place has a unique atmosphere; it's a bit different from the other barracks.
❸ Stipulations?! Just having one more person would be a huge help.
❹ Let's work together! The captain holds monthly flower-arranging classes too!

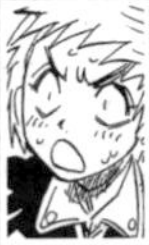

FOURTH COMPANY

ONLY HERE

SPEAKS CANDIDLY!

THIRTEENTH COMPANY
THIRD SEAT

KIYONE KOTETSU

My sister's company is really busy! Sometimes when I go there to pick up medicine for Captain Ukitake, everyone's rushing around hard at work. Captain Unohana may not look it, but she's scary when she reprimands you! Well…that's what my sister told me.

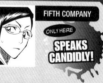

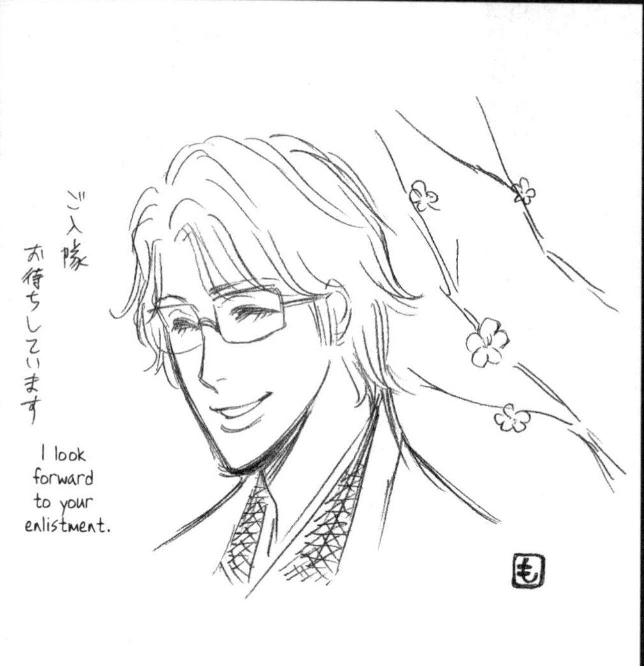
ご入隊お待ちしています
I look forward to your enlistment.

Illustrated by Momo Hinamori

五

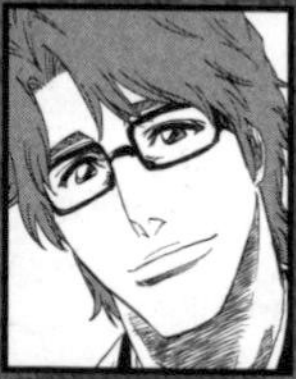

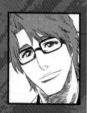

SÔSUKE AIZEN

No entry because his whereabouts are unknown.

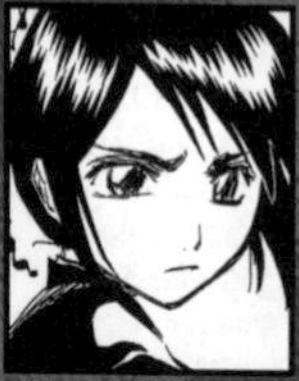

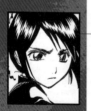

MOMO HINAMORI

❶ Someone cheerful.
❷ The captain is absent, and I'm often confined to bed, but it's actually a tranquil and pleasant company.
❸ Someone who will not betray us…
❹ Let's protect Fifth Company together!

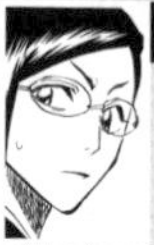

FIFTH COMPANY

ONLY HERE **SPEAKS CANDIDLY!**

EIGHTH COMPANY
ASSISTANT CAPTAIN
NANAO ISE

How have you been feeling, H-Hinamori? If you have any concerns, I'd be glad to lend a sympathetic ear! Let's read a book together again.

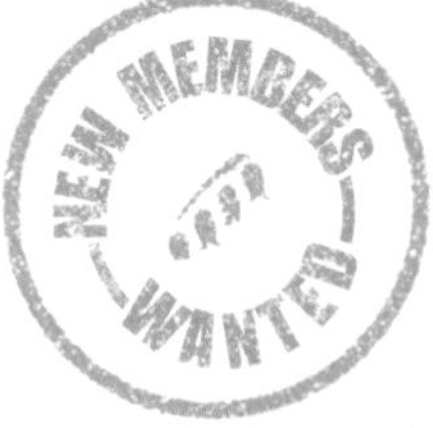
NEW MEMBERS
WANTED

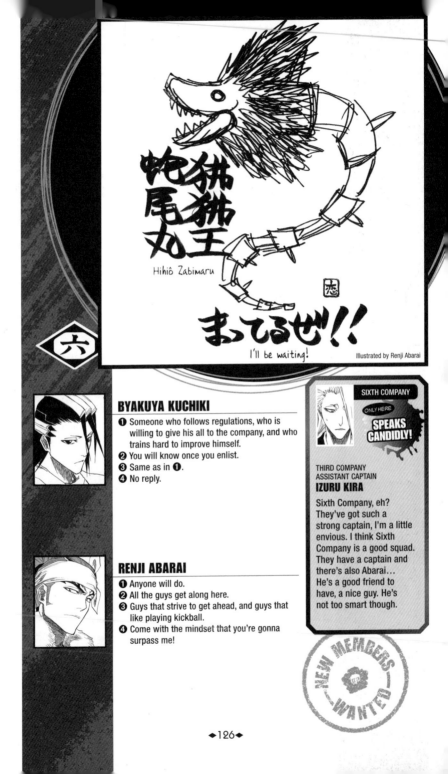

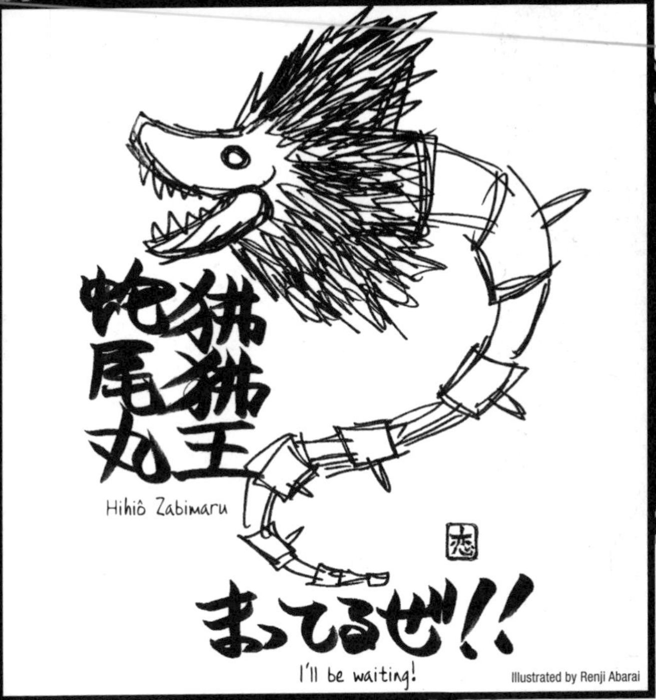
狒狒王
蛇尾丸
Hihiô Zabimaru
恋
まってるぜ!!
I'll be waiting!
Illustrated by Renji Abarai

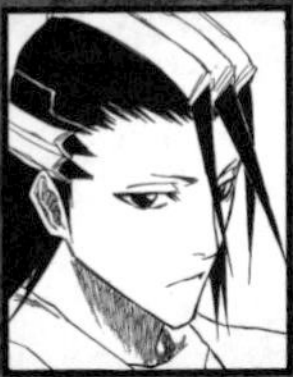

BYAKUYA KUCHIKI

❶ Someone who follows regulations, who is willing to give his all to the company, and who trains hard to improve himself.
❷ You will know once you enlist.
❸ Same as in ❶.
❹ No reply.

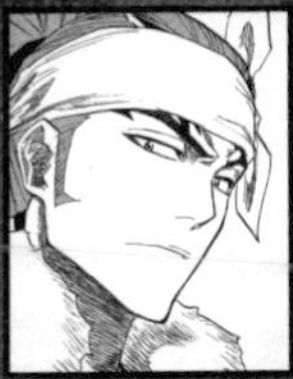

RENJI ABARAI

❶ Anyone will do.
❷ All the guys get along here.
❸ Guys that strive to get ahead, and guys that like playing kickball.
❹ Come with the mindset that you're gonna surpass me!

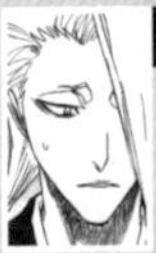

SIXTH COMPANY

ONLY HERE

SPEAKS CANDIDLY!

THIRD COMPANY
ASSISTANT CAPTAIN

IZURU KIRA

Sixth Company, eh? They've got such a strong captain, I'm a little envious. I think Sixth Company is a good squad. They have a captain and there's also Abarai… He's a good friend to have, a nice guy. He's not too smart though.

NEW MEMBERS —WANTED—

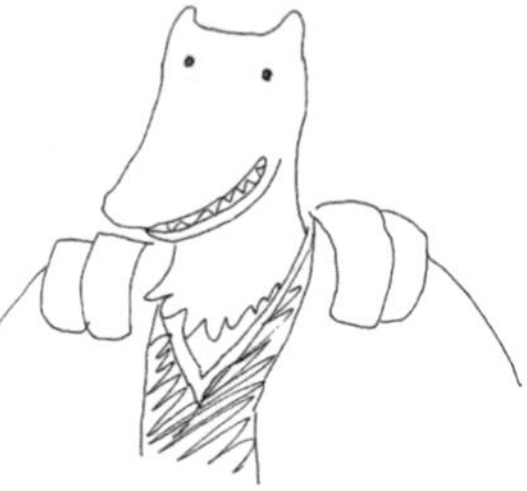

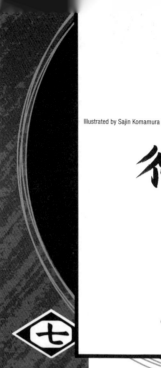

Illustrated by Sajin Komamura

待っているぞ

I'll be waiting for you.

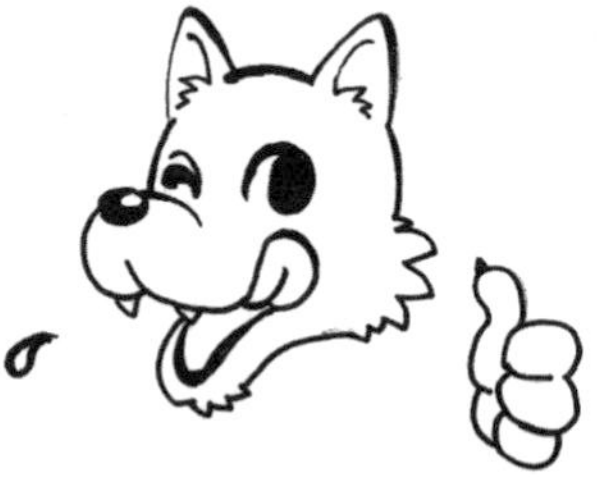

Illustrated by Tetsuzaemon Iba

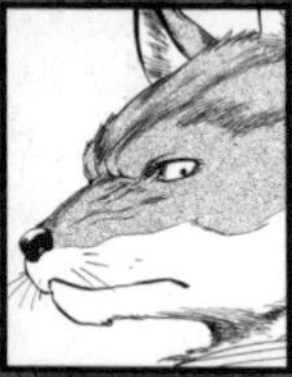

SAJIN KOMAMURA

❶ Someone truly loyal.
❷ I think I can safely say that it has a nice atmosphere, because Tetsuzaemon keeps everyone in line.
❸ We keep a dog named Gorô behind the barracks. I hope you like dogs.
❹ I'm expecting someone easygoing who doesn't panic over every little thing.

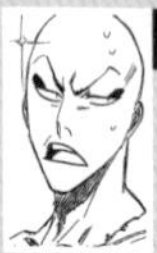

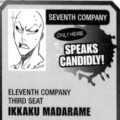

SEVENTH COMPANY

ONLY HERE **SPEAKS CANDIDLY!**

ELEVENTH COMPANY
THIRD SEAT
IKKAKU MADARAME

Seventh Company is so dull. If you wanna be a better man, join Eleventh Company!

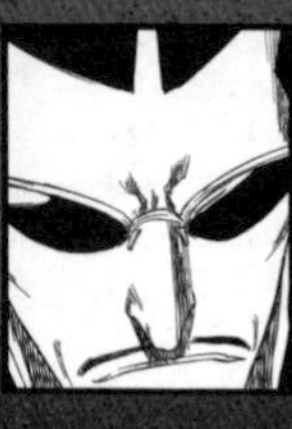

TETSUZAEMON IBA

❶ Someone really manly.
❷ Everyone here speaks in a Hiroshima dialect.
❸ Make sure you read "Men's Section" very carefully.
❹ If you wanna be more of a man, I recommend Seventh Company.

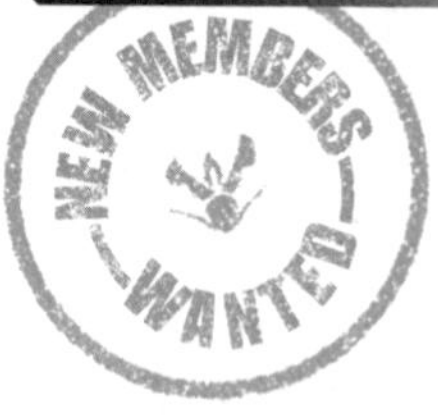
NEW MEMBERS
—WANTED—

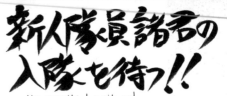

新人隊員諸君の入隊を待つ!!

New recruits, I await you!

Captain
Soi Fon

絵・文 円乗寺屍房

Calligraphy & Drawing: Enjôji Tatsufusa

SHUNSUI KYÔRAKU

❶ We welcome all girls. ♥
❷ It's a fun place. ♥
❸ The company is limited to girls. ♥
❹ Boys can go to another company, girls can apply to Eighth Company. ♥ We have a weekly drinking party.

NANAO ISE

❶ Someone who is diligent in his work.
❷ We're a disciplined and serious company.
❸ Someone who doesn't drink. Male or female, it doesn't matter.
❹ I'm looking forward to your joining us. By the way, we don't throw drinking parties.

EIGHTH COMPANY

ONLY HERE

SPEAKS CANDIDLY!

TENTH COMPANY
ASSISTANT CAPTAIN
RANGIKU MATSUMOTO

Seventh Company is really tough. Given how they are, recruits who would normally come, don't. But Eighth Company is a gorgeous squad that has a mature, sexy captain and a beautiful assistant captain! Come on over. ♥

NEW MEMBERS WANTED

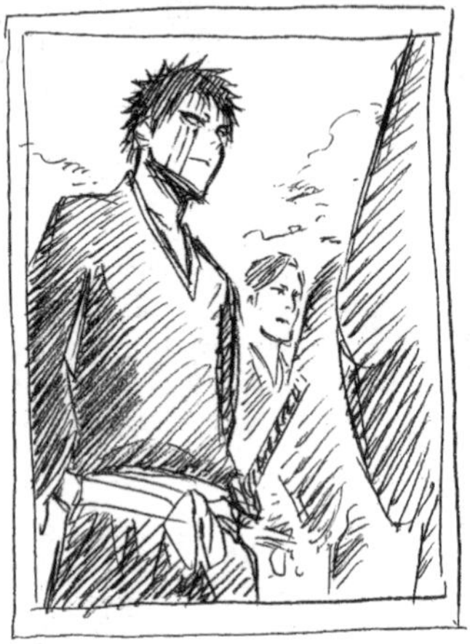

This is a drawing of me when I first joined the Thirteen Court Guards. I was overjoyed to get into my dream company, the Ninth, and went and got a haircut. It was too short and made me look like a school kid. I got teased a lot. But look at me now. I'm the assistant captain of Ninth Company. Together let's do our best!

Illustrated by Shûhei Hisagi

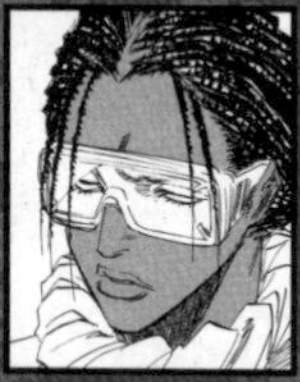

KANAME TÔSEN

No entry because his whereabouts are unknown.

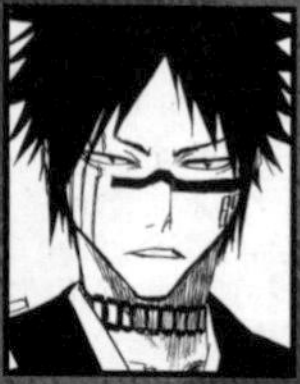

SHÛHEI HISAGI

1. Someone who has literary talent.
2. Ninth Company is cheerful, actually!
3. Cigarettes and pipes are forbidden in the editorial office.
4. Circulation is climbing! Why not come and help us publish *Seireitei Bulletin*?!

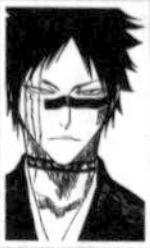

NINTH COMPANY

ONLY HERE

SPEAKS CANDIDLY!

NINTH COMPANY
ASSISTANT CAPTAIN

SHÛHEI HISAGI

We don't have a captain either, but we're doing fine! Protecting Ninth Company is still my goal. Right now, I'm polishing my editing skills, but I'm gonna keep doing my best to fulfill my duties as a Court Guard and editor of Ninth Company! Anyway, I welcome all contributions. I look forward to your enthusiastic work!

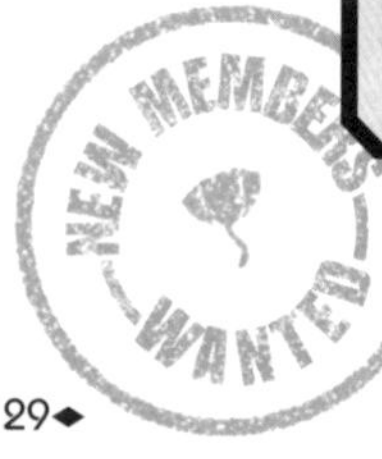
NEW MEMBERS
WANTED

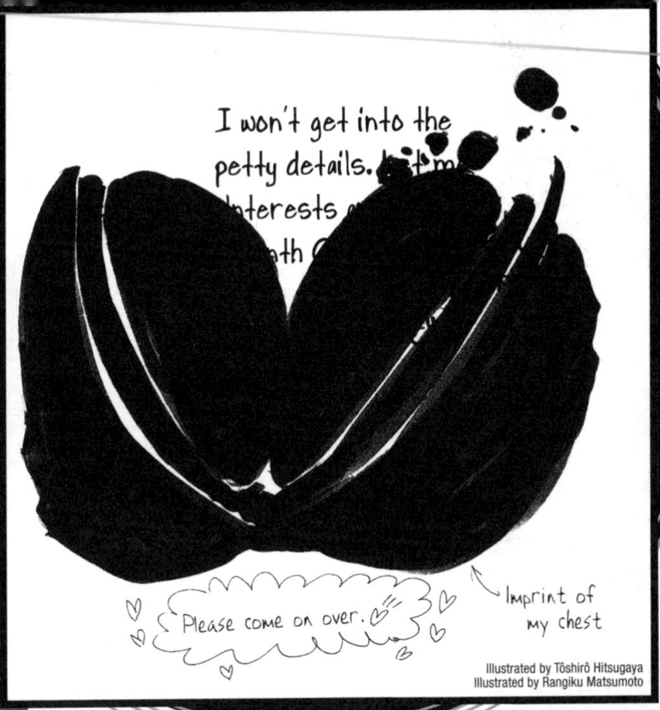
I won't get into the
petty details.
Please come on over.
Imprint of my chest
Illustrated by Tôshirô Hitsugaya
Illustrated by Rangiku Matsumoto

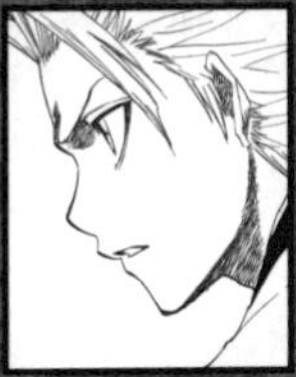

TÔSHIRÔ HITSUGAYA

❶ A hard worker.
❷ Pretty good.
❸ Nothing in particular.
❹ Anyone who's interested is always welcome.

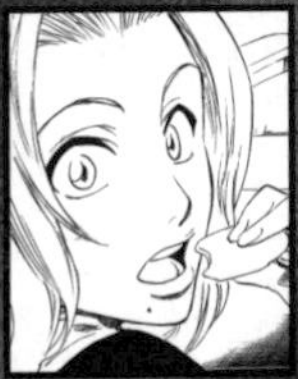

RANGIKU MATSUMOTO

❶ A kid who'll go carousing with me.
❷ I think it's a great company.
❸ Um, nothing in particular.
❹ Only in Tenth Company can you gaze all day long at Captain Hitsugaya, who is extremely popular with both male and female members! I'll be waiting for youuuuu… ♥

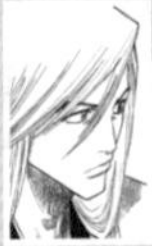

TENTH COMPANY

ONLY HERE SPEAKS CANDIDLY!

THIRTEENTH COMPANY CAPTAIN
JÛSHIRÔ UKITAKE

Tenth Company is a good squad. Captain Hitsugaya is tough and capable, and Assistant Captain Rangiku's gentle support gives the company a nice balance. If you're looking for a place to hone your skills, this is it. Really, Captain Hitsugaya does work hard. And well, don't you think his name sounds a bit like mine? It's like we have a kinship. I want to offer him candy every time I see him. It's a really nice company.

NEW MEMBERS WANTED

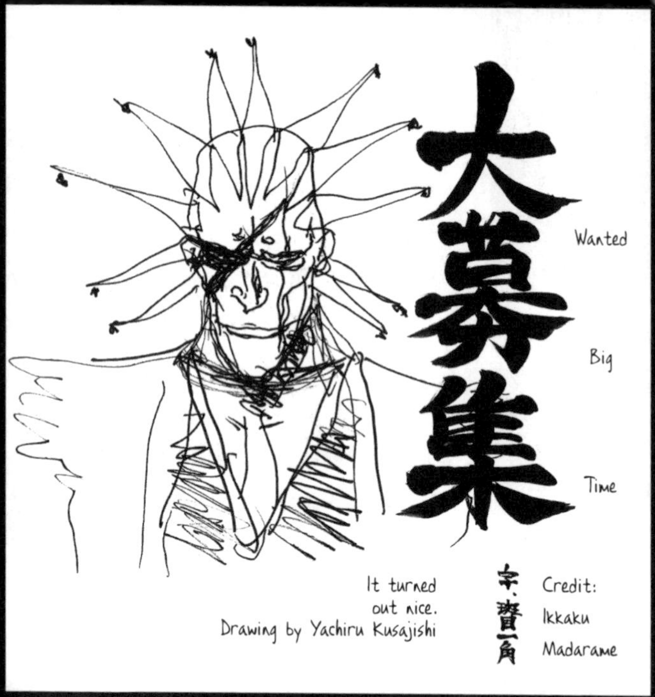
大募集
Wanted
Big
Time
It turned out nice.
Drawing by Yachiru Kusajishi
Credit:
Ikkaku
Madarame

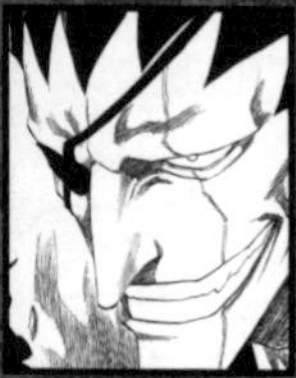

KENPACHI ZARAKI

❶ Someone who loves fighting.
❷ Getting along and being happy is for fools.
❸ Strong guys.
❹ You strong ones, come at me!

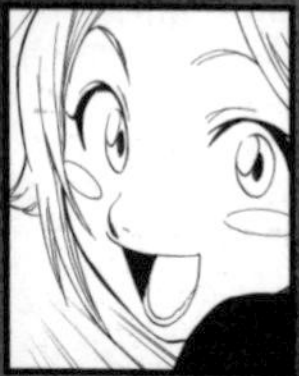

YACHIRU KUSAJISHI

❶ Strong people.
❷ Everyone gets along.
❸ Weak people needn't apply.
❹ I'll think of a nickname for you!

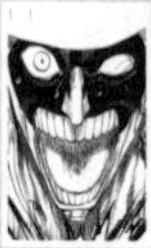

ELEVENTH COMPANY

ONLY HERE

SPEAKS CANDIDLY!

TWELFTH COMPANY CAPTAIN

MAYURI KUROTSUCHI

Eleventh Company? I wouldn't know. Why must I comment on the good things about Eleventh Company? The squad is comprised of people whose intelligence is low and who live only to fight. On top of that, their assistant captain is always barging into my research lab, sitting in my chair, munching on sweets and spilling crumbs everywhere, touching the machines with her dirty hands, deleting my data, and trying to splash water on my face. What is *with* that child? It's all Zaraki's fault.

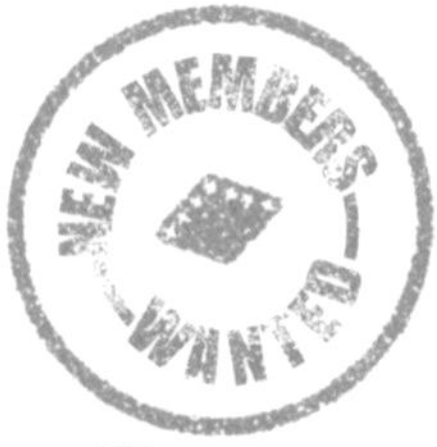
NEW MEMBERS
—WANTED—

I wrote in the questionnaire that I am seeking healthy bodies. Actually, I'm looking for sickly types too. And people with all sorts of injuries. Even dead people. If you've just died, you're welcome here. If you just want to sign up for an organ, organ part or body part, come talk to me. Calming your family, erasing parts of your past, completing your application... we can easily take care of it all. So first, feel free to contact me.

Written by Mayuri Kurotsuchi

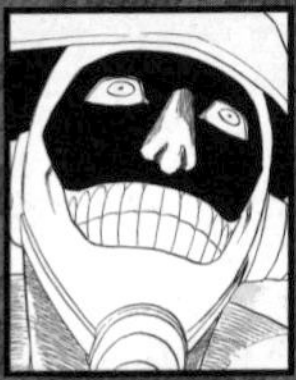

MAYURI KUROTSUCHI

1. Anyone will do.
2. It's a fun place.
3. Healthy bodies.
4. Please do come.

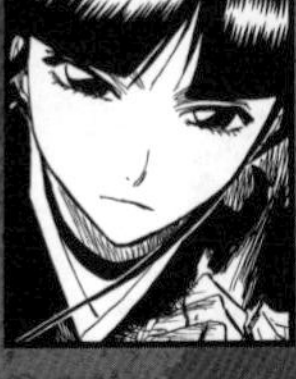

NEMU KUROTSUCHI

1. Nothing in particular.
2. It's a fun place.
3. Healthy bodies.
4. I'll be waiting.

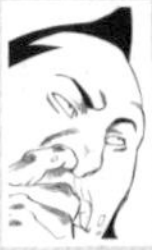

TWELFTH COMPANY

ONLY HERE

SPEAKS CANDIDLY!

SECOND COMPANY
ASSISTANT CAPTAIN
MARECHIYO ÔMAEDA

Huh? Twelfth Company? I wouldn't know, I've never come into contact with them. Could you go through my secretary for anything else that comes up? I am president, after all. Bwa ha ha ha.

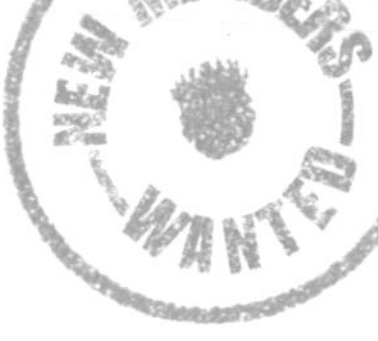
NEW MEMBERS
WANTED

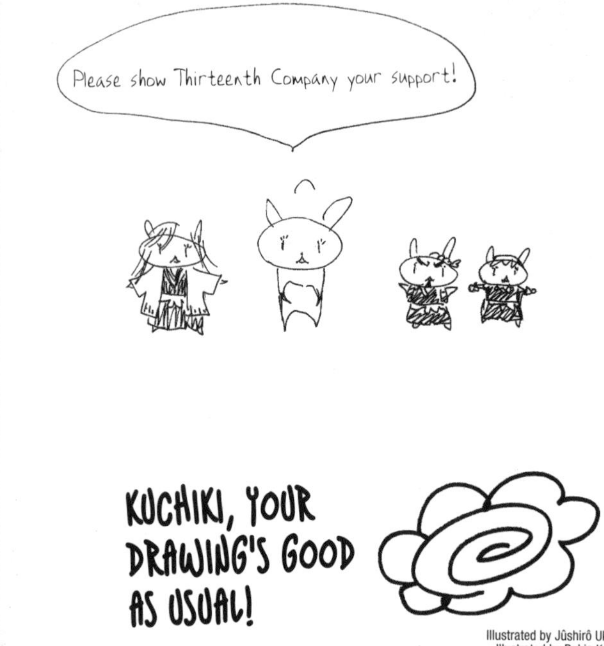
Please show Thirteenth Company your support!
KUCHIKI, YOUR DRAWING'S GOOD AS USUAL!

Illustrated by Jûshirô Ukitake
Illustrated by Rukia Kuchiki

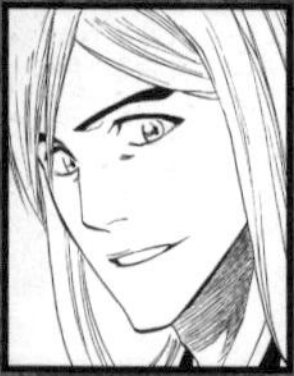

JÛSHIRÔ UKITAKE

❶ Everyone's welcome!
❷ It's a happy company where everyone always gets along!
❸ All you need is strength of mind!
❹ Let's fight together!

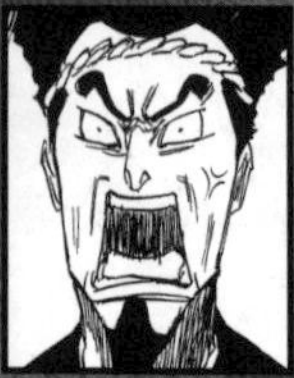

SENTARÔ KOTSUBAKI

❶ Someone gutsy!
❷ It's a great place!
❸ There aren't any!
❹ Our Captain Ukitake is a great guy!

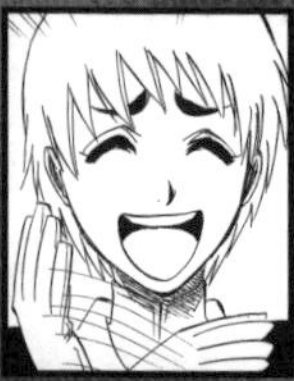

KIYONE KOTETSU

❶ Someone cheerful.
❷ It's always fun!
❸ None whatsoever!
❹ My…our Captain Ukitake really is a great guy!

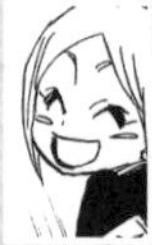

THIRTEENTH COMPANY
ONLY HERE
SPEAKS CANDIDLY!

ELEVENTH COMPANY
ASSISTANT CAPTAIN
YACHIRU KUSAJISHI

Ukki? Ukki always has yummy-looking sweets by his pillow. Outside in the pond, there are huge carp. Heh heh heh, they're the ones I gave him.

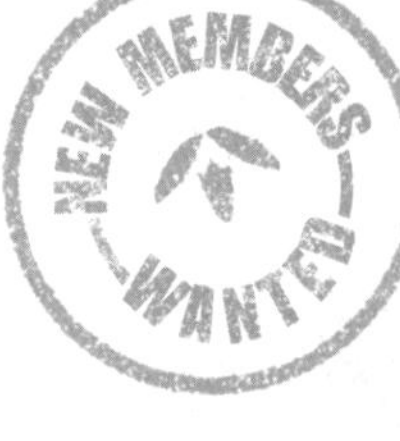
NEW MEMBERS
WANTED

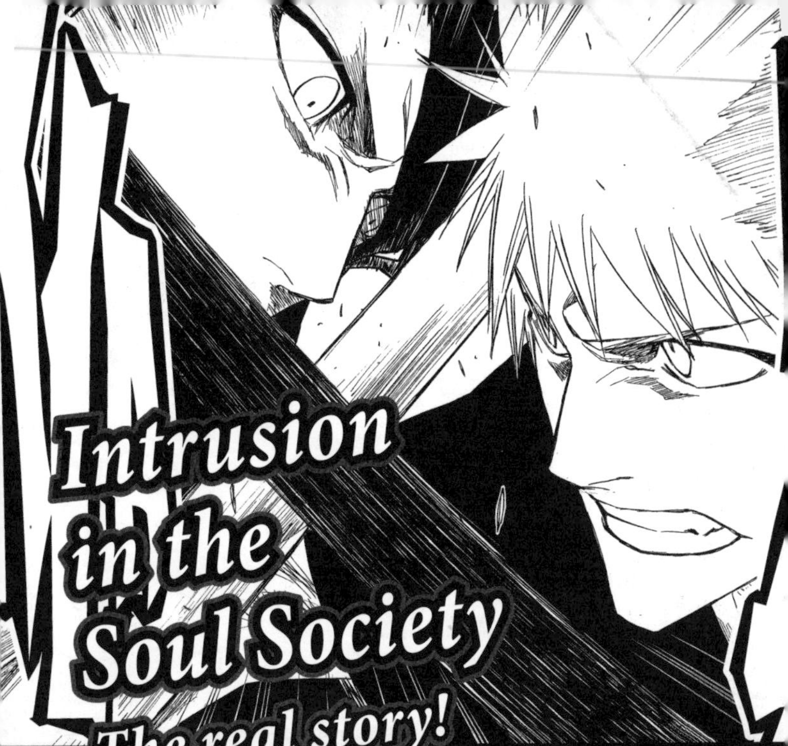

Intrusion in the Soul Society
The real story!

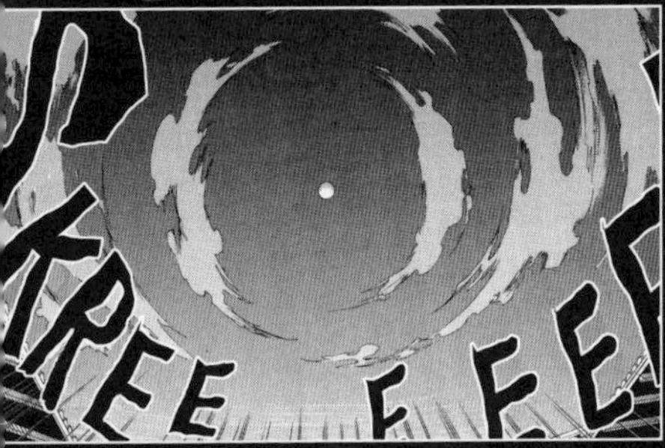

AN EARTHQUAKE IN THE SEIREITEI, INVADERS FROM THE SKY!

The alarm that signaled the ryoka's incursion proved to be false, and the long night was about to end, when suddenly it fell from the sky—the mysterious orb that hit the Soul Shield Membrane. *That* turned out to be *them*.

ONE BY ONE, THE MURDEROUS RYOKA CLAIMED THEIR VICTIMS.

The mysterious orb split into four parts and burst open. Everything was shrouded in mystery—the identity of the invaders, their purpose. Only one thing was certain: the steadily growing number of victims. This was how the unprecedented threat to the Soul Society started.

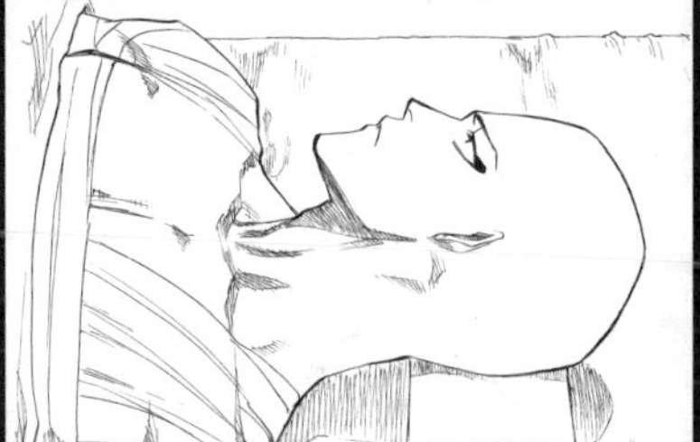

Eleventh Company Third Seat, Ikkaku Madarame, was among those whom the ryoka seriously wounded.

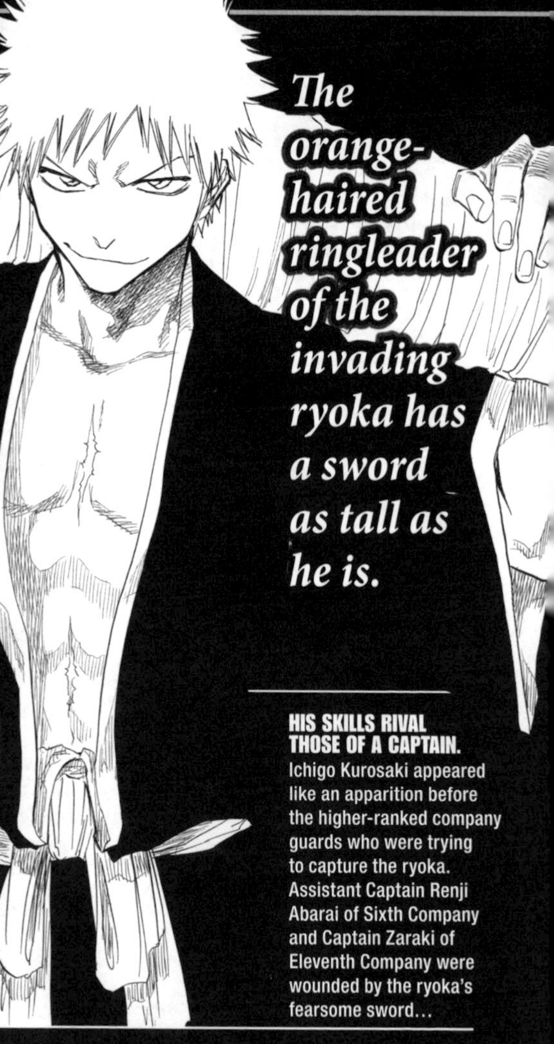

The orange-haired ringleader of the invading ryoka has a sword as tall as he is.

ICHIGO KUROSAKI

The man considered to be the ringleader of the ryoka who infiltrated the Seireitei. Besides having strange orange hair and a crude, giant sword, he wears a smug look on his face. He resembles a Soul Reaper in his appearance.

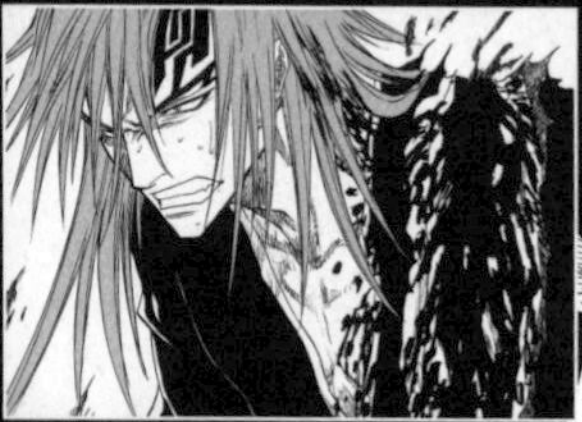

Assistant Captain Abarai sustains a life-threatening gash across his left shoulder. Just who is this ryoka who boasts so much strength?!

HIS SKILLS RIVAL THOSE OF A CAPTAIN.

Ichigo Kurosaki appeared like an apparition before the higher-ranked company guards who were trying to capture the ryoka. Assistant Captain Renji Abarai of Sixth Company and Captain Zaraki of Eleventh Company were wounded by the ryoka's fearsome sword...

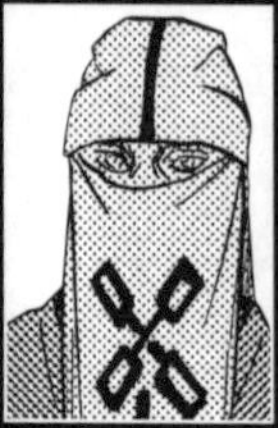

A MEMBER OF THE KIDÔ CORPS

WHAT IS THE RYOKA'S TRUE GOAL?

Central 46 had issued an imperial edict calling for the execution of the Kuchiki woman. The ryoka Ichigo Kurosaki thwarted the execution, according to eyewitnesses at Sôkyoku Hill. Was the ryoka's true goal to rescue the woman? Or was it something else...

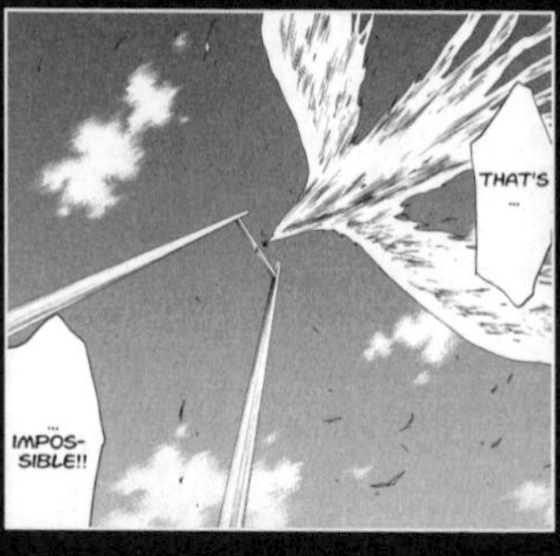
THAT'S ...
... IMPOS-SIBLE!!

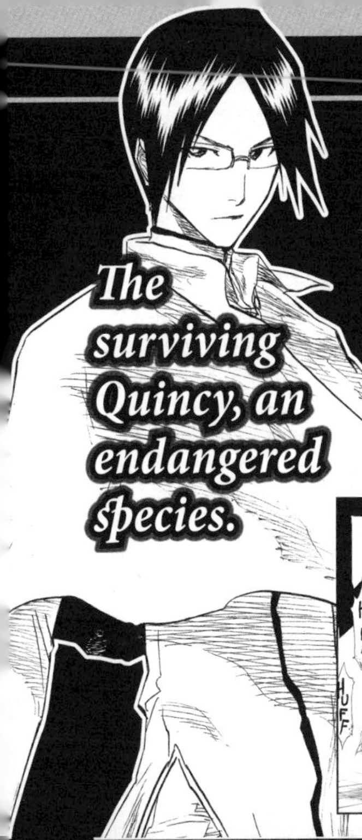

The surviving Quincy, an endangered species.

URYÛ ISHIDA

Clad all in white, he is the last surviving member of a tribe of exterminators known as Quincies. It is remarkable that he has managed to survive alone, but what is his aim? Could it be revenge against the Soul Society?

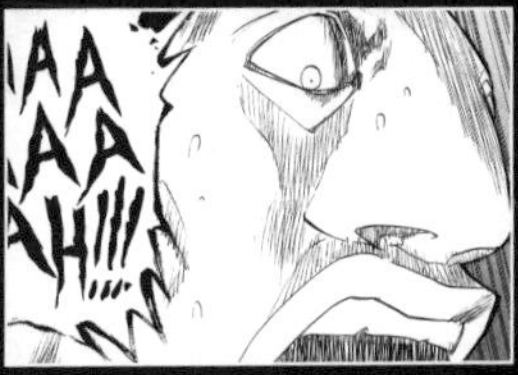

Jirôbô Ikkanzaka, Fourth Seat of Seventh Company, was injured in his encounter with Uryû Ishida. Jirôbô's Soul Chain and Soul Sleep were pierced and his spiritual power lost...

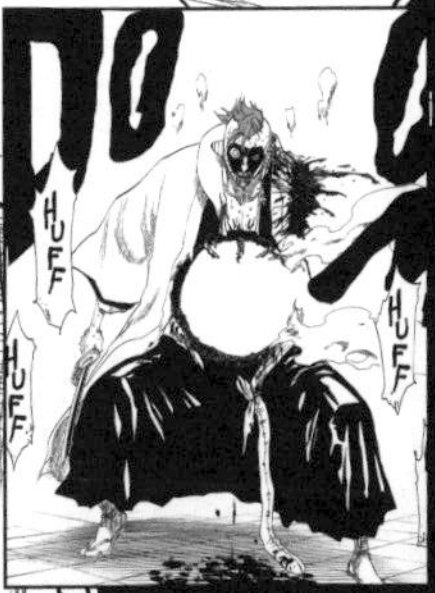
DO
HUFF
HUFF
HUFF

HE BRANDISHES A VICIOUS PROJECTILE WEAPON

The Quincy uses a bow and arrow coated with reishi. Ishida, who defeated Jirôbô's ultimate projectile weapon, Kamaitachi, also attacked Twelfth Company Captain Kurotsuchi. However, Ishida was captured thanks to Captain Tôsen of Ninth Company.

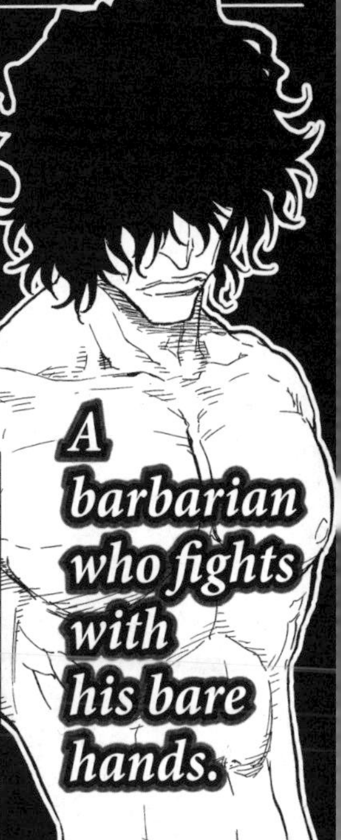

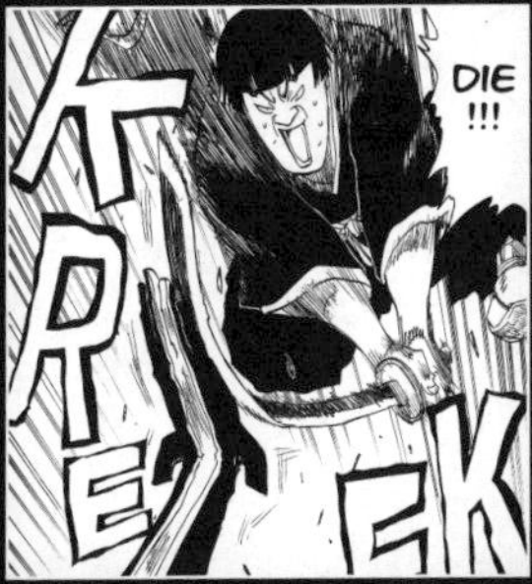
DIE !!!

YASUTORA SADO

Huge in size and with power to match, he is a deadly human weapon that mows down his foes. The destruction of Eleventh Company was due to this man.

THE MAN WITH AN IRON FIST

He is a barbarian who fights unarmed and with his bare hands. Even swords have no effect on his black right arm. He defeated the high-speed sword specialist Tatsufusa Enjôji, Third Seat of Eighth Company, but was apprehended by Captain Kyôraku.

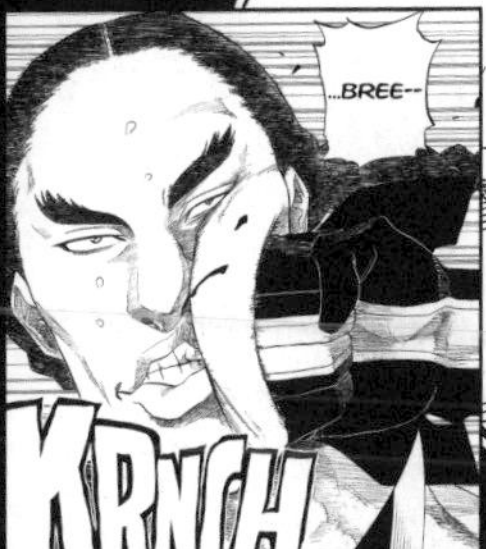
...BREE--
KRNCH

A barbarian who fights with his bare hands.

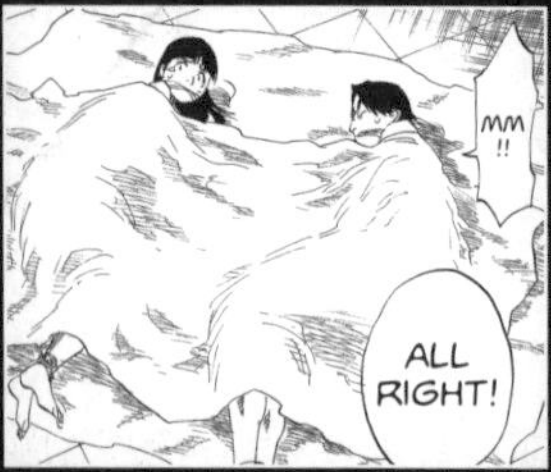
MM !!
ALL RIGHT!

The two victims of Twelfth Company. They discussed the situation fearfully.

ORIHIME INOUE

Don't be fooled by her appearance. She attacked members of Twelfth Company and absconded with their clothes. Her offenses are odious. Do not let down your guard!

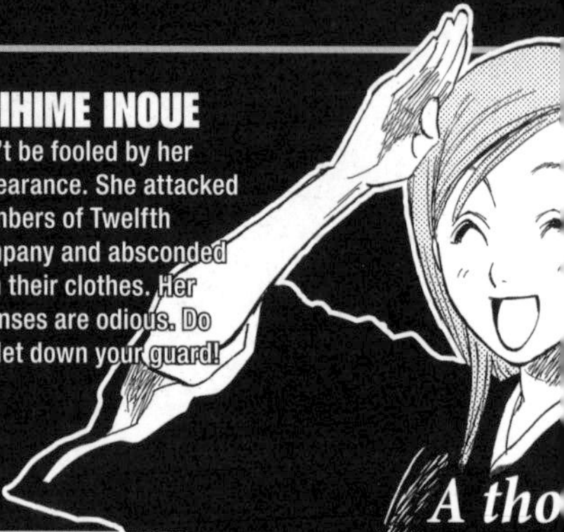
A tho
hidin
insid
beau
flowe

A SINISTER ABILITY TO CONTROL OTHERS

What is most dangerous about Orihime Inoue is her sly way of speaking in order to get close to you—a power that is evil and disarming. Even Captain Zaraki of Eleventh Company fell victim to her poison fangs. How frightening!

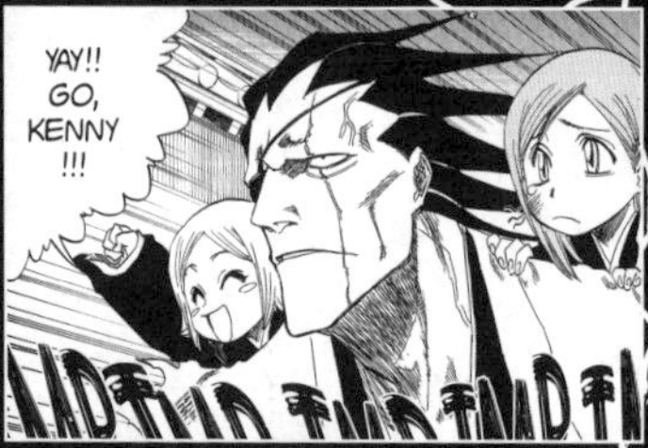
YAY!! GO, KENNY !!!

A Court Guard on patrol took this picture by chance. Even Captain Zaraki was on hand...

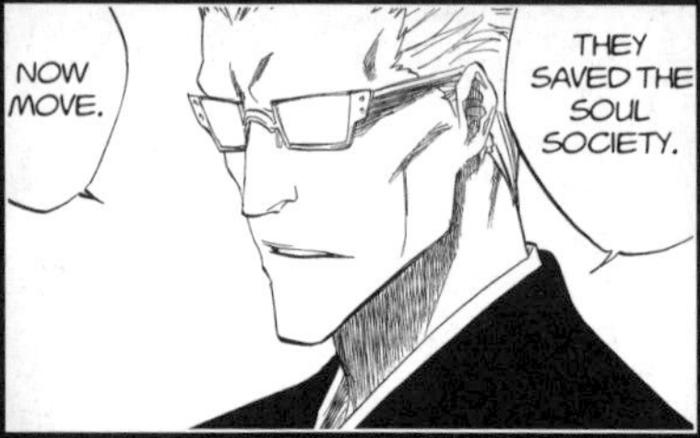
THEY SAVED THE SOUL SOCIETY.
NOW MOVE.

The ryoka were not the enemy. It's rumored that there was far more to the story behind the disturbance, but it is shrouded in mystery.

THE OUTCOME OF THE DISTURBANCE RE

The disturbance, which shook the Soul Society and the Seireitei, came to an end all too abruptly. Captain General Yamamo issued the terse statement, "The ryoka a not guilty." Rumor has it that Isane Kotets Fourth Company transmitted an emergen message through the Tentei Kûra. Howev contents of that message too are not kno

SEEKING INFORMANTS!

Anyone who witnessed the incident or has inside information is asked to contact Ninth Company immediately.

THE MYSTERIOUS THREE MEN

Immediately after the disturbance, a giant explosion rocked Sôkyoku Hill. The figures of three men were seen disappearing into Hueco Mundo. The truth of this incident is consigned to oblivion. This magazine continues to investigate the circumstances.

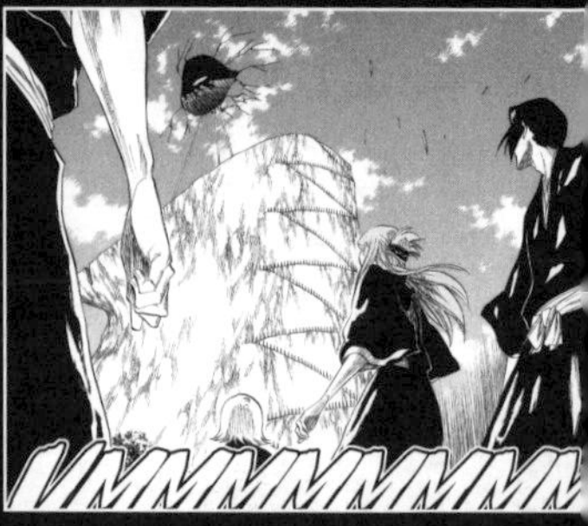

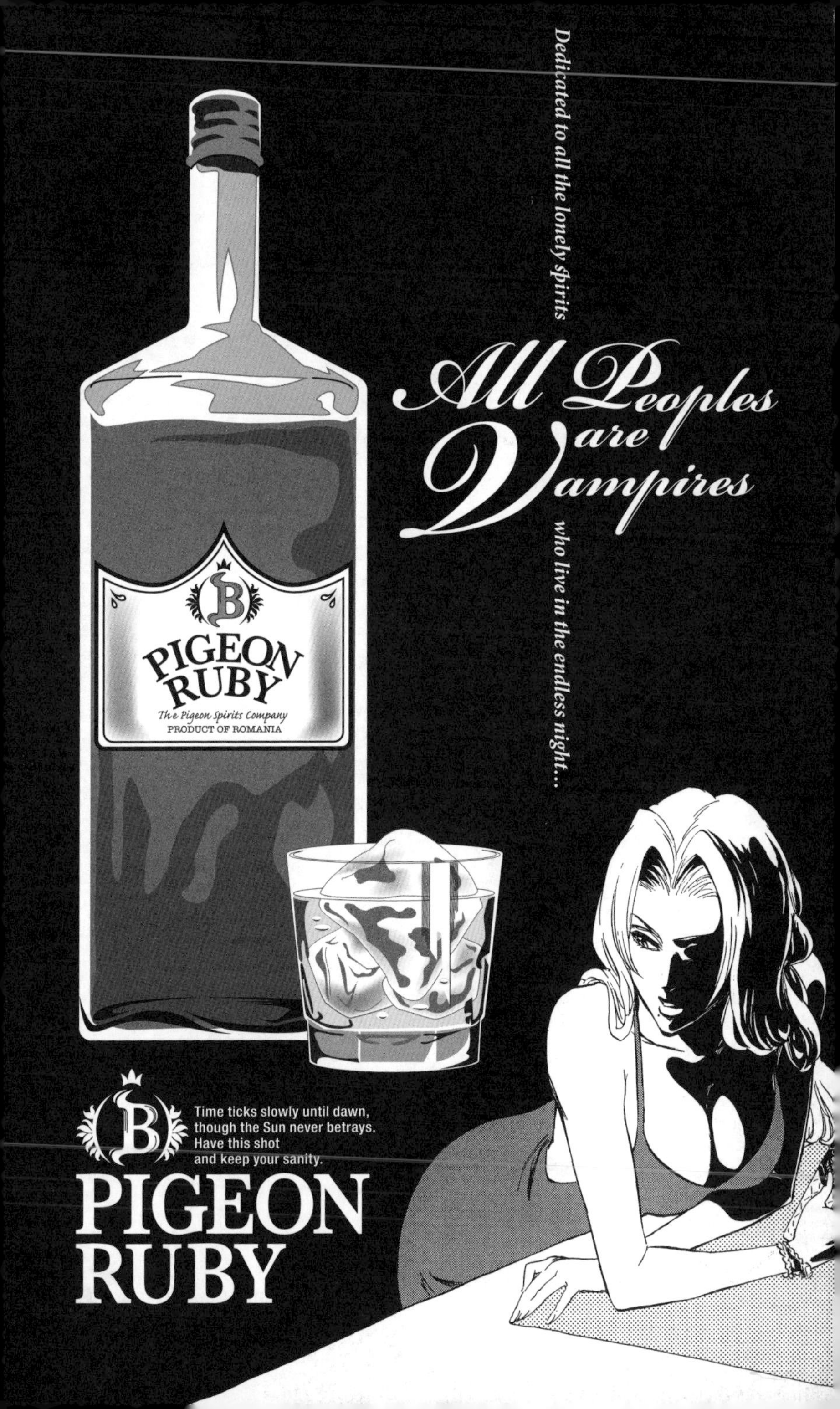
Dedicated to all the lonely spirits
All Peoples are Vampires
who live in the endless night...
B
PIGEON RUBY
The Pigeon Spirits Company
PRODUCT OF ROMANIA
B
Time ticks slowly until dawn,
though the Sun never betrays.
Have this shot
and keep your sanity.
PIGEON RUBY

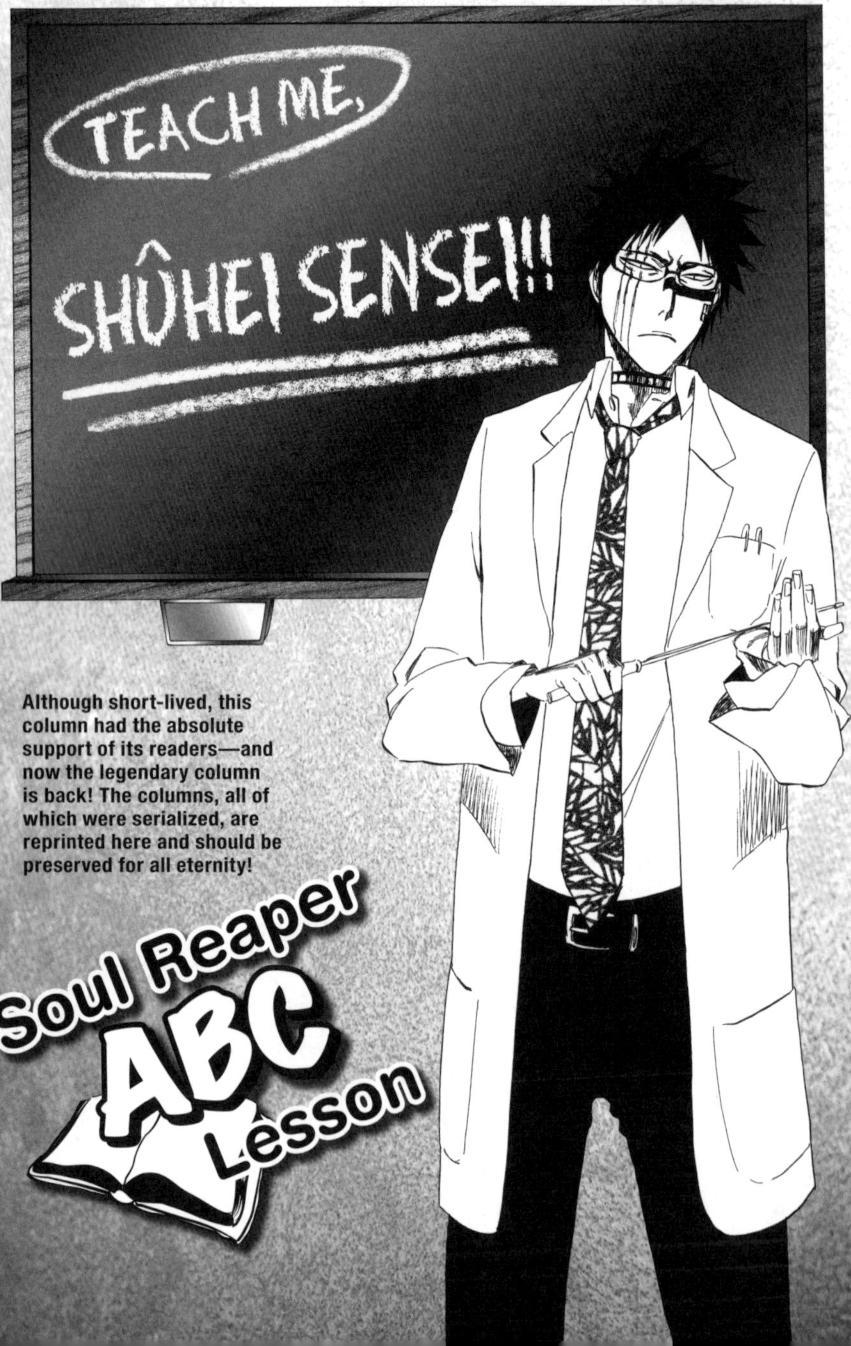
TEACH ME,
SHÛHEI SENSEI!!!

Although short-lived, this column had the absolute support of its readers—and now the legendary column is back! The columns, all of which were serialized, are reprinted here and should be preserved for all eternity!

Soul Reaper ABC Lesson

"Teach Me, Shûhei Sensei!!" Lesson 1 is reprinted from the December issue of *Monthly Seireitei Bulletin*. First published 11/24/2006.

Teach Me, SHÛHEI SENSEI!!

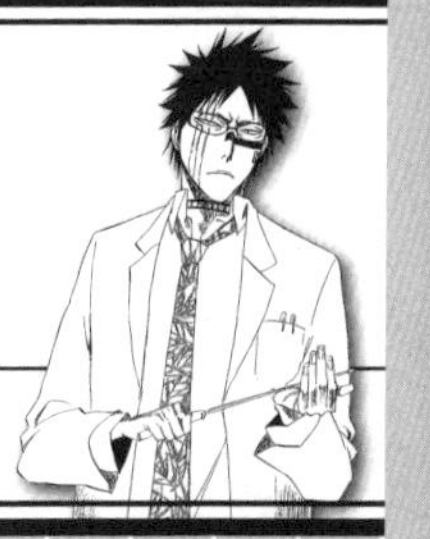

Lesson.1

This new section has finally started! Shûhei Sensei answers a variety of questions from new Soul Reapers!

SOUL REAPER ILLUSTRATION

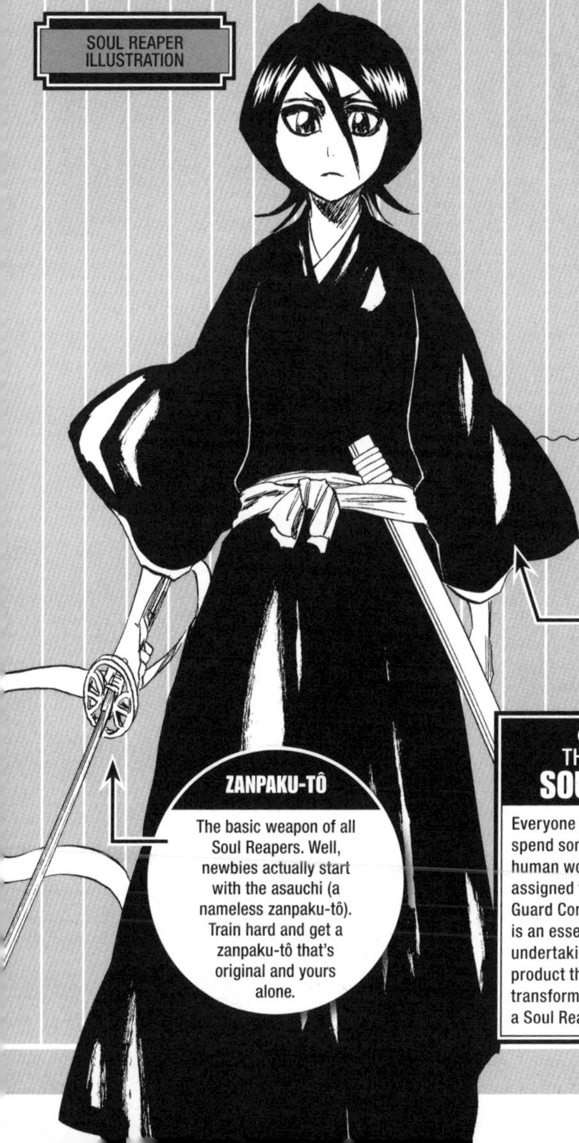

Q 01

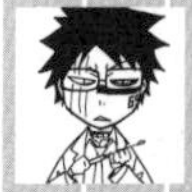

WHAT IS A SOUL REAPER?

Whoa, that's profound. If you don't even know that, you're in trouble. Listen up. Put simply, a Soul Reaper is a guardian of the souls who are going through the circle of transmigration. Namely, they are "balancers." They exterminate Hollows who did evil in the world of the living; they ensure the safe crossing of souls—the Wholes who have lost their way after death—by giving them a soul funeral; and they do all sorts of other things. It's a tough job.

SHIHAKUSHÔ

This black kimono, known as a shihakushô, is like the Soul Reaper uniform. It's cool to create your own look by adding personal touches.

ZANPAKU-TÔ

The basic weapon of all Soul Reapers. Well, newbies actually start with the asauchi (a nameless zanpaku-tô). Train hard and get a zanpaku-tô that's original and yours alone.

❶ ESSENTIAL WHEN IN THE WORLD OF THE LIVING

SOUL CANDY (GIKONGAN)

Everyone is required to spend some time in the human world before being assigned to a Thirteen Court Guard Company. Soul Candy is an essential item for this undertaking. It is the standard product that is used in transforming from a gigai into a Soul Reaper. Don't forget it!

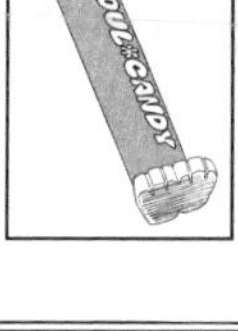
SOUL CANDY

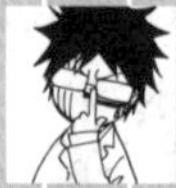

You'll see what I mean when you're in the human world. But that world has many marvelous things you won't see in the Soul Society—like the guitar, for example. I guess it's an advanced version of the traditional Japanese stringed instrument known as the shamisen. It uses a power called electricity and produces all kinds of wailing sounds. I couldn't wait to bring it home and start practicing, but it isn't easy to play. Oh well. I sort of got off the subject, didn't I?

❷ ESSENTIAL WHEN IN THE WORLD OF THE LIVING
SOUL PAGER

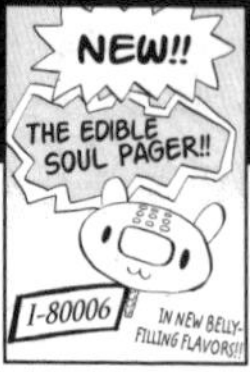
NEW!!
THE EDIBLE SOUL PAGER!!
I-80006
IN NEW BELLY-FILLING FLAVORS!!

It's a convenient gadget that notifies you when and where a Hollow appears. I hear there are many styles these days, so you can choose one that suits your taste.

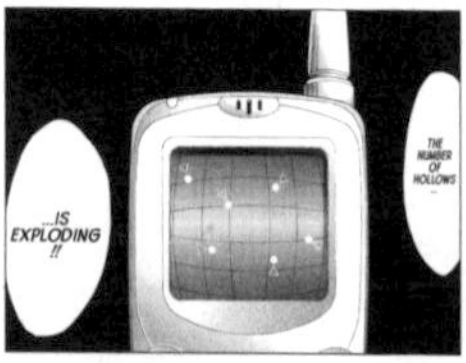
THE NUMBER OF HOLLOWS...
...IS EXPLODING!!

Q 02

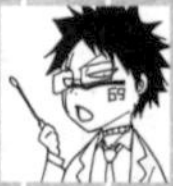

WHAT ARE A SOUL REAPER'S DUTIES?

A Soul Reaper has two main duties. One is to maintain the spiritual order in the world of the living. The other is to protect the Seireitei, the nerve center of the Soul Society. Exterminating Hollows that do mischief in the world of the living, battling the ryoka—much of a Soul Reaper's work requires physical strength. If you don't stay in shape and train hard regularly, you'll end up dead pretty quickly, so be careful.

DUTY ❶
MAINTAIN SPIRITUAL ORDER

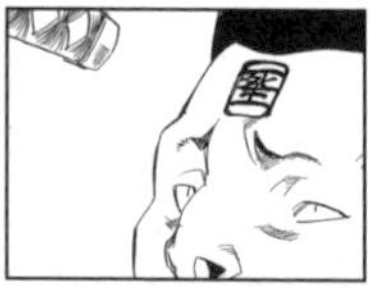

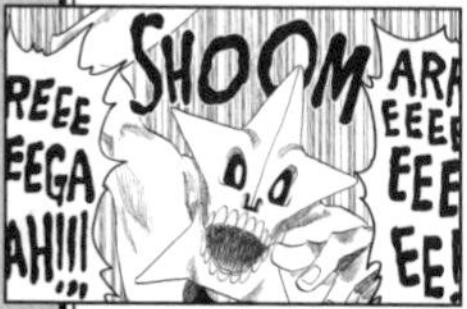
SHOOM
REEEEEGAAH!!!
ARAEEEEEEEEE!

The human world is a world of spiritual disorder, overflowing with Hollows and Pluses, the good and the bad. A street that looks perfectly peaceful can be a battleground where we Soul Reapers fight day in and day out. So tighten your belts and stay alert.

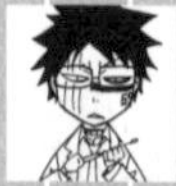

Well, do you think you know a little more about Soul Reapers now? So ends the new column that begins in this issue, featuring me, Shûhei Hisagi. I'm gonna do my best, so I want you all to root for me too!!

DUTY ❷
PROTECT THE SEIREITEI

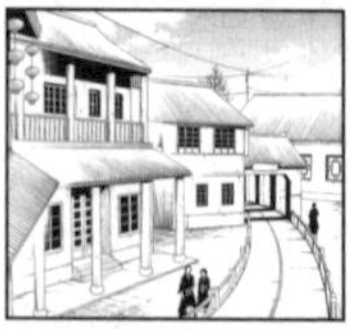

As the name Thirteen Court Guard Companies suggests, our main duty is to *guard* the Seireitei. Well, actually, we rarely encounter invaders because the Seirei Wall and the Soul Shield Membrane are tightly guarded.

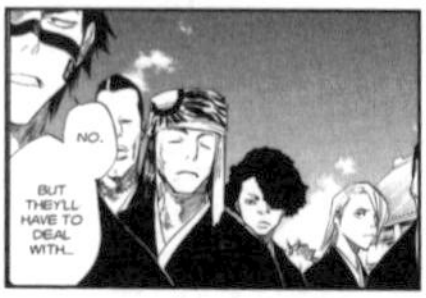
NO.
BUT THEY'LL HAVE TO DEAL WITH...

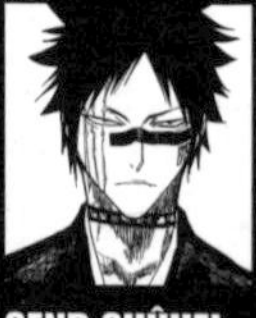

SEND SHÛHEI SENSEI LETTERS OF SUPPORT!

Will reply 100 percent of the time and include a super-rare snapshot!

"Teach Me, Shûhei Sensei!!" Lesson 2 is reprinted from the January issue of *Monthly Seireitei Bulletin*. First published 12/24/2006.

Teach Me, SHÛHEI SENSEI!!

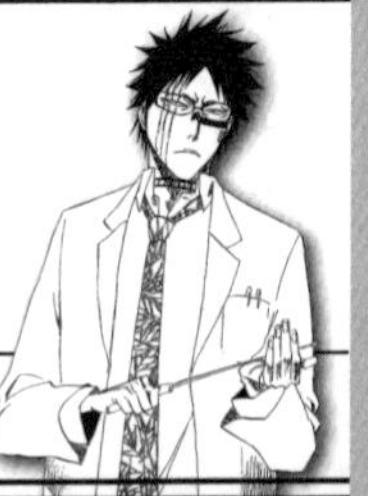

Lesson.2

This new section has finally started!
Shûhei Sensei presents a commemorative second lesson!

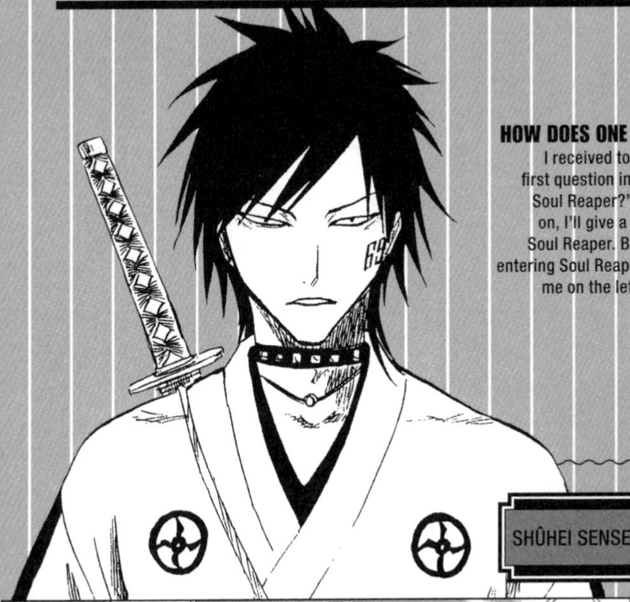

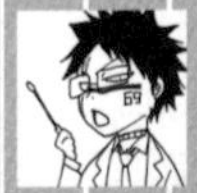

Q 03

HOW DOES ONE BECOME A SOUL REAPER?

I received tons of letters in response to the first question in the previous issue, "What is a Soul Reaper?" Thank you, all! So, continuing on, I'll give a lecture on how one becomes a Soul Reaper. Basically, the fastest route is by entering Soul Reaper Academy. By the way, that's me on the left as a student at the academy.

SHÛHEI SENSEI AS AN ACADEMY STUDENT

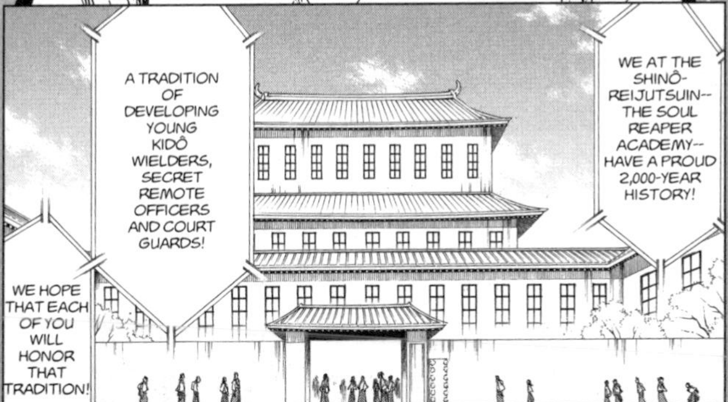
WE AT THE SHINÔ-REIJUTSUIN--THE SOUL REAPER ACADEMY--HAVE A PROUD 2,000-YEAR HISTORY!
A TRADITION OF DEVELOPING YOUNG KIDÔ WIELDERS, SECRET REMOTE OFFICERS AND COURT GUARDS!
WE HOPE THAT EACH OF YOU WILL HONOR THAT TRADITION!

TWO THOUSAND YEARS OF HISTORY AND TRADITION!

SOUL REAPER ACADEMY

Founded by Captain General Shigekuni Genryûsai Yamamoto, this training school for Soul Reapers boasts a two-thousand-year-old history and pedigree. Its doors are open to all, and anyone who passes the entrance exam will be accepted. The curriculum essentially takes six years to complete.

SHÛHEI SENSEI SAYS
THIS WILL APPEAR IN THE TEST!

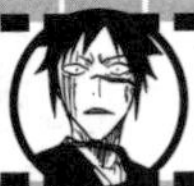

The results of the entrance exam will determine one's grade level. The first group is called the "AP group" (as in "advanced placement") and is made up of the best students.

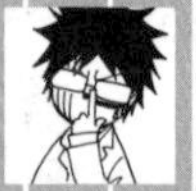

Q 04

WHAT IS ZANKENSÔKI?

It's the general term for Soul Reaper fighting styles. When you first enter the academy, the techniques will be drilled into you. You could focus on one style and master it, but it's best to learn them all equally if you hope to become an assistant captain.

SOUL REAPER FIGHTING STYLE ❶
ZANJUTSU

This is the fighting style for the zanpaku-tô: in other words, sword fighting. It's shameful for a Soul Reaper not to master at least this technique. It's the specialty of Captain Zaraki of Eleventh Company. Or rather, this is the only technique that Captain Zaraki uses.

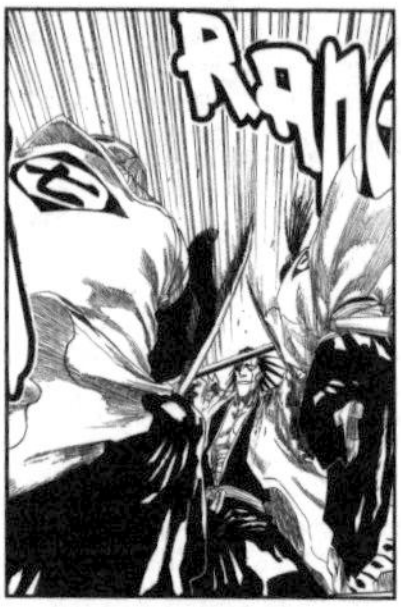

SOUL REAPER FIGHTING STYLE ❷
HAKUDA

A close-combat style of fighting in which one is unarmed and uses only one's body. Captain Soi Fon of Second Company excels in this style. It seems everyone in the Secret Remote Squad's Punishment Force is adept in it.

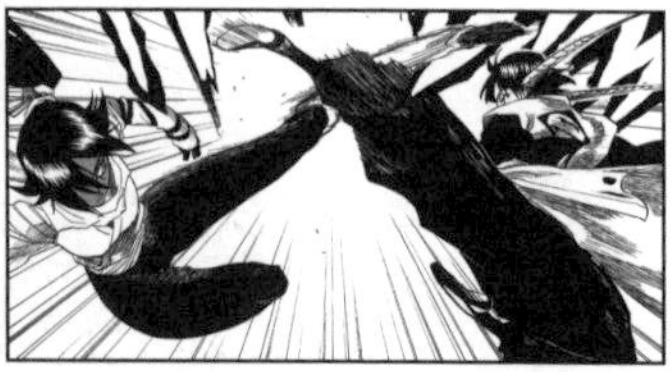

SOUL REAPER FIGHTING STYLE ❸
HOHÔ

Knowing this style will make a huge difference. It encompasses all fighting moves based on shunpo (flash step), which enables one to cover long distances instantly. It requires a great deal of spiritual power and is therefore exhausting.

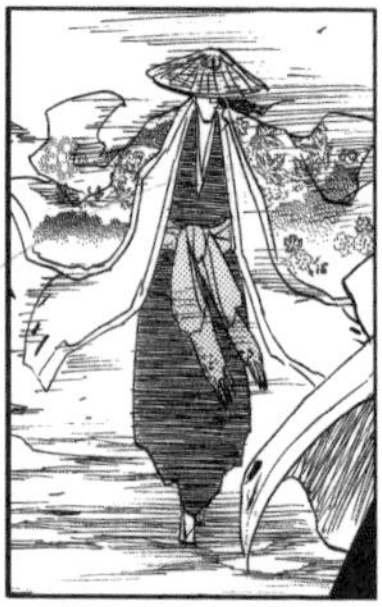

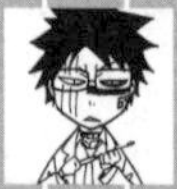

So how was this issue's column? If I could wish for anything, it would be for a bigger show of support, so promise me that. Anyway, see you next time. Ciao!

SOUL REAPER FIGHTING STYLE ❹
KIDÔ

These spells are produced with spiritual power and fall into two main categories: hadô, for direct attacks, and bakudô, for battle support. Assistant Captain Hinamori of Fifth Company is a master of kidô.

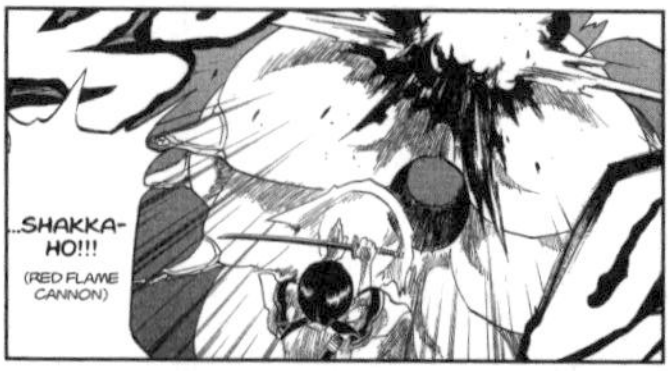
...SHAKKA-HO!!!
(RED FLAME CANNON)

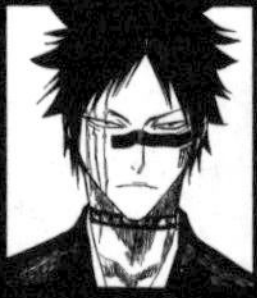

SEND SHÛHEI SENSEI LETTERS OF SUPPORT!

Will reply 100 percent of the time and include a super-rare snapshot!

"Teach Me, Shûhei Sensei!!" Lesson 3 is reprinted from the February issue of *Monthly Seireitei Bulletin*. First published 1/24/2007.

Teach Me, SHÛHEI SENSEI!!

Lesson.3

Here's Mr. Nice Guy, looking great in white. Shûhei Sensei's third special lesson is about to begin!

SOUL SOCIETY RELIEF MAP

DON'T WE GET ANY LINES?
SOUL REAPERS
THE BLUE STREAM GATE (EAST)
SEIREITEI
THE RED HOLLOW GATE (SOUTH)
THE BLACK RIDGE GATE (NORTH)
THE WHITE ROAD GATE (WEST)
JINDANBÔ
RUKONGAI
NEWLY ARRIVED SOULS STAY HERE. ITS RESIDENTS RARELY ENTER THE SEIREITEI AND MUST HAVE PERMISSION TO DO SO.
ICHIGO AND COMPANY

Q 05

PLEASE DESCRIBE THE LAYOUT OF THE SOUL SOCIETY!

Of course, you're curious. The Soul Society is a huge place, and only Soul Reapers and members of the nobility know what it's like inside the Seireitei. All right, I'm gonna answer this question! The Soul Society is made up of Rukongai and the Seireitei, with the latter at the center. There's a diagram of it on the left.

MAP ❶ RUKONGAI

WUZZ
WUZZ
WUZZ
WUZZ
WUZZ

Souls sent from the world of the living arrive here in Rukongai. It is divided into four major zones. Each of these huge sectors is further divided into numerous wards and blocks: the larger the sector number, the more dangerous the sector. Avoid such areas as much as possible.

MAP ❷ THE NUCLEUS OF THE SOUL SOCIETY: THE SEIREITEI

Soaring high above the center of the Soul Society is our headquarters, the Seireitei. It is barrier-free and connects to Rukongai. However, if you approach the Seireitei, be careful of the Seirei Wall, which will come hurtling down.

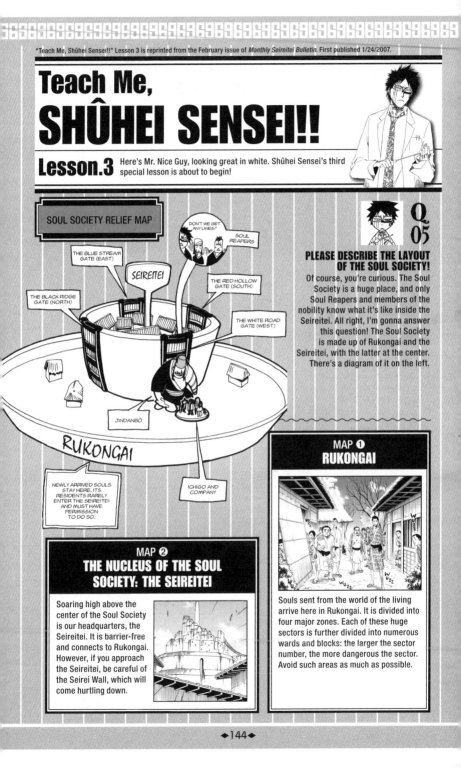

Q 06

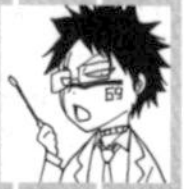

GIVE US MORE DETAILS ABOUT THE SEIREITEI!

Actually, the information is confidential... We're duty-bound not to speak about it, so I can't really tell you any details. Sorry. Well, I feel bad about it, so I'll tell you something harmless. In the center of the Seireitei is a white tower known as the Senzaikyû, where criminals are imprisoned; on the hill adjacent to it is the Sôkyoku.

WHERE SOUL REAPERS LIVE

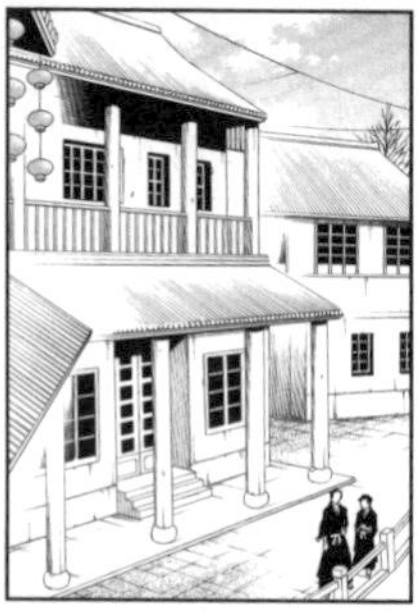

Those permitted to live in the tranquility of the Seireitei are Soul Reapers and the few families of the nobility. We live in the company barracks, while high-ranking officers commute from their own homes.

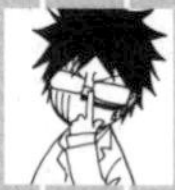

Sôkyoku Hill is also known as the Garden of Judgment, where sentences are carried out with company captains serving as observers. The Sôkyoku is a form of punishment reserved for the most serious offenses and is mainly applied to crimes committed by those with a captain's rank and above. This instrument of punishment, which consists of a giant spear and rack, is said to have a destructive force one million times greater than a zanpaku-tô.

RESTRICTED AREA: NO TRESPASSING

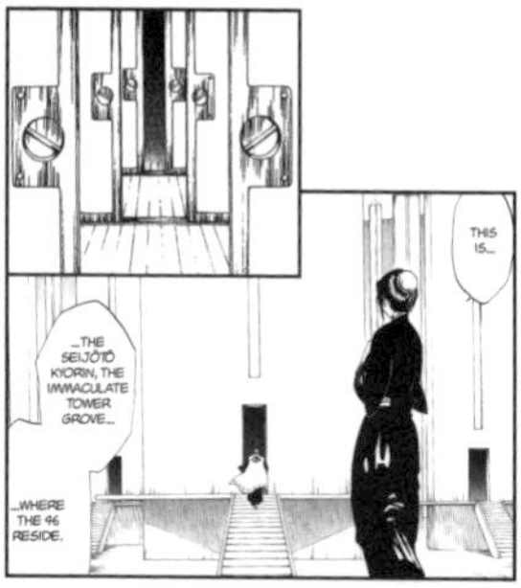
THIS IS...
...THE SEIJÔTÔ KYORIN, THE IMMACULATE TOWER GROVE...
...WHERE THE 46 RESIDE.

Inside the Seireitei are areas that are restricted even to those with the rank of captain. Places like the underground assembly hall or the Seijôtô Kyorin (Immaculate Tower Grove). Not that I have any business there, but I can't help but be curious.

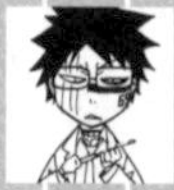

Well? Did you learn a little about the Soul Society? Now then, I have some good news! We have a special guest lecturer for the very first time, and that person is...someone very popular—Assistant Captain of Tenth Company, Rangiku Matsumoto Sensei!

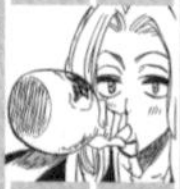

Hello, everyone. ♥ I'm Rangiku Matsumoto. ♥

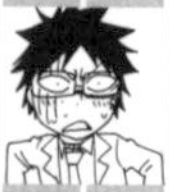

Huh...? Wha--?!!

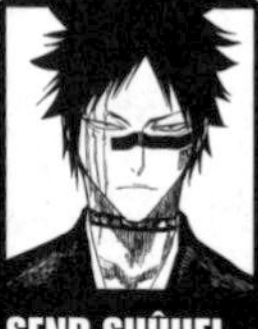

SEND SHÛHEI SENSEI LETTERS OF SUPPORT!

If you write now, the reply rate will be 120 percent. He'll send 20 percent more replies than letters received.

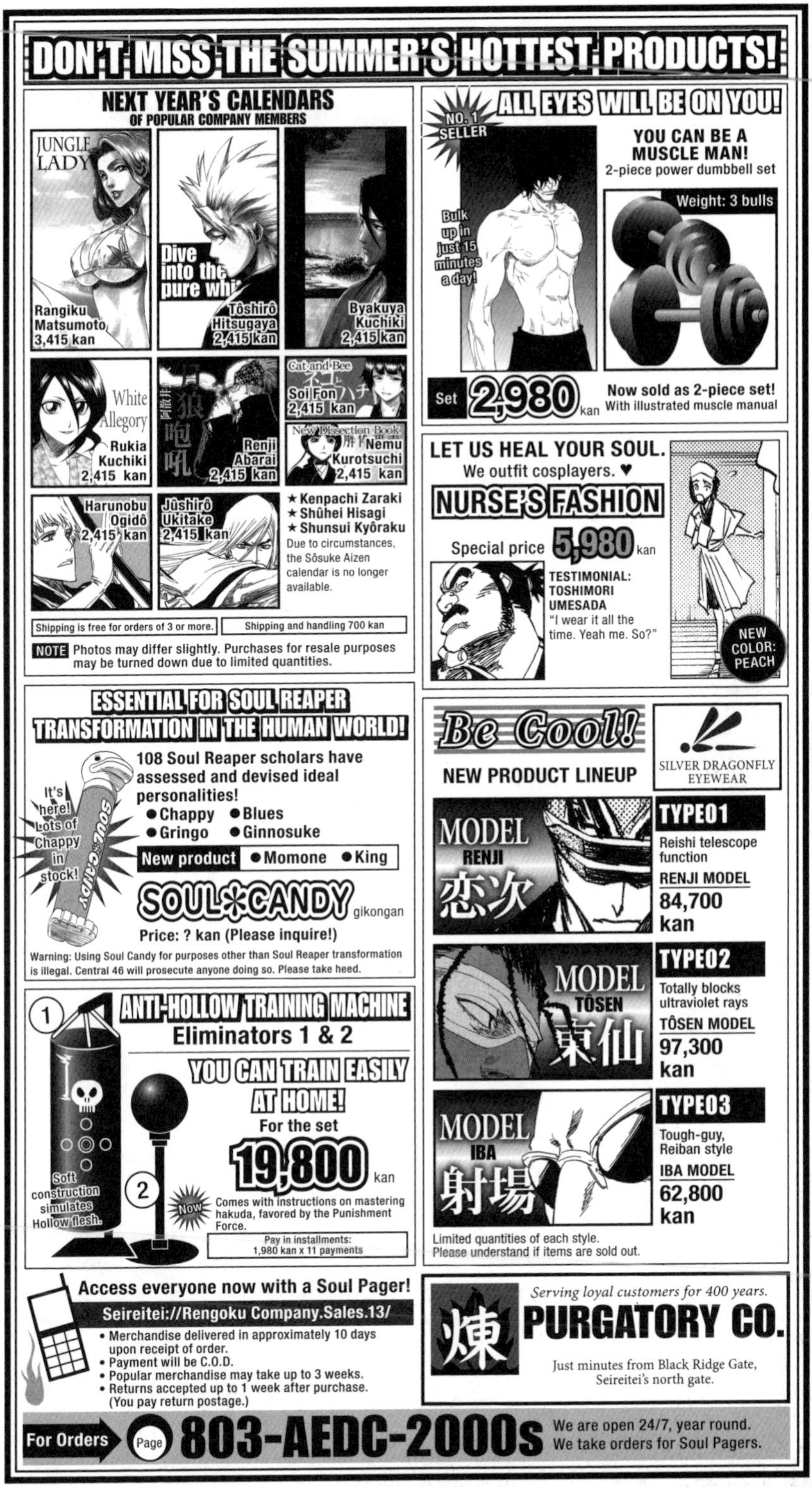
DON'T MISS THE SUMMER'S HOTTEST PRODUCTS!
NEXT YEAR'S CALENDARS
OF POPULAR COMPANY MEMBERS
JUNGLE LADY
Rangiku Matsumoto 3,415 kan
Dive into the pure whi
Tôshirô Hitsugaya 2,415 kan
Byakuya Kuchiki 2,415 kan
White Allegory
Rukia Kuchiki 2,415 kan
Renji Abarai 2,415 kan
Cat and Bee
Soi Fon 2,415 kan
New Dissection Book
Nemu Kurotsuchi 2,415 kan
Harunobu Ogidô 2,415 kan
Jûshirô Ukitake 2,415 kan
★ Kenpachi Zaraki
★ Shûhei Hisagi
★ Shunsui Kyôraku
Due to circumstances, the Sôsuke Aizen calendar is no longer available.
Shipping is free for orders of 3 or more.
Shipping and handling 700 kan
NOTE Photos may differ slightly. Purchases for resale purposes may be turned down due to limited quantities.
ALL EYES WILL BE ON YOU!
NO. 1 SELLER
YOU CAN BE A MUSCLE MAN!
2-piece power dumbbell set
Weight: 3 bulls
Bulk up in just 15 minutes a day!
Set 2,980 kan
Now sold as 2-piece set!
With illustrated muscle manual
LET US HEAL YOUR SOUL.
We outfit cosplayers. ♥
NURSE'S FASHION
Special price 5,980 kan
TESTIMONIAL: TOSHIMORI UMESADA
"I wear it all the time. Yeah me. So?"
NEW COLOR: PEACH
ESSENTIAL FOR SOUL REAPER TRANSFORMATION IN THE HUMAN WORLD!
It's here! Lots of Chappy in stock!
108 Soul Reaper scholars have assessed and devised ideal personalities!
●Chappy ●Blues
●Gringo ●Ginnosuke
New product ●Momone ●King
SOUL*CANDY gikongan
Price: ? kan (Please inquire!)
Warning: Using Soul Candy for purposes other than Soul Reaper transformation is illegal. Central 46 will prosecute anyone doing so. Please take heed.
Be Cool!
NEW PRODUCT LINEUP
SILVER DRAGONFLY EYEWEAR
MODEL RENJI 恋次
TYPE01
Reishi telescope function
RENJI MODEL
84,700 kan
MODEL TÔSEN 東仙
TYPE02
Totally blocks ultraviolet rays
TÔSEN MODEL
97,300 kan
MODEL IBA 射場
TYPE03
Tough-guy, Reiban style
IBA MODEL
62,800 kan
Limited quantities of each style.
Please understand if items are sold out.
① ANTI-HOLLOW TRAINING MACHINE
Eliminators 1 & 2
YOU CAN TRAIN EASILY AT HOME!
For the set
19,800 kan
Soft construction simulates Hollow flesh.
②
Now
Comes with instructions on mastering hakuda, favored by the Punishment Force.
Pay in installments: 1,980 kan x 11 payments
Access everyone now with a Soul Pager!
Seireitei://Rengoku Company.Sales.13/
• Merchandise delivered in approximately 10 days upon receipt of order.
• Payment will be C.O.D.
• Popular merchandise may take up to 3 weeks.
• Returns accepted up to 1 week after purchase. (You pay return postage.)
Serving loyal customers for 400 years.
煉 PURGATORY CO.
Just minutes from Black Ridge Gate, Seireitei's north gate.
For Orders Page 803-AEDC-2000s
We are open 24/7, year round.
We take orders for Soul Pagers.

That red-haired scoundrel Renji Abarai gives tips on the essentials of battle in his popular column, “Let’s Do Shikai!!” The much-touted three-part series is reprinted here!

Men, Claw Your Way Up in the World!!

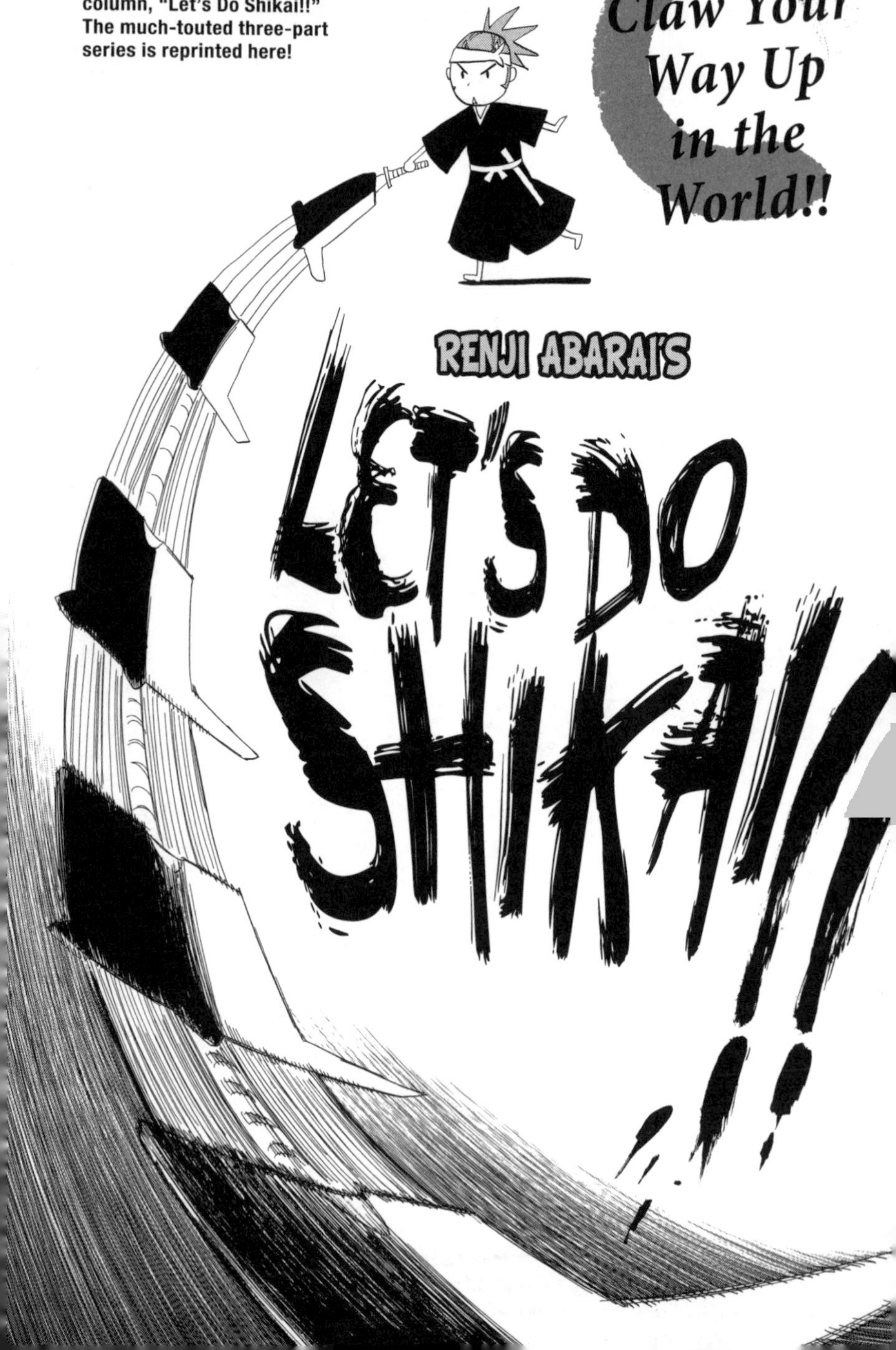
RENJI ABARAI’S
LET’S DO SHIKAI!!

Renji Abarai's
Let's Do Shikai!!

38TH BATTLE

The essence of battle is zanjutsu! Master the zanpaku-tô and seek to become a real man!

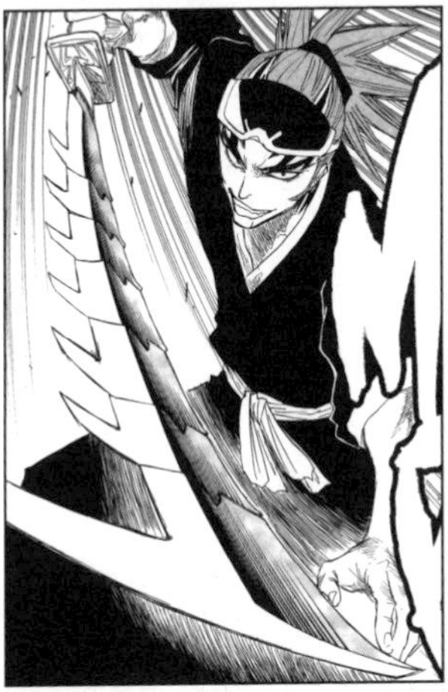

The essential zanpaku-tô battle guide for novice Soul Reapers

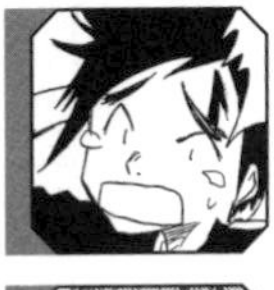

Renji! Ugh, I've had enough. I've lost twenty practice matches in a row. How can I be as strong as you, Renji? Ugh.

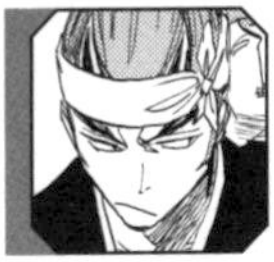

Just because a man loses, that's no reason to cry! No matter how often you may lose, the one who is still standing at the end is the victor! Follow me!

Trained in Zanpaku-tô Techniques!!

Zanjutsu: the basic battle technique of Soul Reapers. Renji will teach you the proper way to wield the zanpaku-tô, which is the cornerstone of every battle! New members, take heed!

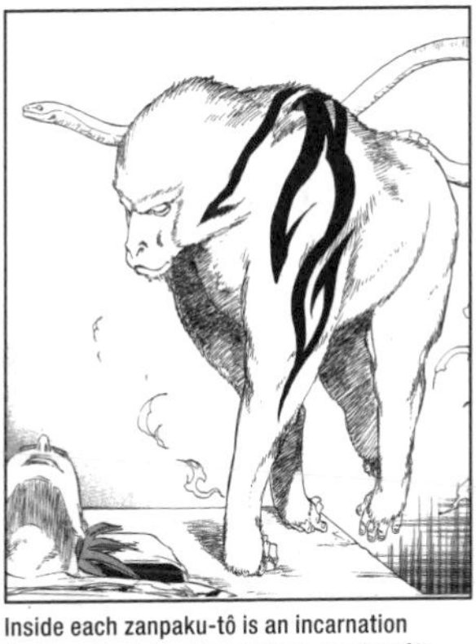

Inside each zanpaku-tô is an incarnation that manifests itself upon the zanpaku-tô's transformation. The first step is to acquaint oneself with this incarnation.

Your heart must become one with your zanpaku-tô. Talk to it, get in tune with it!

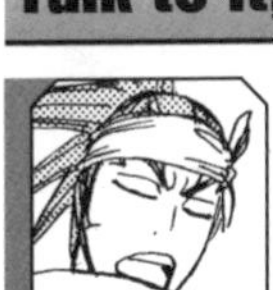

The first basic rule when using the zanpaku-tô in battle is to harmonize with it. Calm your mind and become one with your zanpaku-tô. Go on, try it!

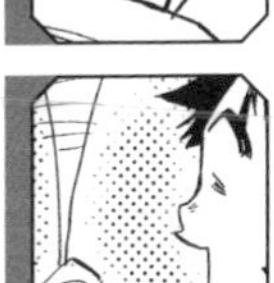

Okay! Hello, zanpaku-tô. Nice weather, isn't it? My name is Rikichi. Please tell me your name...

Renji Abarai's "Let's Do Shikai!!," 38th Battle reprint. First published in *Monthly Seireitei Bulletin*, March Issue, February 24, 2005.

The goal is bankai! Grab the captain's seat!

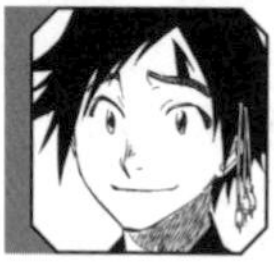

Hey, I think I'm a bit stronger! At this rate, I might easily master bankai. Then I could become a captain too, couldn't I? Huh? Captain...Zaraki?!

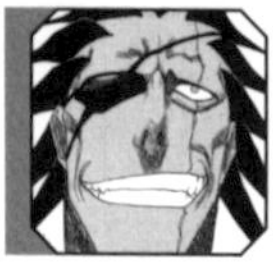

How amusing. So you want to become a captain? Then I'll take you on. What's the matter? Come at me. You'll be a captain if you can beat me!

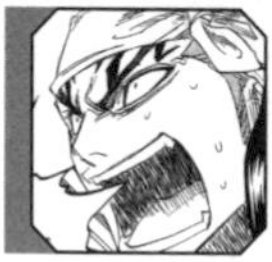

C-C-Captain Zaraki! Um... Ikkaku was over there looking for you. He said something about wanting a bout! Yeah, over there! Well, that's all for today!

Every Soul Reaper Will Be Scrupulously

Zanpaku-tô Chart of Higher-Ranking Officers

Shigekuni Genryûsai Yamamoto	SHIKAI / *Ryûjin Jakka*
Chôjiro Sasakibe	SHIKAI / *Gonryômaru*
Soi Fon	SHIKAI / *Suzumebachi*
Marechiyo Ômaeda	SHIKAI / *Gegetsuburi*
Gin Ichimaru	SHIKAI / *Shinsô*
Izuru Kira	SHIKAI / *Wabisuke*
Retsu Unohana	SHIKAI / *Minazuki*
Isane Kotetsu	SHIKAI / *Itegumo*
Hanatarô Yamada	SHIKAI / *Hisagomaru*
Sôsuke Aizen	SHIKAI / *Kyôkasuigetsu*
Momo Hinamori	SHIKAI / *Tobiume*
Byakuya Kuchiki	SHIKAI / *Senbonzakura* BANKAI / *Senbonzakura Kageyoshi*
Renji Abarai	SHIKAI / *Zabimaru* BANKAI / *Hihiô Zabimaru*
Sajin Komamura	SHIKAI / *Tenken* BANKAI / *Kokujô Tengen Myô-oh*
Jirôbô Ikkanzaka	SHIKAI / *Tsunzakikarasu*
Shunsui Kyôraku	SHIKAI / *Katen Kyôkotsu*
Tatsufusa Enjôji	SHIKAI / *Hôzan*
Kaname Tôsen	SHIKAI / *Suzumushi* BANKAI / *Suzumushi Tsuishiki, Enma Kôrogi*
Tôshirô Hitsugaya	SHIKAI / *Hyôrinmaru* BANKAI / *Daiguren Hyôrinmaru*
Rangiku Matsumoto	SHIKAI / *Haineko*
Ikkaku Madarame	SHIKAI / *Hôzukimaru*
Yumichika Ayasegawa	SHIKAI / *Fujikujaku*
Mayuri Kurotsuchi	SHIKAI / *Ashisogi Jizô* BANKAI / *Konjiki Ashisogi Jizô*
Jûshirô Ukitake	SHIKAI / *Sôgyo no Kotowari*
Kaien Shiba	SHIKAI / *Nejibana*
Rukia Kuchiki	SHIKAI / *Sode no Shirayuki*

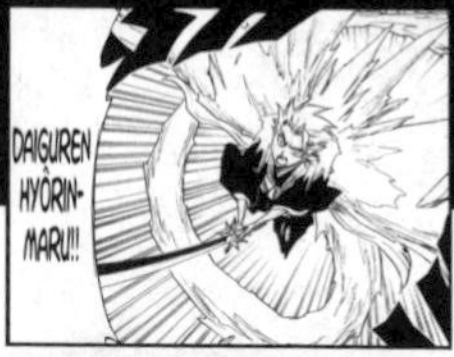
DAIGUREN HYÔRIN-MARU!!

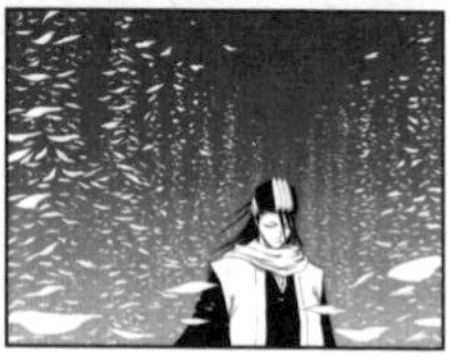

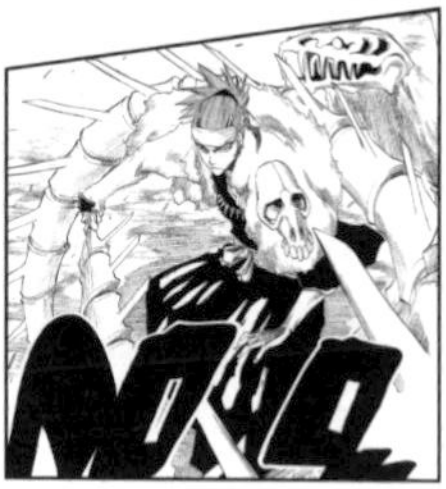

43RD BAT

Let's Do Shikai!!

This special column is brought to you by Renji Abarai, who strives to be a man among men! Here's this month's feature!

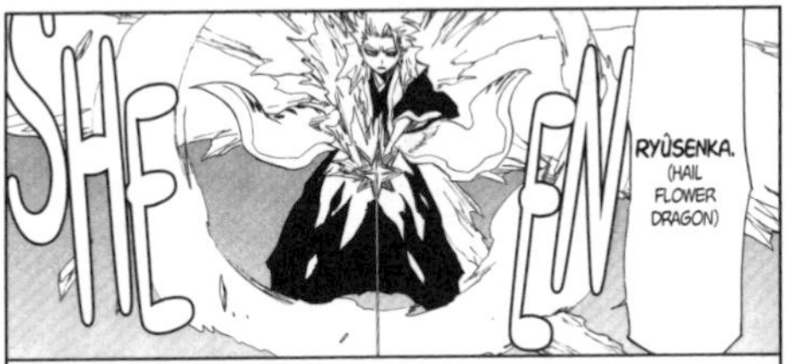
SHE
EN
RYÛSENKA. (HAIL FLOWER DRAGON)

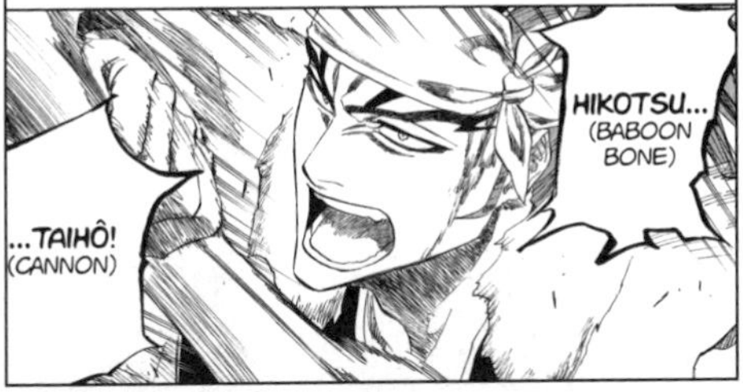
HIKOTSU... (BABOON BONE)
...TAIHÔ! (CANNON)

The beauty of battle: you must master a lethal move!

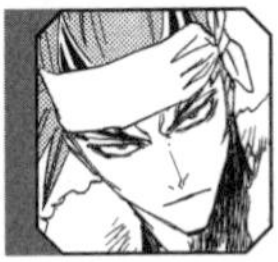

What makes a battle truly exciting is the power of a single blow, a distinctive lethal move. If you're a real man, you'll need to have a couple of them up your sleeve!

Get Your Very Own Lethal Move!

Every man longs to use a lethal move at least once in his life! Having one makes a huge difference in the outcome of a battle. If you're a man, aim for the top!

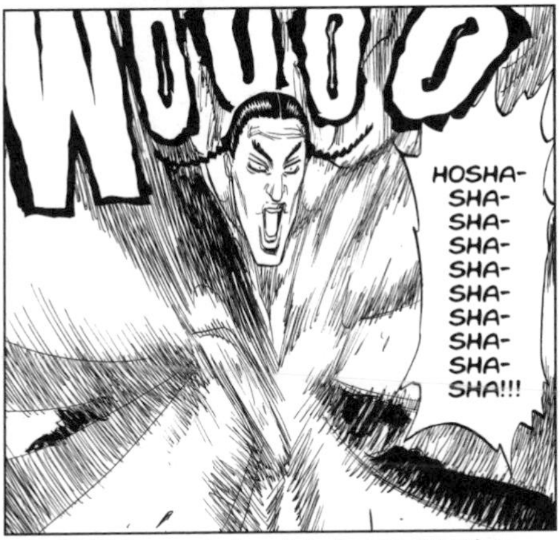
HOSHA-SHA-SHA-SHA-SHA-SHA-SHA-SHA-SHA-SHA-SHA!!!

Enjôji of Eighth Company also has a distinctive move called Hôzan Kenbu.

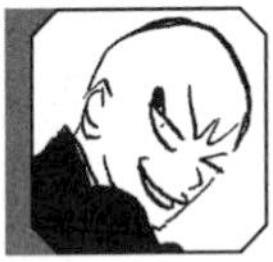

Hey, Renji, you're awfully excited. Want a taste of my distinctive move? How about it? It really is the best. It's called the Luh-Luh-Luh Lucky Dance.

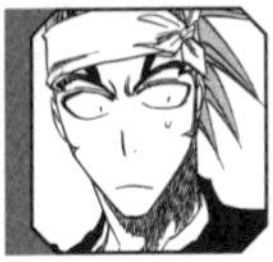

Yeah, yeah... It's that one, isn't it, the weird dance you do when you're feeling good. I don't think you can call it a lethal move.

Renji Abarai's "Let's Do Shikai!!," 43rd Battle reprint. First published in *Monthly Seireitei Bulletin*, August Issue, July 24, 2005.

Steal a lethal move from your superior!

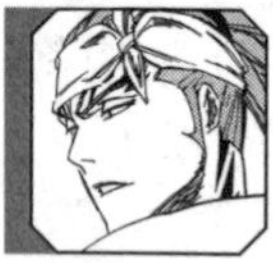

First, take a hard look at a superior's distinctive moves. As the chart shows, every high-ranking officer has his unique lethal move. Why, Captain Byakuya has three.

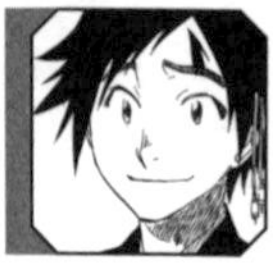

Wow! Even you have two distinctive moves, Renji! All right! I won't fall behind! Um, first...I have the Jennifer Dance. And then...

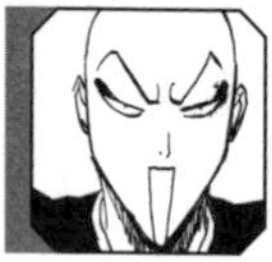

Hold it! Speaking of dancing, it's my turn! Watch me, Ikkaku Madarame! Such supple moves! Now this is the Luh-Luh-Luh Lucky Dance of my family heirloom sword! Luh-Luh. ♪ Luh-Luh-Luh. ♪

If You Aspire to Be a Captain...

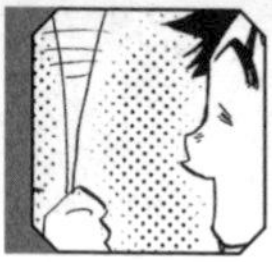

W-wow! The Third Seat of Eleventh Company's fighting squad is cool... All right! I can do it! Luh-Luh. ♪ Luh-Luh. ♪

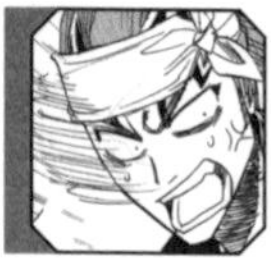

Wake up, Rikichi! That's not even a move. It's a silly dance! C'mon, go home already, Ikkaku. You've ruined everything.

Heirloom Swords: A List of Famous Lethal Moves

Soi Fon	Nigeki Kessatsu
Byakuya Kuchiki	Senka Senkei Senbonzakura Kageyoshi Shûkei Hakuteiken
Renji Abarai	Higa Zekkô Hikotsu Taihô
Kaname Tôsen	Suzumushi Nishiki (Beni Hikô)
Tôshirô Hitsugaya	Ryûsenka Sennen Hyôrô
Rukia Kuchiki	Some No Mai (Tsukishiro) Tsugi No Mai (Hakuren)
Yoruichi Shihôin	Shunkô Hanki Sôsai
Ichigo Kurosaki / ryoka	Getsuga Tenshô
Jidanbô	Banzai Jidanda Matsuri

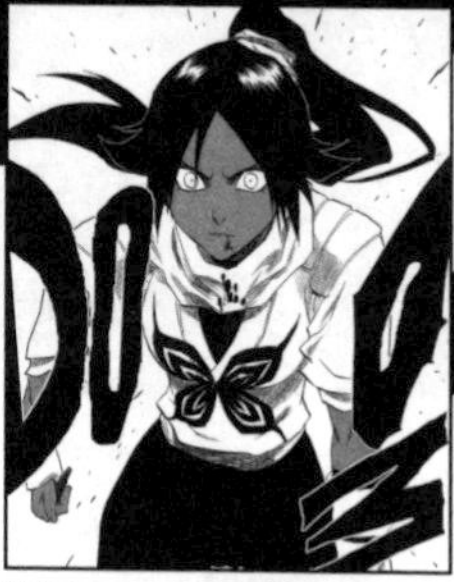

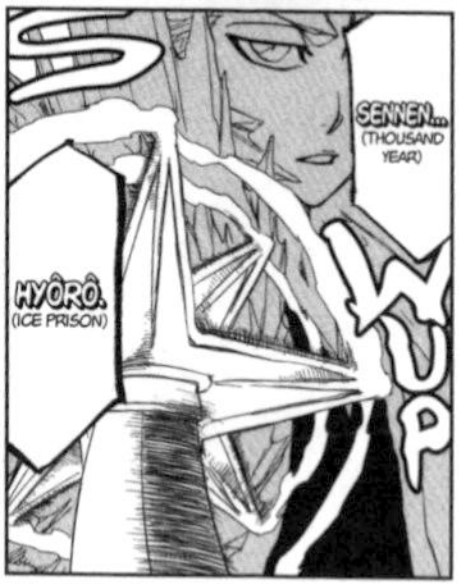
SENNEN... (THOUSAND YEAR)
HYÔRÔ. (ICE PRISON)

Renji Abarai's

Let's Do Shikai!!

51ST BATTLE

The intrusion of the ryoka led to chaos. Let's take a close look at the fierce battles that were fought!

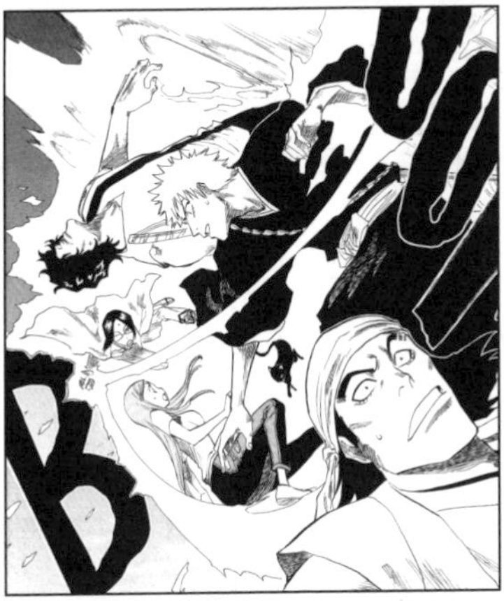

The moment of the ryoka's capture. They look violent.

The Soul Society mobilizes all of its forces in a struggle to the death with the ryoka!

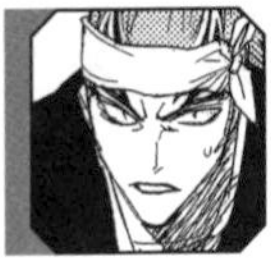

As you'll probably remember, a group of ryoka recently stole into the Soul Society. The warriors of the Thirteen Court Guard Companies beat them back soundly. Now let's look at the various battles. That's the purpose of today's column. Let me just say, it was tough.

The Fierce Battles! Let's Revisit the Memorable Ones!

The insolence of the ryoka, slipping into the center of the Soul Society, the Seireitei, like that. The Thirteen Court Guard Companies stood ready to repel them!

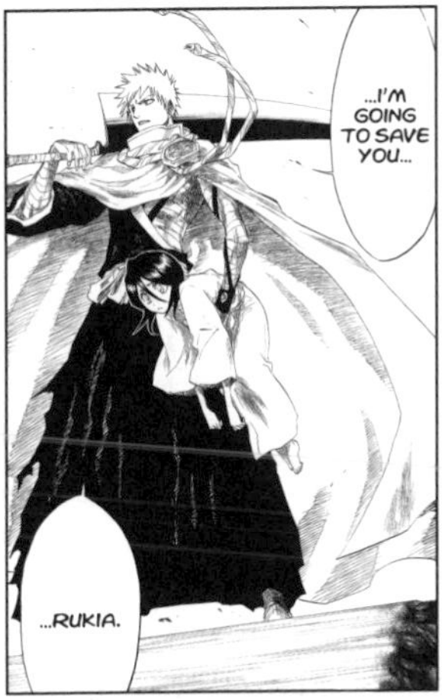
...I'M GOING TO SAVE YOU...
...RUKIA.

A special shot of Ichigo Kurosaki, the ryoka who infiltrated the Seireitei, upon being captured. It appears as though he's holding Thirteenth Company's Kuchiki under his arm.

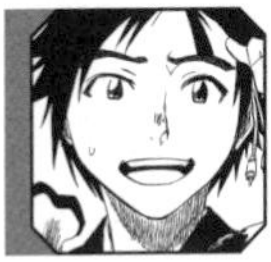

That's true, Renji. You were twice worn out, but you were super-awesome, Renji! Rukia was safe, too, and it's all because of your efforts. You are so cool, Renji!

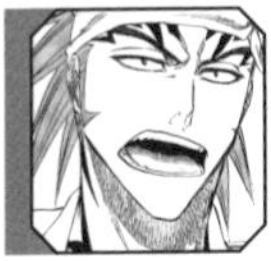

O-oh, well, I wasn't that great! You're overstating it, Rikichi! But the intrusion caused plenty of injuries. Even Captain Kuchiki... It's too bad...really...

Renji Abarai's "Let's Do Shikai!!," 51st Battle reprint. First published in *Monthly Seireitei Bulletin*, April Issue, March 24, 2006.

Famous bouts that will go down in history

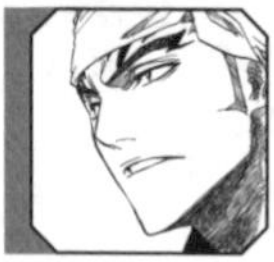

That was the battle in which I faced him head-on for the first time. It ended like that, but the result isn't everything, right? There are times when a man can't hold back!

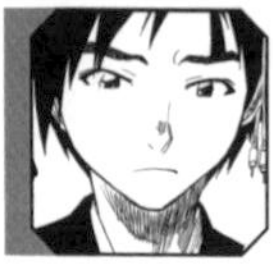

Huh? According to this list, Renji, you had two consecutive losses. You know, I hate to say it, but as the writer of this column, you...

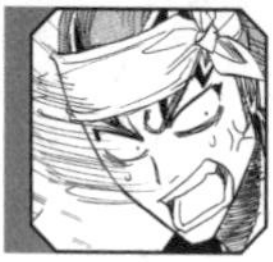

You idiot! A man must always choose the difficult path! There's no meaning in fighting guys you'll always beat! W-what's with the look?! Stop looking at me like that! Hey, you... wait up, Rikichi!

Intrusion in the Soul Society:

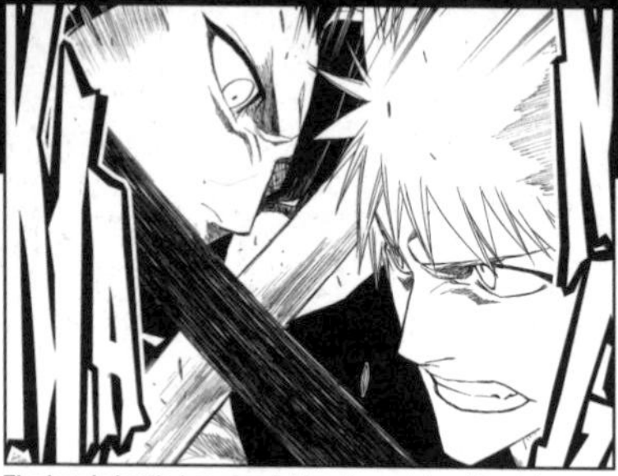

The heroic battle between Ichigo Kurosaki and Captain Kuchiki of Sixth Company! Their swords clashed ceaselessly in a battle that will go down in history.

A lone man, Renji Abarai, bares his teeth at his superior, Byakuya, which is certain to cause a rift between them!

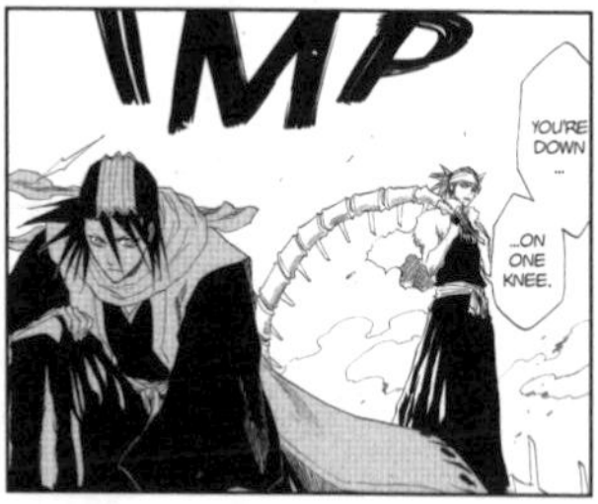
YOU'RE DOWN ...
...ON ONE KNEE.

List of Battles and Results

Gin Ichimaru	△ – △	Ichigo Kurosaki / ryoka
Ikkaku Madarame	× – ○	Ichigo Kurosaki / ryoka
Yumichika Ayasegawa	× – ○	Ganju Shiba / ryoka
Jirôbô Ikkanzaka	× – ○	Uryû Ishida / ryoka
Renji Abarai	× – ○	Ichigo Kurosaki / ryoka
Momo Hinamori	△ – △	Izuru Kira
Kenpachi Zaraki	× – ○	Ichigo Kurosaki / ryoka
Tatsufusa Enjôji	× – ○	Yasutora Sado / ryoka
Shunsui Kyôraku	○ – ×	Yasutora Sado / ryoka
Byakuya Kuchiki	○ – ×	Ganju Shiba / ryoka
Mayuri Kurotsuchi	× – ○	Uryû Ishida / ryoka
Byakuya Kuchiki	○ – ×	Renji Abarai
Shûhei Hisagi	× – ○	Yumichika Ayasegawa
Kenpachi Zaraki	○ – ×	Kaname Tôsen
Kenpachi Zaraki	△ – △	Sajin Komamura
Soi Fon	× – ○	Yoruichi Shihôin
Shigekuni Genryûsai Yamamoto	△ – △	Shunsui Kyôraku / Jûshirô Ukitake
Tetsuzaemon Iba	△ – △	Ikkaku Madarame
Byakuya Kuchiki	× – ○	Ichigo Kurosaki / ryoka

TÔSHIRÔ HITSUGAYA'S

BEAUTIFUL CRYSTAL

ON HIATUS

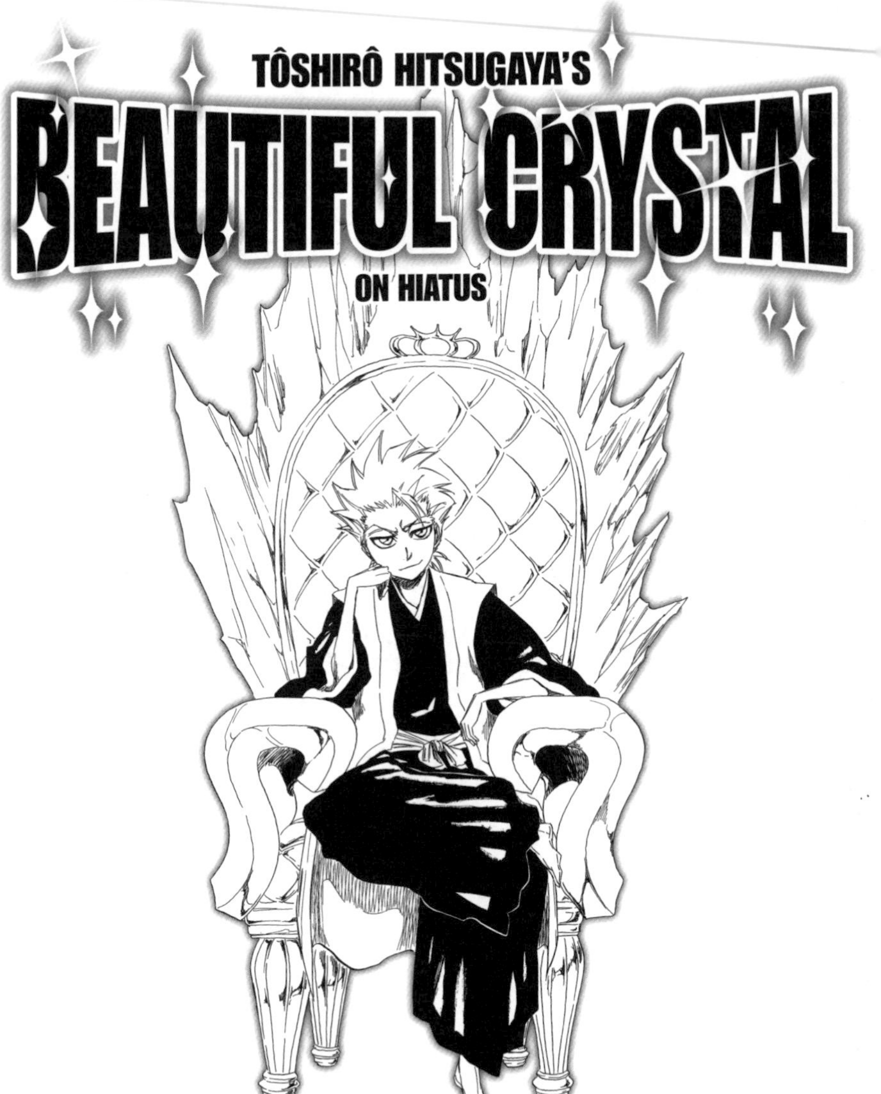

~ Apology and Announcement ~

In every issue, Tôshirô Hitsugaya, captain of Tenth Company, featured items such as carvings and chairs sculpted from ice in his hugely popular serial, "Beautiful Crystal." Every month, we've drawn ideas that readers have submitted and featured them in the magazine. The column will be going on hiatus this summer and will return in the November issue. Thank you for your understanding.

Monthly Seireitei Bulletin Editorial Department

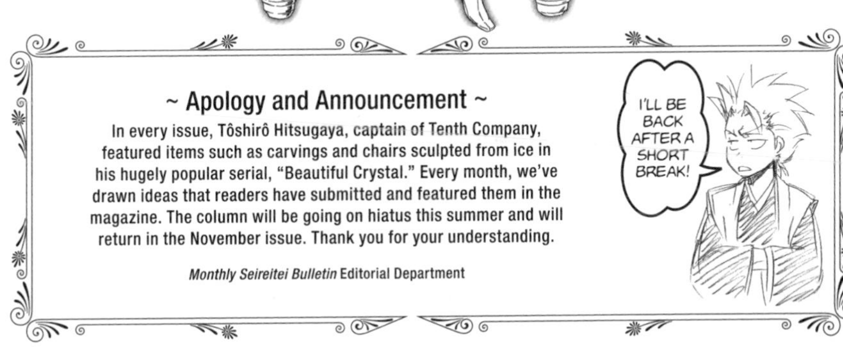
I'LL BE BACK AFTER A SHORT BREAK!

SOUL REAPER ACADEMY
ENTRANCE EXAMINATION QUESTIONS

TIME LIMIT: 60 MINUTES

A WORD OF ADVICE

To all who aspire to enter Soul Reaper Academy:
Past exam questions are now being made public.
Observe the 60-minute time limit and tackle
the questions honestly. Good luck to you.

Fill the blank with the correct word.
(2 POINTS EACH)

1. Those who have infiltrated the Soul Society, like Ichigo Kurosaki and Uryû Ishida, are known as

_____.

2. The name of Thirteenth Company Captain Ukitake's zanpaku-tô is _____.

3. Assistant Captain Yachiru Kusajishi of Eleventh Company gave the nickname "Maki-Maki" to Eleventh Company member _____.

2

Fill in the blank with the correct word.
(2 POINTS EACH)

1. The zanpaku-tô of Sixth Company Assistant Captain Renji Abarai is called _____.

2. The Spiritual Wave Measurement Lab in the Department of Research and Development has been observing the _____ for quite some time.

3. _____ is the great spiritual gate on the east side of the Seireitei.

2

3 **Next is the release (incantation) during shikai. Match each incantation to the correct person in panels A through D.**
(2 POINTS EACH)

1. Show yourself, Wabisuke.
2. Pierce him, Shinsô.
3. Extend, Hôzukimaru!
4. Snap, Tobiume!

A

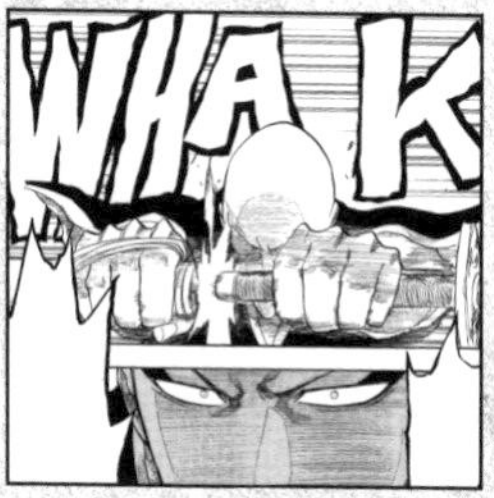
WHA K

B

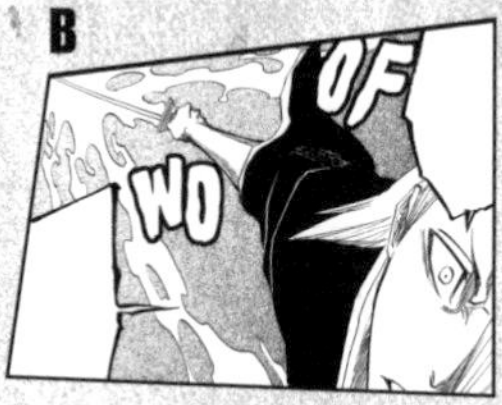
WO
OF

C

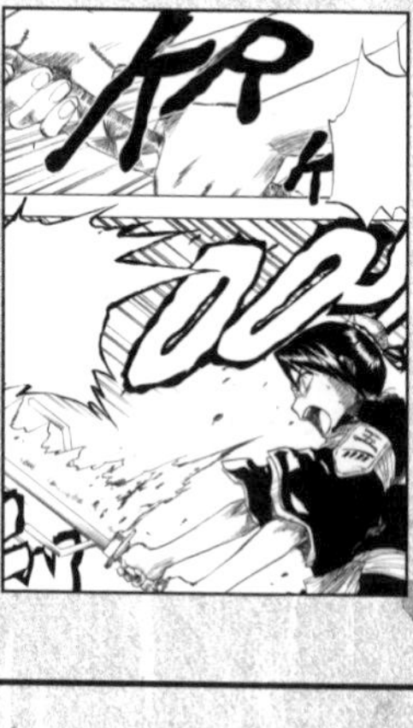
KR
K
OO

D

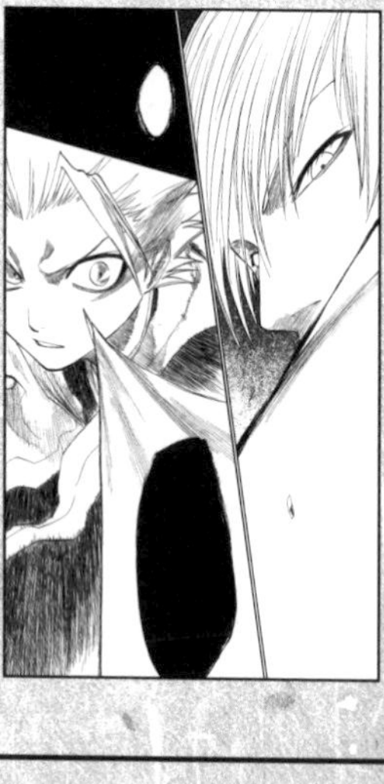

3

4 **Choose the right answer for each question from A through D.** (2 POINTS EACH)

1. Choose the correct incantation and explanation for the bankai of Captain Tôsen of Ninth Company.

   A. Robs his foes of the five senses, except pain, with the incantation "Suzumushi Tsuishiki, Enma Zemi."

   B. Robs his foes of the five senses, except smell, with the incantation "Suzumushi Tsuishiki, Enma Zemi."

   C. Robs his foes of the five senses, except touch, with the incantation "Suzumushi Tsuishiki, Enma Kôrogi."

   D. Robs his foes of the five senses, except spiritual pressure perception, with the incantation "Suzumushi Tsuishiki, Enmakôrogi."

2. Choose the answer that correctly describes the Sôkyoku, which was to be used in Rukia Kuchiki's execution.

   A. The true form of the Sôkyoku spear is called Kikô Oh, and it has the destructive power of 2 million zanpaku-tô.

   B. The true form of the Sôkyoku spear is called Kikô Oh, and it has the destructive power of 1 million zanpaku-tô.

   C. The true form of the Sôkyoku spear is called Zanpaku-tô, and it has the destructive power of 2 million zanpaku-tô.

   D. The true form of the Sôkyoku spear is called Zanpaku-tô, and it has the destructive power of 1 million zanpaku-tô.

4

3. Which answer correctly describes Central 46?

A. The supreme judicial organization made up of 35 technicians and 11 judges brought together from all across the Soul Society.

B. The supreme judicial organization made up of 40 sages and 6 judges brought together from all across the Soul Society.

C. The supreme judicial organization made up of 40 scholars and 6 judges brought together from all across the Soul Society.

D. The supreme lawmaking organization made up of 40 sages and 6 judges brought together from all across the Soul Society.

4. Who has never been a member of the Thirteen Court Guard Companies?

A

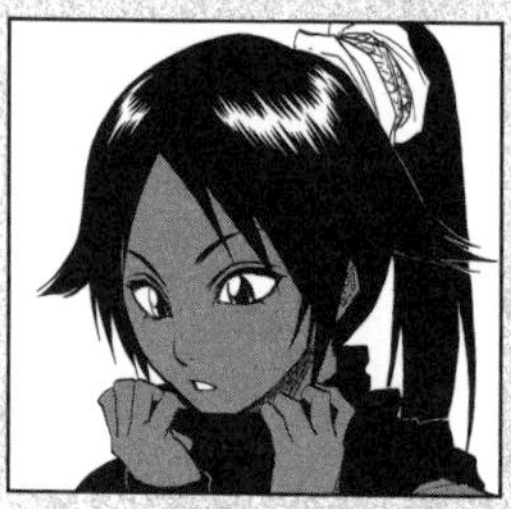

B

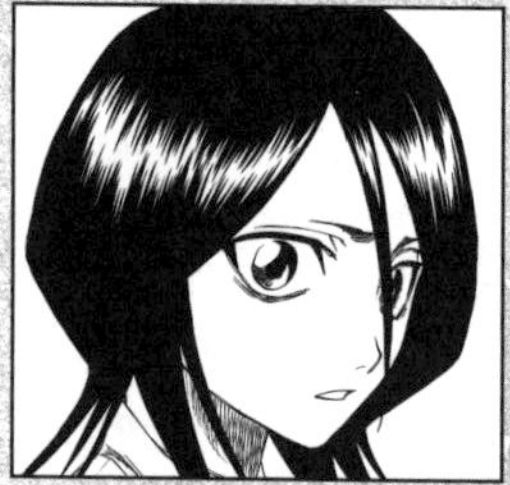

C

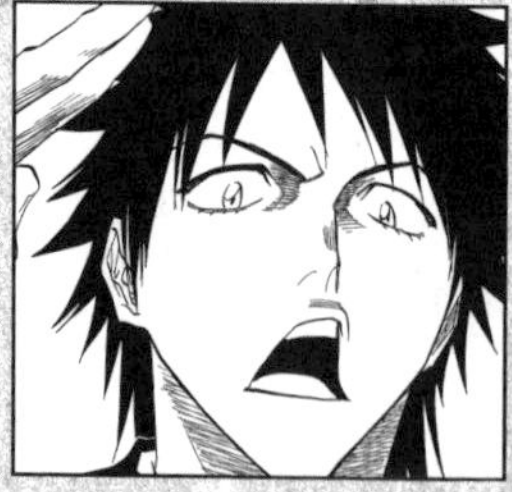

D

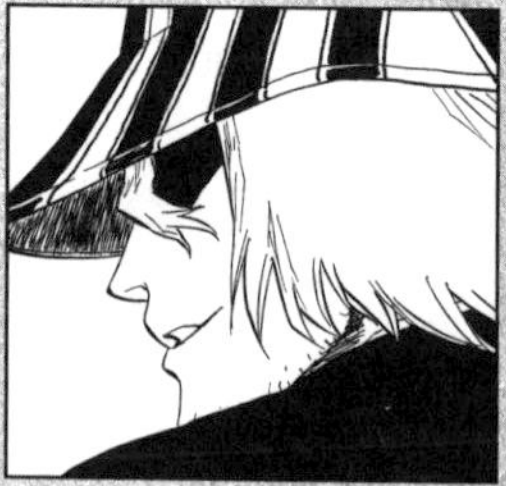

5

5 Answer the following questions about the Thirteen Court Guard Companies.

1. There are three ways in which one can be promoted to the rank of captain in the Thirteen Court Guard Companies. Fill in each blank with the correct answer. (3 POINTS EACH)

  A. By passing the captain's exam in the presence of at least ____ captains, including the Captain General.

   i. 3

   ii. 4

   iii. 5

   iv. 10

  B. By receiving the recommendations of more than ____ captains and the approval of ____ of the remaining captains. (Choose from the numbers below to fill the two blanks.)

   i. 6

   ii. 7

   iii. 8

   iv. 9

  C. By defeating the current captain one on one in the presence of ____ members.

   i. 50

   ii. 100

   iii. 200

   iv. 300

2. Among the current captains, who defeated a sitting captain one on one and took over his position? (3 POINTS)

6

6 **Find the names of these Soul Reapers in the grid below and write their names on the answer sheet.** (3 POINTS EACH)

1
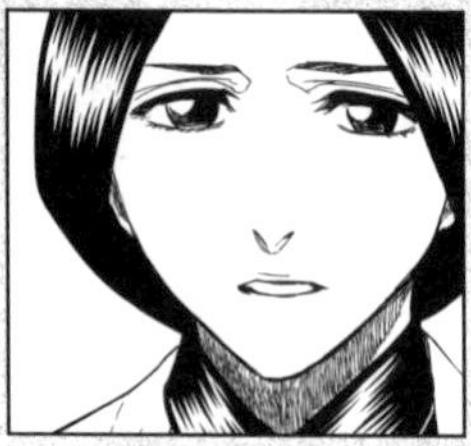

2
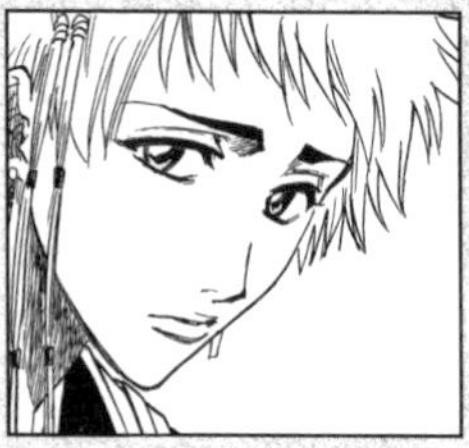

3
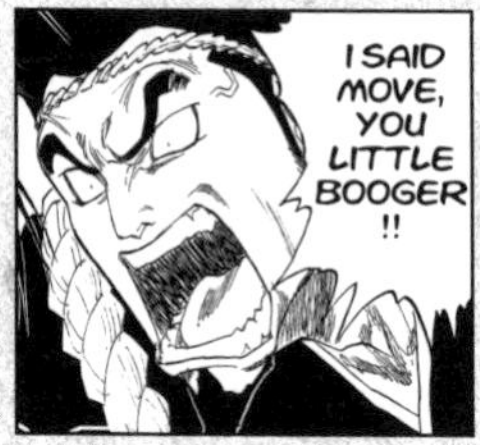
I SAID MOVE, YOU LITTLE BOOGER!!

4
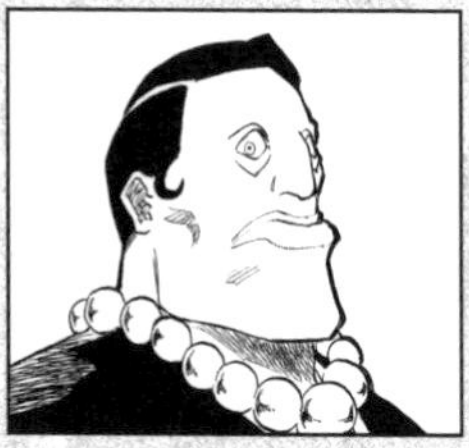

K	A	M	I	N	E	Z	A	K	I	R	Y	A	R	I	M
O	T	K	K	I	Y	O	H	A	K	O	N	O	Y	K	O
S	E	N	A	N	A	H	O	N	U	U	S	T	E	R	B
U	T	A	B	Z	O	K	U	S	I	K	A	R	I	O	M
A	U	E	U	O	N	E	N	O	G	U	K	A	N	B	A
I	B	S	S	U	K	A	I	S	A	H	O	B	O	A	M
E	R	U	T	O	M	O	K	A	S	H	I	A	E	T	T
Z	A	M	O	E	U	A	E	K	O	N	N	O	T	S	U
B	Y	A	K	U	T	H	O	M	I	N	A	K	K	U	C
A	N	K	O	N	S	O	S	E	M	O	B	Y	A	C	H
I	T	E	R	O	B	Y	K	S	Y	A	B	A	C	H	O
S	E	N	A	R	A	J	I	E	O	R	U	O	R	I	M
K	A	Z	T	S	U	O	N	I	N	R	O	S	R	K	N
E	H	O	N	U	I	S	A	M	I	A	A	S	H	I	N
H	S	O	E	N	S	U	R	J	U	R	S	T	O	N	J
T	I	H	S	A	M	M	A	I	T	A	M	I	M	Y	O

7

7 Name the following techniques. (3 POINTS EACH)

1

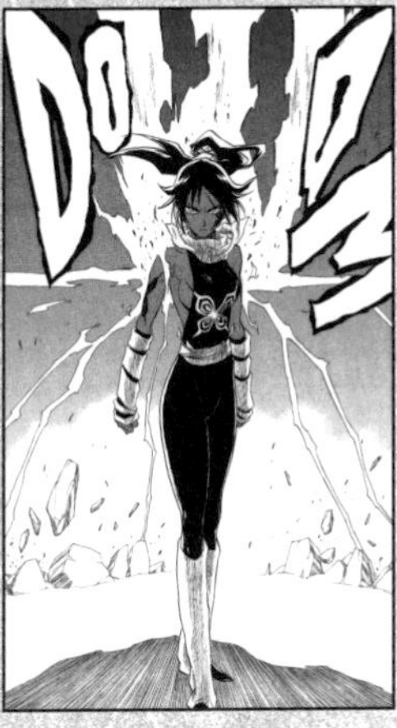

2

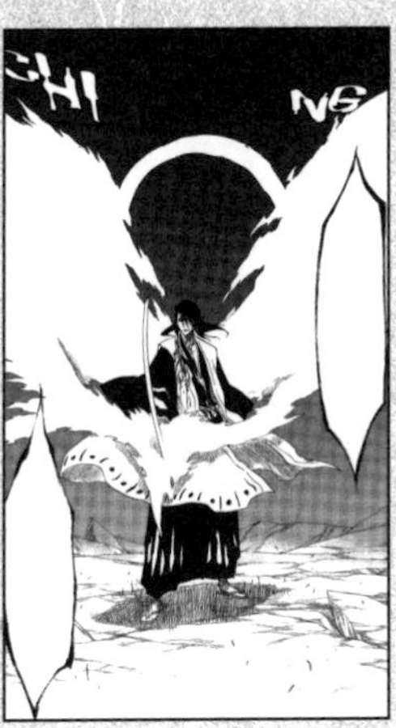

3

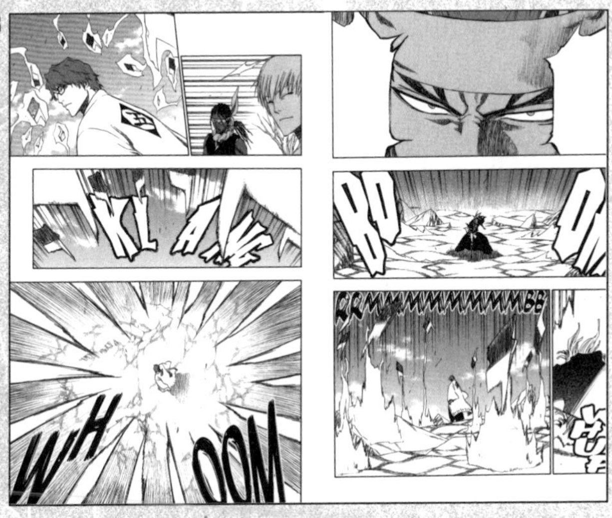

8

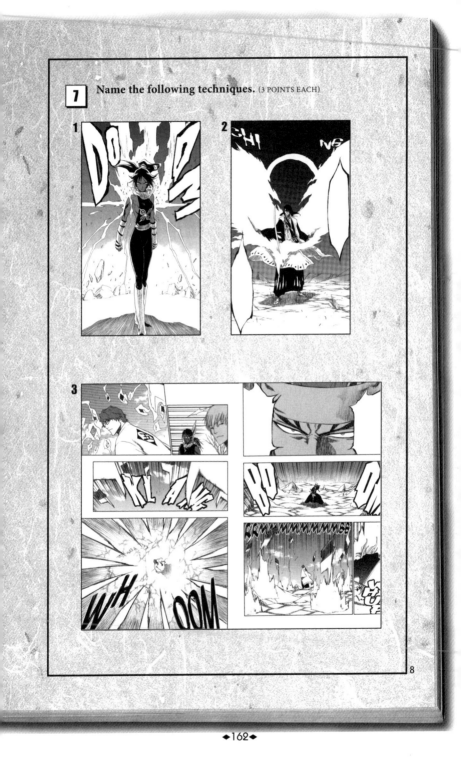

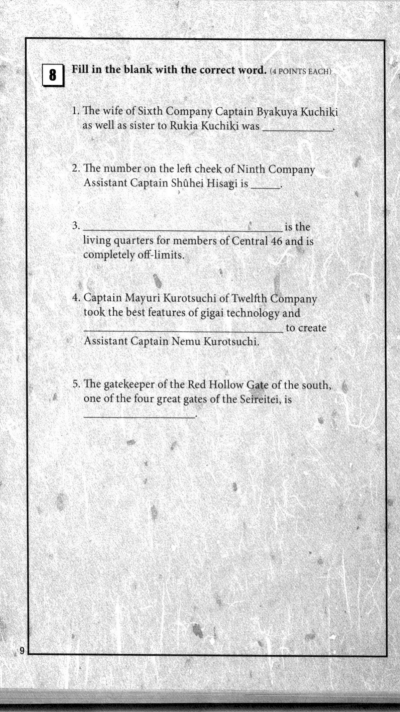

8 **Fill in the blank with the correct word.** (4 POINTS EACH)

1. The wife of Sixth Company Captain Byakuya Kuchiki as well as sister to Rukia Kuchiki was _____.

2. The number on the left cheek of Ninth Company Assistant Captain Shûhei Hisagi is _____.

3. _____ is the living quarters for members of Central 46 and is completely off-limits.

4. Captain Mayuri Kurotsuchi of Twelfth Company took the best features of gigai technology and _____ to create Assistant Captain Nemu Kurotsuchi.

5. The gatekeeper of the Red Hollow Gate of the south, one of the four great gates of the Seireitei, is _____.

9

9 **Pick the correct answer for each question from choices A through D.** (4 POINTS EACH)

1. What is the type of anesthetic that the Seventh Seat of Fourth Company, Hanatarô Yamada, administers to those with low spiritual pressure to make them faint?

    A. Reiten

    B. Sôten

    C. Shinten

    D. Raiten

2. What is the name of the Fourth Seat of Tenth Company?

    A. Tatsufusa Enjôji

    B. Harunobu Ogidô

    C. Toshimori Umesada

    D. Kôkichirô Takezoe

3. Bakudô 58 (Kakushi Tsuijaku) detects where an opponent will move next. An incantation is spoken to activate Bakudô 58. Which of the following incantations is not correct?

    A. Blood Vessels of the South

    B. Eyes of the North

    C. Fingertips of the West

    D. Heels of the East

4. Name the Hadô 33 that Captain Byakuya Kuchiki of Sixth Company used?

    A. Shakkahô (Red Flame Cannon)

    B. Byakurai (Pale Lightning)

    C. Sôkatsui (Pale Fire Crash)

    D. Rikujôkôrô (Six-Rod Light Restraint)

10

Soul Reaper Academy
Entrance Examination Questions
ANSWER SHEET

Test number		Points
Name		

1	1		2		3			
2	1		2		3			
3	1		2		3		4	
4	1		2		3		4	
5	1	A	B1	B2	C	2		
6	1		2					
	3		4					
7	1		2					
	3							
8	1		2		3			
	4		5					
9	1		2		3		4	

11

Cut here

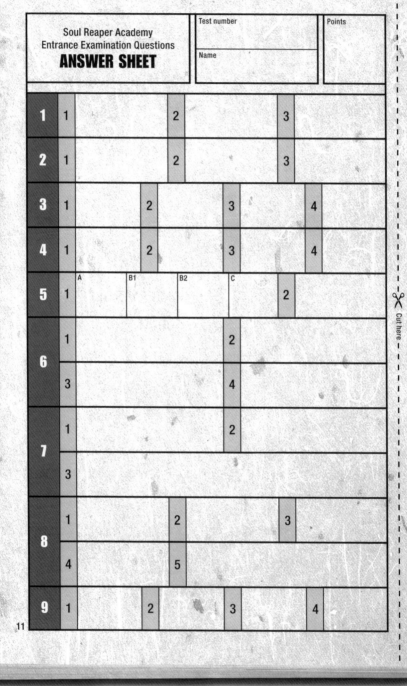

Soul Reaper Academy Entrance Examination Questions
ANSWERS AND EXPLANATIONS

1

1.

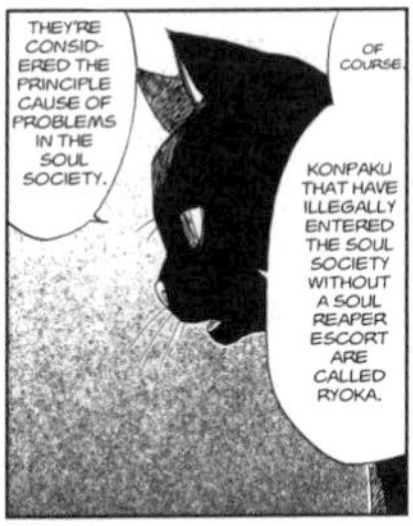

OF COURSE.
KONPAKU THAT HAVE ILLEGALLY ENTERED THE SOUL SOCIETY WITHOUT A SOUL REAPER ESCORT ARE CALLED RYOKA.
THEY'RE CONSIDERED THE PRINCIPLE CAUSE OF PROBLEMS IN THE SOUL SOCIETY.

RYOKA

2.

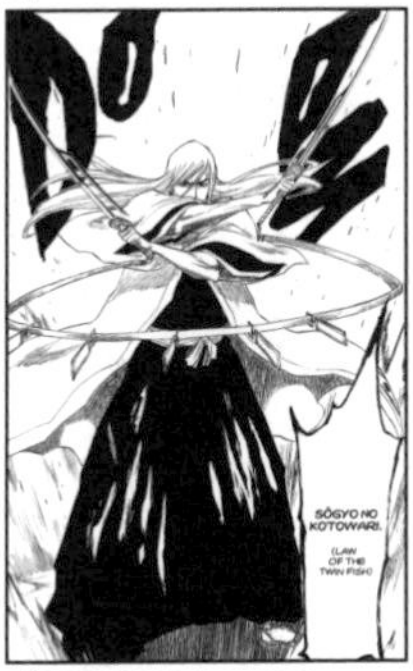

SÔGYO NO KOTOWARI.
(LAW OF THE TWIN FISH)

SÔGYO NO KOTOWARI

3.

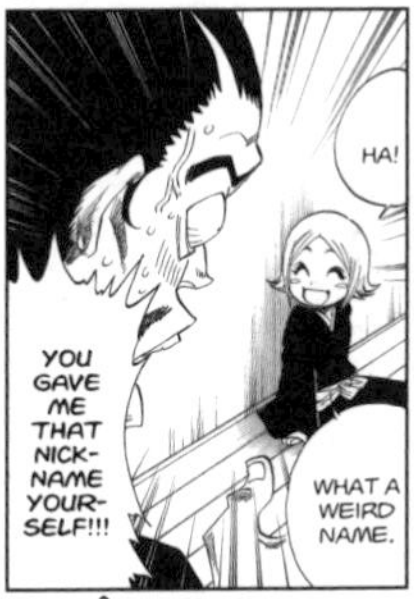

HA!
WHAT A WEIRD NAME.
YOU GAVE ME THAT NICKNAME YOURSELF!!!

MAKIZÔ ARAMAKI

EXPLANATION

The exam has questions about names and terms every year without fail. Names and terms can be easy (like ryoka) or more obscure (like Makizô Aramaki). Remember Aramaki? He's the Soul Reaper in Eleventh Company who Assistant Captain Kusajishi also nicknamed Mustachio.

2

1.

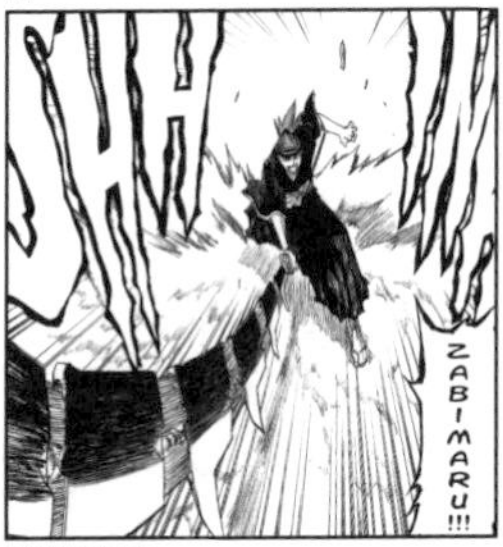

ZABIMARU!!!

ZABIMARU

2.

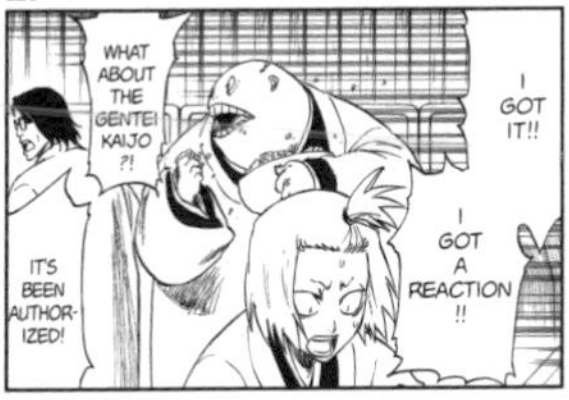

I GOT IT!!
WHAT ABOUT THE GENTEI KAIJO?!
I GOT A REACTION!!
IT'S BEEN AUTHORIZED!

ARRANCARS

3.

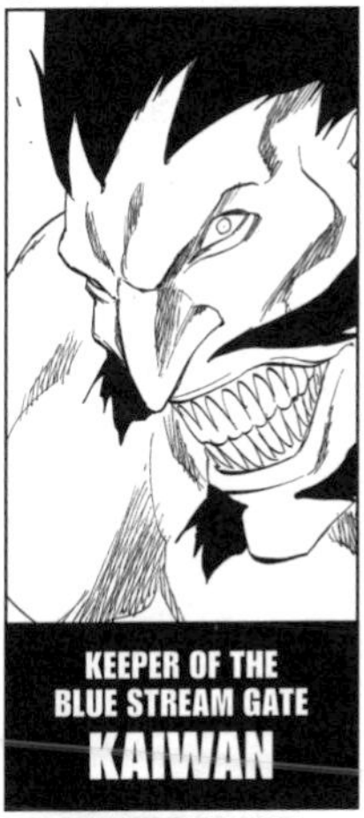

KEEPER OF THE BLUE STREAM GATE
KAIWAN

THE BLUE STREAM GATE

EXPLANATION

Fill-in-the-blank questions aren't as difficult as long answer questions, but it pays to memorize any term you encounter. For example, the exam often has questions about the four great Seireitei gates. Remember them together in order: the Blue Stream Gate (east), the White Road Gate (west), the Red Hollow Gate (south) and the Black Ridge Gate (north).

3

1. B

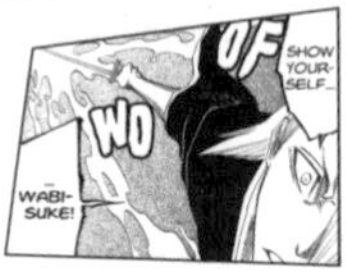
WO
OF
SHOW YOUR-SELF...
...WABI-SUKE!

3. A

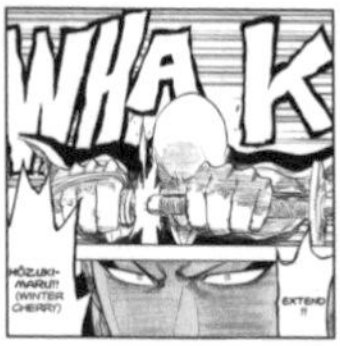
WHAK
EXTEND!!
HÔZUKI-MARU!! (WINTER CHERRY)

4. C

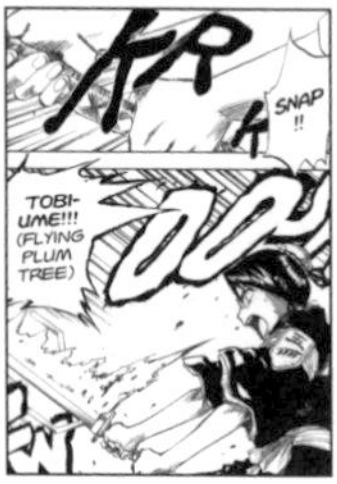
KR
SNAP!!
TOBI-UME!!! (FLYING PLUM TREE)

2. D

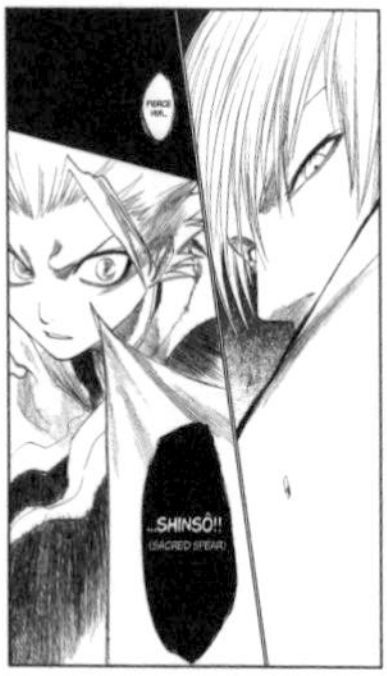
...SHINSÔ!! (SACRED SPEAR)

EXPLANATION

Shikai is the first stage of release of the zanpaku-tô. A special phrase (incantation) followed by the name of the zanpaku-tô activates shikai. It is crucial to memorize each phrase, as every zanpaku-tô has a different incantation. The exam often asks about incantations of Soul Reapers ranked above assistant captains, so keep that in mind.

4

1. C

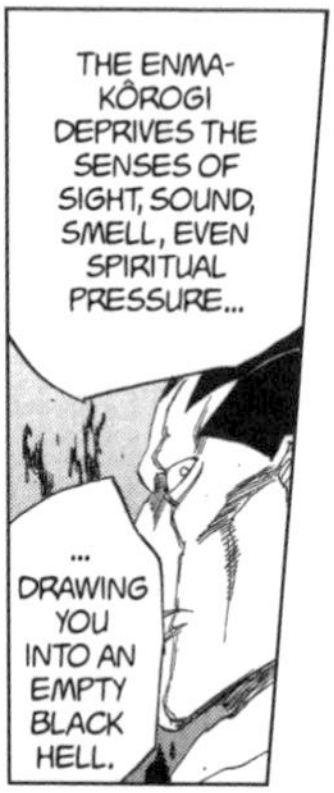
THE ENMA-KÔROGI DEPRIVES THE SENSES OF SIGHT, SOUND, SMELL, EVEN SPIRITUAL PRESSURE...
...DRAWING YOU INTO AN EMPTY BLACK HELL.

EXPLANATION

The sense of touch is the key. You can derive the answer from the clue that the target is aware of Kaname Tôsen's zangeki (sword attack).

2. B

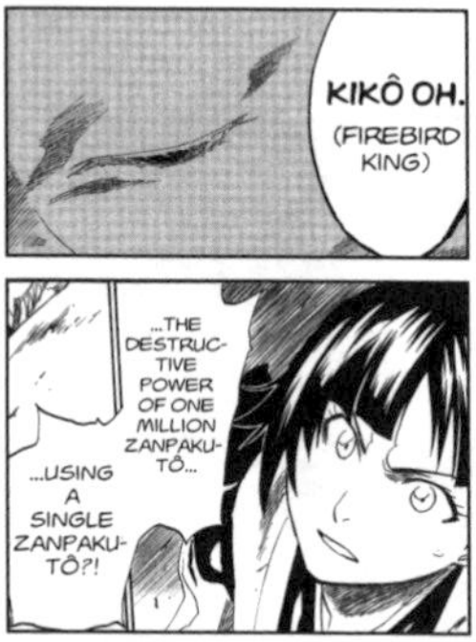
KIKÔ OH. (FIREBIRD KING)
...THE DESTRUC-TIVE POWER OF ONE MILLION ZANPAKU-TÔ...
...USING A SINGLE ZANPAKU-TÔ?!

EXPLANATION

The name is easy to get. Memorize the numbers of the levels of destructive power. The execution frame possesses a power equal to the spear in defending against a zanpaku-tô. This is also a common question, so beware.

3. B

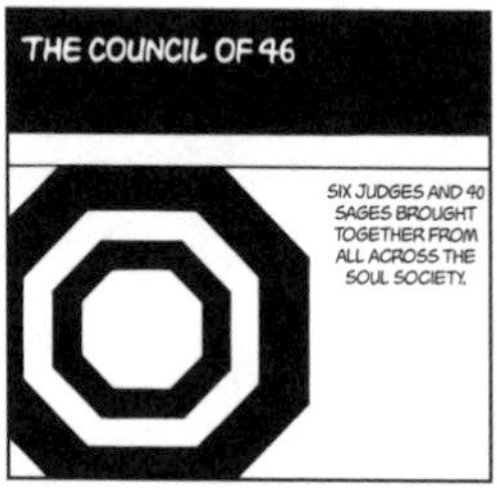
THE COUNCIL OF 46
SIX JUDGES AND 40 SAGES BROUGHT TOGETHER FROM ALL ACROSS THE SOUL SOCIETY.

EXPLANATION

It is possible to get the answer right if you understand the duties of Central 46. Central 46 is the supreme judicial organization that passes judgment on Soul Reapers and konpaku who have broken the law. Their judgments are never overturned. This is an organization essentially made up of rare individuals who analyze every situation rationally and make wise judgments.

4. A

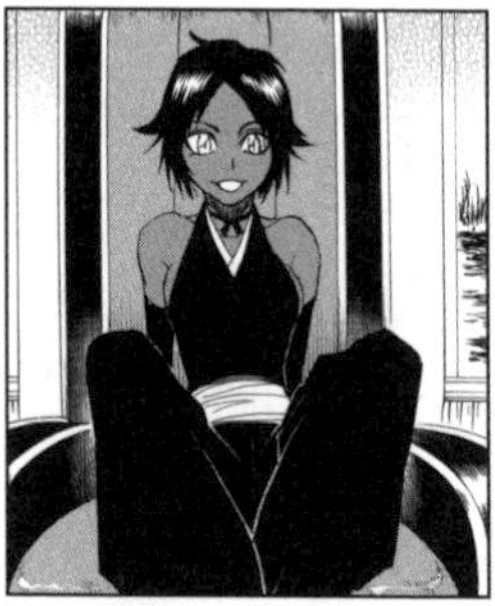

EXPLANATION

Rukia Kuchiki (B) is a member of Thirteenth Company and Kaien Shiba (C) was formerly the assistant captain of Thirteenth Company. Kisuke Urahara was the captain of Twelfth Company. Yoruichi Shihôin is the only one who was assigned to the Secret Remote Squad and has no experience in the Court Guard Companies.

5

A...i) 3
B...i) 6 AND ii) 7
C...iii) 200

THE FIRST WAY IS BY PASSING THE CAPTAIN'S EXAM IN THE PRESENCE OF THREE OR MORE CAPTAINS, INCLUDING THE CAPTAIN-GENERAL.
THE SECOND WAY IS BY RECEIVING RECOMMENDATIONS FROM SIX OR MORE CAPTAINS AND HAVING THREE OF THE SEVEN REMAINING CAPTAINS APPROVE IT.
AND THE THIRD WAY...
...IS BY DEFEATING A CAPTAIN IN THE PRESENCE OF NO LESS THAN 200 GUARDSMEN.

EXPLANATION

Numeric problems appear in the exam every year. It's best to have a sentence for this memorized, but questions like this will be easy to answer if you keep in mind that there are thirteen captains.

2. KENPACHI ZARAKI

"...SPREADING CARNAGE AND THIRSTING FOR BLOOD.
"HE'S NOT LIKE THE REST OF US.

EXPLANATION

Kenpachi Zaraki loves to fight more than anything and believes that going up against strong fighters is the ultimate reason for living. This is why he hoped to duel his company's previous captain. Captain Zaraki is also the only captain who doesn't yet have a bankai.

6

1. RETSU UNOHANA
2. ISANE KOTETSU
3. SENTARÔ KOTSUBAKI
4. JIRÔBÔ IKKANZAKA

K	**A**	M	**I**	N	E	Z	A	K	I	R	Y	A	R	I	M
O	T	**K**	**K**	I	Y	O	H	A	K	O	N	O	Y	K	O
S	E	N	**A**	**N**	**A**	**H**	**O**	**N**	**U**	**U**	**S**	**T**	**E**	**R**	B
U	T	A	**B**	**Z**	O	K	U	S	I	K	A	R	I	O	M
A	**U**	E	**U**	O	**N**	E	N	O	G	U	K	A	N	B	A
I	B	**S**	**S**	U	K	**A**	I	S	A	H	O	B	O	A	M
E	R	U	**T**	O	M	O	**K**	A	S	H	I	A	E	T	T
Z	A	M	**O**	**E**	U	A	E	**K**	O	N	N	O	T	S	U
B	Y	A	**K**	U	**T**	H	O	M	**I**	N	A	K	K	U	C
A	N	K	**O**	N	S	**O**	S	E	M	**O**	B	Y	A	C	H
I	T	E	**R**	O	B	Y	**K**	S	Y	A	**B**	A	C	H	O
S	E	N	**A**	R	A	J	I	**E**	O	R	U	**O**	R	I	M
K	A	Z	**T**	S	U	O	N	I	**N**	R	O	S	**R**	K	N
E	H	O	**N**	U	I	S	A	M	I	**A**	A	S	H	**I**	N
H	S	O	**E**	N	S	U	R	J	U	R	**S**	T	O	N	**J**
T	I	H	**S**	A	M	M	A	I	T	A	M	**I**	M	Y	Ô

EXPLANATION

When you are assigned to a Court Guard Company or the Secret Remote Squad, the first thing you must do is learn the names of your superiors and commanding officers. Learn to spell as many of their names as possible, starting now. For this question, watch out for Isane Kotetsu. Be sure not to mistake her for Kiyone Kotetsu of Thirteenth Company.

7

1. SHUNKÔ

EXPLANATION

Besides the names of zanpaku-tô and shikai, the exam often covers names of techniques. Both the kanji and their readings are often unusual, so learn the names by each kanji character and understand its meaning.

CHI NG
SHÛKEI... (LAST SIGHT)
...HAKUTEI-KEN. (WHITE EMPEROR SWORD)

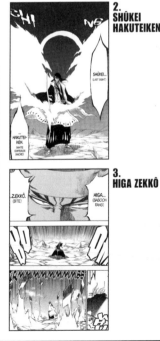

2. SHÛKEI HAKUTEIKEN

HIGA... (BABOON FANG)
...ZEKKÔ. (BITE)

3. HIGA ZEKKÔ

8

1. HISANA

2. 69

EXPLANATION

Tough, detailed questions are on the exam. They also cover things like names or a company member's looks. Study closely.

3. SEIJÔTÔ KYORIN

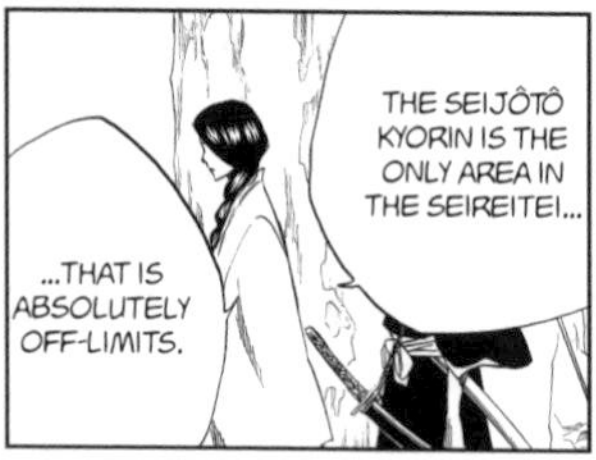
THE SEIJÔTÔ KYORIN IS THE ONLY AREA IN THE SEIREITEI...
...THAT IS ABSOLUTELY OFF-LIMITS.

4. GIKON TECHNOLOGY

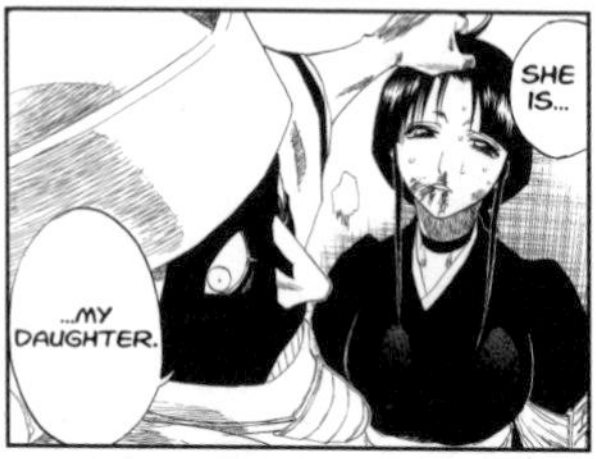
SHE IS...
...MY DAUGHTER.

5. HIGONYÛDÔ

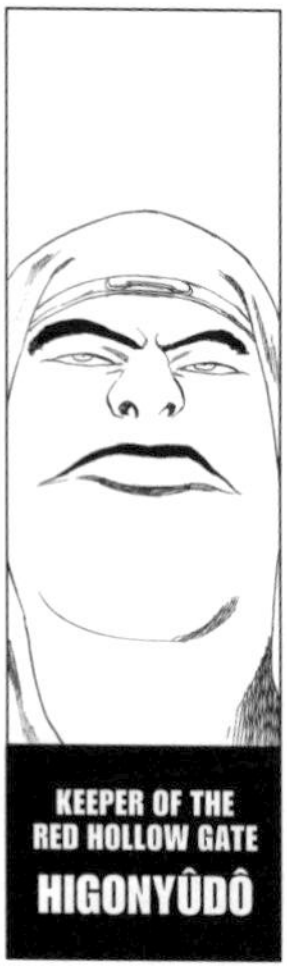
KEEPER OF THE RED HOLLOW GATE
HIGONYÛDÔ

EXPLANATION

Problems 3 and 5 are simple vocabulary questions. If you don't know what a gigai is you may have difficulty answering Problem 4. A gigai is a substitute body that is provided to a Soul Reaper. Once you have a gigai, you'll need an artificial soul. Then you'll be ready to proceed with a gikon substitute soul technique.

9

1. C

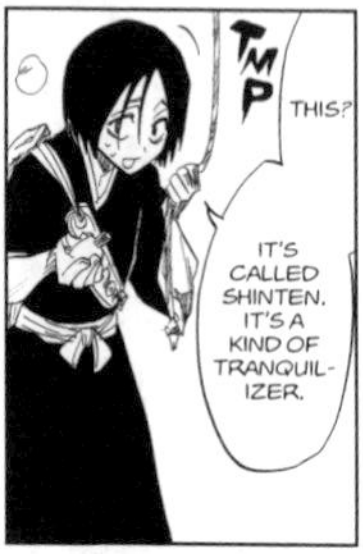
TMP
THIS?
IT'S CALLED SHINTEN. IT'S A KIND OF TRANQUIL-IZER.

EXPLANATION

This question is about the Seventh Seat of Fourth Company, Hanatarô Yamada. Fourth Company specializes in supplies and emergency aid. They also take part in combat. During battles, company members often serve as medics and provide medical assistance.

2. D

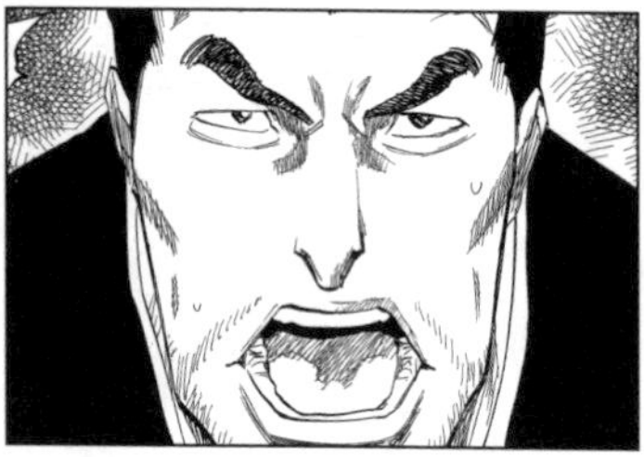

EXPLANATION

Tatsufusa Enjôji is Eighth Company's Third Seat, Harunobu Ogidô is Fourth Company's Eighth Seat, and Toshimori Umesada is the 20th seat in Ninth Company.

3. A

EXPLANATION

Part of the incantation for Kakushi Tsuijaku appears in the image to the right. The correct words are "Hearts of the South." Be sure to study the incantation word for word.

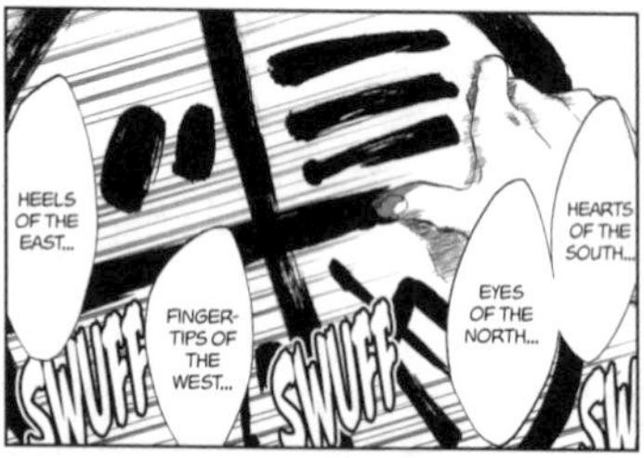
HEARTS OF THE SOUTH...
EYES OF THE NORTH...
FINGER-TIPS OF THE WEST...
HEELS OF THE EAST...
SWUFF
SWUFF

4. C

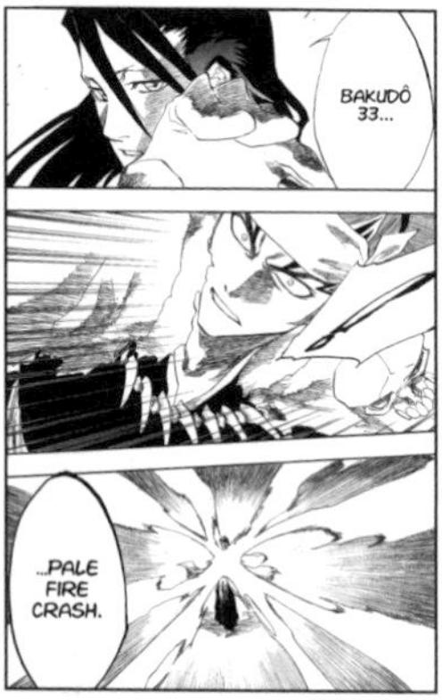
BAKUDÔ 33...
...PALE FIRE CRASH.

EXPLANATION

Shakkahô is Hadô 31, Byakurai is Hadô 4, and Rikujôkôrô is Hakudô 61. Questions about kidô are common in the exam, so know the topic well!

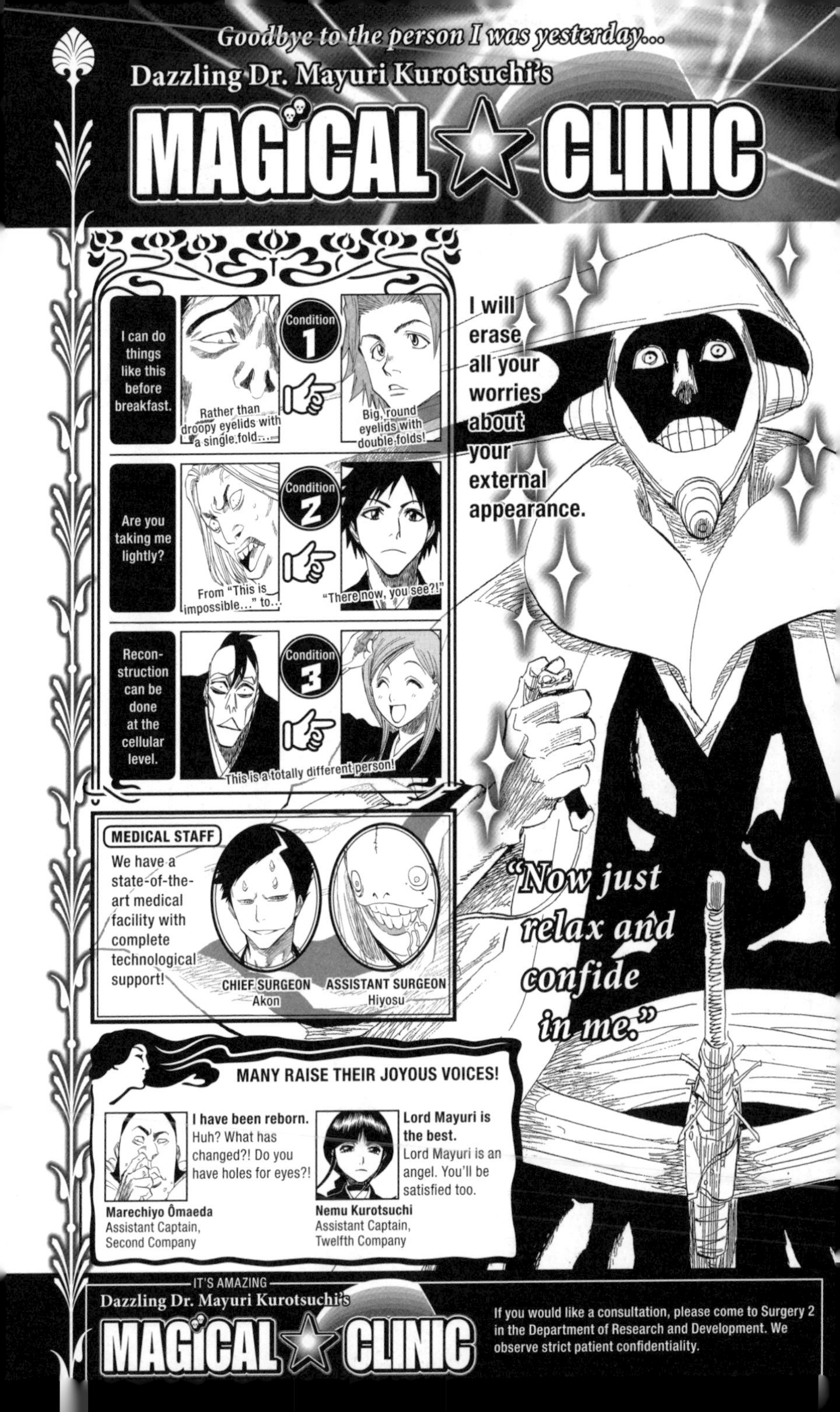
Goodbye to the person I was yesterday...
Dazzling Dr. Mayuri Kurotsuchi's
MAGICAL☆CLINIC
I will erase all your worries about your external appearance.
I can do things like this before breakfast.
Condition 1
Rather than droopy eyelids with a single fold...
Big, round eyelids with double folds!
Are you taking me lightly?
Condition 2
From "This is impossible..." to...
"There now, you see?!"
Recon-struction can be done at the cellular level.
Condition 3
This is a totally different person!
MEDICAL STAFF
We have a state-of-the-art medical facility with complete technological support!
CHIEF SURGEON
Akon
ASSISTANT SURGEON
Hiyosu
"Now just relax and confide in me."
MANY RAISE THEIR JOYOUS VOICES!
I have been reborn.
Huh? What has changed?! Do you have holes for eyes?!
Marechiyo Ômaeda
Assistant Captain, Second Company
Lord Mayuri is the best.
Lord Mayuri is an angel. You'll be satisfied too.
Nemu Kurotsuchi
Assistant Captain, Twelfth Company
IT'S AMAZING
Dazzling Dr. Mayuri Kurotsuchi's
MAGICAL☆CLINIC
If you would like a consultation, please come to Surgery 2 in the Department of Research and Development. We observe strict patient confidentiality.

The Society of Female Soul Reapers Presents

THIRTEEN COURT GUARD COMPANIES
APTITUDE TEST

LADIES !!
MAY I HAVE YOUR ATTENTION ?!
CHAIRWOMAN YACHIRU KUSAJISHI SOCIETY OF FEMALE SOUL REAPERS

You there—the one fretting over your future! Sit quietly and humbly take this test prepared by the Society of Female Soul Reapers! All right, let's do it! ★

➔ ❶ YES

··➤ ❷ NO

Follow the arrow that corresponds to your answer.

START

I am

❶ Literary oriented

❷ Sports oriented

Tea is a man's pastime.

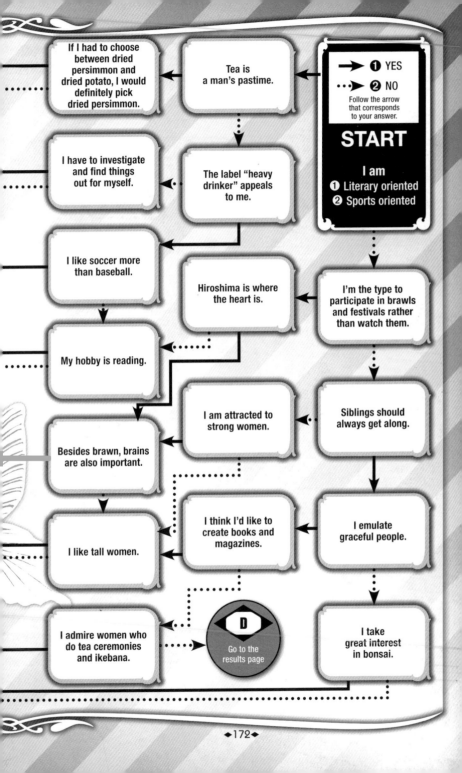

If I had to choose between dried persimmon and dried potato, I would definitely pick dried persimmon.

The label "heavy drinker" appeals to me.

I have to investigate and find things out for myself.

I like soccer more than baseball.

I'm the type to participate in brawls and festivals rather than watch them.

Hiroshima is where the heart is.

My hobby is reading.

Siblings should always get along.

I am attracted to strong women.

Besides brawn, brains are also important.

I emulate graceful people.

I think I'd like to create books and magazines.

I like tall women.

I take great interest in bonsai.

I admire women who do tea ceremonies and ikebana.

D

Go to the results page

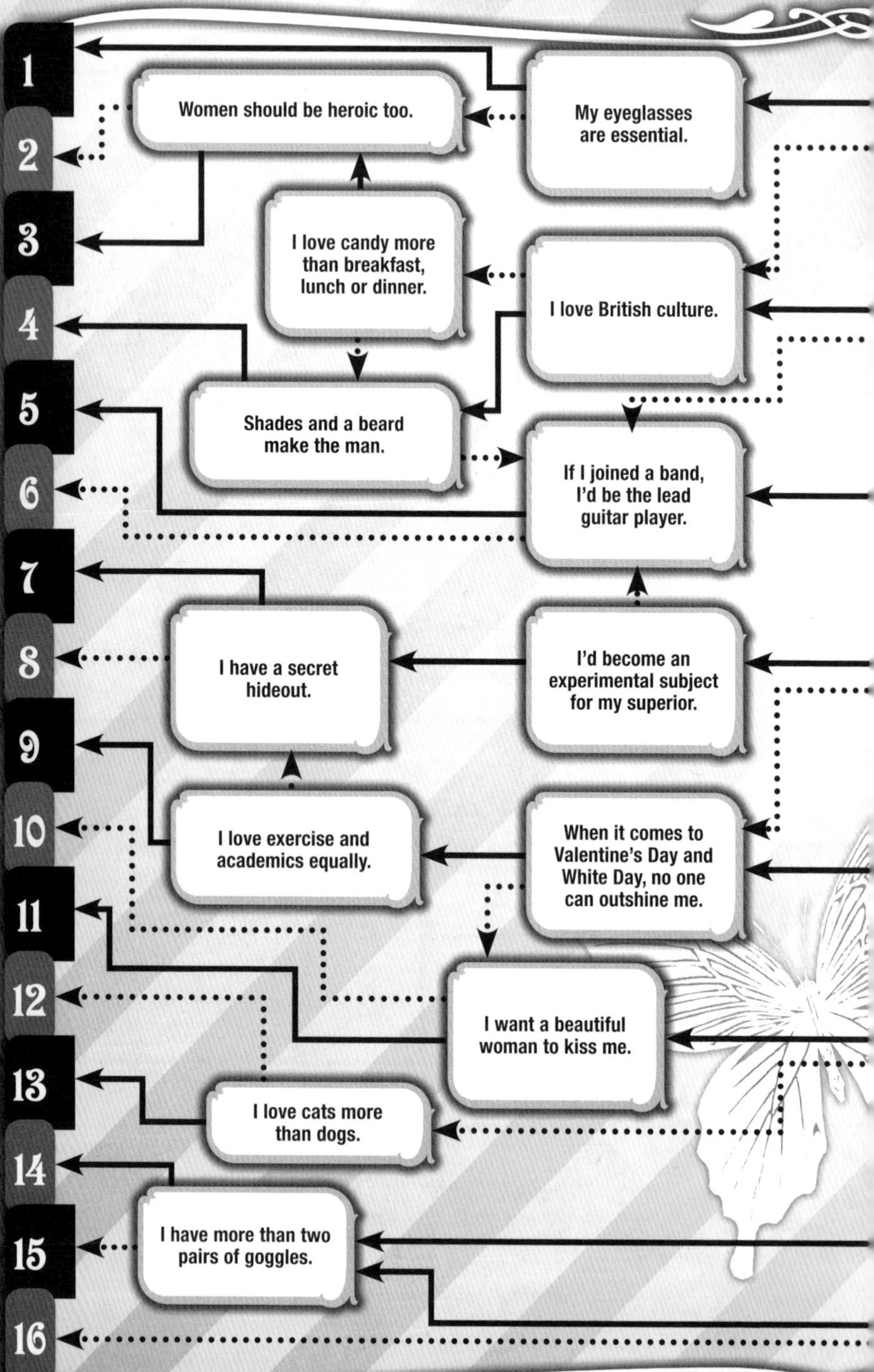
1
2
3
4
5
6
7
8
9
10
11
12
13
14
15
16
My eyeglasses are essential.
Women should be heroic too.
I love candy more than breakfast, lunch or dinner.
I love British culture.
Shades and a beard make the man.
If I joined a band, I'd be the lead guitar player.
I'd become an experimental subject for my superior.
I have a secret hideout.
When it comes to Valentine's Day and White Day, no one can outshine me.
I love exercise and academics equally.
I want a beautiful woman to kiss me.
I love cats more than dogs.
I have more than two pairs of goggles.

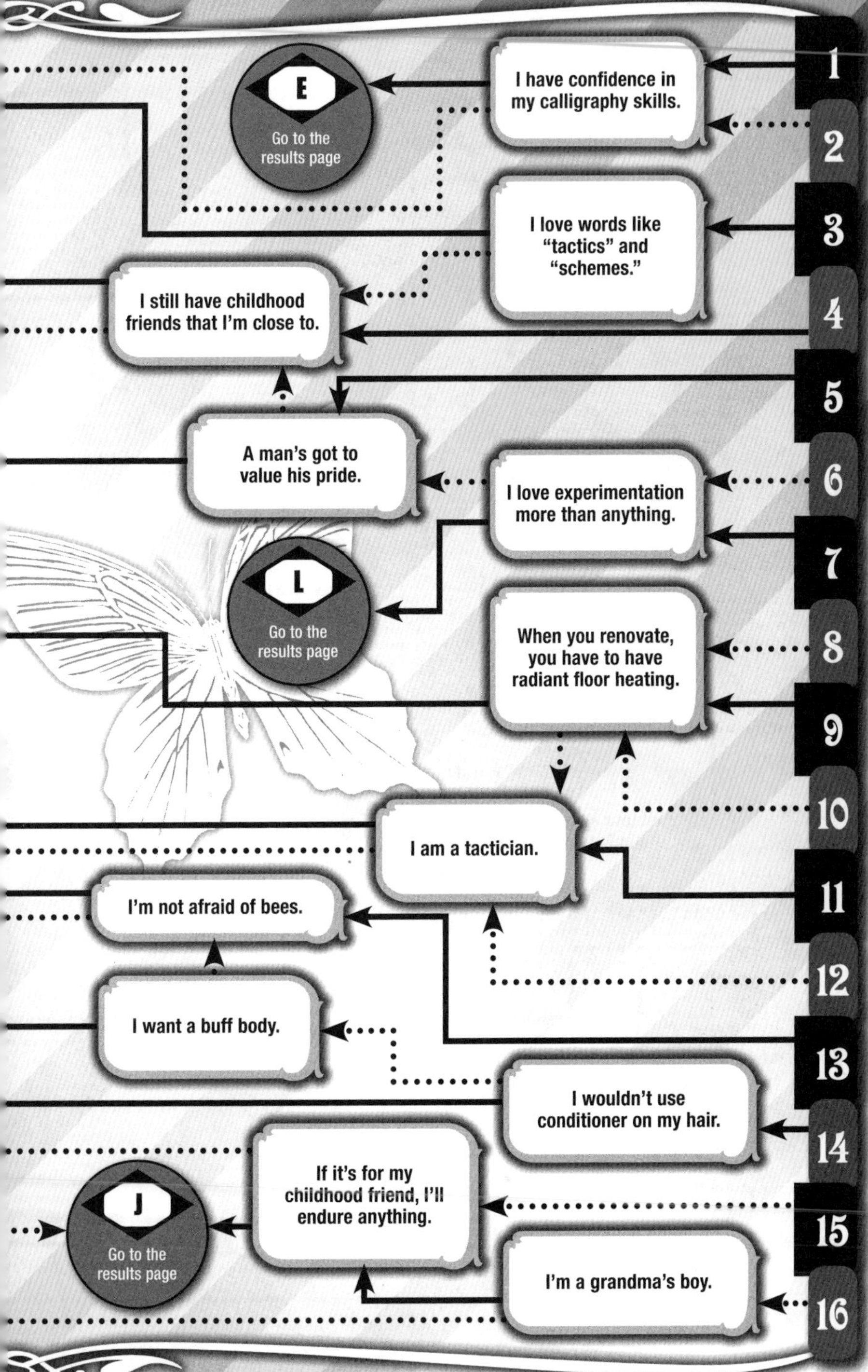
1
2
3
4
5
6
7
8
9
10
11
12
13
14
15
16
I have confidence in my calligraphy skills.
E
Go to the results page
I love words like "tactics" and "schemes."
I still have childhood friends that I'm close to.
A man's got to value his pride.
I love experimentation more than anything.
L
Go to the results page
When you renovate, you have to have radiant floor heating.
I am a tactician.
I'm not afraid of bees.
I want a buff body.
I wouldn't use conditioner on my hair.
If it's for my childhood friend, I'll endure anything.
J
Go to the results page
I'm a grandma's boy.

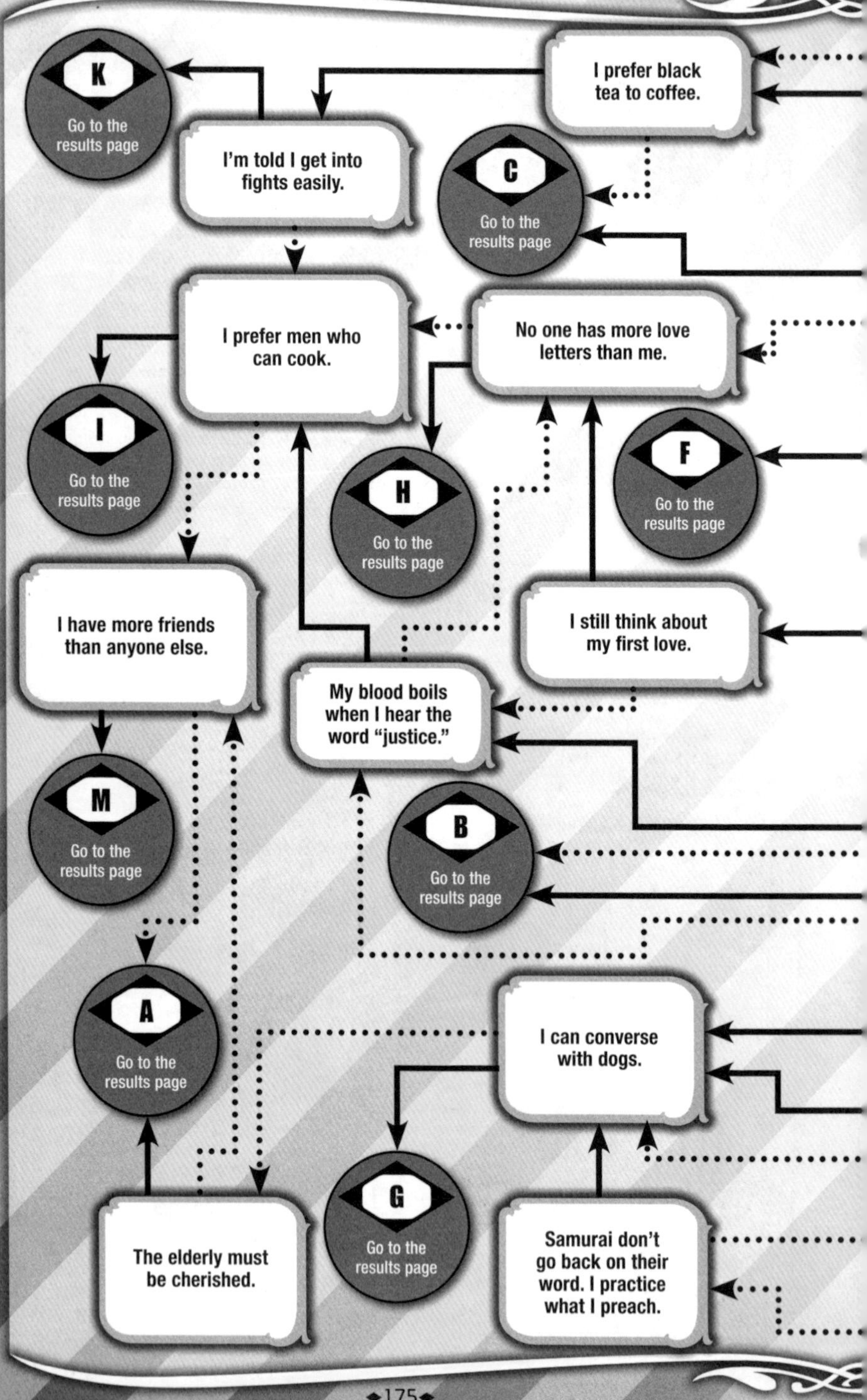
I prefer black tea to coffee.
K
Go to the results page
I'm told I get into fights easily.
C
Go to the results page
I prefer men who can cook.
No one has more love letters than me.
I
Go to the results page
H
Go to the results page
F
Go to the results page
I have more friends than anyone else.
I still think about my first love.
My blood boils when I hear the word "justice."
M
Go to the results page
B
Go to the results page
A
Go to the results page
I can converse with dogs.
G
Go to the results page
The elderly must be cherished.
Samurai don't go back on their word. I practice what I preach.

THIRTEEN COURT GUARD COMPANIES
APTITUDE TEST

Find your perfect match right here!

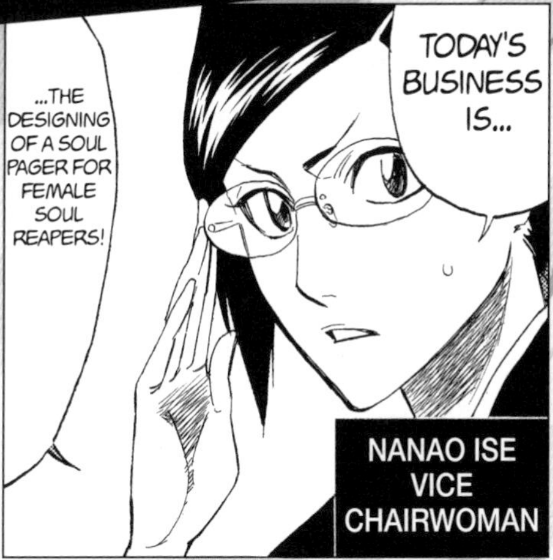
TODAY'S BUSINESS IS...
...THE DESIGNING OF A SOUL PAGER FOR FEMALE SOUL REAPERS!
NANAO ISE
VICE
CHAIRWOMAN

Besides being an assistant captain, she performs her duties as vice chairwoman very seriously.

Highly recommended by the Society of Female Soul Reapers! Find out which company is perfect for you!

Hello, everyone. Do you spend your days and nights agonizing over joining the Court Guard Companies? The results of the test are presented here. We, the Society of Female Soul Reapers, have been strictly impartial in overseeing the aptitude test. I hope that the results prove useful to you. Please don't give up, even if you're unable to find a company suitable for you.

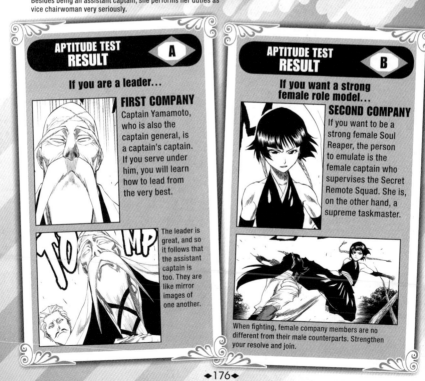

APTITUDE TEST RESULT A

If you are a leader...

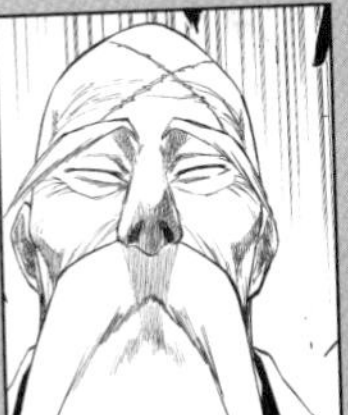

FIRST COMPANY

Captain Yamamoto, who is also the captain general, is a captain's captain. If you serve under him, you will learn how to lead from the very best.

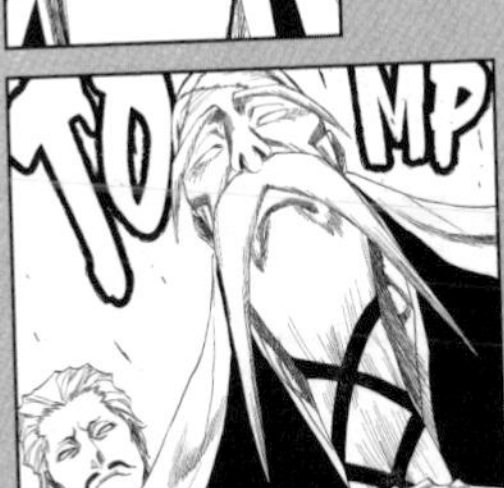

The leader is great, and so it follows that the assistant captain is too. They are like mirror images of one another.

APTITUDE TEST RESULT B

If you want a strong female role model...

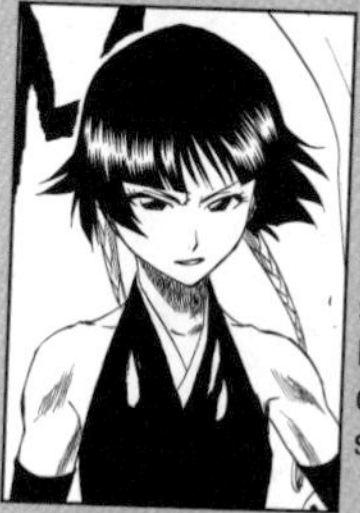

SECOND COMPANY

If you want to be a strong female Soul Reaper, the person to emulate is the female captain who supervises the Secret Remote Squad. She is, on the other hand, a supreme taskmaster.

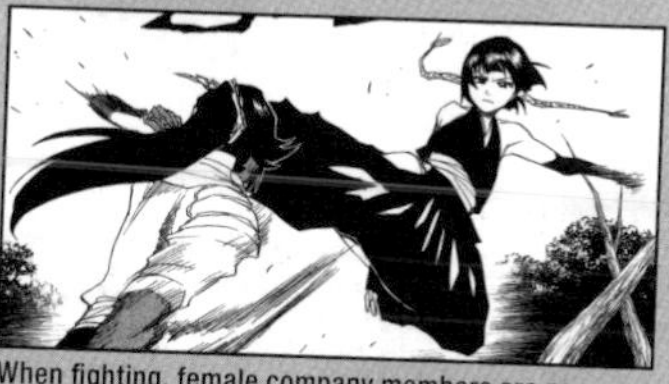

When fighting, female company members are no different from their male counterparts. Strengthen your resolve and join.

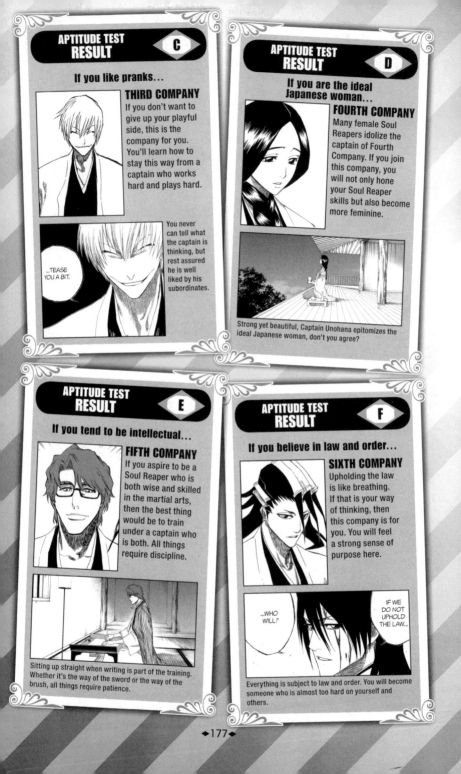

APTITUDE TEST RESULT C

If you like pranks...

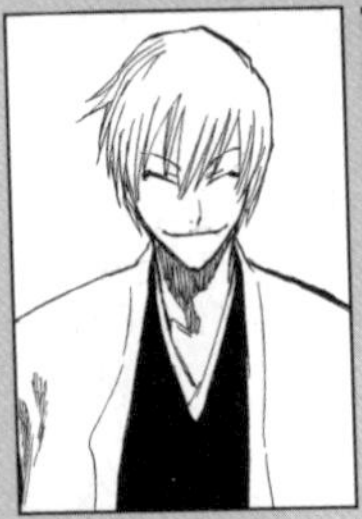

THIRD COMPANY

If you don't want to give up your playful side, this is the company for you. You'll learn how to stay this way from a captain who works hard and plays hard.

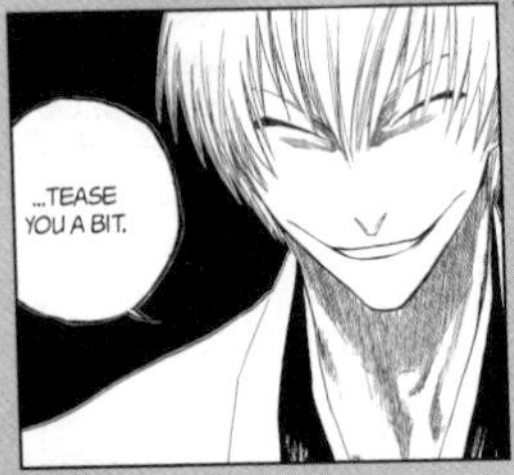
...TEASE YOU A BIT.

You never can tell what the captain is thinking, but rest assured he is well liked by his subordinates.

APTITUDE TEST RESULT D

If you are the ideal Japanese woman...

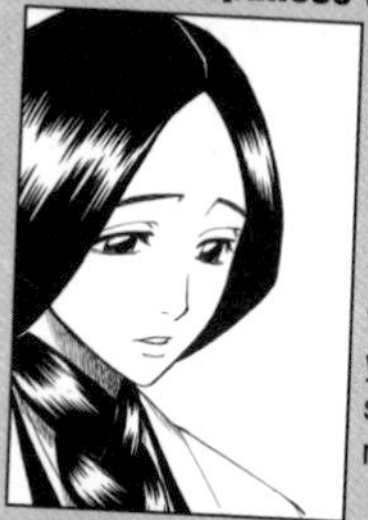

FOURTH COMPANY

Many female Soul Reapers idolize the captain of Fourth Company. If you join this company, you will not only hone your Soul Reaper skills but also become more feminine.

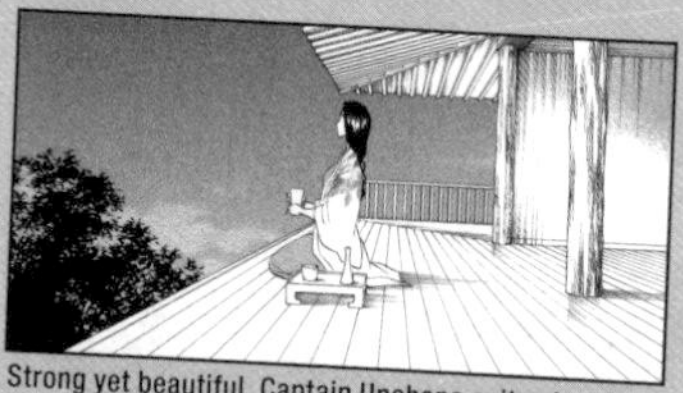

Strong yet beautiful, Captain Unohana epitomizes the ideal Japanese woman, don't you agree?

APTITUDE TEST RESULT E

If you tend to be intellectual...

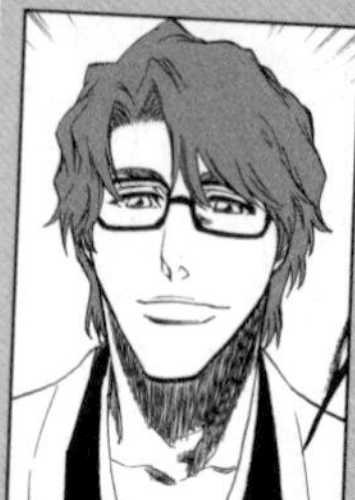

FIFTH COMPANY

If you aspire to be a Soul Reaper who is both wise and skilled in the martial arts, then the best thing would be to train under a captain who is both. All things require discipline.

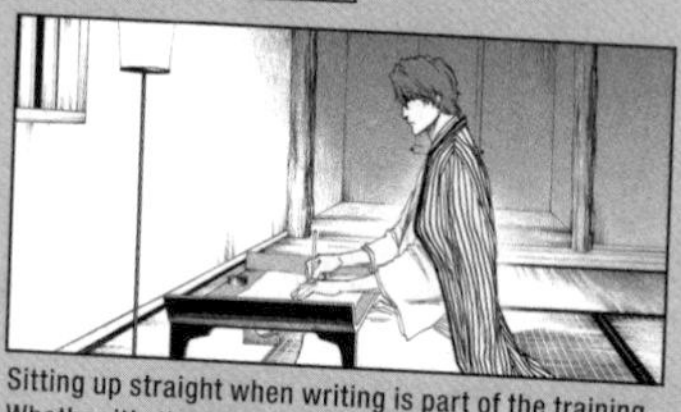

Sitting up straight when writing is part of the training. Whether it's the way of the sword or the way of the brush, all things require patience.

APTITUDE TEST RESULT F

If you believe in law and order...

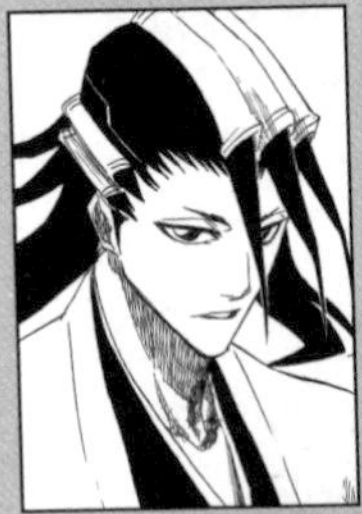

SIXTH COMPANY

Upholding the law is like breathing. If that is your way of thinking, then this company is for you. You will feel a strong sense of purpose here.

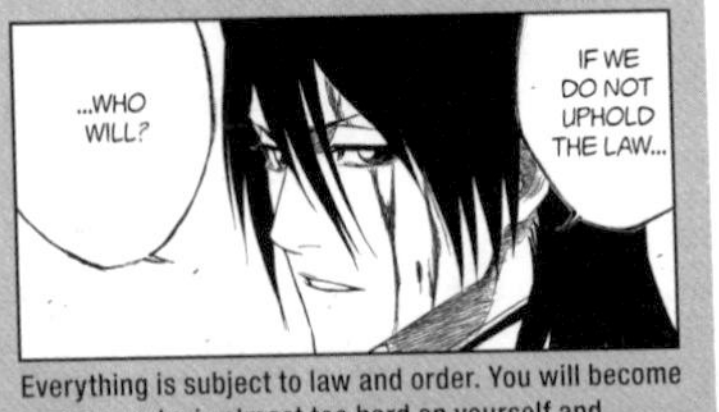
IF WE DO NOT UPHOLD THE LAW...
...WHO WILL?

Everything is subject to law and order. You will become someone who is almost too hard on yourself and others.

APTITUDE TEST RESULT G

If you have a strong sense of loyalty...

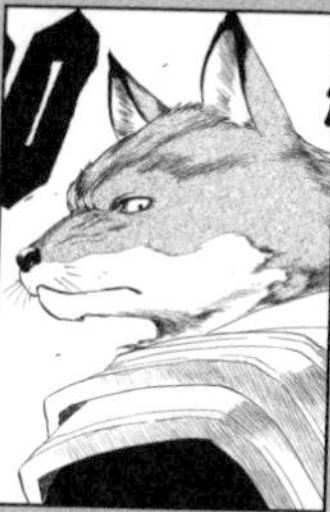

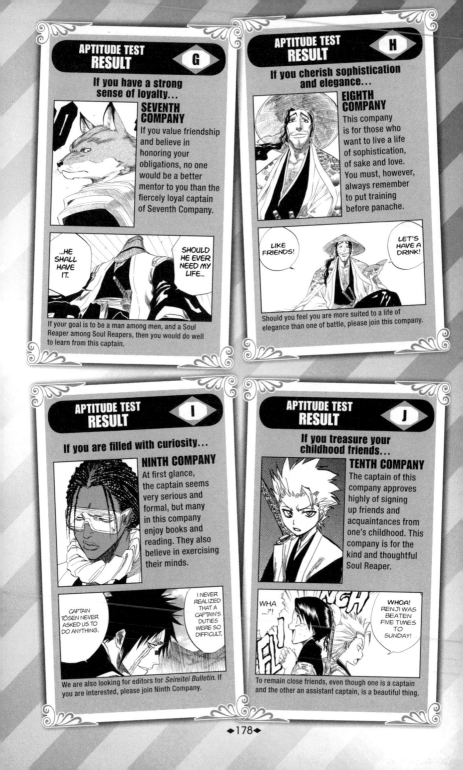

SEVENTH COMPANY

If you value friendship and believe in honoring your obligations, no one would be a better mentor to you than the fiercely loyal captain of Seventh Company.

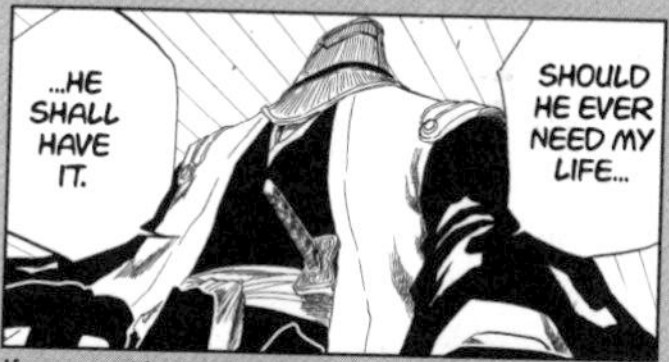
SHOULD HE EVER NEED MY LIFE...
...HE SHALL HAVE IT.

If your goal is to be a man among men, and a Soul Reaper among Soul Reapers, then you would do well to learn from this captain.

APTITUDE TEST RESULT H

If you cherish sophistication and elegance...

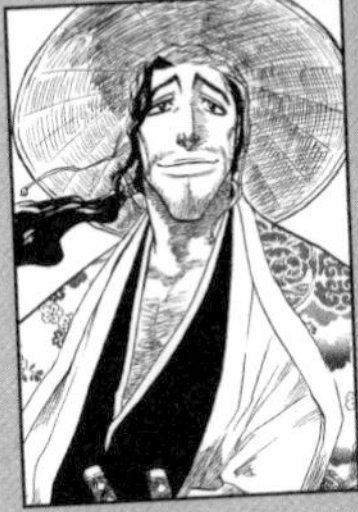

EIGHTH COMPANY

This company is for those who want to live a life of sophistication, of sake and love. You must, however, always remember to put training before panache.

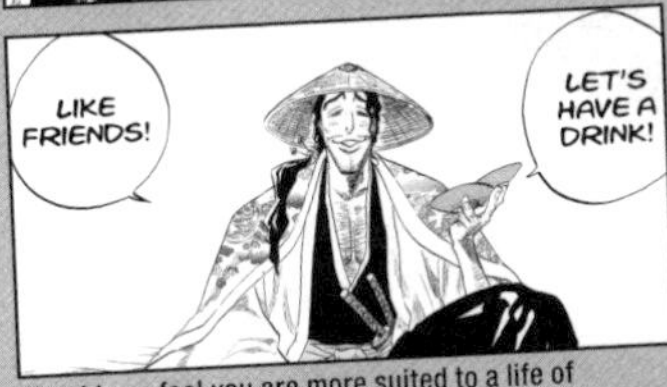
LET'S HAVE A DRINK!
LIKE FRIENDS!

Should you feel you are more suited to a life of elegance than one of battle, please join this company.

APTITUDE TEST RESULT I

If you are filled with curiosity...

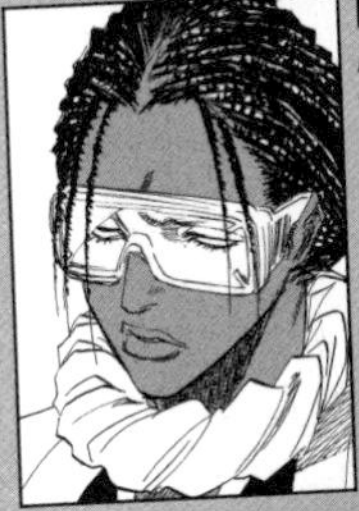

NINTH COMPANY

At first glance, the captain seems very serious and formal, but many in this company enjoy books and reading. They also believe in exercising their minds.

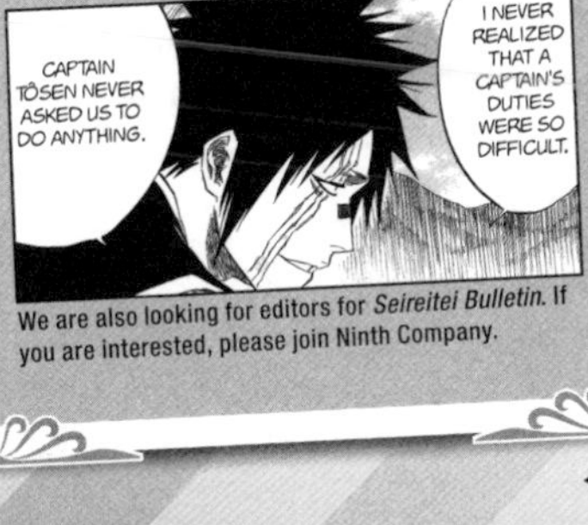
I NEVER REALIZED THAT A CAPTAIN'S DUTIES WERE SO DIFFICULT.
CAPTAIN TŌSEN NEVER ASKED US TO DO ANYTHING.

We are also looking for editors for *Seireitei Bulletin*. If you are interested, please join Ninth Company.

APTITUDE TEST RESULT J

If you treasure your childhood friends...

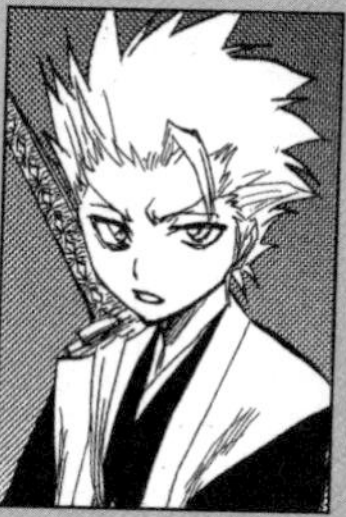

TENTH COMPANY

The captain of this company approves highly of signing up friends and acquaintances from one's childhood. This company is for the kind and thoughtful Soul Reaper.

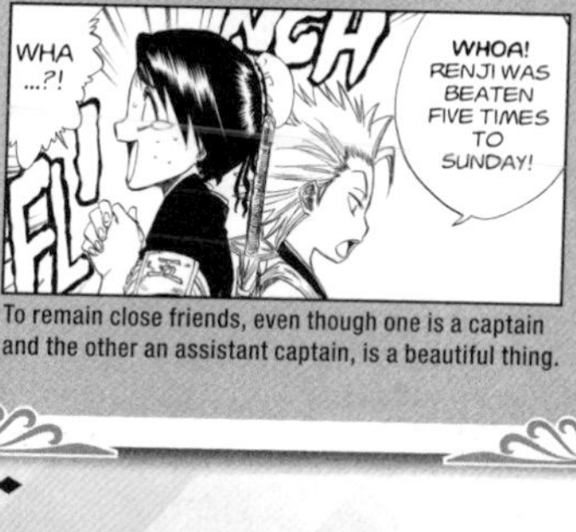
WHOA! RENJI WAS BEATEN FIVE TIMES TO SUNDAY!
WHA ...?!

To remain close friends, even though one is a captain and the other an assistant captain, is a beautiful thing.

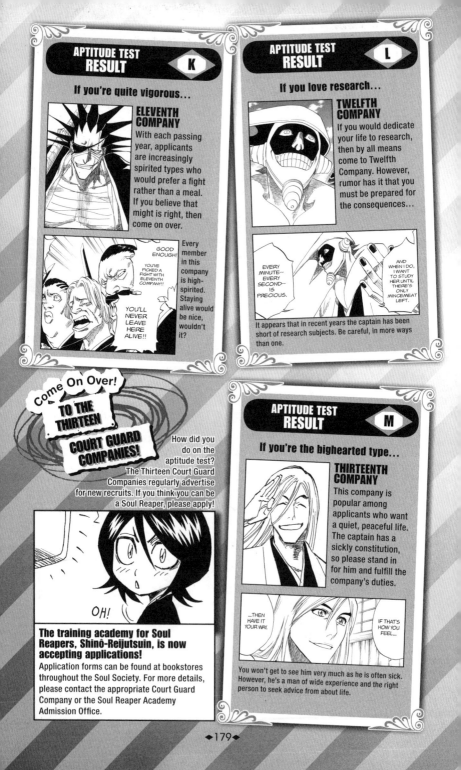

APTITUDE TEST RESULT K

If you're quite vigorous...

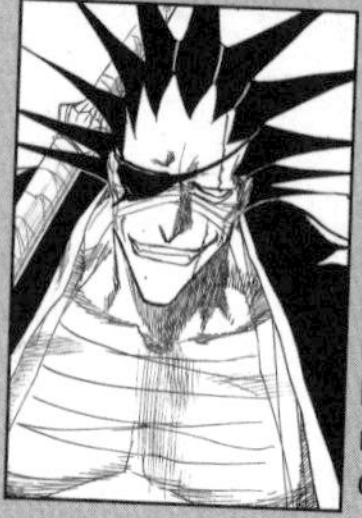

ELEVENTH COMPANY

With each passing year, applicants are increasingly spirited types who would prefer a fight rather than a meal. If you believe that might is right, then come on over.

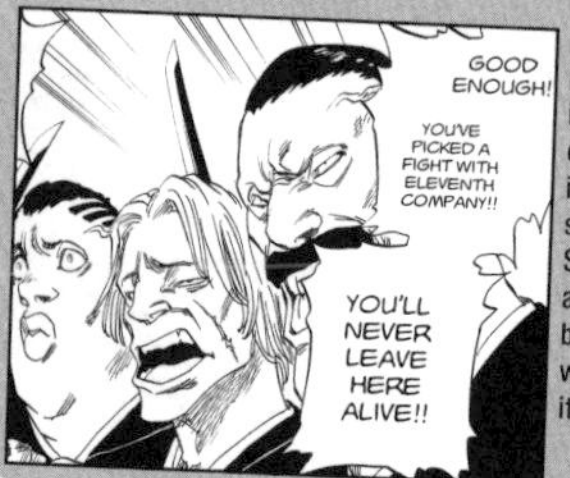
GOOD ENOUGH!
YOU'VE PICKED A FIGHT WITH ELEVENTH COMPANY!!
YOU'LL NEVER LEAVE HERE ALIVE!!

Every member in this company is high-spirited. Staying alive would be nice, wouldn't it?

APTITUDE TEST RESULT L

If you love research...

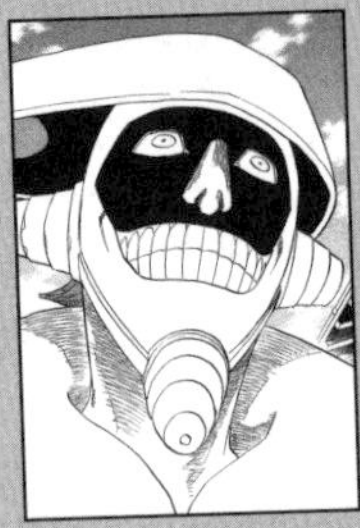

TWELFTH COMPANY

If you would dedicate your life to research, then by all means come to Twelfth Company. However, rumor has it that you must be prepared for the consequences...

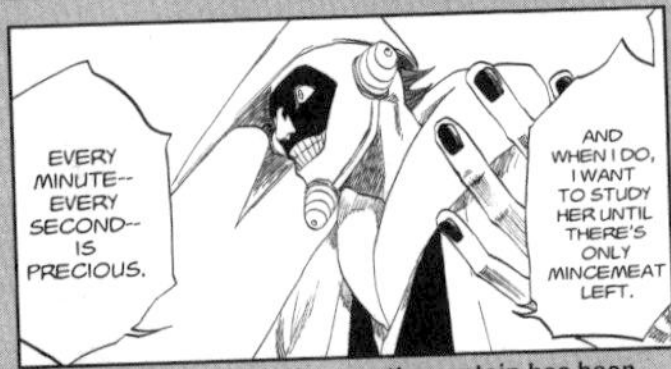
AND WHEN I DO, I WANT TO STUDY HER UNTIL THERE'S ONLY MINCEMEAT LEFT.
EVERY MINUTE-- EVERY SECOND-- IS PRECIOUS.

It appears that in recent years the captain has been short of research subjects. Be careful, in more ways than one.

APTITUDE TEST RESULT M

If you're the bighearted type...

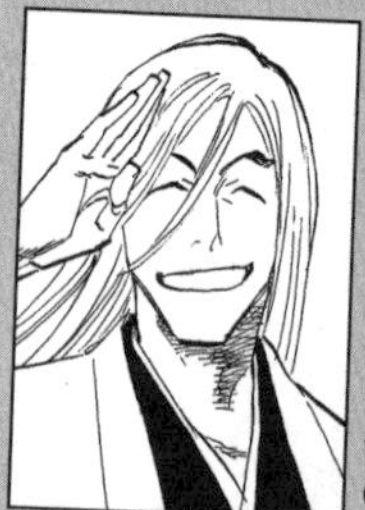

THIRTEENTH COMPANY

This company is popular among applicants who want a quiet, peaceful life. The captain has a sickly constitution, so please stand in for him and fulfill the company's duties.

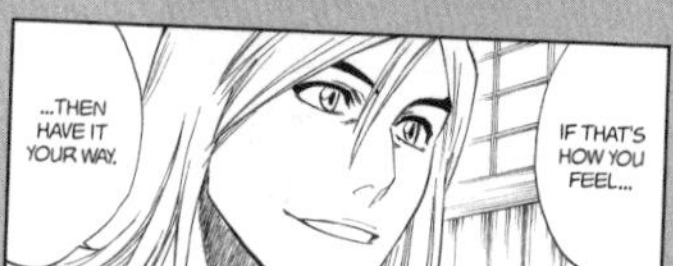
IF THAT'S HOW YOU FEEL...
...THEN HAVE IT YOUR WAY.

You won't get to see him very much as he is often sick. However, he's a man of wide experience and the right person to seek advice from about life.

Come On Over! TO THE THIRTEEN COURT GUARD COMPANIES!

How did you do on the aptitude test? The Thirteen Court Guard Companies regularly advertise for new recruits. If you think you can be a Soul Reaper, please apply!

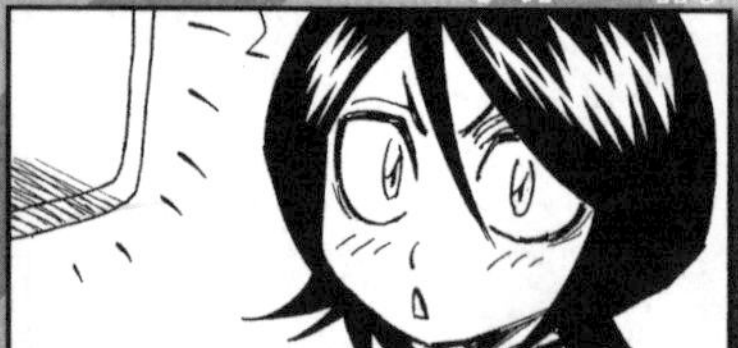
OH!

The training academy for Soul Reapers, Shinô-Reijutsuin, is now accepting applications!

Application forms can be found at bookstores throughout the Soul Society. For more details, please contact the appropriate Court Guard Company or the Soul Reaper Academy Admission Office.

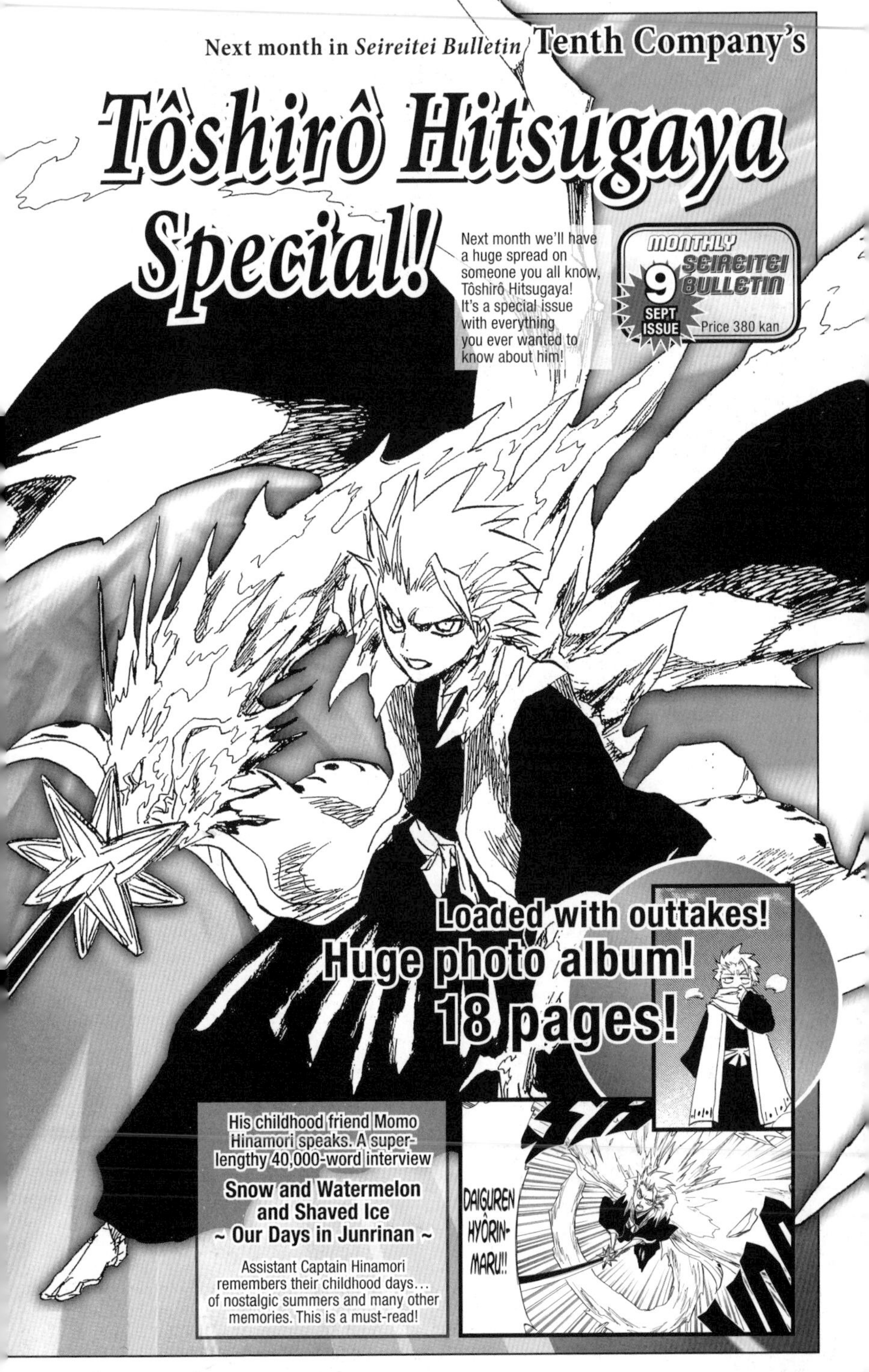

Next month in *Seireitei Bulletin* Tenth Company's
Tôshirô Hitsugaya Special!
Next month we'll have a huge spread on someone you all know, Tôshirô Hitsugaya! It's a special issue with everything you ever wanted to know about him!
MONTHLY SEIREITEI BULLETIN
9 SEPT ISSUE
Price 380 kan
Loaded with outtakes!
Huge photo album!
18 pages!
His childhood friend Momo Hinamori speaks. A super-lengthy 40,000-word interview
Snow and Watermelon and Shaved Ice ~ Our Days in Junrinan ~
Assistant Captain Hinamori remembers their childhood days… of nostalgic summers and many other memories. This is a must-read!
DAIGUREN HYÔRIN-MARU!!

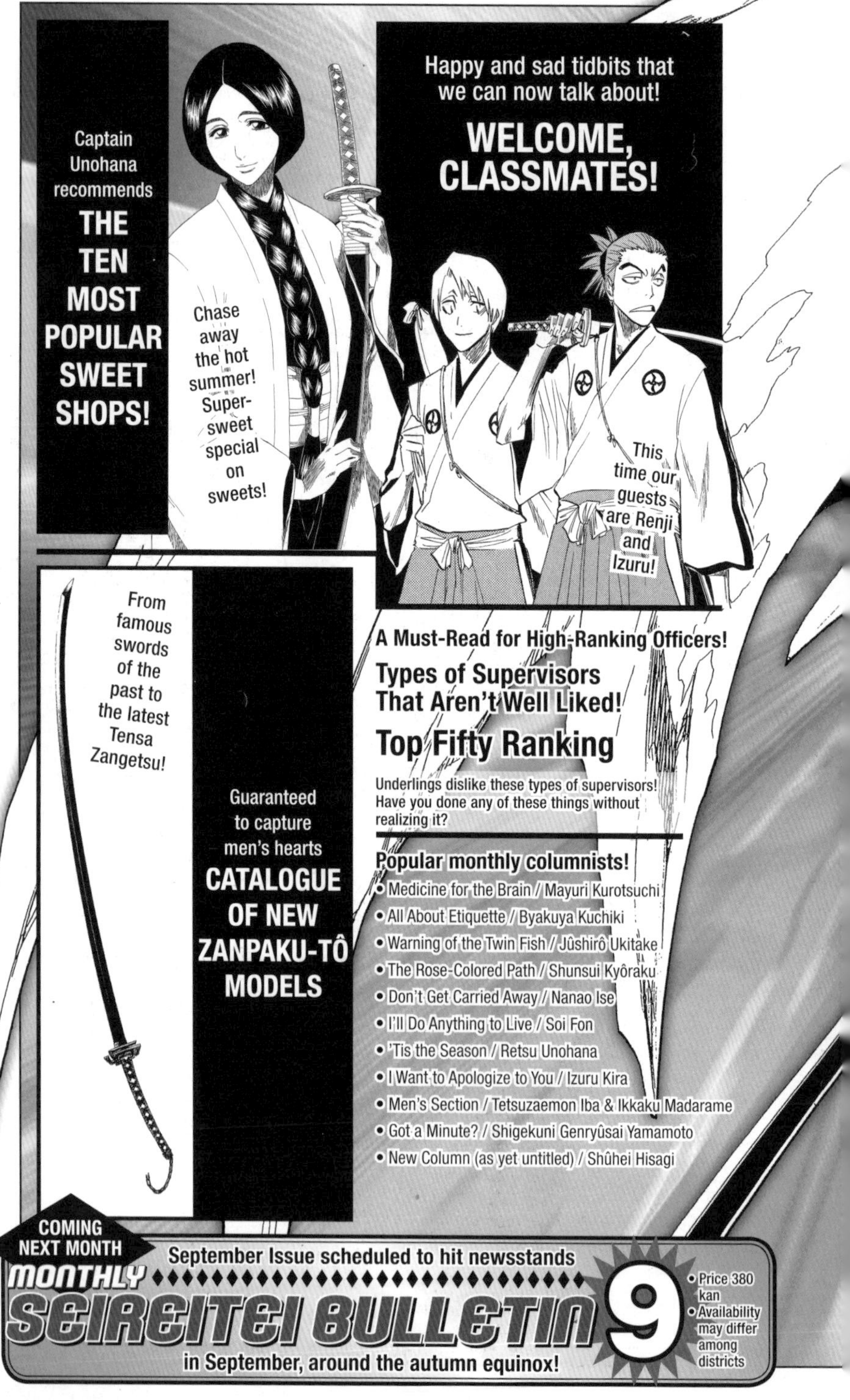
Happy and sad tidbits that we can now talk about!
WELCOME, CLASSMATES!
This time our guests are Renji and Izuru!
Captain Unohana recommends
THE TEN MOST POPULAR SWEET SHOPS!
Chase away the hot summer! Super-sweet special on sweets!
A Must-Read for High-Ranking Officers!
Types of Supervisors That Aren't Well Liked!
Top Fifty Ranking
Underlings dislike these types of supervisors! Have you done any of these things without realizing it?
Popular monthly columnists!
• Medicine for the Brain / Mayuri Kurotsuchi
• All About Etiquette / Byakuya Kuchiki
• Warning of the Twin Fish / Jûshirô Ukitake
• The Rose-Colored Path / Shunsui Kyôraku
• Don't Get Carried Away / Nanao Ise
• I'll Do Anything to Live / Soi Fon
• 'Tis the Season / Retsu Unohana
• I Want to Apologize to You / Izuru Kira
• Men's Section / Tetsuzaemon Iba & Ikkaku Madarame
• Got a Minute? / Shigekuni Genryûsai Yamamoto
• New Column (as yet untitled) / Shûhei Hisagi
Guaranteed to capture men's hearts
CATALOGUE OF NEW ZANPAKU-TÔ MODELS
From famous swords of the past to the latest Tensa Zangetsu!
COMING NEXT MONTH
MONTHLY SEIREITEI BULLETIN 9
September Issue scheduled to hit newsstands in September, around the autumn equinox!
• Price 380 kan
• Availability may differ among districts

OK! THE MEN + WOMEN OF THE SEIREITEI

Editorial postscript

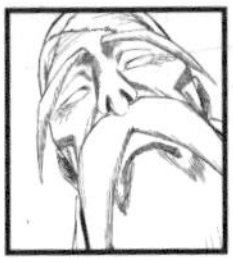

I trimmed my beard the other day. If I left it alone, who knows how long it would grow.
–SHIGEKUNI

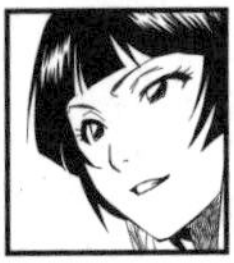

It was fun going to the beach last year for rest and relaxation. I'd really like to go there again this year.
–SOI FON

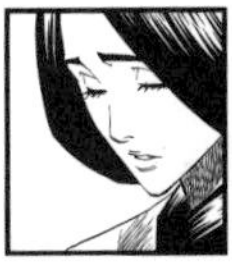

We've been getting lots of inquiries at the barracks, but please do not worry. Assistant Captain Hinamori is well.
–RETSU

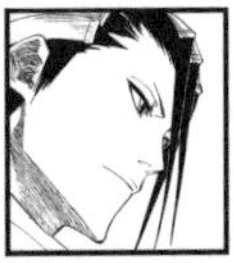

Members of the Society of Female Soul Reapers have been wandering about town lately. I wish they would go away.
–BYAKUYA

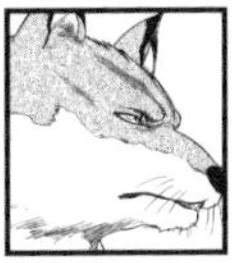

I'm going to visit the family grave. I'll think about that time and ponder the meaning of justice.
–SAJIN

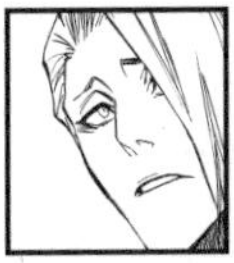

Lately, it's been taking me over 30 minutes to post a comment in this section. People sure have a lot to say.
–IZURU

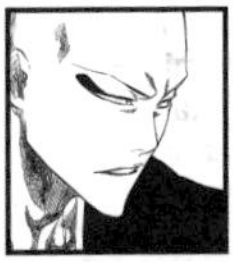

The assistant captain's taking me to visit Tenth Company's barracks. I'll get some ice and make shaved ice. It's good.
–IKKAKU

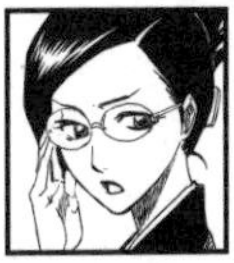

Thank you all for the birthday presents the other day. I'll continue to do my best.
–NANAO

SUBSCRIPTIONS ARE NOW AVAILABLE

We will deliver this magazine to your home on the day of publication. If you subscribe now, you'll get a sake-flavored rice cake dessert in a cup as our gift to you.

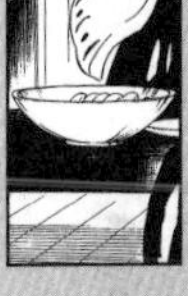

If you subscribe now, you'll get this dessert as a gift!

To order:

Subscription Desk
Editorial Department
Monthly Seireitei Bulletin
2-5-10 Ryûsei, District 1, Seireitei
119 – 0163

◆COVER / Thirteen Court Guard Companies, Ichigo Kurosaki (ryoka), Yoruichi Shihôin, Ganjû Shiba, Kisuke Urahara (intruders)

◆ACTING EDITOR / Shûhei Hisagi

◆DESIGN / Ishinoue Sannen

◆LAYOUT / Ishinoue Sannen, Takehiko Higashiyama (Freiheit) Shunji Harigane (Arrancha)

◆ARTICLES / Akira Ichibanboshi, Umiomi Itô, Shigeru Daidô, Hiroyuki Yagamo, Hiroyuki Ishishiro (Nôdô), Mizuhô Hayakawa (Kurôbâdô)

◆REISHI PRINTING COMPANY

◆The unauthorized spiritual reproduction and transmission of all works, articles and photos in this magazine are prohibited. *Monthly Seireitei Bulletin* is printed on paper that is 100% reishi.

LOOKING FOR STAFF FOR THE EDITORIAL DEPARTMENT!

We're looking for staff to work with us to create this magazine—in particular, those who can go two or three nights without sleeping.

瀞霊廷編集部

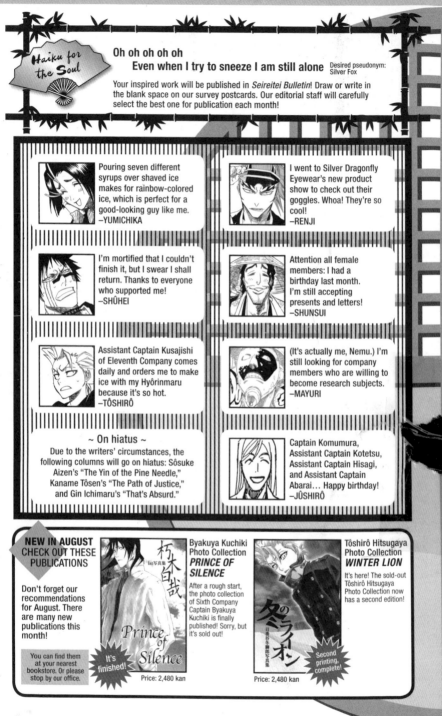

Haiku for the Soul

Oh oh oh oh oh
Even when I try to sneeze I am still alone

Desired pseudonym: Silver Fox

Your inspired work will be published in *Seireitei Bulletin*! Draw or write in the blank space on our survey postcards. Our editorial staff will carefully select the best one for publication each month!

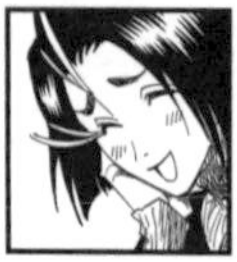

Pouring seven different syrups over shaved ice makes for rainbow-colored ice, which is perfect for a good-looking guy like me.
–YUMICHIKA

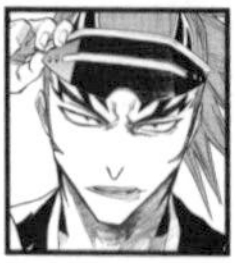

I went to Silver Dragonfly Eyewear's new product show to check out their goggles. Whoa! They're so cool!
–RENJI

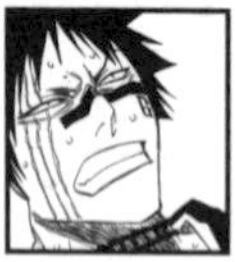

I'm mortified that I couldn't finish it, but I swear I shall return. Thanks to everyone who supported me!
–SHÛHEI

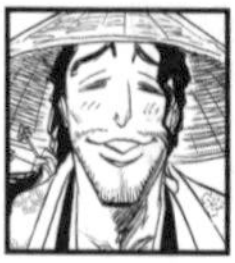

Attention all female members: I had a birthday last month. I'm still accepting presents and letters!
–SHUNSUI

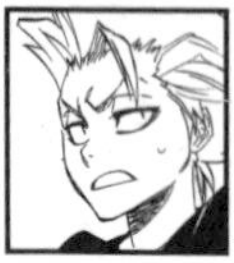

Assistant Captain Kusajishi of Eleventh Company comes daily and orders me to make ice with my Hyôrinmaru because it's so hot.
–TÔSHIRÔ

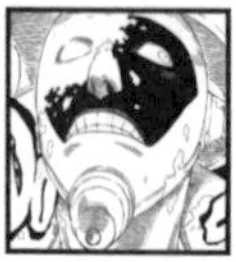

(It's actually me, Nemu.) I'm still looking for company members who are willing to become research subjects.
–MAYURI

~ On hiatus ~

Due to the writers' circumstances, the following columns will go on hiatus: Sôsuke Aizen's "The Yin of the Pine Needle," Kaname Tôsen's "The Path of Justice," and Gin Ichimaru's "That's Absurd."

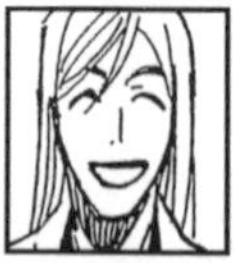

Captain Komumura, Assistant Captain Kotetsu, Assistant Captain Hisagi, and Assistant Captain Abarai… Happy birthday!
–JÛSHIRÔ

NEW IN AUGUST
CHECK OUT THESE PUBLICATIONS

Don't forget our recommendations for August. There are many new publications this month!

You can find them at your nearest bookstore. Or please stop by our office.

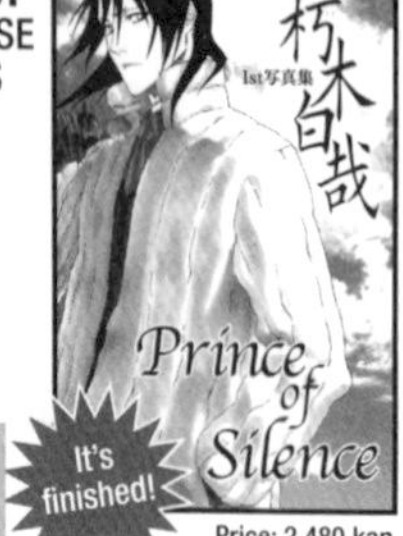
朽木白哉
1st写真集
Prince of Silence
It's finished!

Price: 2,480 kan

Byakuya Kuchiki Photo Collection
PRINCE OF SILENCE

After a rough start, the photo collection of Sixth Company Captain Byakuya Kuchiki is finally published! Sorry, but it's sold out!

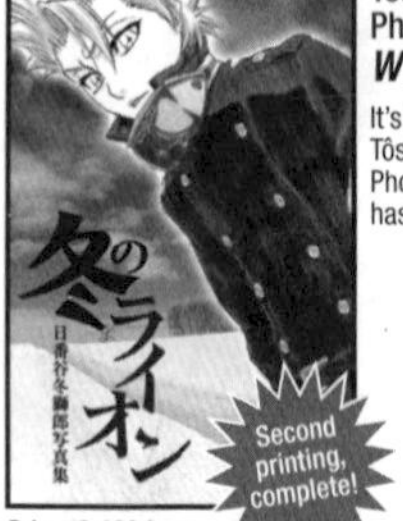
冬のライオン
Second printing, complete!

Price: 2,480 kan

Tôshirô Hitsugaya Photo Collection
WINTER LION

It's here! The sold-out Tôshirô Hitsugaya Photo Collection now has a second edition!

C...
B...
S...

ST...
TI...

E...
T...
LE...

GRAPHIC DESIGN Gerry Serrano
NEW TOUCH-UP ART & LETTERING Mark McMurray
EDITORIAL COORDINATOR Misaki C. Kido
EDITOR Yuki Takagaki

VP, PRODUCTION Alvin Lu
VP, SALES & PRODUCT MARKETING Gonzalo Ferreyra
VP, CREATIVE Linda Espinosa
PUBLISHER Hyoe Narita

BLEACH OFFICIAL BOOTLEG: COLORFUL BLEACH+ © 2007 by Tite Kubo

This book compiles material that appeared in *V Jump* from
January 2005 to September 2007, as well as new material.

The rights of the author(s) of the work(s) in this publication to be so
identified have been asserted in accordance with Copyright, Designs
and Patents Act 1988. A CIP catalogue record for this book is available
from the British Library.

The stories, characters and incidents mentioned in this publication are
entirely fictional.

Printed in Singapore

Published by VIZ Media, LLC
P.O. Box 77010
San Francisco, CA 94107

10 9 8 7 6 5 4 3 2 1
First printing, August 2010

www.viz.com

www.shonenjump.com